MW00997557

THE BIRTH CERTIFICATE

THE BIRTH CERTIFICATE

CERTIFICATE

AN AMERICAN HISTORY

SUSAN J. PEARSON

THE UNIVERSITY OF NORTH CAROLINA PRESS ⋮ CHAPEL HILL

*This book was published with the assistance
of the Thornton H. Brooks Fund of the
University of North Carolina Press.*

Designed by April Leidig
Set in Minion by Copperline Book Services, Inc.
Manufactured in the United States of America

The University of North Carolina Press has been
a member of the Green Press Initiative since 2003.

Jacket image: The standard birth certificate,
issued by the U.S. Census Bureau.

Library of Congress Cataloging-in-Publication Data
Names: Pearson, Susan J., author.
Title: The birth certificate : an American history / Susan J. Pearson.
Description: Chapel Hill : The University of North Carolina Press, 2021. |
     Includes bibliographical references and index.
Identifiers: LCCN 2021021865 | ISBN 9781469665689 (cloth ; alk. paper) |
     ISBN 9781469665702 (ebook)
Subjects: LCSH: Birth certificates—United States—History. | Registers of births, etc.—
     United States—History. | Citizenship—Documentation—United States—History.
Classification: LCC HA38.A5 P43 2021 | DDC 304.6/30973—dc23
LC record available at https://lccn.loc.gov/2021021865

For my mother,
Mary Alyce Pearson
(1941–2016)

CONTENTS

ILLUSTRATIONS

THE BIRTH CERTIFICATE

THE LIFE OF A DOCUMENT

Many years into researching and writing this book, I received a coffee mug from a friend. On one side was emblazoned the birth certificate of President Barack Obama; on the other side, a photograph of a smiling Obama, captioned "Made in the USA." The mug, of course, was an artifact of the "birther" controversy ginned up by a civilian Donald Trump to cast doubt on Obama's citizenship and therefore on his ability to serve as president. As many analysts have noted, birtherism was clearly racist, and President Trump's subsequent treatment of nonwhite, female members of Congress—telling them to go back whence they came despite their U.S. citizenship—demonstrated his basic assumption that the United States is a white man's country. Yet few analysts have noted the powerful political work that Obama's birth certificate (figure 0.1) was summoned to do. Emblazoned on my mug, reprinted in countless publications, and broadcast across the television news, the bureaucratic form mobilized its boxes, its official paper, and its mute ordinariness to supply facts in the face of falsehoods, to offer up the epistemological foundation for citizenship and belonging.

That Obama's birth certificate was summoned to do this work owes not simply to the Fourteenth Amendment and its guarantee of birthright citizenship. Instead, it owes to a function that birth certificates have been made to perform only in the recent past: proof of identity. When the Fourteenth Amendment was ratified in 1868 very few Americans would have had birth certificates to prove that they had been born on U.S. soil. The U.S. government did not yet issue standardized passports, and the Department of State did not ask applicants for a birth certificate to prove their citizenship.[1] Indeed, in 1868 even those few Americans who had had their births registered would have been unlikely to ever use a certificate of birth to establish the facts about themselves: their name, place and date of birth, their parentage, their nativity. Instead, if questioned about any of these, they would have relied on the

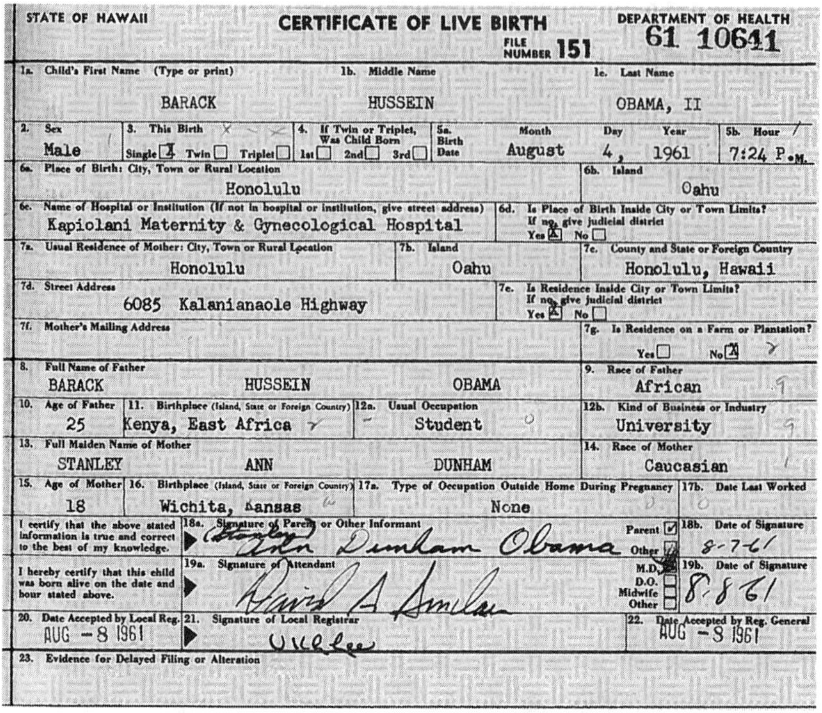

STATE OF HAWAII — CERTIFICATE OF LIVE BIRTH — DEPARTMENT OF HEALTH
FILE NUMBER 151 61 10641

1a. Child's First Name (Type or print): BARACK | 1b. Middle Name: HUSSEIN | 1c. Last Name: OBAMA, II
2. Sex: Male | 3. This Birth: Single [X] Twin [ ] Triplet [ ] | 4. If Twin or Triplet, Was Child Born 1st [ ] 2nd [ ] 3rd [ ] | 5a. Birth Date: Month August, Day 4, Year 1961 | 5b. Hour 7:24 P.M.
6a. Place of Birth: City, Town or Rural Location: Honolulu | 6b. Island: Oahu
6c. Name of Hospital or Institution (If not in hospital or institution, give street address): Kapiolani Maternity & Gynecological Hospital | 6d. Is Place of Birth Inside City or Town Limits? If no, give judicial district. Yes [X] No [ ]
7a. Usual Residence of Mother: City, Town or Rural Location: Honolulu | 7b. Island: Oahu | 7c. County and State or Foreign Country: Honolulu, Hawaii
7d. Street Address: 6085 Kalanianaole Highway | 7e. Is Residence Inside City or Town Limits? If no, give judicial district. Yes [X] No [ ]
7f. Mother's Mailing Address | 7g. Is Residence on a Farm or Plantation? Yes [ ] No [X]
8. Full Name of Father: BARACK HUSSEIN OBAMA | 9. Race of Father: African
10. Age of Father: 25 | 11. Birthplace (Island, State or Foreign Country): Kenya, East Africa | 12a. Usual Occupation: Student | 12b. Kind of Business or Industry: University
13. Full Maiden Name of Mother: STANLEY ANN DUNHAM | 14. Race of Mother: Caucasian
15. Age of Mother: 18 | 16. Birthplace (Island, State or Foreign Country): Wichita, Kansas | 17a. Type of Occupation Outside Home During Pregnancy: None | 17b. Date Last Worked
I certify that the above stated information is true and correct to the best of my knowledge. | 18a. Signature of Parent or Other Informant: Ann Dunham Obama | Parent [X] Other [ ] | 18b. Date of Signature: 8-7-61
I hereby certify that this child was born alive on the date and hour stated above. | 19a. Signature of Attendant: David A. Sinclair | M.D. [X] D.O. [ ] Midwife [ ] Other [ ] | 19b. Date of Signature: 8-8-61
20. Date Accepted by Local Reg.: AUG -8 1961 | 21. Signature of Local Registrar: UKL Lee | 22. Date Accepted by Reg. General: AUG -8 1961
23. Evidence for Delayed Filing or Alteration

Figure 0.1. The birth certificate of Barack Hussein Obama

President Obama's birth certificate was repeatedly scrutinized and published, making clear the often-unacknowledged political work that identity documents perform. Source: State of Hawaii.

testimony of relatives, friends, and neighbors or they would have adduced the family Bible or other personal papers.

President Obama's political advisors hoped that the release of his birth certificate would settle the matter of his citizenship not because birth certificates are inherently citizenship papers but because in the preceding century and a half, a host of individuals, civic organizations, and governmental officials at all levels, from city and county to state and federal, had made them so. These men and women waged a long and iterative campaign that made birth registration universal in the United States and transformed birth certificates into trusted, authoritative identity documents. Today, nearly every baby born in the United States is registered, and birth certificates are the "breeder" documents that generate those that are in even more common use—driver's licenses, social security cards, and passports.

This book describes both sides of that story: how birth registration became universal and how birth certificates were transformed into portable identification long before any other forms of identification were routinized and standardized. Reformers from the 1830s through the 1950s convinced municipalities and states to adopt laws requiring registration at birth; they taught city clerks and state registrars to value "human bookkeeping" and to issue standardized forms; they convinced policy makers that birth registration could be a source of important public health data; they encouraged parents to value birth registration and to cherish the token of that act by pasting their baby's certificate into a baby book or framing it on the wall; they pushed states to make birth certificates into proof of age for employment and old-age pensions or proof of race for access to marriage, schooling, and land; and they argued that, because birth certificates were made by disinterested state officials, these documents were more trustworthy than the testimony of neighbors and more reliable than dates scrawled into the family Bible.

We know that these campaigns were successful not simply because the contemporary United States has universal birth registration. Success is measured also by what it means to fail. Anyone without a registered birth, or without easy access to their birth certificate, is at a severe disadvantage. Indeed, birth registration is considered so fundamental to modern citizenship that the United Nations Convention on the Rights of the Child names it as a fundamental human right. Birth registration affords children official, legal personhood: a name, a birth date (and therefore an age), a family, and a country. Birth registration makes a child known to a state, and a child who is known can be more easily protected from being forced to marry, soldier, or work underage; a child who is known belongs to a country and is entitled to its protections and entitlements. A child who is known can move freely and return to her country of origin. A child who is registered has legal parents who have legal obligations to her.

Across the world more than 290 million children (or about 45 percent) under the age of five do not officially exist. While most of those children live in Asia and sub-Saharan Africa, the undocumented are at a disadvantage no matter where they reside.[2] Around the world, an estimated 1.1 billion people are unable to prove that they belong to their country of birth or residence. In the United States alone, approximately 7 percent of citizens, or 13 million people, most of whom are poor, cannot prove their citizenship.[3] A person who cannot prove who they are and where they were born can easily be pushed to the margins, and beyond the pale, of citizenship. In the modern United States, this is precisely the effect of federal laws such as the REAL ID Act, which mandates that states validate birth certificates for the issuance of driver's licenses or state IDs; voter identification laws in states that require voters to submit state-issued identification at the polls; or federal regulations that require applicants for Medicaid and other benefits to supply state-issued identification. For anyone without a birth certificate, or for anyone who does not know how to obtain theirs or who cannot afford the fee to obtain a certified copy, the most basic rights of citizenship are tenuous.[4] Perhaps 1 percent of all detainees in U.S. Immigration and Customs Enforcement custody today are U.S. citizens who simply cannot prove their citizenship. Just ask Mark Lyttle, who was erroneously identified as Mexican by prison officials in North Carolina. Unable to produce his U.S. birth certificate, in 2008 Lyttle was released into Immigration and Customs Enforcement custody and deported to Mexico, despite having been born in the United States, speaking no Spanish, and having no kin there. Until his brother could locate his birth certificate and fax it to a U.S. consulate, Mark Lyttle was a stateless wanderer, shifting homeless through Mexico and Central America.[5] This is the reason that the word "undocumented" applies to those residents who are said not to belong in the United States. Citizenship may be a birthright, but its documentation is what counts. This is particularly true if, like those whom Donald Trump targets, your skin is not white.[6]

Birth registration does more than provide identification, however. It is also used to create aggregate data about children and their parents that can be used to construct population information and to guide programs of social welfare and public health. It allows a country to gather data about how many children are born annually, where they are born (what towns, cities, or regions), to whom (ethnic or racial groups, single or married mothers), and how (at home, in a hospital, vaginally or by cesarean). Today, birth certificates in the United States are used to record not only identity but also a variety of data about, for instance, prenatal care, maternal habits such as smoking, and whether the birth was covered by public, private, or no insurance. Medical journals are filled with studies that trace the relationship between birth registration and vaccination rates and that use birth registration data to compile infant mortality rates around the world, analyze gestational weights according to maternal age and prenatal care, and track induction of post-term births, to name a few. Indeed, when U.S. reformers began to promote improved birth registration in the 1830s and 1840s, they argued that so doing would provide better public health data and improve public policy.

The single act of registering a birth thus serves two functions: it creates real-time population knowledge and a technology for personal identification. It creates both populations and persons, aggregates and individuals. These functions are linked not only by the act of registration that initiates them both but also by the fact that individuals are made out of the categories that state-issued forms choose to track: name, parentage, place of birth, sex, and race, among others. As such, registration is at the center of how states construct their citizens and apprehend their population. The act of registration transforms a private, familial experience into a political one, linked historically and ideologically with the simultaneous development of both centralized states and individualized identities.[7] The act of registering a live birth, and the certificate that results from this act, is at the foundation of the interface between individuals, identities, and states.

Though all babies born in the United States today are (in theory at least) registered at birth, this is a recent historical development. At the beginning of the twentieth century, only a handful of states had effective systems of birth registration, and most of the U.S. population could not produce an official, government-issued document to prove name, citizenship, birth date, or parentage. It was not until 1933 that all of the then forty-eight states could claim to register an average of 90 percent or more of their live births. Of all the so-called vital events—birth, marriage, and death—registration of birth took the longest to achieve in the United States. Of course, just because babies lacked official registration papers does not mean that their births went unnoticed or unrecorded. As they had for centuries, literate families in the early United States recorded births, marriages, deaths, and other important events in the leaves of family Bibles. Enterprising slave owners recorded "increase" among their slaves in carefully written plantation journals. Likewise, when people had to establish the facts of their birth or other essential elements of their personal identity, nineteenth-century courts and other institutions recognized a variety of legitimate sources of such knowledge. Foremost among these was the individual herself and her family members, all of whom were considered competent to say her birth date or age, her name, or her family connections. If such facts were in dispute, neighbors could be called in to testify as well.[8] Unlike in a system of state-sponsored registration, this knowledge was personal, local, and often oral. Yet by the middle of the twentieth century, not only was birth registration nearly universal in the United States, but the token of this registration—the birth certificate—had become a portable identification paper that displaced oral, local, and personal knowledge as the authoritative source of information about an individual.

This book details how a once locally and unevenly practiced form of record keeping became the most essential mechanism for recording and establishing individual identity. It is a story not only of how birth registration became ubiquitous but also of how birth certificates displaced other forms of knowledge as the state gained a monopoly on epistemological authority. This shift was neither accidental nor inevitable. Indeed, data from around the contemporary world show that rates of birth registration are not predicted by development, modernization, or national wealth. Rather, birth registration is the result of policy: policy that promotes registration and social welfare policy that demands birth documents to function.[9] In the United States, birth registration was the object of reformist attention and its ubiquity the fruit of considerable labor. Reform occurred in two distinct waves. Though some colonies and newly founded states had required that all births be registered, the laws were largely honored in the breach. The first wave of reform, beginning in the 1840s, was led by public health reformers, physicians, and members of the newly founded American Statistical Association, all of whom were interested in improving the nation's well-being. Their interest was less in establishing individual identities than in creating population knowledge. Birth registration, they hoped, would allow the government to know, understand, and manage its population as a whole. Spearheaded by men such as Lemuel Shattuck of Boston, reformers in several states lobbied for new legislation to centralize record keeping and increase enforcement of registration requirements. For men such as Shattuck, the point of vital registration was to provide a more efficient means for a state to know, understand, and govern its population as a whole. Shattuck explained his reasoning in 1850: "We are social beings— bound together by indissoluble ties. Every birth, every marriage, and every death, which takes place, has an influence somewhere [and] a knowledge of these matters alleged to be private, may be an incalculable public benefit."[10] As Shattuck's language suggests, successful registration efforts depended not simply on proper legislation but also on convincing Americans that "private" events had public importance.

Although campaigns to promote birth registration began before the Civil War, the practice was successfully established only along the eastern seaboard. For the remainder of the nineteenth century, birth—which, among vital events, was far less institutionalized than marriage and death (through burial)—remained vastly underreported. With no established churches, no military conscription, and minimal administrative capacity at the state level, the link between birth and governance remained tenuous. By the early twentieth century, a second wave of reformers again tackled the problem of inadequate birth registration. These second-wave reformers coalesced less around an abstract desire for population knowledge and more around the state's growing biopolitical investment in defining and protecting childhood. The underregistration of birth, they maintained, contributed to two central problems facing the state as it tried to foster national health through child protection. First, without birth registration, neither local, state, nor federal government could know the infant mortality rate; without this, policies designed to prevent infant mortality could not be rationally designed or applied. Second, Progressive reformers wanted to use age as an administrative tool to protect children, but they found that without birth registration, children's ages were impossible to determine. Efforts to restrict child labor, raise the age of consent, and mandate school attendance all foundered on the indeterminacy of age. "The obstacles in the way of obtaining correct ages frequently proved insurmountable," complained agents of the U.S. Department of Labor sent to investigate child labor in southern textile mills in 1907.[11] It was not just that parents were free to lie about their children's ages in order that they might work. The larger problem was that there was no external, authoritative empirical basis for adjudicating claims of age. Incomplete and informal documentation of births made age-based restrictions on factory work, marriage, and schooling difficult, if not impossible, to enforce. Early twentieth-century reformers thus wished to know not simply about aggregate populations but about particular individuals: When were they born? Where? To whom? For these questions, the birth certificate held the answer. Kept on file with the state and available as a portable identity paper, it could serve to fix age and identity. As a New York State agent of the National Child Labor Committee explained, the birth certificate was the "most satisfactory proof of age to be obtained."[12]

To achieve the goal of full registration, federal agencies such as the U.S. Census and Children's Bureaus coordinated with national organizations—from the American Medical Association and the American Public Health Association to the General Federation of Women's Clubs—and with state and local voluntary committees. They engaged in a massive, multipronged, multi-agency project to build state capacity. The Census Bureau and private organizations wrote model legislation that they urged on the states so that all vital registration systems would look the same no matter the location. They urged every city and state to use the same forms and office procedures. Federal agencies deployed fieldworkers to states, where they reformed the office practices and record-keeping habits of local clerks and centralized state bureaus.

They fanned out to promote birth registration to parents at churches, state fairs, chambers of commerce, parent-teacher associations, and other local civic organizations. The federal government bolstered states' administrative infrastructure by giving them money through the Sheppard-Towner Act and the Works Progress Administration to hire registration clerks and to mail and process birth certificates. By the mid-1930s, the effort to achieve full registration had been largely successful. States reformed their laws governing vital statistics collection, medical professionals and parents absorbed the notion that a birth was of interest to the government, and a variety of public and private institutions began to rely on the birth certificate as the foundational affixation of identity.

As birth certificates became more common, they also became essential to the functioning of bureaucratic systems such as schooling, employment, military service, social security, and the provision of federal benefits, including land, to the nation's Native Americans. This integration of birth documents into the administration of policy tied the knot between individuals, their documents, and the state. Even then, birth registration was uneven until after World War II. Babies born in a hospital were more likely to be registered than those born at home; white babies more likely than African American; African American more likely than Native American; physician-attended more likely than midwife-attended; and urban more likely than rural. Of course, these demographic categories intersected, and each of these factors could compound another. In a nation with birthright citizenship and no national system of vital registration, state and local systems of birth registration captured birth unevenly, making citizenship itself variegated and unstable. Throughout, when nonwhite Americans interfaced with the state—to marry, enter school, register for the draft, obtain employment, vote, or collect social security—they were more likely to present nonstandardized documentation of identity or none at all (a problem still with us as states pass identification and address requirements for voting). This subjected nonwhites to increased scrutiny and bureaucratic delays and left them at the whim of administrators, who could use personal judgment to decide the accuracy of their identity claims.

But even when they had birth certificates, nonwhite Americans were not necessarily protected by them. White supremacy was one of the bureaucratic systems that birth documents helped states and private employers administer. Southern states used birth certificates to regulate systems of school segregation and prohibitions on interracial marriage. State registrars in places such as Virginia and Louisiana made it their business to personally police racial identification on birth certificates and kept elaborate genealogical records of families they believed would try to "pass" by registering their newborn babies as white. Walter Plecker, Virginia's registrar, wrote to one midwife about a baby whose birth she had recently registered. Though the midwife had marked the baby's race as "white," Plecker wrote that he did not consider the child's father white, "even though he may be white in appearance." According to Plecker's own records, the child's father belonged to a family of mixed racial origins; thus "neither can his child be considered as white." Plecker told the midwife that she must "correct" the baby's race on the birth certificate. "We are warning you," he admonished, "it is a penitentiary offense to make a willfully false statement as to color."[13] Whether functioning to establish age, race, or citizenship, the birth certificate served bureaucracies as a convenient technology of both inclusion and exclusion.

Plecker's careful scrutiny notwithstanding, state administrators did not always get the final say. Precisely because of the birth certificate's increasing power, some Americans began to contest the "facts" that it recorded. The very power of birth certificates—their claim to establish the objective truth about individuals—led to a series of conflicts that showed, ultimately, how epistemologically unstable they were. *The Birth Certificate* traces this dynamic by telling the story of how and why such "facts" as illegitimacy, adoption, and race were removed from the face of birth certificates over the course of the twentieth century. Far from being stable and neutral, the birth certificate's truths were the result of political processes that changed what was possible for the state to know about its citizens.

We know very little about how birth registration came to be compulsory and universal in the United States.[14] Though historians have long used state and ecclesiastical documents (such as birth, death, and marriage certificates, censuses, and passports) as sources of information about populations and individuals, they have too often viewed them as transparent windows onto the past. Recently, however, scholars have argued that we need to "look *at* our archives, not just through them," to interrogate the production and meaning of documents, to recover the logics and concrete practices that lie behind them, and to consider the critical role that such information gathering played in statecraft.[15] To date, much of this scholarship has detailed the development of centralized European states or colonial administration. Recent scholarship on race and immigration in the United States has shown that documentation practices are critical to the construction of basic categories of identity, but accounts of the rise of a documentary regime in the United States are surprisingly thin. When it comes to the politics of government population knowledge, scholars scrutinize the federal, decennial census but ignore vital registration documents, in spite of the fact that census records have no probative value and are not considered a legal form of identification.[16] Despite the absence of scholarly attention to the birth certificate, this apparently humble document is the foundation of individual identity and citizenship in the United States.

The Birth Certificate tells the story of this profound change in how Americans related to the state and constructed identity. As the story of a document that was designed both as a tool of statistical population knowledge and as a form of legal identification, this book takes up several related, yet distinct, historical trajectories. One trajectory is the story of nations' efforts to count or otherwise apprehend their population as a whole through censuses, surveys, and vital statistics. In other words, this is a story about the state: its desire and its capacity to know its population. Both of these elements—desire and capacity—have changed over time. On a grand and transnational scale, historians of western Europe following the lead of Michel Foucault chart the transition from early modern to modern forms of statecraft in terms of changing modes of sovereignty: from the juridical to the biopolitical. Where early modern princes and kings ruled through the force of law and ritualized demonstrations of power, in the Foucauldian schema the modern state is "biopolitical," invested in the health and welfare of its citizens. As such, it rules not through displays of force but through technologies that seek to know, in order to regulate, life and death. The health of the state is identified not with the body of the sovereign but with the bodies of the people; power is bureaucratic and regulatory rather than juridical. This shift in forms of sovereignty is accompanied by the creation of infrastructure for generating knowledge about population and territory. In the words of Bernard Cohn, beginning in the eighteenth century, European states "took control by defining and classifying space, making separations between public and private spheres; by recording transactions such as the sale of property; by counting and classifying their populations, replacing religious institutions as the registrar of birth, marriage, and deaths, and by standardizing languages and scripts." Knowledge, in such tellings, is bound up with power. This account largely intersects with that of the anthropologist James Scott, who credits the "modern" state with the creation of forms of "state simplification" that produce knowledge through categorization and in the service of administrative control. In the creation of territorial maps, censuses, surveys, administrative departments, regulations, and the myriad forms of paperwork that collect information, make citizens visible, and generally grease the wheels of administration, the state uses knowledge to rule. The transition, for Scott, is from blindness to sight through the creation of "legible" subjects who can not only be taxed and conscripted but also become subjects of interventions that promote public health and welfare.[17] In both accounts, the rise of nation-states and the emergence of modern liberal democracies are accompanied by an interlocking network of official forms of knowledge, state population surveillance, and programs to promote social welfare.

The United States is largely left out of such grand historical narratives about the state and its efforts at knowledge production and population management. Partly this is an effect of chronology—born "modern," the United States comes in at the end of the story rather than serving as an illustrative case. Partly this is also because for generations, U.S. historians have done their work under an exceptionalist aegis, the lingering "myth of the weak state."[18] Yet thanks to the work of recent scholars, we know more than ever about the myriad ways that Americans built state capacity from the early republic onward, and we know more than ever about how invested politicians and intellectuals were in knowing, understanding, and analyzing the U.S. population.[19] By turning our attention away from exclusive focus on the federal government and attending instead to the powers, regulations, and activities of states and localities, we find robust forms of governance. The story of universal birth registration extends this revisionist interpretation by focusing on a power, and a duty, denied to the federal government but given to states and localities. As Cressy Wilbur, the chief statistician for the U.S. Census Bureau, explained in 1913, the American constitutional order meant that, from the perspective of universal registration, "we are of course at a disadvantage as compared with foreign countries in which a national registration law can be enacted." Alas, sighed Wilbur, "there is no Constitutional authority for it" and thus no "magic power" to make registration happen by federal fiat.[20] While the federal government had no power to register births or to require their registration, in the twentieth century federal agencies helped private organizations dedicated to child welfare and public health press for registration reform in individual states. The story of the spread of universal and compulsory birth registration therefore illustrates the multilayered, public-private nature of governance in the United States, the functioning of what one scholar has called the "Rube Goldberg state."[21]

Birth registration was a critical function of the modern state because it was part of the emergence of a certain kind of state—one that knows, monitors, and invests in the life of its citizens. But birth registration was also central to the construction of what we might think of as an "aged" state, that is, to the increasing reliance on age as a fundamental organizing category that regulates access to schooling, employment, driving, voting, and retirement benefits (to name just a few) according to precise numerical age. Examining the spread of birth registration and the use of birth certificates as technologies of identification provides the crucial window onto a process that historians have identified as central to the construction of both modern childhood and the American polity: the increasing reliance on chronological age to define the boundary between capacity and incapacity, dependence and independence, innocence and worldliness, and protection and rights. From early in its history, age was particularly important in the United States. As Holly Brewer has shown, consent-based liberal political theory made age (as a proxy for reason) more important than social status to the determination of civil and political rights. Age-consciousness has also enabled the kind of radical rationalization in the interest of bureaucratic efficiency that defines the functioning of modern institutions, including those under the penumbra of the state and its regulatory agencies. And, as the sociologist Judith Treas aptly puts it, "age standards require standards for age." In other words, using age as an administrative standard produced chronological age as an objective fact and contributed to what Treas identifies as the standardization of the life course. By the middle of the twentieth century, birth certificates were the preferred instrument for this epistemological shorthand.[22] And yet, although we know that age has become more important over time, we know strikingly little about the spread of the quotidian practices, forms, and documents that have made this reliance on birth date possible. And we know almost nothing specific about *how* standards of proof of age have changed over time. When early twentieth-century child labor reformers, for example, proposed to replace parental affidavits of age with "documentary proof," not only did they clash with many working people's assumptions about their children's capacity for work, but they radically altered legal notions of proof as well. State-issued birth records—and their use as authoritative statements of identity and age—changed the empirical foundations upon which the state's knowledge about its citizens rested. This book not only documents the fact of such changes but also details the means by which they were institutionalized.

As a paper technology that created both persons and populations, and that standardized the categories that comprise identity, birth registration also forms part of the story of the spread of technologies for creating uniformity and predictability. This story in turn weaves together histories of capitalism, science, and the state. Lemuel Shattuck and the other nineteenth-century men of medicine and science who promoted vital registration were among the earliest American statists—men who believed in the power of statistics to reveal the universal laws of life and health. The "public benefit" to be gained from vital registration was therefore that governments might learn what caused population growth and decline, or low or high rates of fertility and mortality; they might be able to isolate which professions were healthy or injurious and which cities or regions most salubrious to glimpse the interplay between climate and demography. Though such matters had been of interest since the early modern period in Europe, the creation of civil registration systems (as distinct from the ecclesiastical infrastructure of parish registries) was part of the explosion of interest and faith in numbers that swept across the West in the nineteenth century. Alongside this "avalanche of numbers" was a belief that underneath the apparent chaos of events there were regularities that would reveal themselves, if only the right information could be standardized and aggregated. No less than the men who pioneered life and other forms of insurance or crop and weather forecasting, the reformers who urged Americans to create a coherent system of vital registration believed that data could help them tame chance. In the case of the engineers of vital registration, it was population movements, life and death, and sickness and health, rather than economic fluctuations and cycles, that they sought to understand and influence. As a technology of knowledge, birth registration must therefore be considered as part of the "infrastructure of pens and paper" through which data were made.[23]

Like account books, plantation journals, and credit reports, the registers in which local clerks recorded births and the birth certificates they issued to individuals were among the hundreds of types of preprinted standardized forms and fill-in-the-blank books that formed a substrate in the managerial revolution in both business and bureaucracy.[24] Like other kinds of record books and reporting forms, birth registration books and birth certificates were designed to make information standard, uniform, and fungible in order to make human life knowable. Promoters of vital registration frequently analogized the practice as a form of accounting. In explaining its campaign to promote birth registration, the U.S. Children's Bureau lamented that the United States had "no national bookkeeping to account for the ebb and flow of human life as an asset and a liability of our civic organism."[25] This was more than just a metaphor, however. Government interest in population size, fertility, and demographics grew out of a mercantilist "political arithmetic" pioneered by British political economists who did indeed view human bodies as sources of wealth and power for the Crown. Birth was profit, death loss. What is more, like the "bookkeeping" of double-entry accounting, to which such analogies referred, the record keeping of vital registration systems had embedded within it a set of epistemological assumptions and procedures for generating reliable knowledge. As Mary Poovey has argued, accounting gained epistemological authority because it required "writing to rule"—that is, through the use of standardized record books and rules for how to fill them, double-entry accounting "disciplined anyone who wrote in the books" by placing them in "writing positions." This combination produced "facts," statements that were true by virtue of having been produced through rules made manifest in forms.[26]

Like account books and other routinized modes for creating knowledge, birth registration was likewise designed to create reliable, uniform information. It was occasioned by many of the same changes that gave rise to an "information infrastructure" in the United States: territorial expansion, population mobility, urban growth, market economics, and institutional complexity, all of which strained bonds of social trust and long-standing techniques for gathering and assessing information.[27] A small, stable, and residentially fixed population had little need for proof of identity; like the credit reporting bureaus that sprang up to facilitate market exchange across distance and to make strangers legible to one another, the vital registration laws passed beginning in the 1840s provided a means to fix people who were increasingly mobile.[28] They set up an infrastructure for the collection and aggregation of records; this created clear lines of authority about who was responsible for reporting vital events and provided for state production and distribution of record books and standard forms for physicians, sextons, undertakers, and clerks. Irregularity, variation, failure to adhere to systems, lack of similar procedures from state to state—these were the bane of those who labored to establish universal birth registration. Elisha Harris, the registrar of vital statistics for New York City, wrote in 1875 that Americans should strive for "uniformity in practice, and comparable results . . . in the methods and system of registration of Vital Statistics." He averred that the best means of achieving this was to centralize authority over procedure so that local variations in reporting would be minimized. Harris and others also advocated that similar laws, forms, and office procedures be adopted from state to state.[29] Uniformity was both the outcome and the object of the campaign for birth registration.

In 1939, the U.S. Census Bureau issued an illustrated pamphlet entitled *Why Register?* Its pages offered an extended argument for the importance of birth registration to individuals throughout the life cycle. The cover showed a group of babies holding picket signs, as if they were in a march. One read, "Birth Registration is our Protection." The other babies held signs that, taken together, queried, "Parents Can You Prove We Are Your Own?" Expanding outward from the basic fact of establishing maternity and paternity, the contents of the pamphlet explained that parents should register births "to prove date of birth for entrance to school, for first work permit, for automobile license, for right to vote, for right to marry, for right to enter civil service, for entering military service, for settlement of pensions, for social security benefits to blind, dependent children, aged." In addition to all these age-based protections and entitlements that birth registration could help individuals secure, *Why Register?* also argued that birth registration could help prove "the fact of birth," useful for "establishing identity" in cases of disputed parentage, inheritance, insurance settlements, and legal dependency. Likewise, a birth certificate could establish the "place of birth" for purposes of proving citizenship, immigrating or emigrating, and obtaining a passport.

Among the benefits of birth registration, the Census Bureau made scant mention of the state's interest in knowing its population and tracing its increase, decrease, and demographic characteristics; indeed, it pictured the advantages of registration as accruing entirely to the individual (figure 0.2). The creators of *Why Register?* were repeating arguments that had been made for at least three decades about why parents and individuals should care about birth registration: not because it provided aggregate statistical information that might inform policy but because it let individuals prove who they were—when and where they were born and to whom. While the reformers who began to promote American registration laws and practices some 100 years earlier would have recognized some of these arguments—particularly those about establishing legal identity in cases of inheritance and parentage—they could not have imagined the range of uses to which birth certificates would be put by the middle of the twentieth century. In part this is because so many of the programs listed in *Why Register?* did not exist when the first registration

Figure 0.2. Illustration from *Why Register?* (1939)

The view of registration presented here illustrates how important birth certificates had become as identification documents, as well as their role in administering the features of a standardized, age-based life cycle. Source: Records of the Bureau of the Census, National Archives and Records Administration, Washington, D.C.

laws were passed in the early republic—there were few age-based restrictions on labor and schooling, for example, and there were no pensions, no social security or federal aid to dependent children, no driver's licenses, no uniform passports, and not even birthright citizenship. In part this was also because when people were called upon to prove their parentage, age, or citizenship, government-produced identification documents were neither required nor expected. Personal testimony, family records, and community knowledge could tell courts and other institutions who people were. For reformers of the early republic, the problem was not that people could not prove who they were; it was that the state did not know its population in the aggregate, could not discern the laws of life and health that governed its people's health and welfare, and thus could not act to strengthen the nation. The world described by

Why Register? by contrast was more complex, more bureaucratic, and more standardized.

The overwhelmingly individual-centered and positive view of registration presented by *Why Register?* might also surprise scholars, many of whom view the rise of state-sponsored forms of identification with ambivalence. If *Why Register?* presented birth registration as a straightforward mechanism for protection and an instrument for individual rights, scholars often view identity documentation as a node in the system of "mass surveillance and social control" that emerged with the growth of large, complex organizations—industrial capitalism and a bureaucratic, managerial state. Documents are how individuals interface with institutions, and documentation is how institutions rule. This is what Max Weber called "domination through knowledge" or what James Scott would call the creation of a "legible" society through "internal colonization" that proceeds via the creation of "the uniformity of codes, identities, statistics, regulations, and measures."[30] In such accounts, documentary identity appears dehumanizing and oppressive. Through documents, individuals are stripped of complexity, humanity, and ultimately freedom by being reduced to the categories on a form; documents make it possible for governments to know their citizens as a series of abstractions and to render them two-dimensional, capable of being collated, filed, and indexed. In contrast to a politics of recognition, in such scholarship visibility is pictured as inauthentic and disempowering.

In contemporary politics, this scholarly criticism has its parallel in civil disobedience to vital registration. Libertarian author Carl Watner writes that because "effective birth registration lies at the heart of the state's governance of its people," the state has "coercively monopolized the issuance of birth certificates by making it a criminal act for those who are responsible for a birth not to register the newborn." Without the state, Watner argues, most of the reasons to register births would wither away. The sovereign citizen movement, a white nationalist strain of libertarianism, maintains that birth registration makes people property of the state; members of such groups typically refuse to register their children. While state laws already, as Watner notes, make it a crime not to register a birth, children who are not registered at birth can be retroactively registered by submitting documentary proof of birth date and identity. However, as in the case of Texas-born Faith Pennington, who was born at home, homeschooled, and had no other institutional traces, parents do not always cooperate. Pennington's parents refused to help her document her identity later in life when she wanted to get a birth certificate to attend school, seek employment, and obtain a driver's license. Such refusals on the part of sovereign citizen parents led the Texas legislature to create a new law making it a crime for any parent to withhold documentation from a child who asks for it.[31] Whatever we may think of them, protests like those of the sovereign citizens register the ways in which identity documentation is an exercise of the state's power to produce citizens subject to its authority.

Another set of scholars, however, complicate such dour accounts of the rise of documentation. If not reaching the same cheerful conclusions as *Why Register?*, they nonetheless recognize that individuals may benefit from being known by the state and, specifically, by having identity documents. Recent scholarship emphasizes that registration systems have "been the crucial primary instrument for realizing entitlements" and that "large systems of registration, whether of people or of things, tend to work only when they provide an obvious benefit to the people being targeted."[32] In other words, registration works when it works for people, not when it is only an instrument of surveillance and control. Certainly the architects of vital registration and other forms of documentation in the United States labored to convince Americans that these systems were made to help them. Indeed, Americans seemed to welcome certain forms of state knowledge; this was particularly evident when, as in the case of social security, they benefited from being registered, numbered, and documented. (Some even went so far as to tattoo their social security numbers on their bodies.) When citizens stood to benefit from the state's knowledge of their identities, they chose visibility over privacy.[33]

This more positive scholarly account of the relationship between people and the papers that document them has its political counterpart in movements that link documentation to personhood. Most obvious is the UN charter of children's rights. But while the UN charter emphasizes the obligation of the state to provide official registration, more recently groups of individuals have mobilized to seek recognition of identity claims and personal experiences through state records. This is the case with a movement among parents of stillborn infants to receive birth certificates, rather than just death certificates, for their fetuses. The practice in most states until very recently was to issue only a death certificate, which some mothers of stillborn fetuses argued denied them "dignity and validation" of their pregnancy and labor and delivery. Without a birth certificate, parents of the stillborn felt the state was denying their experience of having gestated and birthed a real child. Advocates succeeded in convincing many state legislatures to offer birth certificates for stillbirths, though detractors objected that "birth certificates are legal documents, not memory trinkets or prizes for enduring birthing."[34] Though no entitlements or benefits attach to a certificate of birth for a stillborn fetus, the parents who argue for them proceed within the logic first expressed by Lemuel Shattuck some 160 years earlier: that vital registration depends on understanding "matters alleged to be private" as actually public. Moreover, such parents also express arguments made by Progressive Era campaigners who promoted birth registration as an act of parental love and encouraged parents to prize the birth certificate itself as a token of the child, something to be hung on the wall in a frame or pasted into the baby book as a keepsake of both emotional and legal value. These parents recognize that state documents have a part in constructing reality and validating identity; all they want is to have their experiences of parenthood recognized as real, something they feel that the state's documents have the power to do.

Whether they criticize state identification or clamor for recognition through documentation, both scholars and contemporary political actors recognize that documents are integral to the process of creating identity. Among the most important of these documents is the birth certificate, a document with epistemological authority to establish the original facts of identity. The birth certificate claims a special relationship to time (it is made at birth, not later, so it freezes time) and to authority (it is filled out by persons licensed by the state—physicians, midwives, hospital administrators, or registrars). In the pages that follow, not only do I show how reformers, lawmakers, statisticians, public health advocates, and child welfare workers labored to make birth registration uniform, universal, and routine, but I also attend to the consequences of their actions.

This book is organized into three parts that are roughly but not wholly chronological. In a federal republic with state sovereignty over health and welfare, the story is iterative rather than linear (Massachusetts had a working birth registration system before the Civil War, while Texas arrived at that point only in the 1930s, for example). Part 1, "Building Birth Registration," begins with the interest of early modern rules in population knowledge, follows that to the eastern shores of North America, and traces how white settlers in the early republic built state systems to register birth, usually with the help of civic organizations and the federal government. Altogether, the three chapters in part 1 describe the motivation to register births and trace the creation of infrastructure to do so. Part 2, "Living with Birth Registration," analyzes how states and the federal government began to use birth registration to administer policy: to trace and prevent infant mortality; to prove age for purposes of child labor law; and to classify Americans according to race for programs such as the allotment of Indian reservations and the enforcement of state Jim Crow laws. These chapters demonstrate how the birth certificate, once imagined chiefly as a tool of public health and statistical knowledge, became the most important identity document of the modern U.S. state. Part 3, "Contesting Birth Registration," argues that the more central birth certificates became to identification, the more their basic categories were subject to contest. Quite literally, boxes were removed from the form over time and the standard certificate issued by the U.S. Census Bureau was repeatedly redesigned. Specifically, I examine how categories such as birth status (legitimate or illegitimate) and race were removed from the face of birth certificates, and I tell the story of how unregistered Americans clamored for delayed or post hoc registration during the middle of the twentieth century. These battles over who could obtain a birth certificate and what they should say on them reshaped the documents, the processes for acquiring them, and the underlying rationale for why states are in the business of recording births at all.

Taken together, the chapters trace the career of a document from a marginal, little-used, and poorly attended-to form of record keeping to a central and universal form of identification. Those who promoted birth registration, whether as a form of population knowledge or as a form of identification, hoped that proper laws, forms, and record-keeping practices could create stable, uniform knowledge. In practice, this often failed—not only because doctors, midwives, and clerks often deviated from the letter of the law as they failed to register births or to fill out forms properly but also because ordinary people contested the categories that governments devised to know them by. More than anything, these conflicts remind us that selves are made, not born.

PART 1

BUILDING BIRTH REGISTRATION

CHAPTER 1

THE LAWS OF LIFE AND HEALTH

"If a child is born, if a marriage takes place, or if a person dies, in my house, it is my own affair; what business is it to the public?" This is the question that Massachusetts statistician, genealogist, and public health reformer Lemuel Shattuck imagined that doubters might put to him as he released his 1850 *Report of a General Plan for the Promotion of Public and Personal Health*. Shattuck was perhaps the leading American spokesman for the importance of collecting accurate population information through a combination of vital registration and census enumeration, and he had been commissioned by the State of Massachusetts to devise a plan "to ascertain the causes which favorably or unfavorably affect the health of its inhabitants."[1] A founder of the American Statistical Association, Shattuck had been instrumental in convincing the Massachusetts legislature to reform the state's vital registration laws in 1842. In 1845 he had conducted a widely admired census of the city of Boston, after which he had gone on to advise the U.S. Congress on the (controversial) new schedule for the 1850 federal census. In his efforts to reform Massachusetts's vital registration system, in his 1845 census of Boston, and in his work on the 1850 census, Shattuck's overarching goal was to record exact information about each individual (rather than each household) in the polity to ensure what his defenders called "accuracy in the tables."[2] Individuals were, in other words, the foundation of the aggregate.

In the 1850 *Report* for the State of Massachusetts, not only did Shattuck write as someone with a great deal of practical knowledge about the operation of registration and census systems, but he also used the platform to express his fullest vision of the value of population information to the art of governance. In answering his hypothetical critic, Shattuck explained that anyone who viewed the recording of births, deaths, and marriages as an invasion of privacy had "very inadequate conceptions of the obligations they owe to themselves or others." Such people failed to grasp that "we are social beings—bound together by indissoluble ties." Far from being private matters, "every birth, every marriage, and every death, which takes place, has an influence somewhere." It was the task of public health officials to record these events so that statisticians might determine the patterns in the "revolutions of human life." "A knowledge of these matters, alleged to be private," Shattuck continued, "may be an incalculable public benefit." Without basic population statistics—and particularly those "population movements" reflected in the procession of vital events—governments would not have "a correct basis on which to found remedies for improvement and progress."[3] For Shattuck, population information was the basis for a scientific form of governance; his was a vision of a world in which data would animate the hearts of statesmen who acted not in accordance with the demands of partisan politics but to promote the public health and welfare.

Shattuck's idea that population knowledge was of public benefit, and that it should inform governance, was not in itself new. Since the early modern period, the size, health, and makeup of the population had been of interest to kings and their advisors who believed not only that a large population was the foundation of national and imperial strength but also that rulers should promote population growth. What was new, however, was the idea that population knowledge should come through vital registration rather than through other forms of counting and aggregation. Unlike census taking or other modes of enumeration, vital registration provided real-time knowledge of population movements—birth and deaths—and built aggregates out of precise knowledge about individuals. The idea that population knowledge was important to governance was not new and neither was record keeping about individuals, when they were born, and when they died. For centuries, both families and churches across Europe and its imperial outcroppings kept such records and used them, when necessary, to establish the ties of kinship that governed property transmission. And since the seventeenth century, the colonies of British America had required (though not enforced) some kind of "public" recording of births, marriages, and deaths in either civil or ecclesiastical record books. But the vital registration that Shattuck promoted was different from either of these because it sought to combine these two streams of interest in populations: it braided together the recording of individuals with the aggregation of total populations in order to create statistical knowledge and discern the "laws of life and health."

Many others shared Shattuck's vision and joined him to promote better vital registration in the early republic. Indeed, even as Shattuck composed and released his 1850 *Report*, reformers in several states were waging a campaign to ensure more accurate vital registration. Fledgling statisticians worried that births went unrecorded, lost to both the present and the future. For such reformers, information about births was useful as one link in a chain that also included marriage and death data. They hoped that such vital statistics would reveal the laws of human life and enable governments to ameliorate insalubrious conditions. In Michel Foucault's terms, vital registration reformers sought to advance a "biopolitics of the population"—to develop a state with capacities enlarged to "ensure, maintain, or develop" the life of the social body.[4] What joined the two existing streams of population knowledge—the aggregation of early modern rulers and the individualizing knowledge of lineage record keeping—was an intense interest in reproduction and its links to statecraft. Properly conducted, a system of vital registration showed not only that a population shrank or grew, but how: when and where births happened most often; what kinds of people had babies; and how many of those babies lived and how many died. Promising more than mere numbers, vital registration promised the ability to disaggregate and correlate. Of course, everything depended on "accuracy in the tables," and the tables were built out of data collected on forms that first had to find their way into every birthing room in the nation.

At the time that Shattuck wrote his *Report of a General Plan for the Promotion of Public and Personal Health* in 1850, men had begun to enter the birthing rooms of at least some women. Elite, white women in urban centers such as Philadelphia, Boston, and New York participated in a fad for male doctors, trained abroad in Scotland or at one of the few medical schools in the early republic, to attend their births. For centuries before that, in Europe and among European colonists in North America, birthing was the domain of women. When a pregnant white woman in seventeenth- or eighteenth-century British America went into labor, she would gather with her mother, her sisters, her neighbors, and perhaps a midwife, and together they would wait for the baby's arrival. When the baby arrived, this cadre of women would tend to the newborn and her exhausted, sweaty mother, cleaning and swaddling the baby, changing the bedsheets, bringing the new mother food and drink, and superintending the household so that mother and baby could stay in bed, breastfeeding, sleeping, and recovering.[5] If this new baby was born into a literate household, or a household with any property to transmit, at some point someone might record her birth. This record might be formal, an entry penned into the logbook of a town clerk or a parish priest, or it might be informal, her name entered into a family's account of itself.

Family record keeping was quite common in early America and formed an important part of the "genealogical literacy" of British Americans. Families recorded lineage for a number of reasons, but as Karin Wulf points out, doing so reinforced the emphasis on ancestry (and patriarchy) present in Protestantism, monarchical rule, and British common law.[6] Literate white families recorded and commemorated their births, deaths, and kinship ties in a number of ways. Many, of course, recorded births, marriages, and deaths in the leaves of family Bibles. Bibles, themselves replete with detailed recounting of lineage, provided blank pages at their front and back for such lists, and by the end of the eighteenth century, not only did commercially produced Bibles available in North America have blank pages intended for such use, but many had preprinted family register forms included in the front pages. Enterprising engravers and printers also sold discrete family registers during the same period. These were normally a single, oversized sheet that included four columns, one each for name, date and place of birth, marriage, and death. Wealthier families even produced printed broadside family records that could be shared and circulated among family members. Middling and elite families also purchased family tree lithographs to display in their homes, while many adolescent girls who attended female seminaries in the Northeast were taught to embroider by stitching out decorative, but detailed, family registers and family trees on linen.[7]

Aside from these traditional and relatively structured ways of recording lineage, many families also used whatever was at hand, including diaries, commonplace books, account books, almanacs, and even loose scraps of paper. While records made in family Bibles, stitched in embroidery, or lithographed and hung on the wall might lend a moral significance to the family and its lineage, scratching out births and deaths in these other generic books indicated that keeping such records could also be intensely practical.[8] Toward the end of the eighteenth century, Virginian John Brown, for example, used the back pages of an arithmetic book to record vital events in his family.[9] There is no record of whether Brown ever had reason to consult his records, but we know that one reason families recorded births was to provide evidence of the patrilineal systems through which property flowed in both England and early America (figure 1.1).[10]

Among the forms of property that Americans sought to secure and transmit were slaves. Slavery was genealogical in a double sense: it was a matrilineal

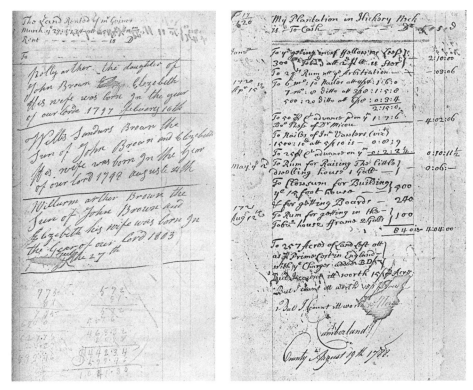

Figure 1.1. Entries from John Brown's arithmetic book (1788)

Brown used the book to keep accounts on his plantation (on the right) as well as to record the births of his children (on the left). Source: Courtesy of the Library of Virginia.

system that transmitted slave status through the mother, while white people's property in people passed from a male head of household to his descendants. Recording the births of slaves preserved both forms of information for the present and the future. John Brown, for example, used the arithmetic book to record the births of his slaves, whom he referred to as "my negro boy" and "my negro girl."[11] Like those of his family, these records, too, were practical in nature and fit neatly alongside his accounting of hogs and sheep killed, boards and nails bought, carpenters paid, and acres of land purchased. Brown's practice was hardly singular. Across the Atlantic world many slave owners kept plantation records that included a good deal of demographic information about their human property: births, deaths, skills, labor output, food rations, illness, and injury. The standardized plantation manuals and account books available by the early nineteenth century contained pages for planters to inventory their slaves by age, sex, and skill, as well as pages on which to record births and deaths. While John Brown may have recorded the births of his own children for a combination of sentimental and practical reasons (the latter having to do with legal matters of lineage and age of majority), in the case of slaves, plantation owners had a different set of practical matters in mind. The list of the total slave population was a list of assets that could be translated into credit. Keeping track of births could yield a host of important information: it told planters which female slaves were most fecund; it gave age information about slaves born on the plantation, which factored into both tasks and value (for either insurance or sale); and it documented the increase of assets for creditors.[12]

Unlike the family Bible or other familial records, these accounts of birth were not intended to establish the legal identity or family relations of the enslaved.[13] Indeed, Frederick Douglass opened his autobiography, *Narrative of the Life of Frederick Douglass*, with a lament that though he knew where he was born, he did not know his birth date. "I have no accurate knowledge of my age, never having seen any authentic record containing it," he wrote. "By far the larger part of the slaves know as little of their ages as horses know of theirs, and it is the wish of most masters within my knowledge to keep their slaves thus ignorant." Denying slaves information about their birth date was, for Douglass, both a symbol of slavery's wrongs and a source of his own awakening to its injustices. "A want of information concerning my own [birth date] was a source of unhappiness to me even during childhood," he continued. "The white children could tell their ages. I could not tell why I ought to be deprived of the same privilege."[14] Douglass was not the only former slave to complain about not knowing his own birthday or age. Indeed, many other slave narratives began with a similar observation. "Like the most of my brothers in bondage, I have no correct account of my age," began Henry Watson's 1848 autobiography.[15] Ex-slave Nat Love opened his autobiography in a similar vein. "The exact date of my birth I never knew, because in those days no count was kept of such trivial matters as the birth of a slave baby. They were born and died and the account was balanced in the gains and losses of the Master's chattels, and one more or less did not matter much one way or another," Love recounted.[16]

Instead, as Douglass noted, slaves marked birth seasonally, telling their children they were born at "planting-time, harvest-time, cherry-time, spring-time, or fall-time." To exist without a birth date was, in such tellings, to be regarded as part of the natural rather than the human world, to exist in a different time horizon. By asserting, as Douglass did, that the erasure of a specific birth date to slaves was deliberate—and by contrasting this to whites' knowledge of their own birthdays—slave narrators connected birth information to individual identity and personhood as a form of racial privilege. In such accounts, unknown birthdays and unknown ages symbolized the harm of slavery: it treated individual human beings as fungible chattel rather than as particular beings. All else that was wrong with slavery—its violence and its separation of families, for example—stemmed from this underlying premise, ritually enacted every time that a slave baby was born and her birth was recorded in the plantation account book but not the family Bible. Family records marked down more than names and dates, but etched with those were marks of status, race, and privilege. And whether a birth was recorded in a plantation book, in a family Bible, or on a scrap of paper tucked into a cabinet or shoved into an account book, these private records functioned as more than internal housekeeping. They also served an important public purpose by tracing the family connections that governed a fundamental political unit: the household and its property.

While the scene of birth may have been the province of women for most early Americans, a father had a role to play in seeing that his child's birth was recorded. He might have been the literate one in the family, the one to write out his new child's name beneath that of those already born. But that might not be the end of his work, for in addition to families, civil and ecclesiastical institutions also recorded births, and if a man's child was to be recorded by the town or the church, he was most certainly responsible for crossing the threshold to see that it was done. Baptisms, and sometimes birth dates, were recorded by priests in both Protestant and Catholic churches. Beginning in the fifteenth century in Spain under the bishop of Toledo, registration of baptisms and burials became an ecclesiastical function, one made official by the 1563 Council of Trent, at which the Catholic Church made the keeping of parish registers a duty of the church.[17] In England's Anglican Church, registration of baptism, marriage, and burial rites began in 1538 under an injunction issued by Thomas Cromwell. As records of religious rites rather than vital events, they did not include the baptisms, marriages, and burials of religious dissenters. And while dissenters may have been few and far between in the 1530s, in the seventeenth and eighteenth centuries, their numbers dramatically increased. During the

30 | BUILDING BIRTH REGISTRATION

mid-eighteenth century, some parliamentary reformers sought to incorporate excluded dissenters in official records by urging new legislation that would require the registration of "natural" rather than religious events—birth, marriage, and death rather than baptism, marriage, and burial. These proposals also called for the creation of a national registry that would collect and aggregate local records. Neither proposal came to pass until the nineteenth century, however.[18]

The ecclesiastical bookkeeping that took place in many countries was hardly just about tallying souls. Like family bookkeeping, ecclesiastical registration fed a growing imperative in early modern Europe: identification of individuals. Indeed, throughout Europe, as both populations and property become more mobile in the early modern period, civil authorities relied more and more on ecclesiastical records to perform the work of identification. As Simon Szreter argues, in England the sixteenth-century system of parish registers was created for "legal and economic" rather than demographic purposes.[19] When Thomas Cromwell issued the original 1538 injunction, he explained that the registers could be used "for the avoiding of sundry strifes and processes and contentsion arising from age, lineal descent, title of inheritance, legitimation of bastardy, and for knowledge, whether any person is our subject or no." The parish registers, in other words, by securing the facts of identity and kinship helped the English—who had more mobile property than other sixteenth-century Europeans—to securely transmit property from generation to generation and, as a bonus, provided this service to religious loyalists over and above dissenters. After the Poor Laws of 1598 and 1601 created a parish-based system of social welfare support, registration created a form of property-in-residence even for the poor and propertyless and made inclusion in the registers a form of legal and social recognition of individual identity that applied to all classes.[20]

Though not ordinarily ordered to do so by civil authorities, many churches in early America did keep records of baptisms. Christ Church of Boston, for example, an Episcopal church, recorded the date of baptism and the names of the baptized person and her parents during the late eighteenth and early nineteenth centuries. However, the records indicate that families often baptized multiple children on a single day.[21] While this might make the records good evidence of lineage, they were not good evidence of birth date or age. St. Michael's Church in Charleston, South Carolina, by contrast, provides a good example of church records that could be mobilized for legal identification. Entries in its baptismal register gave the name of the father, mother, and

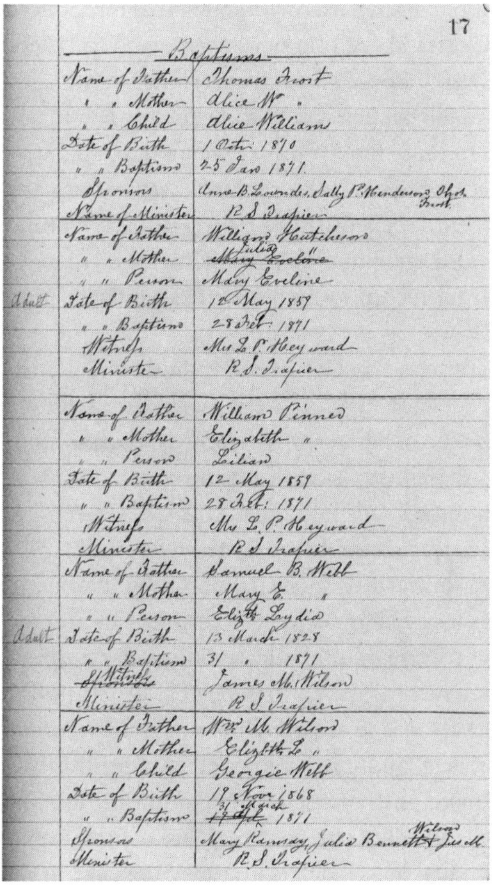

17

Baptisms

	Name of Father	Thomas Frost
	" " Mother	Alice W. "
	" " Child	Alice Williams
	Date of Birth	1 Octr 1870
	" " Baptism	25 Jan 1871.
	Sponsors	Anne B. Lowndes, Sally P. Henderson & Chas. Frost.
	Name of Minister	R. S. Trapier
	Name of Father	William Hutchinson
	" " Mother	~~Mary Eveline~~ Julia "
	" " Person	Mary Eveline
Adult	Date of Birth	12 May 1857
	" " Baptism	28 Feb. 1871
	Witness	Mrs L. P. Heyward
	Minister	R. S. Trapier
	Name of Father	William Pinned
	" " Mother	Elizabeth "
	" " Person	Lilian
	Date of Birth	12 May 1859
	" " Baptism	28 Feb. 1871
	Witness	Mrs L. P. Heyward
	Minister	R. S. Trapier
	Name of Father	Samuel B. Webb
	" " Mother	Mary E. "
	" " Person	Elizth Lydia
Adult	Date of Birth	13 March 1828
	" " Baptism	31 " 1871
	~~Sponsors~~ Witness	James M. Wilson
	Minister	R. S. Trapier
	Name of Father	Wm. M. Wilson
	" " Mother	Elizth E. "
	" " Child	Georgie Webb
	Date of Birth	19 Novr 1868
	" " Baptism	~~17 Apl~~ 31 March 1871
	Sponsors	Mary Ramsay, Julia Bennett & Jas. M. Wilson
	Minister	R. S. Trapier

Figure 1.2. Register of baptisms, St. Michael's Church (1870)

While many church records were not well kept, these could have provided good evidence of legal identification because they recorded the name of the father, mother, and child and the date of birth as well as date of baptism. Source: From the St. Michael's Church Records, 1751–1983 (#320.00) collection at the South Carolina Historical Society.

child and date of birth as well as date of baptism (figure 1.2).[22] Besides official church records, ministers often used their personal diaries to record baptisms, burials, and marriages that they presided over.[23] Absent the legal requirement to keep such records, however, and absent the kind of unified church administrative structure present in many European countries, the clergy seemed, in the words of one antebellum commentator, "not aware of the importance of ecclesiastical records" to "the personal history or identity of individuals."[24]

Given the tradition of parish registration in England, it is not surprising that British colonists also attempted to set up official, legally binding registration systems. Their manner of so doing varied. In 1611, the London Company created a set of rules by which its enterprise in Jamestown should be governed.

Called Dale's Code, these regulations included a requirement that reproduced England's registration system. Clerics in the colony were enjoined to "keepe a faithful and true Record, or Church Booke, of all Christenings, Marriages, and Deaths of such our people as shall happen within their Fort, or Fortresses, Townes or Towne, at any time." In 1619, the Virginia Colony's new legislative assembly passed its own registration bill requiring clergy to keep records and to make annual reports from them. The legislature revisited these requirements again later in the century, and again in the eighteenth century, to make more church officials responsible for recording and reporting baptisms, marriages, and burials.[25]

In the Plymouth and Massachusetts Bay Colonies, by contrast, colonists established a civil registration system, the first in the Western world. Rather than continuing the English tradition of having priests record baptisms, marriages, and burials, the religious dissenters who formed the core migrants to these colonies wrenched registration responsibility away from the church and gave it to secular authorities. This was no doubt motivated by both their experience of exclusion from Anglican records in England and by their arch-Protestant desire to secularize as many church rites as possible.[26] In order to move from ecclesiastical to state control of vital registration, Massachusetts had to create an alternative administrative and epistemological structure. The alternative epistemological structure was to regard the events to be recorded as "natural" events—birth, marriage, and death rather than baptism, marriage, and burial (a change England itself would not make until 1836). The new administrative structure gave the duty of recording these natural events to town clerks and required individual householders to deliver the news to the clerks of the writ. From this civil system's first introduction in 1639 until the consolidation of Plymouth and Massachusetts Bay in 1692, legislators made reforms to increase compliance with vital registration by imposing penalties for failure to report and shifting responsibility for reporting from clerks to householders. Minor changes notwithstanding, this system of registration stood intact until the Revolution.[27]

Though Jamestown and the Massachusetts colonies provided alternative models of registration as either ecclesiastical or civil, other British colonies in mainland North America followed the Massachusetts model, while those in the Caribbean tended to adopt parish registration.[28] Wherever they were, and however they were administered, these colonial registration systems registered at best half of the events they were designed to capture: births/christenings, deaths/burials, or marriages.[29] In the absence of complete civil or ecclesiastical records, individuals, courts, and other administrative bodies relied on both private records and nondocumentary sources to fill the gaps. In courts, when facts of identity such as age or lineage had to be established, defendants and plaintiffs were as likely to provide oral testimony as they were to produce the family Bible or the church baptismal register. Not only were both personal and institutional records unevenly kept, but British legal traditions prized testimony under oath above almost all other forms of evidence. In tight-knit communities, moreover, neighbors could be relied on to testify to basic information about one another. Reputation was often as good as, if not better than, documentation.

To free, white parents, a baby's birth may have been regarded first and foremost as a private family affair, but a father who brought information about his new child to the town clerk in Worcester, Massachusetts, or to the parish priest in Roanoke, Virginia, made his child a part of a list, a serialization of people who were at once particular in their details and members of a collective: Protestants, Catholics, persons born in this or that town. And while churches, colonies, and states never gathered all their lists together to add up their totals, their records formed the nascent elements of something that was of intense interest to early modern rulers: population. Kings, their advisors, and colonial governors cared that women were laboring in birthing rooms and bringing forth new life. These babies belonged not just to their families but to nations and empires.

Across seventeenth- and eighteenth-century Europe, monarchs and their advisors believed that it was important for rulers to know their population, its size, and its makeup. Mercantilist and imperial competition between nation-states provided one stream of interest in population knowledge. Crudely put, in mercantilist thought, populousness—the number of people in a nation—was strength. For seventeenth- and eighteenth-century monarchs and their intellectual spokesmen, the "wealth and strength of the state depended strongly on the number and character of its subjects." A large population provided military strength in the numbers of its fighting men, economic strength in the numbers of its consumers and producers, and easier administration in the density of its settled population. Thus, although international competition between nation-states led to the presumption that population size was important, and important to know, the number of people in a nation was considered so critical to its strength and power that many monarchs regarded it as a state secret.[30] Kings and their advisors had a duty to both know *and* conceal the extent of a nation's peoples.

The notion that kings should not simply command but also know their subjects and regard them as a "population" grew out of sixteenth-century "reason of state" writings and was further developed during the seventeenth and eighteenth centuries.[31] Where mercantilist competition led to the idea that a large population was the foundation of military and economic strength, "reason of state" writings directed monarchs to use population information to make informed decisions about governance. In seventeenth-century England this developed into a form of quantitative population information that came to be called "political arithmetic."

The term was invented by William Petty, an economist, natural historian, and pioneering social scientist who was a member of the Royal Academy and a close advisor to Oliver Cromwell, King Charles II, and James II. The concept of political arithmetic captured Petty's argument that the Crown's political decisions and projects should be based on, and justified by, "reference to quantitative data relating to population, social divisions, and economic activity."[32] A central premise of such work was not just that a nation's population growth was an index of its strength and well-being but more specifically that reproduction served the empire and should be encouraged. Petty suggested that reproduction was not simply a resource for the Crown but also a creature of the state, a function of its policies. While persons formed the basis for "power and wealth," population increase in a nation was a measure of whether "liberty and property have been there well or ill secured."[33] This moved population firmly from the terrain of "natural" to "political" history. People reproduced and died; populations swelled and declined according to divine will, natural laws, *and* the designs of princes.

Like mercantilism as a whole, the population knowledge generated by political arithmetic was inextricably tied to empire. In the case of England, the Crown's ability to expand into new territories depended not only on its military might and the amount of gold bullion in its coffers but also on the ability of its people to colonize land and overpower aboriginal inhabitants. To do this, women needed to have babies—domination of land was bound to fertility.[34] Thus it is no surprise that some of William Petty's first demonstrations of his political arithmetical methods included surveys of newly annexed land in Ireland and quantitative surveys of England's colonies in the Atlantic world. In his survey of England, Wales, and Ireland, Petty proposed to enumerate "how many men and women are prolific" and "in what number of years England and Ireland may be fully peopled, as also all America, and lastly the whole habitable earth." Petty's surveys claimed to show, for example, that the Native American population in North America declined while that of the Irish rebounded after British colonization. Thus he argued that the Irish could form a base of agricultural laborers and possibly intermarry with the British, while Native Americans were robust enough for neither.[35] If the British wanted to people North America, they would have to do it themselves.

Happily, the European women who migrated to North America were exceptionally fruitful, a fact that was an object of fascination and pride on both sides of the Atlantic. Students of Petty and his ilk, such as seventeenth-century Massachusetts minister Cotton Mather, observed that women in England's "plantations" were more fecund than those at home. Mather took this as a sign that New England was more similar to the biblical past—when clerics believed population growth was rapid—than it was to contemporary vice-ridden London.[36] Petty himself proposed repatriating teeming colonials to the metropole to bolster its population. Indeed, compared to women in England, colonists in this new Eden were enormously prolific, a fact that was celebrated by artists who painted portraits of American women with fruit spilling from their laps and children by their sides.[37] Colonial women's reproductive prowess soon drew international attention thanks to the work of Benjamin Franklin, who began publishing (and boasting about) colonial fertility in the 1749 edition of his *Poor Richard's Almanac*. In 1751, Franklin published his essay "Observations Concerning the Increase of Mankind and the Peopling of Countries." He asserted, without offering specific data, that because land was so plentiful in America compared with densely settled England, "marriages in America are more general, and more generally early than in Europe." And such marriages yielded, he surmised, twice as many children as those of the Old World. As a result, Franklin suggested, the settler colonial population in England's North American colonies doubled every twenty years.[38] These "Observations" were published and widely circulated in Great Britain, and popularized at home and abroad, often without Franklin's name attached to them.[39]

Franklin assumed, like so many other political economists, that natural increase measured economic health and opportunity and that a large population was a basis for political strength. For Franklin, pointing out the fecundity of colonial women was hardly a neutral observation—it was an intensely political point because colonial increase was a sign of the political power of the colonies and an argument in favor of reforming Britain's mercantilist economic policies.[40] By suggesting that the colonies' population growth outstripped

England's, Franklin made an argument that looked both to the west and the east. Looking west, Franklin's point implied that colonists needed more land—always a point of contention between colonists and the Crown, which was weary of sending troops and money to protect the colonists, who insisted on continually encroaching on Indian lands and stirring up military conflict. If white women's fecundity continued to outstrip available land, Franklin's boasts implied, settlers would continue their westward march. Looking east, Franklin's observations implied that the balance of power between England and its colonies would soon tip toward the colonies. Indeed, once the colonies declared independence, members of the Continental Congress used population-based arguments to reassure constituents that their cause was just and that they could afford to separate from England.[41] Little wonder, then, that when Franklin and his fellow revolutionaries constructed an independent nation, they not only keyed representation (and thus political power) to population but also instituted the world's first regular census. As keen as Europe's kings and their advisors had been to know the size and increase of their populations, they had always had to estimate how many people they had, how many were born, and how many died. For even in countries with perfect systems of parish registration, the records were neither designed nor ever used to make individuals into a "population."

This was the problem of knowledge that Lemuel Shattuck and others set out to fix in the early republic by reforming or creating state-run vital registration systems. These, they believed, could braid together the aggregating population knowledge of political arithmetic and the individualized records kept by families, churches, and towns. Unlike either the registration books of churches and towns or the snapshot of a population recorded in a census, vital registration would provide both real-time population totals and the ability to break population down into units, to create numerators and denominators at will. The changes that Shattuck and others sought were not simply technical or institutional but also intellectual and political. Shattuck's conviction that "matters alleged to be private" were of public interest rested on the assumption that the events of individual lives, when viewed in the aggregate, conformed to rules not of biography but of society. His was a statistical worldview. While early modern intellectuals and statesmen interpreted population information in terms of a political economy that linked population growth to economic and political power, in the first half of the nineteenth century, by contrast, a worldwide network of statisticians began to amass population, economic, and other data in order to discern the underlying laws of human society and collective health. The emergence of a statistical worldview rested not on new mathematical techniques but rather on the "avalanche of numbers" collected in the early nineteenth-century West. Beginning between 1820 and 1840, western European and American governments, together with scientific societies and other civil organizations, gathered voluminous amounts of information on demography, trade, natural history, geography, mortality, morbidity, and more.[42]

A broad range of constituencies eagerly collected and consumed statistical information, which was as often descriptive as it was quantitative. In the early republican United States, politicians, physicians, actuaries, and reformers in different causes all viewed the aggregation and analysis of information as critical to informed decision-making. Statistically inclined statesmen viewed the federal census as useful for far more than calculating the balance of political representation. In addition to collecting basic information about sex, race, and status (slave or free), by 1840 enumerators were also sorting individuals according to more precise age gradations and inquiring about occupation, nativity, literacy, and disability. Physicians and medical researchers interested in the etiology and epidemiology of disease sought means to better track and tabulate outbreaks of illnesses and death. Along with the growing number of actuaries working in the field of insurance, doctors in the early republic collected bills of mortality and disease information and tried to find the patterns that lay buried within. At the same time, antebellum reformers gathered data on a wide array of social problems: the number of deaths caused by alcohol, the relationship of alcohol to poverty, the amount of money spent annually by Americans on alcoholic beverages, the number of poor who attended church or owned a Bible, the conditions of prisons and poorhouses in major cities, and the extent of insanity and idiocy. The products of these and other data-gathering efforts were disseminated in popular almanacs; newspapers; periodicals such as *Niles' Weekly Register*, *Merchant's Magazine and Commercial Review*, and *DeBow's Review*; and tomes such as *Economica: A Statistical Manual for the United States*, *Statistical View of the Commerce of the United States of America*, and *Statistical Annuals*.[43]

In the United States and elsewhere, the statistical worldview was more political than mathematical. It grew up in the aftermath of political revolutions and was largely the province of liberal reformers who wanted to separate "society" from the state in order to argue both that rulers must legislate in the public's best interest and that this "interest" must be defined by the laws of social life, not by arbitrary authority.[44] In the United States, the political cast was often made from an exceptionalist mold. Founded in Boston in 1839, the American Statistical Association set forth an ambitious program for itself: to collect information from all states on matters of geology, zoology, agriculture, chemistry, medicine, mechanics, meteorology, physiology, population, education, finance, government, and religion. The association noted that statistical labors were particularly important in the United States given "our peculiar civil institutions." The nation's experiment in democracy, the association contended, could only be measured a success or a failure according to "faithful observations and unquestionable facts." This information would serve "the friends of civil and or religious freedom in every country, and in every future age." But such facts would also serve the nation in the present, as its history unfolded. "None of our institutions are in a perfect state," the association admitted, but "every rational reform must be founded on thorough knowledge."[45]

Even as the United States' fledgling statisticians viewed themselves as following in the footsteps of their European brothers, they also viewed their own statistical endeavors as unique in the world. On the one hand, most still believed in the eighteenth-century mercantilist dictum that population was strength; on the other hand, they were becoming more skeptical about whether all population growth was created equal. The United States, they believed, made the equation more complex. University of Virginia professor George Tucker expressed this belief in his 1843 *Progress of the United States in Population and Wealth in Fifty Years*. While Tucker believed that population information was of interest to all statesmen everywhere, he believed the data more salient in the United States because "our changes are both greater and more rapid than those of any other country." Migrants pushed westward to turn forests into farmland, immigrants poured in at the shores, and the nation mixed "different races . . . [in different] conditions of civil freedom."[46] These factors (slavery and immigration) transformed the positive valence of population growth—and its engine, the birthrate—into a more complicated set of questions. For American statists and men of letters, race, nativity, and immigration would trouble the assumption that bigger was always better. Though many might believe, with Franklin, that free institutions and abundant land proved their superiority through numerical growth of the population, they would also pay careful attention to whether such growth occurred through immigration or reproduction, and among slave or free populations.

Whatever they believed made the situation of the United States different, what united the men of the American Statistical Association with their European counterparts was their earnest hope that statistics would improve governance by revealing the laws of human life. No one expressed this idea with more conviction than Belgian astronomer-cum-sociologist Adolphe Quetelet, described by the philosopher Ian Hacking as "the greatest regularity salesman of the nineteenth century."[47] Published in 1835, Quetelet's *Treatise on Man* proposed that human beings, and human societies, obeyed the same statistical laws as planetary bodies. These laws were evidence, however, not of God's design but instead of the laws of social organization, or what Quetelet called "social physics." The *Treatise* introduced the concept of the "average man," or the idea that it was instructive to figure out the mean height, weight, income, and longevity of a Frenchman or a Dane or an American. The average man became not only a descriptive but also a normative type. According to Hacking, Quetelet's "average man" introduced new ways of thinking about population and state intervention. Knowing a nation's population now meant quantifying its people according to measurable physical and moral characteristics. With this also came the idea that governments could "either preserve or alter the average qualities" of a people through their policies.[48]

Quetelet was hardly a household name in the United States, but among the country's statists, his work exemplified the need for population information. In 1844, the editor of the *New York Journal of Medicine and Science* praised the "scientific and popular attention" generated by Quetelet's theory of "social physics." He claimed that Quetelet's proof that "mankind, studied in large numbers, possess certain common qualities, which vary according to determinable laws," demonstrated the importance of collecting vital statistics. In this, however, lamented the editor, "we are obliged to confess that our own country has fallen immeasurably behind those of Europe."[49] Like the anonymous editor, Lemuel Shattuck considered Quetelet's work an inspiration and kept up a correspondence with him. In an 1849 letter, Shattuck asked Quetelet to send him publications "as relate to the population, vital statistics, public hygiene, and other matters." Shattuck explained that he was collecting such information because "the laws of life and health[,] how they are influenced by different agency [*sic*], and how man can be elevated in his physical as well as social nature, are questions, now exciting great interest."[50]

Shattuck's letter to Quetelet indicates that nineteenth-century interest in statistics was motivated by a keen and growing interest in "public hygiene." As cities such as Boston, Philadelphia, New York, and Baltimore swelled in population and as manufacturing took root in the early republic, Americans worried about the immiserating effects of both on the nation's health. John Griscom, a physician and city inspector for New York City, explained that "the constrained gregariousness in which it is the habit and necessity of man now to live, gives rise to totally new conditions of his physical being, and develops laws and influences over his health and life, which were before unknown or disregarded."[51] Cities, in other words, not only made people sicker but also gave birth to a new and different set of laws for human life. Many Americans assumed that the nation was naturally conducive to healthfulness with its wide, open spaces and were apt to blame ill health on personal immorality. But the observable ill health and squalor of the poor crowded into urban slums helped at least some medical men, intellectuals, and reform-minded Americans begin to glimpse that health was the result not simply of individual habits but also of the connection between environment and body.[52] "We believe," wrote Lemuel Shattuck, "that disease and death come not from a mysterious, unconditional Providence, but are the result of the condition of our bodies, and the influences that are brought to bear upon them." In his 1845 *Sanitary Condition of the Laboring Population of New York*, Griscom made a similar point, distinguishing between "Public Health" and "Individual Health." While an individual might be sick with dyspepsia, ophthalmia, or rheumatism for reasons that had nothing to do with external conditions, other maladies were "dependent upon causes which affect large numbers at the same time" and had their root in environmental conditions subject to human control. Among the factors that Griscom targeted for the ill health of New York's poor were crowded, damp, poorly ventilated housing conditions. These fell under the aegis of public health because they were not the product of individual choice but, to Griscom's mind, the product of public neglect, if not public policy. "We are parties to their degradation," Griscom chided. "They are *allowed*, may it not be said *required*, to live in dirt, when the reverse, rather, should be enforced." To Griscom and others, the solution was simple: government regulation and inspection of living and working conditions.[53]

Men such as Shattuck and Griscom were inspired in their view of public health by developments in Europe, which not only urged them to think that governments could and should intervene to improve community health but also ratified their view that vital statistics were the essential form of knowledge upon which government policy should be founded. American vital statisticians particularly praised England, France, Belgium, and Prussia as models of enlightened and active governance. Lemuel Shattuck studied Prussia as illustrative of a thorough system of "medical police"—that is, of regulations promoting public health.[54] "In most of the European governments, it is re-quired that exact returns shall be made of the marriages, births and deaths," noted one envious American author. "Exact knowledge has thus, within a comparatively few years, been substituted for speculation and uncertainty." Exact knowledge had also, in turn, yielded "many sanitary ordinances and regulations highly advantageous to the public."[55] That vital statistics collection led to better public health outcomes was a virtual truism. In Geneva, which had continuously kept a registry since 1549, American public health reform-ers contended that the population experienced greater longevity, lower infant mortality, and increased prosperity. Such good fortune was not by chance but was "derived from the better knowledge and understanding of the science of life and health, the data for which are furnished by the statistics of the Registers."[56]

The creation of England's General Registry Office in 1836 was of particular interest to many American statists and reformer who followed its workings as they unfolded. Unlike the ancient registry systems of many European nations, England's new system was civil in nature. It was based on administrative re-gions created by the Poor Laws that funneled local birth and death records to the centralized General Registry Office, which was headed by one of the nineteenth century's most important statisticians, William Farr.[57] John Forry, a doctor and statist in New York, observed in 1844 that England's General Registry Office "has already repaid, more than ten-fold, the trouble and ex-pense that it has involved." Its value was evident to "the philosopher, the phy-sician, and political economist, to the statesman and legislator."[58] In a letter to Shattuck in 1846, William Farr expressed his "hope [that] you will succeed in getting for U.S. America a correct system of Statistical Registration. The people ought to have it."[59] Shattuck and his fellow reformers could not have agreed more.

It is hardly surprising that many early vital statisticians argued for a greater role for government in matters of population and public health. Lemuel Shat-tuck, for one, did not shy away from this enlarged sphere of authority. Rather, he saw it as absolutely necessary. "To obtain all the needful information on this subject, we must have the aid of government," he wrote. "The Legislature must direct as to the method of collecting and registering the facts in the towns, and the agency by which they shall be returned, digested, arranged, published and spread before the people."[60] To make this expansion palatable, Shattuck and others likened vital registration to other kinds of information gathering that the state already undertook. According to an author in the *American Journal of the Medical Sciences*, vital registration was but one part of a much larger quest on the part of government to amass as much information as possible about its resources, "among which we may refer to the able geological, agricultural, and trigonometrical surveys, including botanical, zoological, and entomological investigations."[61] If the state funded agricultural, manufacturing, and natural historical surveys, should it not also seek to know human life?

Shattuck had reason to feel optimistic about the "great interest" of his countrymen not only in ascertaining the "laws of life and health" but also in their commitment to remedying the woeful neglect of population information. An informal alliance to reform the registration of vital events in the states began in Massachusetts in the late 1830s. In the early 1840s, the American Statistical Association, the American Academy of Arts and Sciences, and the Massachusetts Medical Society all memorialized the state legislature to urge that it reform the state's methods of vital statistics collection. Not only were extant laws inadequately enforced—capturing perhaps only 50 percent of all births, for example—but they had also been written with a mind to the legal rather than statistical utility of documenting birth, marriage, and death. Under the old vital registration system, births and deaths were voluntarily reported by householders to town clerks, who recorded only the most basic information: date of birth or death and the name of the person born or deceased. Such records were kept locally and never aggregated and were thought to be useful primarily in settling matters of probate. After the new law passed in 1842, and after further reformations of the law were enacted in 1844 and 1849, clerks were required to collect much more detailed information about vital events and to report annually to the secretary of state, who would tabulate, analyze, and distribute information about the state's births and deaths in an annual report. In cases of death, clerks now had to report the age and cause of death. In births, clerks were required to report not just the name and date of birth of the newborn but also its sex, the names and residence of its parents, and the occupation of its father.[62]

Both the increase in information collected on registration documents and the requirement that such information be centrally collected and tabulated by the state signaled the waxing of a statistical approach to birth and death. Yet Massachusetts reformers remained unhappy that vital registration was lodged under the control of the secretary of state. As one author complained in the *American Journal of the Medical Sciences*, the secretary of state was a "political" office, not a medical one. Vital registration ought instead to be carried out by "such persons as thoroughly understand and appreciate this branch of vital and statistical science."[63] After 1842, Massachusetts's secretary of state frequently hired Shattuck to tabulate and analyze the vital registration data generated by the new law. In 1845, Shattuck wrote a lengthy letter, later published, to the secretary that explained the value of the statistics that a properly functioning system would generate: "Let the facts which the Registry System proposes to collect . . . be collected, digested, arranged, published and diffused annually, and their effect on the living energies of the people would be incalculable." The statistics would teach the citizens and legislators of the state about the effects of both personal habits and environmental conditions on health and longevity and about the effects of the rise of manufacturing or the "universal thirst for wealth in America" on population increase, disease, and public health. With such data, the state might create a "sanitary map" of the state showing those localities most favorable to health and well-being. "These are not the speculations of a visionary theorist," Shattuck insisted. "We are a statist, a dealer in fact," he explained.[64]

Shattuck's voice was joined by a chorus of others who urged the state to change its vital registration system in ways that were at once practical and conceptual. In his 1850 *Report*, Shattuck had recommended that Massachusetts create a state board of health to oversee "the sanitary condition of the State and its inhabitants," most especially the collection and publication of vital statistics. Throughout the 1850s and '60s, the Massachusetts Medical Society and the American Statistical Association urged the state legislature to create this board of health, which it finally did in 1869. Practically, creating a board of health rearranged the administrative structure for the recording, collection, and dissemination of birth and death information. But this change was conceptual as well. By locating the registration of birth and death under the mantle of "health," the state was signaling that it was important to record such data not because they might settle questions of property but rather because they might, in Shattuck's words, provide "an annual lesson in the laws of human life."[65]

The reforms that Massachusetts made to its vital registration laws were a harbinger of things to come. Not only had the state passed the first modern registration laws in the early republic, but also the 1869 creation of the board of health signaled the wave of the future: birth and death registration under the aegis of health and "vital statistics" rather than law (represented by the record keeping of the secretary of state's office). From the 1840s forward, vital statistics collection caught the attention of state and national medical associations, public health reformers, and the national government. After Massachusetts passed its first reforms in 1842, the first annual meeting of the National Convention of Delegates from medical colleges and state medical societies— the predecessor to the American Medical Association (AMA)—appointed a committee to "recommend and urge" state governments to adopt "measures for a general registration of all the Births, Marriages, and Deaths" among their populations. Indeed, throughout the 1850s, the AMA used its annual meetings to lament the sorry state of vital statistics in the United States and to beg its members to work for legislation in their home states.[66] Between 1857 and 1860, physicians and public health reformers held four National Quarantine and Sanitary Conventions, at which the improvement of vital statistics systems in the states figured prominently. At the second of these conventions, those in attendance tasked the Committee on Internal Hygiene with preparing a report on how to create a functioning vital registration system in the United States. At the fourth convention, in 1860, Edwin Snow, the registrar from Providence, Rhode Island, delivered the report. The same year, a committee from the American Association for the Advancement of Science issued its own report on reform of vital registration.[67]

Before the Civil War, eleven other states followed Massachusetts's example and enacted their own registration laws.[68] Large cities such as Providence, Boston, New York, and Philadelphia also operated their own vital registration systems that were separate from, and often more successful than, those of their states. Passing legislation was not, however, always easy. When Dr. W. L. Sutton of Georgetown, Kentucky, wrote to Lemuel Shattuck in December 1850, he sought advice about how to structure a vital registration system in his state. "You are aware that the subject is a novel one in our states generally," he reminded Shattuck, "and especially in the West." An 1851 news item in the *Western Journal of Medicine and Surgery* reported that when Sutton's bill was presented to the state's legislature, "the members of that dignified body received it as a decidedly rich joke." This was in spite of the fact that Sutton was a leading advocate of registration reform nationally. The article did not specify why Kentucky's lawmakers found the prospect of registration more hilarious than "the threadbare jokes of the circus," but its author speculated that they simply needed education on the value of vital statistics. Georgia's legislature, too, "fairly hooted" at the vital registration bill that the state's medical society put before it in 1849. According to the bill's chief advocate, Georgia lawmakers regarded it as no more than "a trick of the Doctors." Kentucky's lawmakers managed to stifle their laughter in 1852 and pass a vital registration statute, but Georgia's did not do so until 1875.[69]

Legislatures may have looked askance at vital registration for reasons to do with the cost of implementation. Laws typically provided that the government official responsible for receiving birth, death, and marriage registration be paid a fee for his services. In some states, doctors, who were required by law to fill out and sign birth and death certificates, were also paid a fee to report this information. Advocates of vital registration commented that for some legislators "an expense of even five cents or three cents . . . would kill the bill." Moreover, since it was often the county and state medical associations that introduced and lobbied for registration laws, it was easy for legislators to think that doctors were, as one state registrar put it, "doing it for the purpose of making money." This was particularly the case in the antebellum era, when medicine was sharply divided between allopathic and "irregular" practitioners, doctors were regarded with a great deal of skepticism, medical training and licensure were unregulated, and the AMA was only just beginning to try to exert control over the right to practice.[70] In this context, a proposal to pay doctors to report on the occurrence of routine events in their practice—births and deaths—could indeed seem like a "trick of the doctors."

The Civil War interrupted but did not destroy the momentum for enactment of state registration laws. The war taught its own lessons about the importance of standardizing and centralizing information. Faced with an enormous toll of death and injury from the war, the U.S. Sanitary Commission developed its own Bureau of Vital Statistics and a hospital directory that together documented disease and the location of individuals as they shifted from battlefield to hospital.[71] Practically speaking, the provision of pensions to soldiers and their dependents in the years after the war made registration documents, for the few that had them, into technologies of identification that could pay dividends. Even in the midst of the war, the Connecticut state librarian, who was charged with compiling and publishing his state's annual registration statistics, wrote that "the value of a thorough registration will be felt now more than ever in consequence of the war . . . in applications for pensions and bounty lands by the widows and orphans of those who are laying down their lives." He speculated that "had our present system of registration" been in place during the Revolutionary War and the War of 1812, "hundreds of families . . . would have been made comfortable during their lives" because they would have been able to use registration documents to prove their claim to a soldier's pension.[72] Between 1860 and 1883, Alabama, Delaware, Georgia, Illinois, Michigan, Minnesota, North Carolina, and Ohio passed registration legislation for the first time, while several other states amended existing laws.[73] Still, vital registration was concentrated in the Northeast and Midwest, while most of the war-ravaged, cash-strapped, and highly rural states of the former Confederacy either did not require, did not enforce, or did not fund registration in their territories.[74]

The war's end also brought renewed attention to the intersection of race, reproduction, and population growth. The promise of racially disaggregated data was part of the appeal of vital registration in the United States. In every state or municipality that registered births before the Civil War, the forms collected information about the "race or color" of the parents or the child.[75] Because few states had successful registration systems, those that did had their returns scrutinized with great interest for the truths they might reveal about the relationship between race and reproduction. This was evident in Lemuel Shattuck's correspondence with his fellow statists both domestic and foreign. In 1849, for example, John Roberton of Manchester, England, wrote to Shattuck seeking his assistance with research on "the age of Female puberty in different races & in different climates." Roberton explained that Shattuck could assist by "obtain[ing] facts (some hundreds of instances at least) as to the age of puberty in the negroes in your southern states." Roberton had already written a paper on the topic that covered the West Indies, and he was now seeking to fold data on India and the United States into his studies.[76] Likewise Josiah Nott, one of the leading American ethnologists and a proponent of polygenesis, wrote to Shattuck in 1853 that "if, in working over the Statistics of the United States you have anything new about the Negroes, Mulattoes &c. bearing on Races, influence of Climate &c. I would be much obliged for it."[77]

One of the foremost theories that vital registration could help to test was that of racial degeneration. On the one hand, the racialist thinking that justified slavery assumed the greater fecundity of African women; on the other hand, the theory of degeneration posited that primitive races would die out. Before the Civil War, theories of degeneration were mapped onto the difference between the racial health of African Americans in freedom and in slavery. The fecundity of female slaves could demonstrate the benevolent match between African physiognomy and American slavery, while low birthrates among free Blacks demonstrated the ultimate weakness of the race and the impossibility of its full integration into free institutions. The statistical evidence for Black degeneration in freedom was given an enormous boost by the results of the 1840 census, which purported to show that one in every 162 northern Blacks was insane, compared to only one in every 1,558 in the South. That these data were the result of errors in collection and tabulation did not stop proslavery apologists from concluding that "the free negroes of the northern states are the most vicious persons on this continent, perhaps on the earth."[78]

Northern newspapers also reprinted the findings of medical men that the colored population in northern cities had a lower birthrate than did the white population.[79] Throughout the 1850s and '60s, northern commentators never tired of pointing out that deaths among the "colored" population far exceeded births, a fact that seemed to bear directly on the long-popular theory that those of African descent could flourish neither in northern climes nor in freedom. After recording more deaths than births among African Americans in his city, Boston's registrar concluded in 1863 that "there is little probability . . . of the Northern States being overrun by the colored race, bond or free." He went on to explain that "there is undoubtedly an instinctive repugnance on the part of the African to Northern latitudes; and the foregoing facts show very plainly the existence of physical causes, if nothing else, that bar their presence to any great extent."[80] In the midst of a civil war that promised to end slavery and offer occupational and geographic mobility to several million African Americans, the news must have been a relief for many northern whites. For while the fecundity of enslaved African Americans was cause for celebration among southern whites, for whites both north and south the rapid reproduction of a free Black population was cause for alarm. Belief in degeneration and statistical evidence for it, whether in the form of African American insanity or comparatively lower birthrates, suggested that the links between race, reproduction, and national health were durable—the United States was meant to be the home of the English and their descendants.

Once the Civil War was over, leading social scientists considered the accurate collection of vital statistics central to a proper understanding of race and race relations in the United States. Richard Mayo Smith, a professor of political economy and social science at Columbia University and one of the foremost statisticians of the postbellum era, wrote that "the study of [the negro's] condition, its rate of increase, its distribution, its economic progress, its moral characteristics should be one of the constant problems in a properly managed statistical bureau of the United States."[81] This was because, as John S. Billings explained before the College of Physicians and Surgeons in New York City, "one of the most interesting fields of study in vital statistics is the relation of race and color to birth-rate, to certain forms of disease, or to the liability of death at certain ages." Like Virginia's George Tucker many decades earlier, Billings believed that the United States furnished "greater opportunities" for the study of race and its influence on human life than many other nations. He believed that with proper statistics, social scientists in the United States could determine whether the African American population increased faster than that of whites; statists could also compare the fertility and longevity of "mixed bloods" to the "pure blooded" of either race. In all, these findings could help contribute to scientists' understanding of "the relation of race to vital phenomena," an understanding that would help contribute, Billings noted, to the eugenicist Francis Galton's new "science of heredity."[82]

Before the Civil War, many white students of population had taken comfort in statistics showing that Black deaths outnumbered births, and many had rosily predicted the extinction of the African race in the United States. Some held fast to this belief in the war's aftermath as well. In 1869, for example, the State Medical Society of Kentucky petitioned the state legislature to reform its vital statistics collection in light of the end of slavery. In particular, the medical society wished to add "mulatto" to the state's vital statistics classification, in addition to the existing "black" and "white." By way of explanation, a petition from the society explained that "where two races which cannot intermarry are thrown together under one government, it is the tendency of the inferior race to decline in vigor and numbers and ultimately to become extinct." The abolition of slavery in Kentucky offered a chance to study the "practical operation" of this universal law.[83]

While the end of slavery provided an overwhelming opportunity for demographers to use birth registration data to puzzle over the relationship among political economy, race, and reproduction, it was not the only population problem related to "race" on their minds after the war. A series of widely reproduced newspaper articles written by Nathan Allen in 1866 sounded a different alarm about another group that seemed destined to die out: native-born white Americans. After several decades of successful vital registration, the data from Massachusetts's birth registration system showed unmistakably that Irish immigrants had a much higher birthrate than native-born Americans. Allen, a physician from Lowell, was also a fledgling social scientist who served on the Massachusetts State Board of Charities and attended meetings of the American Social Science Association. He had direct contact with Lowell's system of registration when he served in the elected offices of city physician and superintendent of burials, both of which would have required him to make vital registration reports.[84] In making his case, Allen pointed to the annual "report of births" provided by the towns of the state. These showed, he reported, that among the American born, deaths exceeded births. Moreover, the birthrate among the "American population" in Massachusetts was one in sixty-six, twice as low as it should be for "a prosperous or growing state." This, Allen warned, was a "gigantic evil" that would soon kill off "the best stock (the Puritan) the world ever saw," only to be replaced with "a people of foreign origin, with far less intelligence, and a religion entirely different."[85]

When the *New York Observer and Chronicle* reprinted Allen's findings, it speculated that what was occurring in Massachusetts was also likely happening elsewhere, in "other States in which the statistics have not been so carefully gathered."[86] As the first state to thoroughly record vital statistics, Massachusetts demonstrated the value of registration to reveal the changing racial makeup of the United States. More than the decennial census could, birthrate disaggregated by nativity showed the balance between immigration and reproduction in fueling population growth. And while colonial British Americans such as Ben Franklin had been proud of their fecundity and sure that it provided population growth over and above additions through immigration, once it was disaggregated by nativity, pride turned to fear. Tracking births by nativity in the registration reports meant that "population" had been parsed to make some babies more valuable than others. Allen feared that there were too few babies only from Yankees, not from the Irish.

As more states developed vital registration systems after the Civil War, they, too, dutifully reported on the birthrates of their "native" versus "foreign" populations. In his annual report for the year 1870, Michigan's secretary of state, Daniel Striker, took it upon himself to test the theory of "decadence of population in America"—the notion that something in "the climate of the United States was unfavorable to the Caucasian constitution," because white settlers showed a declining birthrate after a few generations. He concluded that while it was manifestly true that the data showed that the foreign born had more children than did the native born, the data could also mislead. There were several reasons for this, including not knowing the age distribution of the foreign-born versus native-born populations and thus not knowing how many people in each population could *potentially* reproduce. But chief among the reasons not to panic about the raw birthrate was that it did not account for infant mortality. It was possible, he reminded his readers, that while foreigners had more babies, more of their babies died. "Multiplication," he wrote with a mixture of gloom and glee, "is not replenishment." Even if such children survived, however, Striker argued that they were most likely to become "the greatest burden upon the State" because of their poverty and criminality. To defend this point of view, Striker cited a report written by the Massachusetts State Board of Charities, on which served none other than Nathan Allen. "Quantity, in this case," the secretary concluded, "is not so important as quality."[87] In the secretary's words there was both reassurance and cause for alarm. Though the native born had fewer children, he suggested, they produced offspring of higher quality.

Nathan Allen's postbellum cri de coeur about the Massachusetts birth registration data put the issue of the foreign- versus native-born birthrate on the national agenda, and in the hands of men who were in a singular position to control the collection and dissemination of national data, it became part of a political program for immigration restriction. Like Allen, Francis Amasa Walker developed his own theories to explain why the foreign born seemed to outpace the "old stock" when it came to population growth. From his post as a professor at Yale and as the superintendent for the 1880 census, Walker continued to track the advance of the immigrant birthrate over that of the native born. In his report on the tenth census, Walker created a whole new set of tables on "foreign parentage."[88] Walker agreed with Allen that immigrants were having more children than the native born. Early in his career Walker had been a population optimist who viewed the fecundity of immigrants as proof of the nation's favorable economic climate, but by the early 1890s he had changed his tune. In his 1891 treatise, "Immigration and Degradation," Walker argued that the problem was not solely the physical degeneration of native-born women but also that immigration depressed the native birthrate by increasing competition for jobs. Unwilling to have their progeny compete side by side with foreigners who lowered wages, the native born instead chose to have fewer children. Walker argued that without immigration, the native born would have continued to reproduce in large numbers and sustain the nation's early record of exponential population growth. Though Walker had no data to support his theory, other than to correlate the decline of native birthrates with immigrant population increase, his argument became a centerpiece of the movement for immigration restriction in the twentieth century.[89] Cobbled together from state registration reports and federal enumeration, birthrate data aided the intellectual construction of a racial order after the war. At the same time, the desire for better data led a growing number of constituencies to advocate for the creation of more uniform, standardized systems of registration.

Increasingly frustrated with slow progress in the states, they began to look to the federal government to provide support.

In the last third of the nineteenth century, national organizations (besides the AMA) and the federal government began to promote vital statistics collection. As national organizations took up the cause of registration, they urged not just that all states pass registration laws but also that laws and practices become standardized and uniform across the states. Founded in 1872, the American Public Health Association (APHA) counted many prominent vital statisticians among its original leadership, and the organization at once created the Committee on Registration. Its first annual meetings were filled with speeches that extolled the "public uses of Vital Statistics" and employed statistics on morbidity, mortality, and birth to make arguments about the etiology of disease or the nature of the American population. APHA leadership also called on city boards of health to regularly conduct vital statistics censuses of their population and undertook a survey of the status of vital statistics registration in every state in the nation. In 1875, the APHA memorialized the U.S. Congress to pass legislation that would "bring about a proper co-operation between the General Government of the United States and the several state governments" in order to create "a uniform and efficient system" for birth, death, and marriage registration. The same resolution was adopted in 1878 and 1880 by the American Association for the Promotion of Science.[90]

The APHA was not content simply to memorialize Congress about national uniformity in vital registration, however. After the 1875 resolution passed, APHA leadership began to organize and lobby for the creation of a national board of health, which, they hoped, would "secure concerted action" across localities in matters of public health including, but not limited to, vital statistics collection. The federal government could not itself register births, deaths, and marriages, but it could encourage states and municipalities to take up the responsibility and to do so in a manner that would produce reliable statistics. In 1879, Congress created the National Board of Health (NBH), the first federal health agency, and installed members of the executive board of the APHA as its leaders.[91] As one of its first acts, the NBH created the Committee on Registration and Vital Statistics with the aim to foment a "scheme of uniform registration throughout the country." Acting on the order of the board, several months later NBH vice president Dr. John S. Billings began organizing "a convention for all registrars of vital statistics and others interested in that matter" to be held in May 1880. In his correspondence with state public health officials, Billings expressed hope that his conference would "effect some good in securing uniform methods of collecting and presenting statistics." Massachusetts and the handful of other states with registration laws notwithstanding, Billings lamented that no state was, in his mind, "yet educated to the proper degree in this respect."[92]

As much as the men of the APHA and NBH believed that national uniformity was essential to the collection of birth and death records and to the production of accurate statistical knowledge about the population, localism and federalism made this dream difficult to achieve. The NBH convened its Conference on Vital Statistics in Washington, D.C., in May 1880 in the hopes of creating a document that would spell out the best registration practices that could be adopted in every state. Some twenty-seven men attended, nearly all of them doctors and nearly all of them the head of a municipal or state registration system. When the discussion turned to the second agenda item, "Basis of Complete Individual Records as Statistical Units," the attendees quickly discovered many points of disagreement about how a registration system should actually function. While all agreed that doctors should certify the cause of death on a death certificate, attendees could not agree that doctors should be held responsible for reporting births. The Committee on the Best Methods of Securing Numerical Exactness in Returns of a City recommended that in every city, doctors and midwives be required to register with the city registrar of vital statistics. This would enable the registrar or his staff to visit doctors and midwives every thirty days to inspect their patient records and to record any births that had not already been reported. James Steuart, the commissioner of health in Baltimore, explained that this system would serve as a check on the "leading practitioners of medicine," who, he claimed, "are the most negligent." Edwin Snow, the highly prominent registrar of a nationally acclaimed registration system in Providence, Rhode Island, replied that he thought it unwise to rely on doctors for birth reports. Instead of requiring doctors to bring reports of births to a town clerk or a city registrar, Providence (and other large cities in New England, such as Boston) relied on a biannual house-to-house census of the entire city. At each door, a canvasser would inquire whether a baby had been born to the family in the past six months and, if so, would record "all these particulars" about the birth and turn them in to the registrar. "Under these circumstances," boasted Snow, "we get almost complete returns of births." While in the plan advocated by Steuart physicians were considered the most logical—if highly fallible—source of birth reports, in Snow's plan doctors had no responsibility whatsoever. Rather, the onus fell entirely on the municipal government to collect and record its own vital records.[93]

The differences between these two reporting avenues revealed that uniformity in registration methods would prove illusory. Conditions in different parts of the country were too different. No sooner had Snow finished evangelizing about the reliability of canvassing for births than J. H. Rauch, the head of Illinois's board of health, objected that such a plan would never work in Chicago because it was too large and the population too transient. John Billings, from the NBH, agreed. The Providence plan, he argued, would not work "in one of our western towns—in a town where there is very rapid immigration, emigration, or both." The unreliability of physicians and the infeasibility of a birth census in all towns and cities led some attendees to conclude that making householders responsible for birth registration was the only way to achieve a uniform standard. Whether the birth took place in the country or the city, or in the East or the West, it always happened in a household. "The only party who everywhere exists," argued Azel Ames of Massachusetts, "is the head of the family." Yet, as Ames lamented, even this system would fail "in the remote counties of the Southwest and elsewhere where there are numbers of foreigners" who do not know the law. "It is useless to expect these foreigners to make returns," he grumped. Only education would remedy this, but that would take time. In the meantime, the conference ended without a recommendation for a standard method of reporting births. "It must be evident to every gentleman here," said one attendee, "that uniformity . . . would never be reached if we were to take six months." Instead, the convention passed a resolution calling on the NBH to invite recommendations for a method that would achieve "the nearest approach to uniformity and completeness."[94] A year later, the APHA's own Committee on Vital Statistics reached much the same conclusion: though it was imperative that every locality and every state collect the same *categories* of vital information, the methods of so doing would remain "quite as diverse in their details as are the forms of local government administration."[95]

After the rather tepid outcome of the 1880 convention, John Billings of the NBH undertook a study of state systems of vital registration in the hopes not only of understanding how the most efficient systems worked but also of figuring out how the federal government might help promote the uniformity that statists so desired. For their part, the APHA and other national organizations continued to call for a greater role for the federal government in coordinating vital statistics collection in the states. As a result of his study, Billings reported to the board of the NBH that though many states had registration laws on their books, he believed "practically nothing had been done under a great majority." He concluded that the only way the United States could achieve comprehensive registration was "by paying a certain limited amount for reports, to be made upon forms to be dictated by the General Government." That is, the federal government should create birth, death, and marriage registration forms for use in every state and should pay states for the reports they actually filed. In his remarks to the NBH and in the published report resulting from his study of state laws, Billings urged Congress to take up the matter and give the NBH the power to create forms and compensate states—either that or create a "permanent census Bureau" to do the same. In 1883, thanks to internecine squabbling about its quarantine regulations, the NBH was defunded.[96] But the "permanent census Bureau" was on the horizon.

Even though it had no authority to register births, deaths, and marriages, the federal government had long tried to use the decennial census to collect vital statistics of the population (beyond aggregate total). Beginning in 1850, the year that Lemuel Shattuck helped design the census schedule, census enumerators were instructed to ask if there had been a birth or death in the household in the past year. While this method would not identify which specific individuals were born or had died, it would enable census takers to calculate the birth and death rates and to determine whether the U.S. population grew mainly from natural increase or immigration. The results of these initial inquiries, however, were considered so unreliable that Congress refused to publish them and the AMA begged Congress to appoint a physician to help collect vital statistics during the 1860 census.[97] In subsequent years some of the leading statisticians in the United States—men such as Francis Amasa Walker and the NBH's John Billings—attempted to improve the census's vital statistics collection. The 1880 census, for example, switched from household enumeration of deaths to a system that gave doctors forms to report the deaths in their practices in the preceding year. Birth information was still collected through household heads, however.[98]

By the turn of the century, statists all agreed that the federal government's attempts to track "population movements" through the census had been a miserable failure. They also agreed on the solution: a permanent census bureau. In 1891, Carroll Wright, the U.S. commissioner of labor and a leader in the use of statistics in federal administration, reported for the American Economic Association's Committee on Statistics in words that echoed Billings's call nearly a decade earlier. Wright deplored the still-incomplete nature of birth and death registration in the states and noted how attempts to use the census to secure this information had failed. His committee recommended that the federal government adopt a system that would cooperate with the states and yield comprehensive and reliable vital statistics. This would require, Wright noted, a permanent census bureau.[99] Throughout the 1890s, other leading statists, along with organizations such as the APHA, the American Economic Association, and the American Statistical Association, sounded the call and urged Congress to pass legislation establishing a permanent census bureau with the power not only to conduct the decennial census but also to collect vital statistics. "Besides giving us more timely population data," urged Michigan's state registrar, a census bureau "will greatly improve the collection of vital statistics in non-registration states."[100]

The U.S. Congress created a permanent census bureau in 1902. Under the terms of the legislation that created it, the U.S. Census Bureau was required to annually collect birth and death registration information from all states and cities that "maintained a satisfactory system of registration." Anyone who was interested in population statistics knew that, in practice, this meant the bureau would actually collect very few vital statistics. William King, the bureau's first chief statistician for vital statistics, explained to Congress that it also meant the bureau would initially only collect mortality statistics. Whereas a few states and cities had fairly effective death registration, almost none did a thorough job of birth registration. While births, King testified, are "of almost equal importance, experience has demonstrated that it is impracticable to secure their return as completely as deaths." This was because "in cases of death the disposition of the body can generally be controlled. Physicians and undertakers may be licensed or registered, cemeteries incorporated, and transportation or interment of bodies prohibited except upon official permit issued by proper authority, etc." Even when it came to death registration, the Census Bureau considered only a handful of states good enough to include in the group from which it would collect statistics, an entity that it called the "death registration area."[101]

Because the bureau was now required to collect vital statistics, its staff picked up the project begun in the 1880s by the NBH: the creation of uniform registration laws and methods across the states. In its first annual report, the Census Bureau declared that the poor state of vital registration combined with the bureau's mandate to collect vital statistics compelled it to "take the lead in a movement for the extension of registration areas, for improvement in records and methods, and for greater uniformity."[102] In other words, the bureau would not simply wait for states to create "satisfactory" registration but rather work to make sure that they did so. It did this in two ways. First, as John Billings had suggested in the 1880s, the bureau created a financial incentive for states to share their vital registration with the federal government: it would pay states by the piece to transcribe their death (and, later, birth) certificates and send them to Washington, D.C. For this the bureau sought, and was granted, funds from Congress. Second, the bureau worked with the APHA, the AMA, the American Bar Association, and the Conference of Commissioners on Uniform State Laws to design and promote what it called the "model law." Initially, in keeping with its focus on mortality statistics, the bureau and the APHA only prepared a model law for death registration. Both state registrars and statisticians, however, clamored for the bureau to include birth in its efforts to reform and standardize vital statistics collection. "I hope that your division can make a beginning with its birth statistics," wrote Walter Willcox, a prominent statistician at Cornell University, to the head of the Census Bureau's new Division of Vital Statistics. Only then, he jibed, will the division "have begun for the first time to deserve the name which you now employ perhaps a little unjustifiably."[103] After just a year, the bureau and the APHA jointly issued a model law that included provisions for both death and birth registration.

The model law for birth registration sought to control the conditions under which birth certificates were produced and to centralize and standardize the knowledge they collected. The bureau and its partners in the APHA, AMA, American Bar Association, and Conference of Commissioners on Uniform State Laws stressed that births should be "registered immediately after their occurrence," typically within three days. A good state law would also require that births be recorded on certificates of birth rather than simply in a logbook. This would ensure uniformity of information from all reporters and also across states. Along with the model law, the bureau issued a standard certificate of birth that it suggested all states and cities adopt. The model law instructed states to clearly fix the responsibility for reporting births and to enforce penalties for failure to report. The law sought to create standardization and centralization of registration practices within a state, calling for the "central registration office" to have "full control of the local machinery." Finally, the law urged centralization of information by providing that local registration offices should transmit their certificates to a central, state office that would preserve birth registration information in perpetuity. Cressy Wilbur, the chief of the Census Bureau's Division of Vital Statistics after William King, stressed that the model law differed from existing state laws mainly in how quickly it required births to be reported and in its emphasis on centralizing registration returns in a state, rather than a local, office of vital statistics. "The advantage of uniform certificates and methods in all parts of the same state will at once be appreciated," the bureau confidently predicted, "and a little consideration will make it clear that a uniform system in all states will be equally advantageous."[104]

Some states already had laws that conformed to the main principles and practices of the model law. "It is not intended to recommend the model bill to states having satisfactory laws in effect," explained Cressy Wilbur.[105] Though it had initially eschewed collecting birth registration from the states on the grounds that most births were not registered, as early as 1907 the bureau began to contemplate establishing a birth registration area, a collection of states and cities from which it could reliably collect and collate complete birth information. In order for a state to be included in the registration area, the bureau required that it register at least 90 percent of live births.[106] This standard proved too high. It was not until 1915 that the Census Bureau felt confident that enough states had a functioning birth registration system for it to create a birth registration area and begin collecting birth statistics. Between 1903, when the model law was first drafted, and 1915, when the birth registration area was first established, twenty-six states and the District of Columbia revised their laws to conform with the model law, while ten other states passed birth registration laws for the first time. Still, as the bureau learned, there was often a lag of several years between when a state passed the model law and when it had a functioning vital statistics system. The original birth registration area included just ten states—Maine, New Hampshire, Vermont, Massachusetts, Rhode Island, Connecticut, New York, Pennsylvania, Michigan, and Minnesota—and the District of Columbia.[107]

Though it represented just 31 percent of the nation's population, the creation of the birth registration area was a significant marker. What had begun in Massachusetts as the dream of a few eager statists inspired by developments in England and on the European continent was now being promoted nationally by the federal government and public health and medical organizations. The systems being created in states from Massachusetts to Minnesota merged the counting and aggregating impulses of political arithmetic with the identifying and individuating aspects of parish and personal records. And yet in jurisdictions across the United States, registration—and especially birth registration—often failed. Parsimonious legislatures laughed at vital registration bills or refused to pay doctors for reporting births and deaths. Midwives, only tenuously connected to the state, failed to report the births they attended. Doctors blanched at a task they saw as outside their professional duties. Even the officials of the state in its local incarnations—town, village, city, and county clerks—did not view registration as particularly pressing among their many duties. And when registration laws were enforced, the local lawyers and judges responsible for bringing cases viewed the failure to report a birth or death as a trivial offense. Perhaps they failed to grasp, as Lemuel Shattuck did, that the only way to ensure "accuracy in the tables" was to have a full accounting of every person who was born and every person who died.

CHAPTER 2

HONORED IN THE BREACH

I t was one thing to convince a state legislature to pass a vital statistics registration law but quite another to convince doctors, midwives, and even local recording officials such as town clerks that they should take the duty of reporting births seriously. Birth registration laws, quipped the *St. Louis Globe-Democrat* in 1879, were "more honored in the breach than the observance."[1] Whether a state passed its registration law in 1850 or 1915, many of the barriers to achieving complete registration were the same: neither midwives nor doctors nor registrars seemed to take the reporting requirement seriously enough. And beyond the dilatory behaviors of mandatory reporters, there were other barriers to full reporting that stemmed from the structural position of reporters in relation to the law. Midwives feared being caught without a license, physicians believed they should receive a fee for their services, and local clerks contested the boundaries of their responsibility.

As we have seen, reformers in organizations such as the American Public Health Association and the American Medical Association (AMA) looked with hope toward the federal government to provide centralized procedures and forms and to aggregate data on the national level. Such optimism was born of the frustration that many felt with the patchwork of practices, and even outright resistance, that bungled the functioning of registration laws in the states. Yet the one arena in which the federal government did have direct control of vital registration—in the administration of Indian policy on federal reservations—should have given reformers pause. Any efforts on the part of the Office of Indian Affairs (later the Bureau of Indian Affairs) to count and register Native Americans during the nineteenth century were beset by the same problems that plagued the states—weak infrastructure, little commitment to registration on the part of low-level officials who had to actually implement the laws, and, worse still, outright resistance on the part of those whose lives were to be recorded.

The difficulty that both states and the federal government had in administering birth registration throughout the nineteenth and early twentieth century points toward the complexity of any straightforward story that historians might wish to tell about "the state." In important ways, the story of the spread of vital registration in the United States conforms to well-trod tales of political development. Vital statistics collection is a kind of "biopolitics" that emerges from the mercantilist, body-counting logic of early modern states and flowers into the public-health- and welfare-promoting modern state that not only counts but tends the bodies of its people. And vital statistics collection is part of the process of "state simplification" integral to modern bureaucratic administration, of a piece with the creation of legible citizens through the invention and assignation of surnames, addresses, and other markers of knowability.[2] And yet in other ways this was more dream than reality. In 1915, thirty-six states had "model laws," but only ten actually administered those laws with any success. The distance between a house where a baby was born and the clerk's office where its birth was to be registered was apparently, in many places, too great to be overcome. This distance was not only physical but also ideological and administrative. It was one thing to write laws requiring registration, and it was another thing to make them function. As it turned out, the very people whom the law entrusted to report births—local clerks, physicians, and midwives—sometimes could not and often would not.

For midwives, reporting births was often practically difficult. Many midwives, complained a New York doctor at the state medical society's meeting in 1867, "cannot read or write."[3] Thus the task of filling out a birth certificate would be impossible. Sometimes what observers regarded as illiteracy was more likely lack of fluency in English. From the nineteenth century through the first four decades of the twentieth century, in ethnically European enclaves in urban areas or in rural areas settled mainly by recent European immigrants, most births were delivered by midwives who were countrywomen of the parturient mother. In an article ridiculing the city's midwives, the *Milwaukee Sentinel* listed the improper answers that such women gave on birth forms. On one form, the paper reported, a midwife filled out the baby's sex as "Catholic girl," and "in another certificate the sex was given as 'Bavi,' which, it is believed, meant 'boy.'" Still another midwife had listed "German" for sex. Clearly, the paper concluded, midwives were struggling with "a lack of knowledge of English."[4] Less demeaning than the *Sentinel*'s mockery, a study conducted in 1911 by Gertrude Barnes, a visiting nurse in Cleveland, found that all of that city's midwives were foreign born. And though most were literate in their native language, nearly one-third were illiterate in any language. Only one of the city's midwives could read English. Barnes's findings are not surprising given that the population of Cleveland was, in 1910, three-quarters foreign born.[5]

· Rural areas were little better. In states such as Minnesota, where rural counties were populated by foreign-born homesteaders, births were likewise often attended by countrywomen. Correspondence between Otto Hoffman, the town clerk of rural Granite Township in Minnesota (population 487 in 1910), and Dr. H. M. Bracken, the state's registration executive, illustrated the problem. Bracken wrote to Hoffman in July 1911 to complain that none of the birth reports Hoffman sent in were signed by the birth attendant, as the law required. Hoffman replied that "most time the people around here don't use no physician and . . . the midwifes (without examination) can neither read nor write the english language." As a result, Hoffman filled out the birth reports himself but could not convince midwives to sign them, because they "refused to sign any paper, what they cannot read."[6] As Hoffman indicated, the midwives in his community were not licensed ("without examination") and were likely largely untrained but instead were women whom friends and neighbors regarded as particularly helpful with birthing and who could be called in to attend mothers during labor. "It seems a real necessity to have such women in a community," wrote one town clerk in Minnesota, "as it is so far to go for a doctor and very bad roads that it is an utter impossibility to get one in time and a life or perhaps two might be lost during that time."[7]

New York's state Department of Health found such women delivering babies in "mountain districts remote from any medical service, little groups of foreign people near quarries or mountain camps, settlements on the fringe of larger communities." While New York State required midwives to be licensed, in such out-of-the-way places health inspectors found nearly as many licensed as unlicensed midwives delivering births, none of which were reported.[8] In rural North Carolina, U.S. Children's Bureau agents discovered a similar situation. In a lowland farming community, fewer than half of the midwives were registered with the state, and of all the midwives the agents interviewed, only one of them could read (but even she could not write). In the mountains of the state, fewer than one-quarter of the midwives were registered with the state. Of the thirteen midwives interviewed, only five could read and write.[9] As late as the 1930s, some rural counties in Georgia had as few as one general practice physician (never mind an obstetrician) for every 4,000 people.[10] So long as rural areas wanted for adequate numbers of doctors, and so long as poor county roads made travel slow and cumbersome, farm women would turn to neighbor women to assist with birth, whether or not those women were licensed or literate.

Among African Americans both rural and urban, the use of midwives was even more common than among ethnic Europeans, and here, too, illiteracy created a barrier to midwives' reporting of births. In 1909, an anonymous physician writing in the *Atlanta Constitution* complained that Atlanta's vital statistics were incomplete because the African American population's births were entirely attended by midwives who were "often so ignorant and untutored as not to be able to fill out the required form."[11] Virginia's state registrar made similar complaints. Under his state's new law, he claimed, the main barrier to complete birth registration was the "colored midwives," because they "do not receive mail regularly, cannot read, and cannot be reached readily from our office."[12] This was a problem throughout the rural South. In 1918, a study of maternal and child health in two rural Mississippi counties found not only that 88 percent of African American births were delivered by midwives (compared to 21 percent of white births) but also that of the seventy-nine Black midwives interviewed, nearly two-thirds were illiterate. The study concluded that midwives were the "greatest obstacle" to complete birth registration in the state.[13]

Complaints about midwives' illiteracy must be viewed skeptically, because they were often made by those who already viewed midwives as unsanitary, unscientific, and otherwise backward. Indeed, allegations like this formed the core of the discourse on the "midwife problem" in discussions of maternal and child health. Whether they were discussing the European immigrant midwife who attended births in a crowded urban area or the rural, African American "granny" midwife, public health reformers and physicians promoting the new specialty of obstetrics routinely characterized the midwife as "filthy and ignorant."[14] The lament that some midwives failed to register their births because they were illiterate both was undoubtedly true *and* served as one more way of painting a portrait of midwives as irredeemably outside the bounds of modernity.

In spite of the allegation that midwives failed to report the births they attended because they could not read or write, it is also clear that many non-literate midwives found ways to report their births through proxies. In the same survey in which she complained about Cleveland's illiterate midwives, Gertrude Barnes also reported that one midwife explained how she would have her husband write "the answer on the birth blanks, and later took them to one of two physicians of their own nationality, who puts his signature to the certificates before sending them to the City Hall."[15] A 1912 study of midwives in Providence, Rhode Island, conducted by the American Association for the Study and Prevention of Infant Mortality concluded that two-thirds of the city's midwives had a "friend or relative" report the births they attended.[16] In rural Wisconsin, Polish and German midwives were in the habit of having a baby's father file and sign the birth report.[17] Mississippi's African American midwives likewise got "some one else to fill out the certificate or report by word of mouth when they happened to go to town."[18]

Just as serious as illiteracy, however, was the issue of licensure and registration. Between 1910 and 1930, the years during which the campaign against midwives was at its peak, many municipalities and states began to train, license, or otherwise regulate midwifery. In 1923, nineteen states still had no regulation of midwifery at all, but by 1930, that number had dropped to ten.[19] Many midwives nevertheless continued to operate without training or a license and thus without any government supervision. Without licensure or registration, midwives were often unaware of state rules about the reporting of births. Because many states regarded simple education and instruction in registration requirements to be the best and most effective tool in combating low registration rates, health departments sent out circulars to physicians and midwives and posted copies of registration laws in prominent places such as local post offices. In New York, for example, the director of the Division of Vital Statistics sent notices to all registrars, physicians, and midwives warning them that the registration law was to be strictly enforced (figure 2.1).[20] Unlicensed midwives—the very people who most needed to be reached by such information—would not, however, receive such notices. The queries of G. W. Smith, a town clerk in Germania, Minnesota, illustrate the problem. Smith wrote to the state's health department that "there are a number of women that act as midwives[. A]re they not as responsible for the report of a birth as a regularly licensed midwife or a physician?" If so, reported Smith, "they do not know it." He wondered if he should send "a notice to all of them I know of."[21] Because such women were not licensed, Smith could not consult a registry to reach them but rather could only evangelize to "them I know of." Practicing midwifery without a license meant that some midwives were likely to miss the registration reminders and instructions that many states regularly sent out to licensed physicians and midwives.

But lack of license meant more than just lack of knowledge; it could also

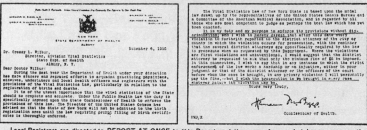

Figure 2.1. Notice to midwives, physicians, and registrars

Passing vital registration laws was only one step in a much larger process. Once laws were passed, states had to convince professionals to comply with the laws. Handbills and posters such as these, issued by the State of New York, put those responsible for registering births on notice that the state aimed to enforce its laws. Source: Willcox Papers, Library of Congress.

mean fear of reporting. In states where midwives were required to be licensed and registered, reporting a birth as an unlicensed midwife was tantamount to confessing a crime. In Connecticut, the state's head of vital statistics estimated that 85 percent of the state's unregistered births were due to the fact that unlicensed midwives "will not report for fear of prosecution for practicing without a license." Because birth certificates asked who attended the birth, even the parents involved in such births would not register them for fear of incriminating a neighbor and countrywoman.[22] In neighboring Massachusetts the situation was even more convoluted. The state's medical practice laws forbade the practice of midwifery, yet the state's registration laws required midwives to report the births they attended. Many midwives, not surprisingly, declined to report births they were not legally allowed to attend for fear of calling attention to their illegal behavior.[23] In Nevada, field agents for the Children's Bureau found many birth attendants who were "afraid to be known as midwives" because they were not licensed and "are afraid that they will get into trouble if it is known that they are practicing" without a "diploma." After many visits and much convincing, one agent reported that she had convinced some of the women to report their births to the local registrar. "One old woman," however, "insisted on having my name and address so that if she got into trouble by reporting the births I could come and defend her."[24] Unlike allopathic obstetrics, the practice of midwifery was loosely organized, professionalized, and licensed, and as many of its practitioners fell outside legal lines as inside them. So long as this situation persisted, unlicensed midwives were unlikely to report the births they attended.

Since at least 1880 (when the matter was discussed at the National Board of Health meeting), it had been axiomatic among advocates of vital statistics collection that a functioning system depended upon "some system of registration of physicians and midwives." A registry of doctors and midwives gave the local registrar or town clerk a list of people from whom to expect birth reports; the ideal clerk would periodically write to each registered birth attendant to check whether he or she had any births to report. Though many clerks, registrars, and health departments did just that, the strategy was more effective for doctors than for midwives.[25] While most physicians and their representatives in the AMA took the position that midwives should be eliminated, many public health administrators and child welfare reformers recognized that licensing midwives would improve not just infant and maternal mortality but also birth reporting.[26] Maryland, for example, decided to start licensing midwives in 1912. The licensure law required that a midwife pass an exam administered by the state health board and file her license with the registrar of vital statistics in her locality. The licensure law also specified that midwives "must at least know how to read, write, and be able to make out correctly a birth certificate as required by law."[27] Licensing midwives meant that registrars could reach them with information about birth registration and also conduct annual checks to inquire if a midwife had performed any births during the year. It also meant that midwives and their equipment were open to inspection. In 1915, New York City issued new regulations that required a midwife's home to be open to inspection, including her "equipment, record of cases, and register of births."[28] In Mississippi, the state board of health created a registry card for each midwife in the state and recorded information not only about whether she was clean and sterile in her instructions but also about whether the midwife was willing to follow instructions, could read and write, or had a "record for prompt reporting of births."[29] Some states not only used licensure to improve midwives' birth registration practices but also worked in reverse, using birth registration to license and regulate midwives. Michigan's health department reported that whenever it received a birth certificate signed by an unlicensed midwife, it mailed the woman a copy of the state's "regulations governing midwives."[30] Birth registration thus acted not only as the consequence but also as the cause of state regulation of midwives.

In studies of infant mortality in places as diverse as rural Georgia or Gary, Indiana, researchers found that licensure did successfully bring midwives into the ambit of the state. Not only did licensure regulate their practice, but also it made them responsive to the laws requiring that they report births. Among births attended by licensed midwives in Gary, for example, 89 percent were registered, "a showing only slightly below the percentage of registered births among those attended by physicians." Births attended by unlicensed midwives were, by contrast, "nearly half" unregistered.[31] In Mississippi, where the state board of health conducted midwife education classes and organized its midwives into "clubs," some of which functioned to perform proxy birth registration, registrars and physicians both agreed that such supervision by the state improved birth reporting.[32] One advocate for birth registration put the matter succinctly: "Improved reporting of birth has been credited to the midwife as soon as she comes under supervision."[33]

Midwives were not the only birth attendants, however, who failed to report births. Many doctors also refused to fill out certificates for the births they attended. No advocates of vital registration attributed doctors' errancy to illiteracy, but it is possible that in the late nineteenth and early twentieth centuries this was a part of the problem for at least some physicians. Even as the AMA sought to regulate the practice of medicine more strictly, state licensure laws often grandfathered in practicing physicians, many of whom had little to no formal training and may have been functionally illiterate.[34] Most commentators, however, were more likely to characterize doctors as careless or forgetful. Still others claimed that doctors actively refused to report births. A New York doctor complained to his brethren that "many physicians prefer to make no report rather than let it appear how small their practice is."[35] For doctors who delivered babies, reporting births was, in effect, a public record of popularity. Besides protecting their reputation as practitioners with a robust client base, "physicians often assert," reported the *Boston Globe* in 1910, "that it is none of the public's business who is born or dead."[36] Whether protecting their own or their clients' privacy, some doctors apparently viewed reporting births as a form of publicity that it was illegitimate for the state to demand.

Reporting requirements ran up against doctors' relationship with the state in another way, too. Many doctors viewed filing birth certificates as a form of uncompensated labor demanded by the government.[37] In 1855, Connecticut's chief registration officer complained of the "positive unwillingness" of doctors to file their birth certificates because "no compensation" was given them. At a convention of county health officers held in Indiana in 1887, several officers reported that local physicians refused to report births because they believed, as one officer put it, that "it was not right to demand something from them for which they received no remuneration. They think they have a right to be paid for making these returns."[38] Norman Teal, an Indiana doctor who also served in the state's legislature and was the chairman of the legislature's Committee on State Medicine, Health, and Vital Statistics, made the case more fully in 1891. "The physician's time does not belong to the State any more than does that of the wood-chopper," claimed Teal. The obligation to collect vital statistics "rests entirely upon the State, certainly not upon one class of citizens alone, but upon all alike. In short, it is public business and should be carried on by public officers at public expense." Teal suggested that if the state wanted to have a record of its births and deaths then it should have public officials, not private practitioners, perform that duty. "It would be best," Teal advised, "to require Township Trustees to collect these reports and return them to County Recorders for public record."[39] It was well and good, in Teal's view, for the state to want to collect records of births and deaths, but it was not fine to do so on the backs of private citizens.

Doctors may have also sensed that the uncompensated labor they were asked to perform for the state was beneath them. At a time when allopathic physicians were trying to consolidate their professional power and authority, states proliferated preprinted forms for them to fill out. As Lisa Gitelman has pointed out, preprinted forms instantiated a mental division of labor by separating the act of deciding what is important to know from the act of obtaining and transmitting knowledge. Doctors were turned into clerks for the state when they filled out birth certificates. Physicians also performed routinized exams using preprinted blank forms for the life insurance industry beginning in the early twentieth century, a process that historian Dan Bouk describes as "disciplining" physicians in order to create an "observational community" that acted on behalf of life insurers. Like vital registration systems, insurance companies' risk-making data were only as good as the compliance of the physicians who filled out their forms. The difference between the insurance industry and state boards of health, however, was that private industry paid physicians for these services.[40] Like vital registration, this model limited the independent judgment of the physician and co-opted his labor, but unlike the state, private industry recognized the process as work and paid for it.

Some localities responded to physicians' complaints about the matter by offering a fee for each birth certificate filed.[41] The general consensus among public health advocates, however, was against the practice on both practical and philosophical grounds. Practically speaking, for the doctor who "can get $15 for telling a man that he is sick, improving and well, the smaller [reporting] fee has few temptations."[42] The ten or twenty-five cents a doctor might earn for a birth report was, in other words, too trivial to motivate him. In a column considering the "ethics of registration," Marshall Price explained that doctors were not ordinarily paid for registering vital statistics because "experience has shown that a fee commensurate with the services performed has little influence in improving the quantity or quality of the birth and death returns." Effectiveness aside, Price also claimed that states did not offer to pay doctors for their reports because "legislatures are too parsimonious to spare money for the trivial questions involving the life, health and happiness of their citizens."[43] Whether it was because legislatures were too cheap or doctors too rich, many of those interested in improving registration agreed that paying doctors on a fee-for-service model was unlikely to help the cause.

Philosophically, advocates of vital registration disagreed that asking doctors to file birth certificates was an undue burden or a form of uncompensated labor. Instead, they believed that birth registration inhered in doctors' duty to their profession, their patients, and their country. Fees, objected John Trask of the U.S. Public Health Service, suggested that vital registration was not a duty but a choice, something optional rather than required.[44] The head of Indiana's state board of health, Dr. John Hurty, likewise insisted that reporting births was a duty. In his correspondence with county health officers, most of whom were physicians, Hurty told them to deal with recalcitrant doctors by calling "the attention of the profession to their legal duty, which is likewise their duty to the science of medicine, and to their patients."[45] Hurty was fond of pointing out that doctors' refusal to report births later harmed their patients. In a speech before the AMA, Hurty told of a daughter in a poor family who stood to inherit $12,000 if she could only prove that she was the daughter of her dead father (and hence the niece of the wealthy uncle who had left her the money in her will). Because she lacked a birth certificate, the courts would not recognize her kinship to her uncle and denied her the money. "What a cruel and unnecessary blow was this," Hurty intoned, "from the hand of a practitioner of this learned and benevolent science of medicine."[46] Health officials in other states agreed with Hurty. "I have no patience with the individual who is lacking in patriotism, and who is so careless of the welfare of his patients, that because he believes he should be paid to make the report he refuses or neglects to make it," declared Ohio's state registrar.[47]

Beyond maligning the patriotism and professionalism of dilatory doctors, public health officials also liked to remind doctors that they enjoyed state protection through the laws governing medical licensure. Throughout the second half of the nineteenth century, the AMA fought to marginalize "irregular" medical practitioners, and by the turn of the century every state had a medical licensure law on its books.[48] Given this, state officials reasoned, it was not too much to ask, in return, that doctors perform simple services such as vital registration. Minnesota's chief health officer, H. M. Bracken, explained such reasoning in a letter to a fellow doctor. Complaining physicians, he wrote, "seem to overlook the fact that the government gives them certain privileges, and has a right to expect something in return. . . . It would seem that he might fill out a few birth and death certificates to offset this great advantage."[49] William Deacon, the Kansas state registrar, after finding that the doctors in his state resented reporting births without compensation, traveled to county medical society meetings to remind the assembled physicians that "the state protects the physician in his practice, and on ethical grounds has a right to expect him to comply with the laws affecting his practice," including the law requiring attendants to file birth certificates.[50] If organized medicine was itself a creature of state laws, it could not object to the demand that it serve the public interest. Indeed, states such as Wisconsin and Indiana went so far as to pass legislation stipulating that no midwife or doctor could collect payment for the delivery of a baby until and unless that baby's birth was registered. Such legislation made it clear that reporting births was not a task separate from delivering babies but a basic feature of the job.[51]

Advocates of vital registration liked to point out not only that the state was responsible for the privileges that physicians enjoyed in the medical marketplace but also that decisions by state attorneys general and courts routinely supported the right of states to conduct vital registration under their police powers. "It has been ruled by the Attorney General," wrote Minnesota's head registrar, "that, for the reason that physicians have certain privileges, such as exemption from jury duty, etc., the state can demand certain services from them in return."[52] Such confidence notwithstanding, vital registration laws were occasionally successfully challenged in court. In the 1911 case of *Ohio v. Boone*, a doctor challenged his prosecution for failure to report births on constitutional grounds, and Ohio's highest court agreed with the defendant. It found that under the terms of the Northwest Ordinance of 1787, "the state has not the right to draft a citizen into particular service without substantial compensation." And while the court felt that requiring a physician to report the fact of a birth or death to public authorities was acceptable, requiring him to report what it called "nonprofessional" information, such as whether the birth was legitimate or illegitimate and the parents' races, addresses, birthplaces, occupations, and more, went beyond the state's just exercise of police powers. "The provisions of this statute which require a professional man to search out non-professional information and certify it to state authorities," wrote the court, "is unnecessary, unreasonable and arbitrary, and is not, therefore, a valid exercise of police power."[53] The decision in *Boone* made those in the public health community extremely anxious because it seemed to give credence to doctors' long-standing complaint that the state was extracting uncompensated labor from them. At the very least, it suggested that Ohio would have to either stop asking physicians to report "nonprofessional" information or begin offering its physicians a fee for reporting the details of a baby's parentage. Ohio resolved the problem by making it optional for a physician to supply most of the personal information about parents on the birth certificate. In case a doctor left that information blank, the local registrar, who *was* paid for handling certificates, had the responsibility to obtain it from the child's parents.[54]

As Ohio's eventual reliance on the intercession of the local registrar indicates, a functioning vital registration system depended not only on the diligence of those who job it was to report births—birth attendants such as doctors and midwives—but also on the enthusiasm and capacity of the local clerks and registrars whose job it was to receive, collate, and transmit vital registration documents on behalf of state boards of health. The local registrar was, opined one state health official, the "first cog" in the state's registration machinery.[55] Just as they ran into trouble with midwives and doctors, new state laws often faltered because of problems with such local officials. Some of these problems were structural: while town clerks or subregistrars were essential to the registration system, many were only tenuously connected to the machinery of government. In the small towns and cities of Minnesota, for example, local recording officials often performed a variety of functions in addition to their work as town clerk. As Otto Pierson canvassed the state in the early years of the twentieth century, he found a village recorder in Little Fork Township who "did not understand when he took the office of village recorder that this birth and death reporting would be part of his duty." In Rosemont, the clerk was also a postmaster. In Millersville, the town clerk was a blacksmith and a wagonmaker "with a shop at the country cross-roads." In Odessa, the clerk owned a furniture store, while the clerk of Correll was also the hardware, furniture, harness, paint, and oil dealer in town. Another clerk owned a creamery "in the center of town." Still others were farmers who spent long days out in their fields, lived far from the center of town, and would be hard to reach. "There is people in the Town," wrote Sinnott clerk Henry Hoper, "wich [sic] I do not meet for the whole year, therefore it may be that they do not all report."[56]

Having a blacksmith shop at the crossroads or a creamery in the center of town might, in some ways, be ideal for a town clerk. In the words of the creamery owner who served as his town's clerk, "people from all parts of the town come with their milk so I get a chance to see or hear from every corner of the town," including hearing the news of the latest births in local families. At the same time, the clerk who was busy making his living as a blacksmith, a farmer, or a merchant might not consider the meticulous care of state records as his first priority. When Otto Pierson visited Mr. Lenz, the town clerk and furniture dealer in Odessa, for example, he found "a large accumulation of papers" in the store's roll-top desk. Among the "heap," Pierson found nine death and sixteen birth certificates, some of which were more than two years old and none of which were "transcribed in the local register" and so none of which had been transmitted to the state's central registry.[57] A survey of records kept by local registrars in the 1930s revealed that many of Minnesota's birth and death registers were being stored in attics, basements, barns, and granaries around the state.[58]

In some states, registration responsibility was placed upon those who already had another official duty: a city auditor, a village or township clerk, or the tax assessor, for example. Unlike the town furniture dealer or a rural blacksmith, such officials could reasonably be expected to feel somewhat more connected to the functions of local, if not state, government. Nevertheless, registration machinery faltered in many of these instances as well. Virginia's first state registration law, passed in 1853, provides a good example. The law gave the responsibility for birth and death registration to commissioners of the revenue, local officials whose primary job was to survey the taxable personal property in their district. Commissioners were required not only to record the births and deaths in each family that they surveyed but also to annually transmit this record to the clerk of the county court.[59] From the outset, commissioners resented this new duty. They complained that the auditor of public accounts, under whose aegis they worked, failed to give them adequate instructions, forms, time, or compensation. In 1854, Mr. Graves, a commissioner, wrote to the auditor that "I do not believe that any one in the world can take all the lists now required." Not only did he have to list taxable property and register voters, but recent legislation meant that he now also had to enroll the militia and record the births and deaths in his district. "It takes just as long," Graves complained, "where there are any deaths and birth in a family to get all the information which the law requires . . . as it does to get the list of Taxable property, and whether there are any or not, the inquiries have to be made." Other commissioners agreed. "I find that due to this additional duty, it takes much time & patience & a *great deal* of writing," wrote Commissioner Lands. Lands ended his letter with a query: "Are we to receive no pay for this extra labour?"[60] Many commissioners felt that the legislature unfairly burdened them by giving them extra work without extra pay. "This law is a most iniquitous one from beginning to end, in requiring clerks to perform all this labour without one cent compensation," protested another commissioner, who concluded by sarcastically quipping that he and other commissioners nonetheless "have to submit to our Master." Even though they, unlike the physicians who complained about performing the state's registration work, were public servants, commissioners chafed no less at bearing the burden of the state's increasing bureaucratic enumeration of its citizens. A post that had been designed to survey and register property now included voter registration, militia enrollment, and birth and death registration.

This was not simply a nineteenth-century problem. Well into the twentieth century, states expanded their functions without expanding their capacity, relying instead on local officials who had multiple duties. In Progressive Era North Dakota, for example, the state delegated birth and death registration to city auditors and clerks of villages and townships, but researchers studying public health administration in the state found that these functionaries did not take "sufficient interest" in vital registration "for the reason that they have other duties to occupy their time."[61] This was also true in rural Kansas, where township, village, or city clerks served as registrars. Not only were such men often busy with other duties, but their registration districts were sufficiently large that a man could not "keep track of events through his own acquaintance."[62]

The matter of a birth that occurred outside a clerk's "acquaintance" but inside his registration district was a matter of contestation. Like physicians, local clerks and registrars also questioned the boundaries of duty that inhered in their position. Many clerks took the position that their duty was simply to receive and transmit the birth certificates that were submitted to them by local midwives, doctors, and parents. State officials, on the other hand, believed that clerks should actively seek out births to register and report. Beginning in the mid-nineteenth century when Massachusetts began to publish its collected vital statistics, commentators lamented that local clerks reported "only such of these facts [of birth and death] as happened by accident or otherwise, to come to their knowledge. They had taken no pains to obtain them, and had put in operation no active inquiry."[63] Town clerks, in other words, reported the vital events that were brought to their attention by diligent doctors, midwives, and householders, but they did not seek to find out whether other, unreported births and deaths had occurred. In 1860, Massachusetts began instructing each clerk that his duty went beyond merely receiving returns but extended to discovering "all deficiencies, by '*obtaining*' the facts respecting events not so returned—so that his record may faithfully represent all the cases of deaths, births, and marriages, which occur in his town." Even when a clerk found it impossible to obtain all the information that a form required, he should still report what he could so that "*the event itself should never escape unnoticed.*" The state recommended that each clerk perform a canvass of his town "either personally or by agent" at least once a year, visiting each home to inquire if a birth or death had occurred there in the previous year.[64]

What was true in Massachusetts in the mid-nineteenth century was equally true in early twentieth-century Minnesota. In 1903, H. M. Bracken of the Minnesota Board of Health wrote to each of the state's local registration officials asking them to double-check whether there were any unreported births or deaths in their jurisdictions. Many were offended by the request. A clerk from Polk County responded to Bracken that "it is almost impossible for the Town Clerks to get this report without first making inquiries and then sending blanks in every instance. The people seem to have forgot all about this law. It is to [sic] small pay for the Clerks to go and make inspection for every case." In other words, people rarely remembered to report births and deaths but depended on the clerk to find out about these events and then deliver the appropriate forms. But for this clerk, the fee of twenty-five cents he received for each report could not compensate for the labor required. As another clerk wrote in irritation, "I haven't time to hitch up a team every time a child is born." A clerk from Milaca, Minnesota, sent a similar reply. He noted that it would take him more than a week to canvass his entire jurisdiction, and he complained that "at this time of the year I could hardly afford to make the Canvass without some Recompense." Because the clerk wrote in July, he likely would have had to take time out from working his farm to visit neighbors, and this, he felt, was too much to ask. In Livonia, the town clerk began to canvass his neighbors at Bracken's request but gave up after realizing how much time it would take him to reach his entire district. "This canvassing of the Town is something I can not do," the clerk explained to Bracken, for "I have to work for my living and as there is nothing in it I can not waste my time for this purpose alone."[65]

State officials despaired over the apparent lack of commitment to vital registration on the part of midwives, doctors, and local clerks, but they did not remain passive in the face of it. Instead, they tried to make registration requirements seem more incumbent by prosecuting those who flouted the law. It was a truism among state health officials that making an example of a delinquent midwife, doctor, or clerk was an effective way to get all reporters to do their job. "One of the best ways to secure birth reports without prosecution," advised New Jersey's chief registration official, "is to prosecute a few physicians who fail to report, and then other reports will begin to roll in."[66] In his correspondence with county health officers, the head of Indiana's state board of health, John Hurty, advised them to go after recalcitrant doctors. Those who refuse to report births violate the law and "are not good citizens" and should be "made to feel its penalty." "Inform the prosecuting attorney," Hurty recommended, "giving him all of the facts."[67] In some localities, this strategy was a proven success. Beginning in 1916, New York State's Division of Vital Statistics vigorously enforced the birth registration law. In less than one year, the promptness of birth reports increased by 75 percent for physicians and 57.6 percent for midwives. Such numbers showed, in the division head's words, "the marked evidence of success in the actual enforcement of the birth registration law."[68] Registration officials considered the *ability* to prosecute to be a critical feature of the model law and likewise considered *actual* prosecution a mark of their own commitment to the public good.

While registration officials agreed that prosecution of scofflaws was necessary to grease the wheels of the registration machinery, securing convictions was easier said than done. For one thing, it required discovering an omission rather than the commission of a positive act. In places such as New York City, registrars discovered unreported births by checking the death certificates of children under the age of one against the birth certificates filed during the previous year. Since deaths were better reported than births, this checking often turned up many unreported births.[69] In Pennsylvania, the state selected "certain squares, districts or localities" and conducted "a birth census" in them, knocking on the door of each house and writing down the name, birth date, and birth attendant of any baby born in the previous year. These birth census reports were matched against the birth certificates on file in the state office, "and if the original report is not found, the physician attending is prosecuted."[70] In Minnesota, the state's field agent for vital statistics traveled the state to discover unreported births by visiting local communities and checking their newspapers for birth announcements, visiting the schools and health officers, checking local church baptismal registers, and surveying hospital records of births.[71] Rounding up unreported births, in other words, required having access to alternative sources of information and took much time and effort on the part of often underfunded and understaffed state and municipal health departments.

Even when vital statistics officers managed to secure evidence that births had gone unreported, they often encountered local hostility to enforcement of the registration law. In Princeton, Minnesota, a small town fifty miles north of Minneapolis, Gladys Casady, the state's vital statistics field agent, found herself unable to prosecute errant doctors. After discovering several births that were not reported by two of the town's doctors, Casady paid a visit to the justice of the peace to inform him that she intended to press charges. Mr. Keith, the "spineless" justice of the peace, "was very reluctant to handle the matter" and conveyed that "he did not want to impose a fine upon these doctors." The county attorney, meanwhile, was sympathetic to Casady's desire to enforce the law but told her that "it would be impossible to get a jury" to convict one of the doctors, Dr. Cooney, because "there was hardly a family in that part of the country that had not had at least one life saved" by him.

Dr. Cooney, meanwhile, blew his top, "said some very harsh things about the State Board of Health," and told Casady that he would never file another birth certificate "so long as I live, and I'll never pay a fine." Reluctant to confront a hostile jury in front of a spineless judge, Casady instead extracted a promise from Cooney that, his previous outburst notwithstanding, he would file all birth certificates in the future. She considered this the best she could do under the circumstances.[72] In another small town, Casady successfully prosecuted a doctor; after he complained, however, that "we could not enforce the law until we embodied it in a physician's fee," she found that the local judge imposed a minimal fine "because he considered it a technical offense."[73] In towns where judges, county attorneys, and even village recorders were all elected positions, reports of local indifference and hostility to state enforcement of vital registration were commonplace.

While the problem of dilatory reporting on the part of midwives and doctors could be solved, reformers hoped, by a combination of education, licensure, regulation, and prosecution, the case of government officials who slacked in their duties called for solutions that attacked what many saw as the root of the problem: patronage. As a sign, "patronage" gathered under it a host of late nineteenth-century and early twentieth-century complaints about the failure of governments large and small to function in the public interest. Even before the Civil War, public health reformers and statists in cities such as New York and Philadelphia complained that the men appointed to administer vital registration were party hacks who mixed "science and humanity with politics" to ill effect. John Griscom, displaced after an election as New York's city inspector, complained that his replacement was an uneducated party functionary who would not enforce the city's registration laws. "We tremble for the results," Griscom gushed angrily, "in observing the foul spirit of partisanship [that] now attempts to lay its Vandal grasp upon the sacred temple of science." Griscom claimed that for his part he felt only shame when he read vital statistics reports from abroad, while he, in his attempt to "expose to the light the mysteries of life and death," had instead become "a mark for the bullet of party warfare."[74] When it came to vital statistics collection, replacing politics with public interest was both the object—to create data for a science of human life—and, as the nineteenth century wore on, also the subject. Politics could not replace public interest in legislation until public interest replaced politics in vital registration.

The solution in vital registration, as in so many areas of governance, appeared simple to reformers: the right administrative structure combined with the right sorts of men to do the job. As the struggle in Massachusetts to shift vital statistics collection from the secretary of state to a newly created board of health shows, reformers believed that new administrative structures could create better results. State health boards would be mirrored by county and city boards of health and these, ideally, would be staffed by doctors. Instead of town clerks or village assessors recording birth and death registrations, county health officers would do the job. When Pennsylvania's legislature proposed a bill to create a state board of health in 1874, the Philadelphia County Medical Society delighted at the prospect that vital registration might now be released from the control of men whose chief qualification was "political favoritism." In a resolution, the society asked that the state appoint only men familiar with "State medicine" and "the theory of statistics."[75] Through the model law, the U.S. Census Bureau also recommended that states create boards of health to replace existing registration structures. By 1915, most states had a state-level board or department of health.[76]

Yet administrative reform was not a cure-all. As late as 1916 in New York State, which had a robust state board of health, prosecution of nonreporting physicians and midwives created political turmoil for the appointed head of the state board of health, Dr. Biggs. The state's doctors, together with their state assemblymen, lobbied Biggs to amend the state's laws to relieve doctors from prosecution. Dr. Biggs seemed inclined to heed the message. The head of the state's Vital Statistics Division, who was behind the prosecution campaign, lamented that Biggs exhibited "servile acquiescence to foolish and ignorant designs rather than [to] the reasonable and independent action of a competent statistician."[77] The day was yet to come when statisticians would operate independently to provide reliable data on which to base rational public policy.

Much as many interested in vital registration might have regretted it, the federal government had no jurisdiction over registration within a federalist system. Unlike England's General Registry Office, there was no centralized bureau that could create a registration infrastructure and command obedience to it. Even after the Census Bureau was created in 1903, the best it could do was promote the model law and create forms that states could use if they wanted, but it could compel neither of these. There was, however, one group of people over whom the federal government had direct jurisdiction: Native Americans living on reservations. From the era of Indian removal, beginning in the 1830s, through the 1880s, the federal government coerced the Native Americans in

U.S. territory to live on reservations.[78] Administering reservations, the Office of Indian Affairs sought population knowledge but engaged in no systematic registration of births, deaths, and marriages. In practice, there were several reasons why the federal government gathered population information about Native Americans, nearly all of which facilitated the advance of settler colonialism. Demographic information was intimately tied to questions of military conquest, sovereignty, land, and assimilation. Yet even though the federal government had practical reasons to track Indian populations, the issues that beset administration of registration in the states plagued the Office of Indian Affairs to an even greater degree. Besides the federal government's feeble registration infrastructure and diffuse sense of responsibility for vital events, Native Americans had every reason to resist being registered. For when Office of Indian Affairs agents on reservations counted resident Indians, they asserted U.S. sovereignty over them, demonstrating starkly the relationship between power and knowledge.

From the formation of the Office of Indian Affairs in the War Department in 1824 forward, the federal government was interested in assessing the numbers of the Indian population in its territory, and it was particularly interested to understand the number of warriors in this population. These were nations with whom the federal government conducted diplomatic affairs and sometimes engaged in military conflict, so knowing the military strength of Indians made political sense. While all such knowledge was fairly conjectural, it nonetheless factored into politicians' and Indian administrators' thinking about the relationship between policies of removal, for example, and the line of white settlement in the 1830s. In administering removal, Secretary of War Lewis Cass calculated the total Indian population of the United States and the total number of warriors in striking distance of white settlers.[79] Knowing the military strength of Native Americans was important again after the acquisition of territories from Mexico in 1848. Here the U.S. government faced Indian nations with whom it had no treaties and who occupied lands that it wanted to clear for white settlement. Though the Indian Office had been transferred to the newly created Interior Department in 1848, the reservation system in the far West was the product of a series of military campaigns after the Civil War, conducted under Ulysses S. Grant's "peace policy." This policy maintained that the United States was at peace with all Indians who accepted the boundaries of reservations and at war with all who transgressed them. In the midst of this renewed military engagement with Native nations, the U.S. Census Bureau conducted its first comprehensive enumeration of all Indians in the

1870 decennial census. Led by none other than Francis Amasa Walker, who simultaneously served as the director of the census and the commissioner of Indian Affairs under Grant, the results were published as the *Statistical Atlas* (1874) for public consumption. Working with a lithographer, Walker produced detailed maps showing the line of white settlement as well as the location of Indian reservations.[80] Population knowledge gave information about where Indians were located, which lands would need to be cleared, and which were available for white settlement. In the context of the peace policy, demographic information *was* military intelligence.

Though politicians and bureaucrats in the Office of Indian Affairs might wish for population information about Native Americans, federal knowledge was highly inexact. Even the conclusion that Indians were not a vanishing race was based on conjecture. The Office of Indian Affairs had ambitions, however, to enumerate the Indians it treated with. Beginning in 1846, Congress required that agents of the Indian Office, then located in the War Department, "take a census, and . . . obtain such other statistical information" about the tribes under their jurisdiction as the secretary of war might request. In 1847, twelve Indian agents conducted censuses of their reservations. The same year, Henry R. Schoolcraft, who became a statistician in the Office of Indian Affairs, began an elaborate census of reservation Indians.[81] Schoolcraft's pan-reservation census was not repeated, but individual Indian agents administering reservations were required to regularly enumerate their populations. Often guaranteed by treaty, reservations granted tribally held land and payments to Indian nations in rations or annuities, goods or cash. Payments to Indians in cash or kind required some knowledge of who was entitled to such goods, and for this reason, reservation superintendents were required to conduct an annual census of the tribal population. These censuses organized Indians into Euro-American nuclear families that did not reflect Native customs regarding marriage, property, or inheritance. The censuses also formed the basis for the tribal rolls, where births could be added and deaths subtracted.[82]

Connecting the annual reservation census to distribution of provisions made population knowledge into a form of accounting and made plain the link between enumeration and sovereignty. It could also encourage Native Americans to cooperate with the census. As the agent in charge of the California superintendency reported to the commissioner of Indian Affairs in 1870, the Indians on his reservation "understood that the census was taken as a basis for the purchase of supplies, and seemed willing to be enumerated and anxious that all should be included."[83] On the other hand, when Indians refused to cooperate with the census, agents withheld their rations, making the relationship between being known and being ruled explicit. In 1880, the superintendent of the Sac and Fox Agency in Iowa reported that he had been withholding annuities from the Sac and Fox for nearly four years because they were refusing to cooperate with the census. The problem, from the Native Americans' point of view, was that the census had changed. "The new form requires each family to be entered separately, commencing with the head of the same and followed by the names and a brief description of all the persons for whom he or she is entitled to draw the per capita payment," the commissioner of Indian Affairs explained. The old form had only required that the head of household give his name and the total number of others in the household without giving their names and ages. In exasperation, the commissioner wrote that "the whole difficulty in this lies in their perverseness and objection to being enrolled and to taking of a proper and accurate census." The agent, meanwhile, reported that he had given the Sac and Fox "every explanation and argument" to agree to the new census but claimed that they refused because it "conflicts with their religious opinions in regard to counting of time or ages and of enumerating the number of their people."[84] The next year, the agent conducted a census of the tribe without their consent but still withheld annuities from the heads of household until they signed the roll to confirm that it was correct. Rather than comply, the Sac and Fox sent a delegation to Washington, D.C., to meet with the secretary of the Interior and the commissioner of Indian Affairs. The commissioner explained that Congress had mandated the new forms and nothing could be done to change them. After this, the agent reported, they then "very reluctantly consented" to sign the new rolls.[85]

While the Sac and Fox objected to enumeration for religious reasons, other Native Americans did so because they understood the relationship between being counted and being ruled militarily. Two examples from 1874 illustrate this. In that year, the superintendent of the Arickaree, Gros Ventre, and Mandan Agency in the Dakota Territory explained that he had trouble completing his annual census because, "like most other Indian tribes, these have steadily refused to be counted, believing the object to be their gradual and final extinction by means of such diseases as the whites from time to time may desire to introduce." The agent elaborated that just as he had tried to conduct his census, deadly whooping cough had appeared among members of the tribes, and his last attempt at a census had been followed by an outbreak of smallpox. "They insist all these deaths are the consequence of being counted," he lamented.[86] Though the superintendent clearly believed that the link between disease and counting was no more than irrational superstition, he ignored the larger logic within which enumeration was part of a set of policies designed, if not to literally infect Indian bodies, to extinguish Indian sovereignty. To be counted was to accept one's status as a ward of the U.S. government, in exchange for which rations or annuities might be granted.

The same year, enumeration at the Red Cloud Agency in Nebraska turned into a scene of military conflict. The commissioner of Indian Affairs reported that the agent had, in years past, been forced to distribute rations without taking a census, presumably because the Sioux there had threatened him. In September 1874 when the agent was prepared to distribute annuities to those Sioux who accepted the treaty of 1868 (which led to the creation of the Red Cloud Agency), bands of "hostile," nontreaty Sioux rode into the agency, also demanding rations. The agent insisted that they must be added to the census rolls. But "they resisted every effort to count them." Like the agent at the Sac and Fox Agency would later do, the agent at Red Cloud attempted to count the "hostile" bands against their will. As he described it, he walked among their lodges counting them but was "arrested by some three hundred of these wild fellows and returned to the agency for trial." Resident, or treaty, Indians protected him. "Unable to induce them to comply with the orders of the Government for a census to be taken," he wrote, "I appealed to those who had lived long enough at the agency to understand the necessity of a compliance with these orders." Some five months after he had first attempted to take a census, the treaty Sioux agreed to comply, at which point they were attacked by the nontreaty bands. As part of these skirmishes, a "hostile" Indian killed the agency clerk, and the superintendent summoned federal troops to the agency. When they arrived, "all of the hostile and many of the resident Indians left the agency for the north." A short time later, however, the agent reported that many former residents had returned, and with the U.S. military still present, "I commenced a registration of the people."[87] Those Native Americans who had not made treaties with the U.S. government and had not consented to live under U.S. sovereignty understood that if they agreed to be counted, they agreed to be ruled, and that their continued military strength lay in the refusal of both.

The events at Red Cloud Agency notwithstanding, for most employees of the Office of Indian Affairs, census taking was a routine but often unsuccessful affair. Indeed, in 1887, the commissioner of Indian Affairs complained in his annual report that most censuses were inaccurate. He blamed challenging conditions and inadequate funding and infrastructure for the problem.

He noted that in 1884, Congress had passed a new Indian appropriations bill with a provision requiring an annual census at each reservation, but "no special means are provided for taking the census." The commissioner generously concluded that "Congress when framing this law could not have fully comprehended the magnitude of the extra labor thereby imposed on the agent and his employès." The reasons for the "extra labor," the commissioner explained, included the facts that reservations were vast in area; Indian residences might be thirty to fifty miles apart from one another; houses and tipis might not have a road leading to them; many Indians were mobile, not sedentary; most did not speak English, and Indian interpreters often could not write; and it was impossible to "induce many to visit the agency office for enumeration." Thus most censuses were but "unreliable estimates, compiled from such information as can be picked up by the police or other employès from whatever sources may be available." The commissioner recommended that Congress provide special funds for census taking and that the censuses be conducted triennially rather than annually.[88] Though the annual reports from agency superintendents were littered with examples of the kinds of problems the commissioner described, Congress never heeded his request for more money or support for census taking.[89]

Along with conducting the annual census, during the second half of the nineteenth century, the Office of Indian Affairs periodically prodded agents to record and reports the births and deaths that occurred under their jurisdiction. Recording births proved even more difficult than taking a census. Beginning in 1874, the Office of Indian Affairs asked its agents to report births and deaths, and it published the information in its annual reports in subsequent years. But agents often reported, as they did with the census, that the results were highly incomplete. The superintendent of the Warm Springs Agency in Oregon, for example, noted in his 1878 report to the commissioner that "there have no doubt been a number unknown to us, as it is rarely that we are informed of a birth, and the physician is seldom called in to render assistance."[90] Likewise the agent for the Kiowa, Comanche, and Wichita in Indian Territory suspected a high infant mortality rate on the reservation but could only conjecture because "neither the birth or death of these infants is reported, hence the fact does not appear upon the records of this office."[91]

The same sorts of challenges that encumbered census taking also affected birth recording. Moreover, unlike with the census, responsibility for reporting births and deaths was diffuse. The postbellum reservation system included a bare-bones administrative staff, any of whom could be called upon to register a birth. Agency clerks and superintendents had ultimate control of the records and kept the census rolls. One way to record vital events was simply to note it on the census rolls. Agency physicians kept medical records, though often not systematically, and they infrequently attended either births or deaths.[92] Indian police forces, composed largely of resident Indians, patrolled reservations and served in the capacity of what one historian has called the "reservation handyman." Police performed a variety of tasks from distributing rations to taking the census, from building infrastructure to reporting births and deaths to the superintendent.[93] Without a clear infrastructure for vital registration, such as that being constructed in the states during the same years, and without a separate federal infrastructure, agents of the Office of Indian Affairs were left with little to help them accomplish the task at hand.

Perhaps just as important as the diffusion of responsibility and the absence of administrative infrastructure was the lack of any clear relationship between the collection of birth information and the policies of the Indian Office as they operated either on particular reservations or nationally. While for much of the nineteenth century the office was interested in the aggregate increase or decrease of the Indian population, and it needed to know to how many people, and to whom, it owed rations and annuities, neither of the functions that birth registration served—as a tool of public health or as a form of legal identification—dovetailed with the operations of federal reservations. That would change in the 1880s when federal Indian policy began to emphasize civilization through education and allotment of land in severalty.

Where the "peace policy" had pursued the confinement of Indians on reservations where adults might be taught to farm and children might be educated by missionaries, consensus about the policy began to fracture in the late 1870s. Ongoing graft in the administration of the Office of Indian Affairs, brutal and well-publicized military action against Indians in the West, and the exposure of near starvation among many who received rations and annuities from the government led reformers active in the Women's National Indian Association, the Indian Rights Association, and the annual Lake Mohonk Conference of the Friend of the Indian to work with politicians and Office of Indian Affairs officials to promote a new solution to the "Indian problem." Reservations, these reformers began to argue, were the problem, not the solution. They preserved tribal relations and kept Indians segregated from contact with civilization. If reformers had once believed that reservations protected

Indians from encroaching whites and provided a place within which the seeds of civilization could be planted, they now seemed like prisons that held Native Americans in a state of savagery and denied them the chance to become equal citizens with their white neighbors. Freedom and equality would require assimilation. Assimilation, in the view of the reformers of the Women's National Indian Association, Indian Rights Association, and Lake Mohonk Conference, would require education for children, the adoption of Christianity, the reformation of gender roles through the institution of legal marriage and the end of matrilineal systems of descent, and the allotment of private property to individual Indians.[94]

Incomplete though it was, information about Native American population size underwrote the federal government's dramatic change in policy during the 1880s. Indian policy had long rested on two contradictory assumptions, between which it vacillated. One was that as Indians came into contact with civilization, they would die out. The other was that Indians could and should be "civilized" by being taught to farm and assimilate into the larger U.S. population. The basic question, therefore, of the size of the Native American population—whether it comprised mainly "Indians not taxed," who belonged to tribes and might or might not live on reservations, or "taxed" Indians, who lived outside the auspices of tribal government or the reservation system—gave lawmakers and administrators statistical fuel to stoke arguments about policy. An iteration of this debate was part of the lead-up to the transformation of federal policy from reservations to the allotment of land to individual Indians. In 1877, the commissioner of Indian Affairs included a special section in his annual report to the secretary of the Interior Department. Entitled "Are the Indians Dying Out?" the section collected information that had been prepared by Maj. Selden Clark of the federal Bureau of Education. While the report admitted that nearly all information about the historical size of the Native American population was but an estimate, it explained that it was important to try to reckon anyway. "If they are a vanishing race," the report read, "then it makes little sense to try to civilize them." On the other hand, it reasoned, if the population is increasing rather than decreasing and Indians "are destined to form a permanent factor, an enduring element of our population," then civilize them we must. The report concluded that there was no evidence for a "a rapid decrease of the Indian population from natural causes."[95] This sentiment was echoed the same year by the ethnologist Garrick Mallery in a paper before the American Association for the Advancement of Science. Such ideas became widespread. By 1878, the *New York Times* declared the debate was over—Indians were not going anywhere. As Tim Rowse has argued, this population knowledge underlay the federal government's turn from reservations to allotment; reformers and their political allies made the continued strength of the Indian population an argument for assimilation through property ownership rather than for containment through reservation.[96]

Allotment happened in fits and starts until the passage of the General Allotment Act in 1887, commonly known as the Dawes Act after Henry Dawes, the Massachusetts senator and chairman of the Committee on Indian Affairs who shepherded the bill through Congress. The Dawes Act authorized the president to order the allotment of reservations. Under its terms, each head of a family would receive a 160-acre plot of land; minors and single persons would receive smaller plots of land. Allotments were to be held in trust by the U.S. government for twenty-five years, after which time they would be converted to fee-simple property. During the trust period, allotted land could be conveyed only to an heir; no other sale or transfer was permitted.[97] As Frederick Hoxie has argued, the passage of the Dawes Act represented the triumph of optimism. Clinton Fisk, the chairman of the Lake Mohonk Conference, called it "the beginning of a new epoch in Indian affairs."[98] Some years later, the president of the same organization lauded the act as a "mighty pulverizing engine for breaking up the tribal mass" to "get at the individual" Indian.[99]

Though Dawes and his allies among white reformers imagined that allotment would spell the end of the federal Indian bureaucracy because it would transform Indians into citizens who had no special relationship to the federal government, in reality assimilation through allotment led to an "increasingly complex bureaucratic structure" in the Indian Office. This was in part because, as Cathleen Cahill has shown, allotment was accompanied by the delivery of "social programs" to Indians in lieu of rations and annuities. Agencies were staffed with farmers to teach men to till their fields, with field matrons to instruct Native women in the arts of housekeeping, and with teachers to instruct children in English, home economics, agriculture, and elements of "civilization." But this was also because allotment itself was a huge administrative undertaking that involved what one historian calls the "bureaucratic reorganization" of Indian families. Though allotment policy centered on land, it was a form of "intimate colonialism" that attempted to construct citizens not only by breaking up tribal land and governance but by breaking down Indian kinship structures and reformulating them as nuclear, patriarchal households.[100] The process of allotment also instructed Indians in the practical epistemology of American legal culture, including what counted as a true fact and why.[101]

Because allotment combined property transmission with family reorganization, it made population registration important to the Indian Office in new ways. As a documentary process, allotment began with the creation of a census roll, not unlike that used for rations and annuities in years past. This established a baseline register of who was eligible for an allotment. The office not only wanted to know exactly to whom it was deeding land, but it also wanted to document the legal relationships that governed any subsequent transmission of property—from husbands to wives or from fathers to children. Documenting family relationships also ensured that no one received land illegitimately—that a woman who lived as married did not register for land as a single person, for example. This required not just scrupulous record keeping but also the imposition of legal marriages duly registered and the documentation of parentage.[102]

One of the first allotting agents was the pioneering ethnologist Alice Fletcher, and her description of the challenges she faced allotting land to the Omaha clearly demonstrates how allotment remade Indian families through record keeping. In a speech to the Lake Mohonk Conference, she told fellow supporters of allotment that "the family within the tribe is not only differently organized, as to the relationship of its members," from those of Anglo-Americans, "but the laws of the descent of property are widely dissimilar from those we maintain." She went on to say that "when the Indian is allotted he is taken out of the tribal relation and placed in families, according to our custom," and that this was "new and strange" for those men and women suddenly thrown into legal relations of husband and wife, mother and father. Once in legally formed families and in possession of property, "the allotted land shall descend according to the laws of the State or Territory in which the land lies." But such laws were, Fletcher recognized, "foreign to the tribal customs with which the Indian is familiar." Because of the distance between Indian and American forms of kinship, patterns of inheritance, and marital relations, allotting agents had, therefore, to take special care in making their records lest they end up with incomplete or inaccurate records. For an example, Fletcher pointed out that the terms "mother" and "father" meant different things to the Omaha than they did to white people. For an Omaha, "father" referred to the man who sired a child and also to all of his brothers. Likewise, a "mother" was the woman who gave birth to a child, plus all of her sisters. When filling out a family schedule, therefore, that showed not only to whom a plot of land was being allotted but also that household head's wife, parents, and children, an agent could not simply ask a person to name his "mother" or "father."

Agents would run into problems with Indian naming traditions as well, Fletcher cautioned. The Omaha considered names sacred, and a man would never speak his to a white person. A man might also change his name several times over the course of his life. A woman's name usually stayed the same, but this was also confusing since she would not take her husband's name upon marriage. And children were named without reference to their parents' surnames. This in particular would cause problems in the future. "We must be able to trace the family through the children," Fletcher cautioned, or title to allotments would become hopelessly clouded. It was essential, therefore, not only to correctly record family relations but also to require parents to follow European surname customs.[103] While Fletcher recognized the profound differences between Omaha systems of kinship, inheritance, and naming and those that would prevail under the government-sanctioned system of individual landholding and patriarchal marriage, she urged the Indian Office to understand these differences only to be able to effectively undermine them. The Omaha might still continue to believe that a child had many mothers and multiple fathers, but only one could transmit property to the child through legal marriage.

In her study of the allotment of the Cherokee, Rose Stremlau shows how the creation of the "Dawes roll" sought to restructure Indian relationships. The roll, she argues, served three functions. First, it determined who was eligible for land, and in so doing transferred the power to determine tribal membership from the Cherokee to the U.S. government. Second, the roll "was intended to organize the population of the tribal republic into categories that facilitated the management of tribal property." It did this through the "symbolic language" of blood quantum. Third, the roll looked to the future transmission of allotted land, and "for this reason, the documentation of paternity and maternity was essential." The allotting agents in Cherokee Territory, known as Dawes commissioners, set up shop and held public hearings at which Cherokee heads of household were to come and present themselves for enrollment. Commissioners asked heads to list themselves and their family members. The commission insisted that enrollees be entered onto the rolls in nuclear families organized by biological and marital relations even though the Cherokee were often not living in those formations. The commissioners then sought evidence to verify the household head's claims about his relations. They did this by checking previous tribal rolls to see if individuals had been enrolled in the past and in the same family formations. The commission also "requested documentation of marriages, births, and deaths," something that few Cherokee could give. Commissioners therefore had to rely on oral testimony from neighbors and midwives to verify something of especial concern to them—"whether or not the children living in a household were the biological offspring of the adults caring for them." In some cases, applicants for enrollment returned to the commission with sworn affidavits of birth for their children. Enrollees toward the end of the commission's process were also more likely to present themselves with birth or marriage affidavits in hand, suggesting that knowledge of the commission's desire for documentation was becoming more commonplace among the Cherokee. Like the possession of individual title to land, commissioners considered documentation a sign of civilization and were likely gratified that among other things, they taught the Cherokee to record vital events on paper and not in memory.[104]

The creation of the original registration roll for allotment was but the beginning of a documentary process that the Indian Office and its allies in private reform hoped would become routinized and self-perpetuating. While the agents who made the rolls often had to content themselves with oral testimony or post hoc affidavits to determine the family relations that they should record on the allotment documents, they wanted more certainty in the process going forward. For this reason, both the government-sponsored Board of Indian Commissioners (BIC) and the Lake Mohonk Conference reformers beat a steady drum about securing vital registration for Indians. In November of 1899, the secretary of the BIC surveyed all Indian agents about the process of allotment, and he requested written replies to his circular letter. He wanted to know how they thought it was working in practice. Among the areas of inquiry, he asked agents to describe whether they kept a register of marriages, births, and deaths of allottees and also to note any "evils from lack of registration and records" that they might encounter. In its annual report, the BIC printed the responses of the agents. Respondents who worked on allotted agencies were more likely to report that they kept records of births, marriages, and deaths, with some noting that the practice had begun only with allotment.[105] Many agents also detailed the "evils" of improper or inadequate registration. Like Alice Fletcher, the agent from the Sisseton Agency noted that "an Indian does not trace his relationship as a white man would, but he is liable to adopt a father or a mother," and this would cause trouble "when the time comes to deliver deeds to this people." An agent at the Pueblo and Jicarilla Agency claimed that "on account of lack of registration and records, it has been impossible to deliver a larger number of the patents." Still others complained of another problem Fletcher noted: the inconstancy of Indian names.

At least one agent was content, however. At the Mescalero Apache reservation, the agent reported that "these Indians adopted white people's mode of naming children in 1896, being forced to by the agent."[106] This meant that wives and children took the husband's name, and it had helped keep the record books straight.

Whether they claimed to keep accurate records or not, most agents echoed the opinion of the Siletz Agency superintendent, who wrote that "the Department should issue an order giving the form and manner in which the records of births, deaths, marriages, and divorces should be kept on each reservation, thus securing a uniformity of record for the whole service." The BIC and the Lake Mohonk Conference concurred. In its summary of findings on the process of allotment, the BIC argued that there were both "moral and economic" reasons to seek better vital registration for Indians. From a moral point of view, one of the aims of allotment was to "lead the Indians to self-supporting industry in their own homes, and to strengthen that family life which alone can fit people for good citizenship." Without marriage registration, the marital tie was not "sacred and binding," and without proper birth registration "family ties" were rendered weak. The U.S. government also had a moral obligation to protect the legal relationships that created inheritance rights in allotted land, something that proper registration alone could do. From an economic vantage point, the commission asked, "is it wise for a Government to bring upon itself such a mass of litigation as this lack of records invites?"[107] Clearly not.

A year later, the Lake Mohonk Conference adopted a plea for vital registration as part of its platform. In his address to the conference, President Gates echoed some of the BIC themes. He professed shock that the federal government had done "nothing to render family life sacred" among Indians by creating marriage and birth registers. These, he argued, were agents of "social purity" that created and perpetuated family groups. Proper registration would have a "marked influence in civilizing the Indians by adding dignity to family life." To the moral arguments, Gates also added economic ones, as registration would "save the Government great expense and trouble in preventing a mass of litigation to determine the heirs" of allotted lands. On 15 May 1900, the chairman of the Senate Committee on Indian Affairs, John Thurston of Nebraska, introduced Senate Bill 4713, a bill for the regulation of marriage among Indians and the registration of vital events. The bill would have required the Office of Indian Affairs to provide every agency with a record book; agents would be required to record all existing marriages, complete with all children, and to link the registrations to allotments. The legislation also made it the agent's duty to record all births and deaths in the future but made it the responsibility of Indian parents to report births to the agent. Like the model legislation that many states adopted for their vital registration systems, Senate Bill 4173 also made the information recorded in the agent's registry book "prima facie evidence of the facts contained therein." As legislators introduced a new regime of private property, the act of registration would create a form of legal identity that would remold Indian naming, kinship, and inheritance practices into Anglo legal traditions. Thurston's bill never made it out of committee, but both Gates and the BIC urged the commissioner of Indian Affairs to use his executive powers to put in place the legislation's provisions by fiat.[108]

In 1901, Commissioner William Jones did just that. In a circular letter to all U.S. Indian agents and superintendents of Indian schools, Jones instructed them to "keep a permanent register of every marriage" between Indians under their charge. The register should record the Indian and English names of both husband and wife; the name by which each was listed on the allotment roll; the age, tribe, blood quantum, and citizenship of each; the date of marriage; and the names of each party's parents. Jones's regulations also required that marriages be licensed according to the laws of the state or territory in which they occurred—meaning they must use the legal forms of the state but also obey state laws with respect to miscegenation and polygamy. Making records of and requiring marriages to be legalized was part of a larger system of family record keeping. In the same circular letter, Jones instructed his agents to also keep a permanent family register of all Indians under their charge. This would link marriages to their offspring to facilitate both the assignment and transfer of allotments and rations. Jones reminded his agents that "rations may be withheld from Indians who refuse to obtain proper marriage licenses or to give truthfully the information needed for the proposed records." Unlike the legislation introduced in the Senate, Jones's regulations did not provide for birth or death registration. In his annual report to the secretary of the Interior, however, Jones commented that "to complete the system, books for recording births and deaths are needed and will be shortly furnished."[109]

Jones stepped down in 1901, and the reports of his successor, Francis Leupp, do not specify whether the birth or death registers that Jones promised were ever supplied to agents. But other evidence suggests that they were. In subsequent years, some agents reported that they had worked on "the establishment of a register of families . . . [and] the keeping of records of births and deaths."[110] In 1907, the Office of Indian Affairs sent a clerk to the Shawnee

Agency in Oklahoma specifically to "complete the family register of the Citizen [allotted] Pottawatomie Indians" there.[111] Likewise, in 1905 the BIC once
again surveyed all agents about the progress of allotment on their agencies
and to inquire about their record-keeping habits. The BIC's 1905 annual report
summarized the results of this survey and specifically chastised agents for *not*
keeping accurate family registers despite Jones's 1901 circular. The BIC worried about this not only because of the "moral and economic" issues that it had
identified in its earlier plea for marriage, birth, and death registration but also
because the commissioner of Indian Affairs was now endorsing a plan to end
tribal annuities and make treaty payments directly to individual Indians.[112]
Like allotment, this was an effort to end tribal sovereignty, and like allotment
it would require the government to adjudicate the transmission of federal assets through lineage. Committed to requiring Indians to live in monogamous
nuclear families, the new payment scheme would require the same attention
to documenting marriage and paternity as did allotment.

Better registration of families dovetailed not only with allotment but also
with another of the Indian Office's planks in its assimilation program: the
education of Native American children in federally run boarding schools.
Just as allotment was designed to break up tribal relationships and substitute
them with family ties maintained and expressed through the preservation
and transmission of property, so too education was meant to snuff out the
tribal affiliations of children. During the Dawes era, the federal government
ran over 150 boarding schools designed to assimilate children by stripping
them of their Indian names, clothing, and dress, requiring them to read and
write in English, and training them in a program of vocational education. In
order to plan, build, and fill such schools, the Indian Office had to have some
knowledge of how many children were born and thus how many school-age
children there might be in any given year. Missionaries, federal agents, and
local reservation employees annually descended on reservations to round up
children and take them away to boarding schools. During such roundups,
many families and communities hid their children.[113] And while there is no
evidence that Native American parents kept children off of tribal rolls or refused to register their births in order to keep them out of such schools, it must
not have been lost on many families that the same documents that gave them
land took their children.

In spite of the directives of the Office of Indian Affairs, the repeated pleas
of the BIC, and the apparently earnest efforts of some agents, neither marriage
nor birth and death registration became uniform across Indian agencies in the

late nineteenth or early twentieth centuries. Allotment initiated a new legal and gender regime that rested on legal marriage, patriarchal households, and the adoption of Anglo-American naming, kinship, and inheritance patterns. The BIC and the commissioner of Indian Affairs wanted marriage, birth, and death registration to help this system function. To the extent that agents put some form of registration in place, it became a part of the "intimate colonialism" of allotment, a technology that, along with private property and schooling, sought to individuate and assimilate Native peoples. But directives from Washington, D.C., the distribution of record books, and threats to withhold rations were not enough. As was the case for most other rural and nonwhite people in the United States, it took local, state, and national government the better part of the twentieth century to approach full birth registration for Native Americans.

Writing in 1845, Lemuel Shattuck approvingly quoted an article in the *American Journal of Medical Sciences* that complained that the states of America had "legislated for property, but not for life." To Shattuck and his fellow advocates of vital registration, birth and death registrations were a form of legislation for "life" because their aggregate data would reveal what Shattuck called "the laws of human life." Such laws, so revealed, would lead to better governance, better health, and greater prosperity. Statistics were the heart of statecraft. Yet vital statistics themselves were a creature of the state, and in many areas of the United States, including those under federal control, the administration of vital registration was "honored in the breach." This was partly a problem of state capacity; registration laws largely functioned by co-opting citizens (doctors and midwives) to perform the labor of reporting births. Even for local clerks, vital registration was often tacked on to a laundry list of other duties, and it was seldom at the core of how they understood their functions. On federal Indian reservations, this problem was particularly acute since registration there operated without even the guiding legislation or minimal infrastructure that prevailed in many of the states. This was true even when policies such as allotment depended on the kinds of identification that vital registration could provide.

Getting registration to work required not just laws, forms, and delegated duties but also ideological investment in registration as a public good. For a new generation of reformers, this meant taking the case not just to doctors, midwives, and clerks but also to the public, especially to parents and most especially to mothers. Led by the women who founded and ran the U.S. Children's Bureau and staffed by volunteers, many of them women too, a campaign for full birth registration fanned out across the states. And while this campaign did its fair share of infrastructure building, it also focused on creating public events to attract attention to birth registration, and it advanced a new set of arguments centered around the ways that a birth certificate was a form of protection for each and every child. As one Children's Bureau employee put it, the publicity was meant to teach citizens that "vital statistics are not merely a technical necessity, removed from the common interests of every day life, the concern only of officials and statisticians, but a matter of most intimate concern to every individual."[114]

CHAPTER 3

A COOPERATIVE MOVEMENT

B eginning in 1913, the U.S. Census Bureau had a new partner in promoting birth registration: the U.S. Children's Bureau. Founded in 1912 and housed in the U.S. Department of Labor, the Children's Bureau was tasked with "investigating and reporting upon all matters pertaining to the welfare of children and child life." The first subject the new bureau chose to investigate was infant mortality, which it called a "national disaster."[1] Like the statistically minded men who promoted vital registration laws during the mid- and late nineteenth century, the men and women who staffed the new bureau also believed in the power of data to reveal the laws of human life and direct wise government policy. Infant mortality was not, for them, a natural occurrence in the Malthusian struggle for existence but a failure of both personal habits and public policy. It was, in other words, preventable.

Gaining a proper understanding of the problem was easier said than done, however. In order to investigate the causes and cures for infant mortality, the bureau first had to know the infant mortality rate in each community, in each state, and in the nation as a whole. But without comprehensive birth and death registration, this proved impossible. To calculate the infant mortality rate, statisticians take the number of deaths under one year of age, divide it by the number of live births in a year, and multiply by 1,000. Trying to understand how many babies died, where, and why led straight to the problem of inadequate birth registration. The bureau was, one of its early publications explained, "hampered at every step by the limitations created by the imperfect collection of birth statistics in this country." Instead of acting as a source of information, birth registration instead became a variable that the bureau had to consider when conducting studies of infant mortality. It could only really study the factors that contributed to infant death in places it knew had effective vital registration. Its workers could not, the bureau complained, conduct investigations based on the variables that most interest us, such as "location, industrial conditions, racial composition . . . but must consider the effectiveness of birth registration."[2] Without complete birth registration, the bureau quite literally could not know the extent of infant mortality and could not disaggregate the effects of factors such as housing, sanitation, infant feeding and other child-rearing practices, household income, race, and immigration on a baby's chances for survival. How, then, could it formulate policy to redress the problem?

In order to use birth registration as a tool of child welfare, the Children's Bureau promoted it through two related strategies. On the one hand, the bureau and its allies tried to create public awareness of and demand for birth registration. They did this by disseminating publicity about birth registration directly to parents, arguing that a parent's first duty to their child was to see that her birth was registered. On the other hand, the bureau teamed up with a variety of other public and private organizations to build registration infrastructure and state capacity. As it had in the nineteenth century, the effort to achieve vital registration in the first half of the twentieth century crossed the lines between state and civil society.

Despite a half century's work to define and combat infant mortality through sanitary reform and maternal education, by the early twentieth century, the infant death rate showed no signs of abating. The problem received renewed attention in the early twentieth century because "infant mortality" provided a language within which several allied problems could be articulated. For a growing child welfare movement, infant mortality was the most dramatic evidence of the perils that faced the nation's children. At the same time, national attention to the declining birthrate among native-born Americans fueled a discourse about "race suicide" and a larger panic about not just the quantity but also the quality of the population. This, in turn, fed into the burgeoning eugenics movement, at the center of which was reproduction. All of these merged into a public discourse about population size and health, the quantity and quality of babies being born, and what remedies governments should offer. Though these discourses were not seamlessly integrated with one another, they all coalesced around attention to infant mortality as a source of national weakness and a preventable problem.[3]

Swelling public interest in infant mortality was expressed institutionally by national conferences as well as by the creation of two new organizations: the American Association for the Study and Prevention of Infant Mortality

(AASPIM) and the U.S. Children's Bureau. The AASPIM grew out of a two-day-long conference on the prevention of infant mortality held in New Haven, Connecticut, organized by the American Academy of Medicine. On the last day of the conference, delegates voted to organize the AASPIM, the first national organization dedicated exclusively to infant mortality as a single issue. The AASPIM's first annual meeting, held in 1910 at Johns Hopkins, was attended by representatives from a wide range of organizations, attesting to the coalitions that had formed as infant mortality prevention had expanded beyond sanitarians and sanitary reform. Delegates from nursing schools and visiting nurses' associations, milk dispensaries, general women's organizations, children's missions, health departments, settlement houses, life insurance companies, and physicians all gathered at the sessions in Baltimore. The association defined its work as a "twofold task of investigation and of education." Investigation comprised the work of finding the causes and cures for infant death, while education embraced both general publicity about the extent of infant mortality and outreach to individual mothers. To aid investigation, the AASPIM created the Committee on Birth Registration, chaired by Cressy Wilbur, the chief statistician of the U.S. Census Bureau, and also passed a resolution approving the model law and calling for the "thorough *enforcement* of such laws" by public officials.[4]

At the same meeting, the AASPIM passed a resolution calling for the establishment of a national department of health, an idea that had been circulating for some years among those interested in medicine and public health.[5] Though this did not come to pass, within two years, another kind of federal agency, the Children's Bureau, was established in no small part because of interest in combating infant mortality. Like the idea for a national department of health, the idea for a federal agency for children had been percolating for several years. Florence Kelley, a major figure in the settlement house movement, the chief factory inspector for the State of Illinois, and the secretary of the National Consumers League, suggested the idea in her 1905 book, *Some Ethical Gains through Legislation*. Kelley called for a U.S. Commission for Children, which she said would be similar to the Department of Agriculture, and she enumerated ten problems she thought the commission could tackle. Number one was infant mortality; number two was "registration of births." Kelley spoke in terms both of children's rights—the first chapter of the book was entitled "the right to childhood"—and in the biopolitical terms of population health, strength, and national reproduction. Kelley framed the latter in democratic terms, speaking of the importance of the citizenry in a republic. "The noblest duty of the Republic," she wrote, "is that of self preservation," which meant ensuring that the children born to it lived to become its citizens. "For if children perish in infancy they are obviously lost to the Republic as citizens. If surviving infancy, children are permitted to deteriorate into criminals, they are bad citizens; if they are left devitalized in body and mind, the Republic suffers the penalty of every offense against childhood." Here the Department of Agriculture provided not simply an organizational model for a federal bureau but also an analogy for the kinds of investments that governments could make to foster the nation's material wealth and strength. Kelley's friend and fellow settlement house worker Lillian Wald put it this way: "If the Government can have a department to look after the Nation's farm crops, why can't it have a bureau to look after the Nation's child crop[?]"[6] With the support of President Roosevelt, bills to create a federal children's bureau were introduced annually beginning in 1906. After intensive lobbying efforts from major national reform organizations including the National Consumers League, the National Child Labor Committee, the General Federation of Women's Clubs (GFWC), the Daughters of the American Revolution, and the National Congress of Mothers, a bill authorizing the creation of the Children's Bureau was finally passed in 1912. The legislation tasked the new bureau to "investigate and report . . . upon all matters pertaining to the welfare of children and child life among all classes of our people." The bureau began operation in 1913.[7]

Just as Kelley's list in *Some Ethical Gains* had suggested, the new bureau and its chief, Julia Lathrop, made the interrelated issues of infant mortality and birth registration their first priorities. The first studies the bureau conducted were of infant mortality, and the first publication it issued was its monograph *Birth Registration: An Aid in Protecting the Lives and Rights of Children* (1914).[8] In 1915, the Children's Bureau partnered with the Census Bureau, the GFWC, State Federations of Women's Clubs, and the Association of Collegiate Alumnae (ACA) to conduct "birth registration tests" in towns and cities across the United States. In participating communities, volunteer committees conducted house-to-house canvasses in search of all babies under one year of age. They then compared this list of names with those on file with the local registrar of vital statistics. This gave communities a measure of how many births went unreported; it also gave parents of unregistered babies a chance to correct the situation. Tests were designed both to measure how well communities were registering their births and to act as "an advertisement . . . to put before the public the value of birth registration."[9] As part of their campaign, the tests expressed several elements of the Children's Bureau's approach to combating ineffective registration. The bureau was convinced that the machinery of law and administration was only one side of the problem: without public awareness of the value of birth registration, the laws would never function. "Birth registration will never be complete in this country unless individual fathers and mothers know about it and want it," argued Julia Lathrop. Teaching the public to value birth registration was half the battle, and among other benefits, the bureau believed that the tests did just that. In addition, the bureau's collaboration with civil society groups such as the GFWC and the ACA expressed its approach to problems of state capacity. By partnering with nonstate actors, the bureau filled in the gaps left by inadequate state administration and wagered that greater public demand for birth registration would encourage government actors, from local registrars on up, to do a better job. Between 1915 and 1933, the bureau formed a node in a multifaceted campaign to achieve full birth registration in the United States.[10]

In a speech delivered before the National Conference of Charities and Correction in 1913, Lewis Meriam, the second-in-command to Julia Lathrop, announced the campaign that the bureau was about to launch. He explained that the bureau was going to begin a "co-operative movement with the women's organizations throughout the country" to conduct tests of birth registration in "selected towns and districts." Each woman who participated might get the names of, say, ten babies in a given neighborhood and then go to her town's registration office to see if the babies were registered. Meriam predicted that while this would involve little labor for each individual woman, in the aggregate it would give the bureau a wealth of valuable data about where registration functioned well and where it faltered. Criticism of current administration of registration systems was implicit in the coordinated campaign. Meriam told his audience that, ideally, every registrar should be engaged in what amounted to an ongoing test of his own systems. Every time he received a death certificate for a child under the age of one, he should check to see if the birth of the child had been registered. Since death registration was more reliable than birth registration across the country, this was a simple way to provide what Meriam called an "audit" of the "birth account." When the bureau selected a community to test, it essentially declared that, among other sources of administrative failure, the registrars there were not engaged in such self-audits.[11]

The volunteer-staffed birth registration tests were conducted largely between 1915 and 1919, though in some communities they lasted into the 1920s. In 1912, the GFWC passed a resolution at its biennial meeting calling on the Children's Bureau, which then existed "only on paper," to prepare a pamphlet on the value of birth registration. The first monograph, *Birth Registration: An Aid in Protecting the Lives and Rights of Children*, was the result. In 1913, the Children's Bureau began talks with the Census Bureau and the GFWC to conduct tests of birth registration.[12] While Lathrop addressed the national meeting of the GFWC about their joint venture, she also took her appeal directly to the states. *Florida Health Notes*, for example, reported in 1914 that Lathrop had "taken up the matter of tests in Florida cities with the State Federation of Women's Clubs."[13] State and local chapters of the GFWC, meanwhile, continually reported on their activities to promote and test birth registration in their communities.[14] Besides the GFWC, the ACA (the predecessor to the American Association of University Women) responded to an appeal from Julia Lathrop to assist in the tests. At its annual meeting in 1913, the ACA passed a resolution calling on its branches to participate in the bureau's birth registration campaign. In subsequent years, branches in Illinois, Michigan, Ohio, West Virginia, New York, Pennsylvania, and Connecticut reported that they conducted tests of birth registration.[15] Though the Census Bureau had initially identified twelve states in which to encourage clubwomen to conduct tests, by July 1915, some 3,303 women in 674 town and cities in twenty-six states had investigated nearly 14,000 births and found about a quarter of them unregistered.[16] Local chapters of the ACA and GFWC also recruited other organizations to assist with the tests, including the Camp Fire Girls, the Boy Scouts, Little Mothers' Leagues, the Sunday School Association, the League of Women Voters, and extension divisions of state colleges and universities. During World War I, the Women's Committees of State Councils of Defense also incorporated birth registration tests into their work. By 1918, these volunteers had conducted tests of registration in thirty-seven states; of the 38,000 births they collected information about, an average of 22 percent were not registered.[17]

The Children's Bureau took great pains to ensure that tests were conducted in a uniform fashion across the country. The chief statistician for the Census Bureau prepared detailed instructions for conducting a test, which the Children's Bureau distributed to participating organizations and, eventually, published as a booklet. The instructions recommended that volunteers form a committee and try to canvass births in "as wide a range in social environment as possible" and not just in the poor districts of their community. The scope of the test could range from a house-to-house canvass of the entire town to a house-to-house canvass of a limited district, or volunteers could choose instead to work from an existing nonstate list of births—such as a baptismal register or a church cradle roll. In cases of house-to-house canvassing, volunteers would be given a "definite territory," or list of addresses to visit. At each house in her territory, the volunteer was to inquire whether a baby had been born to the family in the past year. Using either a form supplied by the Children's Bureau or a blank certificate of birth, volunteers recorded information about the child and her parents: names, races, and nationalities of parents; name and birth date of the child; whether the child was still living; and the type of birth attendant (physician, midwife, neighbor, etc.). The instructions were clear that canvassers should *not* ask about the child's legitimacy even though it was a feature of the standard birth certificate. Canvassers would turn over all their forms to the committee chair, who would check the forms against the birth registrations on file with the relevant registrar. The chair would tabulate the results and report them to the Children's Bureau, paying special attention to facts about the unregistered births such as the number attended by physicians versus midwives and the proportion of native- versus foreign-born parents.[18] Collecting these facts plugged the bureau's registration tests into the ongoing discussions about the fecundity of different populations and the reliability of different types of birth attendants. In both cases, birth registration was the key data source.

Conducting the tests required coordination and cooperation not only between agencies of the federal government—the Census Bureau and the Children's Bureau—and national, state, and local women's organizations but also with municipal and state health officers who kept vital records. This multilayered coordination is illustrated by the tests conducted by the Minnesota State Federation of Women's Clubs in 1914 and 1915. Julia Lathrop directly asked the state federation to conduct a birth registration test in Duluth in 1914, which it did. When the test's results were publicized, the head of the state health department, H. M. Bracken, wrote to Lathrop asking her to conduct "similar work in other sections of the state." He suggested she activate committees immediately in Minneapolis and St. Paul and when the winter was over and the roads passable, send out the women of the state federation into the rural sections of the state. He appended a list of towns and counties he believed the statewide tests should cover. Bracken also wrote to the head of the state federation and asked to address its annual convention about the importance of birth registration. Lathrop was enthusiastic about the suggestion "to bring the matter before the clubs more forcibly." She appointed Bracken and Jessie Marcley, the chair of the state federation's Public Health Committee, as special agents of the Children's Bureau so that they could use the bureau's letterhead and materials in appealing to local chapters. Marcley put the matter to the women of the state federation at their annual meeting and also sent out a letter on bureau letterhead to women in the counties Bracken had identified as good candidates for testing. She asked each recipient to spearhead the test in her county or to send to "Miss Lathrop" the name of another clubwoman who could do the job. Bracken would supply volunteers with a list of registrars in each county and a form letter explaining the work. Lathrop "will provide blanks and explain the work to you in detail." "This is the first time," Marcley concluded her letter, that "our women's clubs have been asked to perform a national service." She urged Minnesota's women to join those in other states such as Ohio, Kentucky, Tennessee, New York, Indiana, and Florida who were already performing tests. Lathrop herself wrote another appeal to the state's clubwomen, and then Marcley forwarded to Bracken the list of women who agreed to serve. Bracken sent these names on to the Children's Bureau, which then sent the women the instructions and forms they would need to carry out the tests.[19]

While the Children's Bureau intended the tests to serve as a barometer of registration effectiveness and to stimulate better enforcement of registration laws, local and state officials did not always appreciate the intrusion of external agents in their internal operations. The bureau recommended that before beginning the test, clubwomen "secure the interest and cooperation of the local health officer and local registrar." The clubs would need to convince these officials to provide them with access to the local birth records free of charge and allow them to work in their offices to tabulate their returns. In private correspondence, bureau employees recognized that this was an imposition on registrars' space and time. Estelle Hunter wrote to her bureau colleagues on this point. She explained that it was imperative to impress on clubwomen that they "make arrangements with the registrar when the work should be done" and that they inquire also as to "how many persons could work in his office." She also recommended that the canvassing committee select "one person who has had office experience," someone who could appreciate the filing systems that the registrar had in place. "Nothing can more quickly kill the interest of a registrar," she wrote, "than to have several untrained women disarranging his files." Hunter was so emphatic on this point that she suggested they stress it in their published instructions for tests. If nothing else, doing so would show registrars that the bureau understood the potential inconvenience and was taking pains to avoid it; "otherwise the Bureau will be given the discredit for sending out a large number of untrained people to upset the registrars' offices."[20]

In addition to bristling against the possible interference with their files and daily operations, registrars also resented how the tests implicitly criticized their work. This kind of tension erupted in the test conducted by the Minnesota State Federation of Women's Clubs in Duluth. In conducting their test, a committee led by Mrs. F. L. Barrows sought to collect information on 100 births in Duluth and compare them to the records on file at the city health department. The committee reported that it found only seventy-five births on file with the city, a very low rate of registration. When the results of the test were made public, Bracken, of the state board of health, wrote to the city's director of health, Dr. H. E. Webster, expressing alarm that Duluth's unreported births by themselves could keep the entire state out of the birth registration area. He also questioned why Webster did nothing to punish birth attendants who failed to report births. In his reply to Bracken, and also publicly, Webster challenged the methods, motivations, and qualifications of the federation's test committee. He accused the women of deviating from the procedures of the test, purposefully seeking out births they knew were unregistered, and rejecting those they knew were registered in order to make the city health department look bad. Mrs. Barrows defended her methods and pointed out that all of the women on her committee were "of middle age and trained workers" with "responsibility and integrity." Moreover, all the women were dyed-in-the-wool Duluthians, so "there could be no object in our distorting facts to the discredit of Duluth." Bracken also defended the women, pointing out that they were following the steps outlined by the federal Children's Bureau, not acting as rogue agents.[21]

The bad publicity led the county medical association to appoint a committee to investigate the federation's report and see whether the city's doctors were to blame. In the end, the number of unregistered births was reduced from twenty-five to nineteen, and the federation's methods and motivations were absolved. Even Webster had to admit they had done nothing wrong. Nevertheless, after defending the Duluth committee and begging Lathrop to help him organize a statewide birth registration test through the State Federation of Women's Clubs, H. M. Bracken later complained to Lathrop about their work. "The returns secured through these women were very inaccurate and incomplete in most cases," he groused in 1916. He questioned whether volunteers could really do the work unless they were closely supervised, because "there is a great opportunity for mistakes . . . by people who are not familiar with the work."[22] The test in Duluth was one of the first conducted in the nation, and the Children's Bureau's subsequent instructions to clubwomen sought to prevent this kind of friction.

The bureau's instructions also reminded volunteer committees to assure the local health officers that "the investigation is not intended as a critical test of the work of registration authorities" but was primarily "propaganda to stimulate public interest."[23] Indeed, the publicity tests brought was considered by the bureau equal in importance to any data gleaned from them. The process was educative by design. Lathrop said as much in an address to an annual meeting of the GFWC. "While the mass of material gathered by the test is valuable statistically," she told the gathered women, "we who are not statisticians realize that the mere fact of gathering it produces an invaluable byproduct of interest which is a sure aid to better laws and better enforcement."[24] First among those educated by the tests were the volunteers who conducted them. Bureau employee Etta Goodwin said as much in an article she wrote for the *Kentucky Women's Clubs Magazine* describing the tests that 186 Kentucky clubwomen had conducted in sixteen towns across the state in 1915. Participating in the tests taught clubwomen "that vital statistics are not merely a technical necessity, removed from the common interests of every day life, the concern only of officials and statisticians, but a matter of most intimate concern to every individual," Goodwin wrote.[25] The bureau hoped that clubwomen would turn their experiences into action beyond the test itself. If a community's registration was hampered by an inadequate law—one that deviated from the model law, for example—then the clubwomen should offer their assistance to the state health officer to lobby for a new and better law. Likewise, if inadequate funding for vital statistics work was the problem, the clubwomen should lobby the legislature for a better appropriation.[26] In other words, clubwomen had to be committed to turning their education about birth registration into political action. In his speech before the National Conference of Charities and Correction, Lewis Meriam joked that in the "suffrage states," where women could vote, the bureau could not guarantee the "peace and comfort" of any officials found by an "organized body of women" to be denying babies their legal right to registration.[27] Tapping the GFWC and other "organized women" was predicated on the assumption that educating such women would pay dividends beyond the test itself.

The bureau also hoped that the tests would reach parents and convince them of the value of birth registration. It knew that the tests would likely receive press coverage in local communities, and this often led parents to the local registrar's office to check up on their children's birth registration. Just as important, every time a clubwoman knocked on a door, she had a chance to educate those inside about the value of birth registration. Instructions for the tests included talking points about why the test was being conducted and why parents should care about whether their baby was registered. One clubwoman who participated reported, "I think this [test] will stimulate the interest in favor of birth registration. Many mothers said they were not sure whether their children were registered or not, but would see that they were at once." Volunteers also told mothers that it was the doctor's or midwife's responsibility to report the birth and that they ought not to be paid any fees for the delivery until they had done so.[28] They were thus educating parents not only about why their children should be registered but also about the mechanics of the law, which made it the duty of birth attendants to file reports.

The bureau also encouraged test committees to educate their entire community by holding a "mass meeting at which the results of the investigation" could be put before the public. "Graphic charts and posters should be used," the bureau instructed. It also recommended that committees help their communities understand the significance of unregistered births by recruiting speakers who could address registration "from different angles": a lawyer to discuss the legal value; a doctor to explain the public health value; a social worker to explain how registration fit in with infant welfare work; a school board official to talk about registration's role in compulsory schooling; and someone to address how birth certificates prevented "premature labor." Moreover, the committee should draw the public's attention to the trouble spots in registration so they could be remedied—was it among midwives or foreign-born parents that registration was neglected? If so, the town would have to find a way to reach foreign-born parents or midwives to help them see the value of birth registration.[29]

Besides coordinating the birth registration tests, the Children's Bureau also promoted birth registration in its other work. Beginning in 1915, it worked with the GFWC to sponsor a "baby week" in towns and cities across the country, an event that was repeated in subsequent years. In 1918, the bureau partnered with the Woman's Committee of the National Council of Defense to conduct a Children's Year campaign. Both the baby weeks and the Children's Year aimed to reduce infant mortality through a broad program of education aimed at parents and the broader community. For parents, the programs taught "the facts with regard to the care of their babies"; for the larger community, the aim was to teach "the importance [of] its babies" and "the need of permanent work for their welfare." As part of both parent and community education, the baby weeks and Children's Year incorporated birth registration into their programs in a variety of ways. The bureau instructed those who wished to organize a baby week that "the need for better vital statistics should be emphasized throughout the campaign." It recommended a series of themed days throughout the week culminating in birth registration day. On this final day, organizers should seek press cooperation to publish stories about the importance of birth registration and should also send a letter asking every physician in the city to register all the births he attends. The Census Bureau aided the cause by having its chief statistician send a letter to physicians across the nation asking them to publish births in the town papers and to encourage their local women's clubs to help promote birth registration as part of baby week.[30]

Communities across the country responded by making birth registration a focus of baby week. In 1917, the organizers of baby weeks in Mississippi, Ohio, Illinois, Washington, Louisiana, and Wisconsin all made birth registration the "special object" of their baby weeks. In places such as Kankakee, Illinois, the baby week committee made a birth registration test part of its program. Some towns conducted a canvass of registration before baby week began and publicized the results in order to promote registration during baby week itself. In one Idaho town, the health officer printed up a list of all the births registered in the past five years and made it publicly available as part of baby week. In Grand Rapids, Michigan, schoolchildren were paid twenty-five cents for every unregistered birth they turned over to the health department. State health departments in New York, Florida, Illinois, and Louisiana all included information about birth registration in their traveling child welfare exhibits, which they loaned to baby week organizers. Other states such as New Jersey, Pennsylvania, Texas, and Virginia gave pamphlets on the subject to be distributed at baby week events. In other states, parades were part of the celebration; in Louisiana one parade banner read, "Louisiana babies' first plea: Doctor I want a record for me."[31]

Promotion of birth registration was incorporated not just into the general program and publicity for baby weeks and Children's Year but also into some seemingly unrelated features. Child health conferences, or weighing and measuring tests, were a central part of both campaigns. Child health conferences were derived from a popular form of baby health contest called the better baby contest, which weighed, measured, tested, and scored babies in order to rank them. Such contests were a wildly popular part of infant welfare work across the country and were promoted by the Committee on Women's and Children's Welfare of the American Medical Association (figure 3.1). The Children's Bureau did not like the competitive aspect of the contests but saw that they had

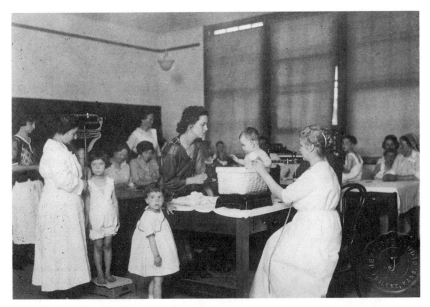

Figure 3.1. Weighing and measuring at Baby Welfare Week, Abilene, Kansas (1921)

The Children's Bureau incorporated birth registration into its broader effort to measure and promote child welfare. At the child health conferences promoted by the bureau in local communities across the country, volunteers weighed and measured babies and asked mothers a series of questions about child-rearing practices, including whether their baby's birth was registered. Source: American Red Cross Photograph Collection, Library of Congress, Prints and Photographs Division, Washington, D.C.

great potential as a form of education and publicity. The bureau instead promoted "conferences" that involved many of the same features of contests without the ranking and prizes. They worked with the American Medical Association to create a noncompetitive scoring card that could be used during baby weeks.[32] For a conference, a mother would bring her child at an appointed time to be examined by a physician on a series of points. The exam also involved questions for the mother about her child-rearing practices. The mother would leave with a record of her child's health and any recommendations from the doctor about how to improve it or her own habits. Like the house-to-house canvasses, the health conferences brought volunteers into direct contact with parents and gave them an opportunity to check on birth registration and explain its value. At many of the conferences, physicians queried mothers not only about child-rearing habits such as whether they had been or were

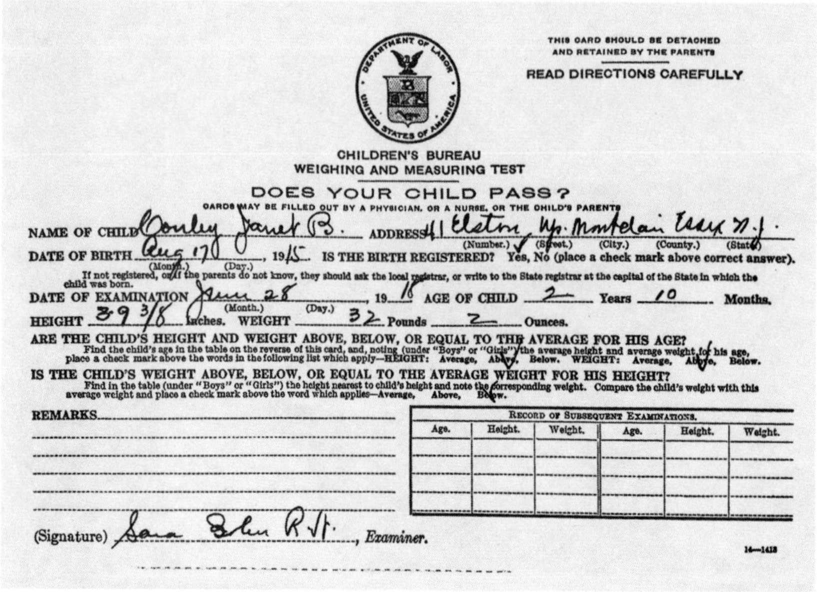
DEPARTMENT OF LABOR
UNITED STATES OF AMERICA

THIS CARD SHOULD BE DETACHED AND RETAINED BY THE PARENTS

READ DIRECTIONS CAREFULLY

CHILDREN'S BUREAU
WEIGHING AND MEASURING TEST

DOES YOUR CHILD PASS?

CARDS MAY BE FILLED OUT BY A PHYSICIAN, OR A NURSE, OR THE CHILD'S PARENTS

NAME OF CHILD Conley Janet B. ADDRESS 41 Elston, Up. Montclair Essex N.J.
(Number.) (Street.) (City.) (County.) (State)

DATE OF BIRTH Aug 17 (Month.) (Day.), 1915. IS THE BIRTH REGISTERED? Yes, No (place a check mark above correct answer).

If not registered, or if the parents do not know, they should ask the local registrar, or write to the State registrar at the capital of the State in which the child was born.

DATE OF EXAMINATION June 28 (Month.) (Day.), 1918 AGE OF CHILD 2 Years 10 Months.

HEIGHT 39 3/8 Inches. WEIGHT 32 Pounds 2 Ounces.

ARE THE CHILD'S HEIGHT AND WEIGHT ABOVE, BELOW, OR EQUAL TO THE AVERAGE FOR HIS AGE?
Find the child's age in the table on the reverse of this card, and, noting (under "Boys" or "Girls") the average height and average weight for his age, place a check mark above the words in the following list which apply—HEIGHT: Average, Above, Below. WEIGHT: Average, Above, Below.

IS THE CHILD'S WEIGHT ABOVE, BELOW, OR EQUAL TO THE AVERAGE WEIGHT FOR HIS HEIGHT?
Find in the table (under "Boys" or "Girls") the height nearest to child's height and note the corresponding weight. Compare the child's weight with this average weight and place a check mark above the word which applies—Average, Above, Below.

REMARKS

Record of Subsequent Examinations.					
Age.	Height.	Weight.	Age.	Height.	Weight.

(Signature) Sara Blu R.N., Examiner.

14—1413

Figure 3.2. Weighing and measuring test form (1915)

Parents received their children's health data forms when they participated in the child health conference weighing and measuring tests. Some pasted them into their children's baby books. Source: Baby book of Janet Blake Conley, *Baby's Life*, arranged and illustrated by Evelyn von Hartmann (New York: Barse and Hopkins, [1913]), Baby Book Collection, UCLA Biomedical Library, History and Special Collections, Los Angeles, California.

breast- or bottle-feeding their baby but also about whether the baby's birth had been registered. The scoring card distributed by the Children's Bureau for use in the conferences included a question about registration (figure 3.2).[33]

In Wheeling, West Virginia, weighing and measuring tests revealed that 48 percent of the participating children did not have their births registered. In these cases, the child's mother was given both a talk about "the advantages of birth registration" and a blank birth certificate to fill out and return to the city health department.[34] In Indiana, which ran the conferences as contests for many years, all contest scoring cards contained an inquiry about whether a baby's birth was registered, and in some towns only registered babies were admitted to the contests, thus "calling the attention of parents to a very important matter." Ada Schweitzer, who served as the director of Indiana's Department of Child Hygiene, used the weighing and measuring tests conducted in her state during Children's Year as a way to promote birth registration. In 1919, she helped organize sixty-three chapters of the Tri Kappa Sorority to conduct a follow-up canvass on the children who had been examined during the 1918 health conferences. The Tri Kappas were supplied with forms to fill out, just as clubwomen were during a birth registration canvass, and among the queries they were to make was whether the child had her birth registered.[35] Though they were not designed primarily to promote birth registration, the health conferences during baby weeks and Children's Year were so successful in doing so that public health officials came to regard them as an important tool. This was particularly the case in helping to promote rural registration because baby week celebrations tended to cluster otherwise scattered farm women in the nearest town.[36]

In addition to conducting its own birth registration tests and promoting birth registration through baby weeks and Children's Year, the Children's Bureau got a boost in its efforts from several directions in the late 1910s and the '20s. The first was the passage of the Sheppard-Towner Act. The second was the American Child Health Association's role in promoting birth registration in the states. The third was a campaign coordinated among the Census Bureau, the Children's Bureau, and numerous private organizations designed to bring all remaining states into the birth registration area by 1930. As part of the culmination of Children's Year in 1919, Julia Lathrop put forward a proposal to combat infant and maternal mortality by expanding access to health care for pregnant women and newborn babies. Known by the name of its sponsors, Sheppard-Towner passed in 1921 and provided matching grants to states be-tween 1922 and 1929, when its funding was not renewed by Congress. In order for a state to receive its matching funds, it had to have (or create) a state agency to administer funds and programs; usually this was a child hygiene division of a state health bureau. States created plans and submitted them for approval to the Children's Bureau; the federal legislation stipulated that no funds could be used to provide material assistance and all programs had to be voluntary. Forty-five of the forty-eight states accepted the matching grants, which they used to administer a variety of outreach and educational programs.[37] When the states submitted their plans for approval, twenty-one proposed to use funds to promote birth registration—eleven of these were not in the birth registration area, and another ten were but used funds to bolster their regis-tration systems.[38] In a radio address broadcast in 1922, the bureau explained why many states were using their funds for birth registration. "Some [states] cannot even tell where to center their work because they have not good birth registration. They do not know where the greatest proportion of babies die." Such states thus chose to "start at the beginning" of the problem and "use the interest in the Sheppard-Towner Act to improve the registering of births."[39]

States used the federal matching funds to continue practices that had begun as part of the birth registration tests, weighing and measuring conferences, and other promotional programs encouraged by the Children's Bureau. Beyond publicity and education, however, states used federal funds to increase their administrative capacity and bolster registration infrastructure. In Pennsylvania, for example, the state spent $7,800 of its budget in 1926 to hire twenty-six "birth registration clerks," who processed birth registrations and sent out notifications to parents. California spent some of its funds to employ a clerk whose sole job was to check physicians' own rosters of the births they had attended against birth certificates on file with the state. In Idaho, Sheppard-Towner funds paid for a "field worker" who could canvass the state visiting homes and checking birth registration. In Kentucky, a full-time worker visited local registrars to investigate their birth registration practices. Colorado, South Carolina, Tennessee, and Wisconsin all placed an additional clerk in the state registrar's office. West Virginia paid for both an additional clerk in the state registrar's office and a roving field agent to stimulate birth registration.[40]

Thirty-one states also used Sheppard-Towner funds to create more infrastructure for the supervision of midwives by establishing licensing requirements and conducting outreach and education. Among other things, midwife-education programs taught that it was the midwife's legal duty to register the births she attended.[41] While use of proxies to fill out registration forms figured in reformers' accounts of why birth registration remained incomplete, when it came to improving birth registration by midwives, reformers encouraged the practice. In Texas, for example, the bureau sent Dr. Whipper, an African American female physician, out to work with the state's "colored midwives." In addition to conducting educational classes for midwives, Whipper organized the women into local groups so that each nonliterate midwife could have a literate midwife partner to "help her make out birth certificates."[42]

In their reports to the Children's Bureau, states emphasized that midwife education and increased birth registration went hand in hand. Indeed, in some states, the use of Sheppard-Towner funds to get the state into the Census Bureau's birth registration area was virtually indistinguishable from the use of Sheppard-Towner funds for midwife education. In Georgia, for example, the state used federal money to employ "negro nurses" to instruct "negro mid-wives." The state also instituted a certificate system in which midwives had to be licensed. In order to receive and maintain a license, the midwives had to not only complete the course of education but also report all their births to the local registrar. When the state finally got into the birth registration area in 1928, it reported that "the work with the midwives in securing better registration of births was an important feature of the campaign."[43] Delaware, Kentucky, Arkansas, Virginia, Tennessee, Louisiana, Alabama, Mississippi, and Texas all claimed that midwife education had improved birth registration. In Kentucky, the Bureau of Maternal and Child Health reported that its education campaign resulted in birth registration forms that were now more likely to be completed correctly "from the midwives, who as a rule are uneducated and who submit very incomplete and illegible certificates."[44]

Midwife education and infrastructure building also went hand in hand. When the director of the New Mexico State Bureau of Public Health requested, as part of his budget, a "field representative to work in the most backward parts of the state for the purposes of bringing up registration to a higher level," the Children's Bureau sent one of its agents, Anita Jones, to the state in 1928. This was the second time that the bureau had put one of its employees on the ground in the state.[45] Fluent in Spanish and English, Jones combined building infrastructure with midwife education. One of her tasks was to find and appoint more registrars to decrease the distance that anyone reporting a birth might have to travel to file a certificate. One registrar, for example, lived up in the mountains, eight miles from the nearest town. Remote as she was, when Jones went to find her and check on her registration records, she was not there; she was working as a cook at a school and would be gone for the entire school year. "It seems queer that she was ever appointed . . . when she lives in such an inaccessible place," never mind that she was not even around, mused Jones in a report to the central office. Jones solved this problem by finding another registrar, the postmaster in the nearby town. In addition to his central location, the postmaster's mother boarded the town priest and kept the keys to the church, "so she will know of baptism and deaths." As she traveled around the lightly populated and remote sections of the state, Jones built up infrastruc-ture not only by appointing new registrars but also by instructing existing registrars in how to fill out forms, how to keep their files organized, and how to integrate locally generated registration forms with the state's centralized re-cords of births and deaths. In Tierra Amarilla, Jones spent a day sorting birth and death certificates that the county clerk had accumulated in "unorganized packages" since 1907. Together with the clerk, the town registrar, and the registrar's son, Jones made folders for every year and helped sort the certificates by year and then "completely explained" the "system of filing" to the county clerk. Jones then hand-delivered twenty-one years' worth of birth and death certificates from the county to the state Bureau of Public Health in Santa Fe.[46]

Registration infrastructure, however, was only as good as the birth attendants who were willing to use it. This was where midwife education and registration intersected. Jones made a point of seeking out midwives wherever she could find them, which was often no small task. In Cebolla, New Mexico, the local registrar, Mrs. Rivas, took Jones around to visit the midwives in the area. "All promised . . . to report all births and deaths in the future."[47] Around Monero, Dulce, and Lumberton, Jones found the midwives "scattered and inaccessible." Trying to drive up a wagon road to the home of one, "I broke the crank of my ford"; to reach another, Jones had to "leave the car more than a mile away and climb a mountain" using a burro trail, as there was no road. She talked with each midwife about basic sanitation and medical care for birth and newborns and taught each how to fill out a birth certificate. One midwife said "she had never made out a birth certificate but was glad to learn how." Another, however, "was very suspicious and kept saying she did not have a 'Diploma.'" Since midwife education and outreach often went hand in hand with licensure and state control, it made sense for this midwife to regard Jones with suspicion. Still, though this midwife could "neither read nor write," her daughter, who was literate and spoke English, "promised to help her with the birth Certificates."[48] In San Miguel County, Jones gave a speech to the Woman's Club on the importance of birth registration; she arranged to have the secretary of the "Spanish Child Welfare Society" bring the area midwives to the meeting and agree to "help the midwives to fill out birth certificates and get them properly filed" in the future.[49] Jones also did more traditional types of registration promotion to interest parents in their children's registration status—chiefly giving out blue ribbons to registered babies at county fairs—but in her work appointing and training registrars and connecting midwives to the registration machinery, Jones was like a spider spinning a web whose strands formed a functioning state.[50]

During the 1920s, states received assistance with registration not only from the federal Sheppard-Towner funds but also from a second source: the American Child Health Association (ACHA). Led by former secretary of commerce (and future president) Herbert Hoover, the ACHA was a rechristened and expanded version of the AASPIM. Startled by the poor health of World War I draftees, members of the AASPIM decided that they should expand their focus to child, and not just infant, health, and they renamed the organization the American Child Hygiene Association and, eventually, the American Child Health Association. In 1923, just as Sheppard-Towner funds were making their way into the states, Lathrop's successor as chief of the Children's Bureau, Grace Abbott, wrote a letter to Hoover suggesting that his organization devote some of its money and personnel to helping the Children's Bureau and the Census Bureau expand the birth registration area. She suggested a model not unlike that of Sheppard-Towner: direct cash infusions to state bureaus of health for registration work.[51] The ACHA did not give states cash, but it did supply personnel. The ACHA organized a meeting in Washington, D.C., with staff from the U.S. Public Health Service, the Children's Bureau, and the Census Bureau to learn what they had been doing to promote birth registration. The ACHA then sent letters to the head of every state bureau of health offering its assistance. Between 1923 and 1926, the ACHA provided aid to registration in Arkansas, Colorado, Iowa, Louisiana, Missouri, New Mexico, North Dakota, Oklahoma, South Carolina, South Dakota, Tennessee, and Wyoming.[52] To support birth registration in the states, the ACHA had a staff of three roving consultants who largely focused on the administrative side of the problem. They conducted birth registration tests and surveys of the registration systems in states and embedded themselves in state vital statistics offices to reform "office procedure" and bring it up to standards suggested by the Census Bureau.[53]

Besides treating birth registration as a single issue, the ACHA, like the Children's Bureau, incorporated it into its other projects. The organization sponsored child health demonstration projects in cities such as Fargo, North Dakota, a state that was not in the birth registration area. One of the things the demonstration project did was work to improve birth registration in Fargo by inquiring about the registration status of all the children who came under its auspices and registering those who were not already registered. Mary Dempsey, a former employee of the Children's Bureau, served as the statistician on the Fargo demonstration project, and she kept in close touch with the bureau about the problems with birth registration in the city and the state as a whole.[54] Likewise, when the ACHA conducted a public health survey of eighty-six cities in 1924, it included the effectiveness of vital registration among its metrics for assessing how well or poorly cities promoted the health of children.[55] Just as infant mortality was considered an index of community health, the ACHA made birth registration into an index of a community's commitment to child well-being.

The Children's Bureau also participated in a multipronged, cross-organizational effort known as the Committee to Aid Completion of the Registration Area before 1930. This was a fourth source of support for birth registration. In 1924, the Census Bureau adopted a slogan, "Every State in the Registration Area before 1930," which it began stamping on all its official correspondence.[56] In 1925, a committee designed to make this slogan a reality was formed as a subcommittee of the Vital Statistics Section of the American Public Health Association.[57] Louis Dublin was appointed chairman. Dublin was the chief statistician for the Metropolitan Life Insurance Company. Both Dublin and Metropolitan Life had a long-standing interest in accurate vital statistics. Dublin was an active member of the AASPIM and the American Public Health Association and regularly delivered papers on birth registration, infant mortality, and the importance of accurate vital statistics. He established the Statistical Bureau at Met Life, and at his urging the company promoted birth registration by issuing pamphlets on the topic to its subscribers, asking them to verify that their children's births were registered, and lobbying for the model law when it was before state legislatures.[58] The committee Dublin convened included representatives from the Children's Bureau, the Census Bureau, the U.S. Public Health Service, the U.S. Chamber of Commerce, the American Red Cross, and the National Tuberculosis Association and also included Dublin's fellow statistician Frederick L. Hoffman of Prudential Life Insurance.[59] Though the committee relied on federal agencies and private organizations that already had staff and funds dedicated to promoting vital registration, it also raised its own funds to help pay for fieldworkers, clerical staff, and promotional materials. Much of this money Dublin raised from "six or seven of the large insurance companies." The Rockefeller Foundation also contributed matching funds in select states.[60]

Like the work already being done by the Census Bureau and the Children's Bureau, the committee's basic strategy focused on increasing both administrative capacity in the states and public awareness of, and demand for, registration. When its work began, fifteen states and roughly 25 percent of the population remained outside the Census Bureau's birth registration area. Most of these states were in the South and the West: Idaho, South Dakota, Nevada, Arizona, New Mexico, Colorado, Texas, Oklahoma, Missouri, Arkansas, Louisiana, Tennessee, Alabama, Georgia, and South Carolina. By contrast, 90 percent of the population was in the death registration area.[61] Different states required different things. In some, the committee focused its energy on getting the state to pass the model law to create what the Census Bureau considered a functional administrative and legal apparatus. In others, the legislation was adequate, but the practice was not. The first task of the committee's field agents, therefore, was to diagnose the nature of the problem in each state and secure an "invitation" to come work there from the chief health officer. The field force was led by Pennsylvania's former state registrar W. R. Batt, who understood that convincing state health officers to invite advisors in "requires the utmost tact, patience, and perseverance."[62]

In the committee's assessment, South Dakota, Georgia, Nevada, and Texas were the states that needed new legislation. In South Dakota, for example, the committee was unhappy that state law organized the registration system on the basis of counties. That is, each county had one registrar. As William Davis of the Vital Statistics Division of the Census Bureau explained in a letter to Grace Abbott, counties were an arbitrary and irrational registration unit. In South Dakota, counties varied from a low of 403 to a high of 3,491 square miles in area. In larger counties, "no registrar can possibly know personally about the births and deaths which are occurring daily." And even if a registrar did manage to make registration function in a large county, "just as soon as a new crop of physicians or midwives locates in these counties, or just as soon as the new country registrars take office there is a grave danger that registration will drop back to an unsatisfactory condition."[63] A good registration system required good infrastructure that would function over time and did not depend solely on the character of those who staffed it. And good infrastructure was the product of a good law. Of course, the head of the South Dakota State Board of Health, Dr. Cook, disagreed, arguing that his state's system functioned just fine and that counties were an acceptable registration unit in a state "vast in area and sparsely settled."[64] A staff member from the National Tuberculosis Association, Mr. Strawson, was loaned out to work in South Dakota "to try to get this legislation over."[65] On the ground, chapters of the women's auxiliary of the American Legion and the Parent-Teacher Association threw their weight behind passage of new legislation. Though the law did not pass until 1932, Cook, his earlier protests notwithstanding, asked his state's legislature for a reformed law beginning in 1927.[66]

The committee's efforts to pass the model law in Nevada showcased a variety of strategies. In Nevada, the committee dispatched Miss Whitney, also from the National Tuberculosis Association, to promote the model law. She met with state legislators and convinced one of them to sponsor a bill. "I sort of prodded them along and since then I have tried to keep in touch with them," she reported to the committee. She also tapped networks of lobbying influence and intelligence among female child welfare activists, including the head of the state's Bureau of Child Hygiene, who had helped convince the state to accept Sheppard-Towner funds. The commercial infrastructure of the insurance industry was also useful in lobbying because a national company such as Prudential or Met Life could tap its network of local agents. Dublin suggested that "constant pressure might be brought on the legislators in Nevada by the insurance companies on the Pacific Coast."[67]

While only four states lacked the model law, many more had registration systems that failed in one way or another. For these states, the committee supplied fieldworkers, usually employees of the Census Bureau's Vital Statistics Division. Their first task was to visit the central registration office in each state's department of health. Fieldworkers examined office procedures "with a view to suggesting improvements or to detect any serious flaws in the office routine." Information in the state office also helped the field force determine where to direct their energies in the state by showing which registration districts had the lowest rates of birth reporting. The subsequent work depended on the nature of the state's problems, but like Anita Jones's campaign in New Mexico, it involved everything from publicity and education with birth attendants to making sure there were enough registrars in every part of the state. In a letter to the committee and at meetings of the committee in Washington, D.C., the chief of the field force, Dr. Batt, described how he did his work. He was adamant that though work had to begin and end with the registration procedures in the central state office, nothing could be changed without understanding conditions on the ground. During fieldwork in Arkansas and Louisiana, for example, Batt drove from Little Rock to New Orleans conducting informal research to see how well people understood registration. "I stopped in 15 places in three days," he told the committee. "I wanted to see how registration was sold to the people." In each town he would stop at the bank "and tell them I had a baby I wanted to register." Then he would try the same at stores in town. No one ever knew where the registrar was, he claimed.[68]

In Arkansas, Batt's team distributed 2,000 posters advertising birth registration to hang in post offices. They sent out 10,000 directories that listed the name, address, and territory of every registrar in the state. Two hundred and twenty of those were sent to newspapers along with an article describing the importance of registration. To registrars, they gave lists of every physician, midwife, and casket dealer in the state. They mailed every physician and every midwife in the state a list of the births they had registered in 1925 so that they could check whether it matched their own record books. Batt also managed a team of seventeen who "combed that state," working with the state Bureau of Education to use the school census to find children. "We had records of over 20,000 children born in Arkansas gathered through school enumerators," Batt told the committee.[69] State campaigns also used all the promotional tools familiar from Children's Bureau work: outreach to local organizations such as women's clubs, local medical societies, and schools; booths at county fairs; posters; and speeches. In states without the model law, such as Texas, fieldworkers also organized birth registration tests that mobilized numerous local organizations.[70]

The committee failed to reach its goal of having every state enter the birth registration area by 1930, but by 1933 the task was complete when Texas, the final state, entered. From the beginning of the Children's Bureau's efforts to promote registration in 1915 through 1933, expanding the practice of birth registration was a project that worked on both the supply side and the demand side. Working across lines of federal and state authority and combining the efforts of state and civil society actors, the campaign for full registration sought both to convince ordinary Americans that their children's births should be registered and to increase the capacity of the states to actually meet the demand for registration by suturing the gaps in their administrative infrastructure.

Besides promoting birth registration as a singular cause, the incorporation of birth registration into larger child welfare campaigns—such as baby weeks, Children's Year, the Sheppard-Towner funds for maternal and child health, and the demonstration projects and surveys of the ACHA—made the argument that was at the heart of the Children's Bureau's interest in the subject: that birth registration was the foundational element of a broader agenda of child welfare. But because the bureau believed that universal birth registration would only be achieved when individual parents demanded it, it also promoted the idea that registering a baby at birth was the parent's first duty to the child, an essential act of love. Throughout the 1910s and '20s, the bureau, state health departments, and nongovernmental organizations supplied press releases and stories to newspapers to illustrate the importance of birth registration. While these usually included the argument that vital statistics were a public health necessity and a form of child protection, they also tended to use dramatic stories to illustrate that unregistered births had personal costs.[71] As a result, the idea that the parent's first duty toward the child was registration of her birth became a standard part of child-rearing manuals, newspaper child-rearing and advice columns, Americanization campaigns, and child welfare curricula prepared for high schools, colleges, and women's groups.[72]

The human interest stories circulated by birth registration promoters often emphasized that proof of identity protected parents' investment in their children. In one story that the ACHA released to the press, and which was published in over 117 newspapers in nine different languages, the immigrant Antino family lost its farm and its citizenship because two of its seven children were not registered at birth. As the story went, Tony Antino, an immigrant from Italy, worked a piece of land on Long Island with the help of his wife and children. One year, "at the end of a prosperous harvest," Tony took his family back to visit Italy. When they tried to return to the United States, the two youngest children were discovered to have trachoma while in quarantine at Ellis Island. Port officials said they could not enter the country. Tony protested they had been born in the United States and thus "that they had a right to the land of their birth." But he could not prove this, because "unfortunately Tony and the doctor who had officiated at the birth of these two children had neglected to register their births." The Antinos were sent back to Italy. There they were also denied admission because the Italians regarded them as Americans—foreigners—and likewise refused to admit the sick children. The story concluded somberly, noting that the Antinos were now "wanderers" who could have been saved by a "scrap of paper recording the birth of the two sick children." Meanwhile, the farm (and with it the better life that Tony had tried to establish for his children in the United States) was "rapidly slipping into ruin."[73] Here citizenship and economic security were bound up together in a "scrap of paper." Both the negligent physician and Tony as father were blamed for turning the children, and as a result the rest of the family, into stateless paupers. Protecting the investment he'd made in his children's future by immigrating to America and growing a successful farm also meant registering their births. Like a deed to land, a birth certificate gave children a deed to their citizenship.

Failing the child's future was also the theme of a movie made to illustrate the importance of birth registration. Called *The Error of Omission*, the film was produced in 1912 and distributed throughout the 1910s and '20s. The movie contrasted the registration of blooded animals with neglect of human birth registration. On the day the film's main character, Tommy, was born, his father was also given a pedigreed bulldog. Tommy's father took care to file papers on

A CONTRAST IN BIRTH REGISTRATION
Scenes from "The Error of Omission"
Copyright by Essanay Film Mfg. Co.

DOG REGISTRY OFFICE   BABY REGISTRY OFFICE
Speaking of dogs and babies—Many are registered, but few are babies.

Figure 3.3. *The Error of Omission* (1912)

Publicity to promote birth registration featured human interest stories and showed registration as a parental duty born of love. The movie *The Error of Omission* was distributed for birth registration campaigns and contrasted the care taken to register pedigreed dogs with the neglect to register children. While the Kennel Club's office is bustling, the vital registration office is moribund. Source: *Bulletin, Chicago School of Sanitary Instruction*, 5 October 1912, 159.

the dog at the dog registry office but failed to register his own son, crumpling up the birth registration form as just a bunch of "official nonsense" (figure 3.3). Having failed to register his son's birth, Tommy's father finds it difficult to enroll the boy in school and is able to do so only after kicking up a fuss. Later, when Tommy's father dies and leaves the boy and his mother destitute, Tommy cannot secure an employment certificate because he cannot prove his age. When he wants to vote and marry, he cannot prove his eligibility. When he receives an inheritance from an uncle, he is unable to prove his right to it until he searches his family's records and finds that his father had noted his birth on the back of the dog registration papers he had faithfully filed. When his own son is born two years later, Tommy rushes the boy's birth certificate to the vital registration office, determined not to repeat the "error of omission" made by his own father.[74] The film forcefully made the point that a birth certificate was an entry ticket to a range of basic institutions and showed that parents who denied their child this ticket were guilty of neglect. Like the story of the Antino family, the fictional Tommy's story stressed the importance of birth registration to children's future security and prosperity rather than the importance of public health or infant mortality prevention. The appeal was to parental love rather than to abstract statistical information.

Incorporating birth registration into parenting duties was also the aim of a tactic that both federal and state agencies considered critical to their campaign: getting physical birth certificates, or notifications of registration, into the hands of parents. Some states and cities began the practice before the Children's Bureau began promoting registration, but the Children's Bureau staff viewed this as an ideal part of a functioning registration system, and both it and the Census Bureau encouraged municipal and state vital statistics offices to adopt the practice whenever practicable.[75] On the one hand, the Children's Bureau suggested to parents that having the certificate was the only way to know for certain that their child's birth had been registered. This suggested that sending parents a notification of birth registration was a way of checking up on local registration authorities and rested on the bureau's assumption that an informed public was crucial to making vital registration work.[76] On the other hand, public health officials and those in the bureau considered that the certificate itself served as a form of publicity that taught parents to expect registration in the first place. In some states, such as Wisconsin, the board of health sent a notice of registration to parents after a certificate had been filed. The notification was didactic. It was emblazoned with the instruction to "Preserve this Record." The rear face explained the importance of birth registration to the child's future ability to inherit property, prove citizenship, marry, vote, work, attend school, and so on.[77]

Even when the birth certificates sent by the state did not contain such explanations, promoters assumed that the very fact of the certificate served as an advertisement for registration. The certificate as an object was a talisman for the child herself, and promoters believed that as such it would stir envy, pride, and desire. During a baby week celebration in Cleveland, Ohio, branches of the State Federation of Women's Clubs arranged to have an engraved and printed "handsome certificate of birth registration" presented to each woman who brought her baby in to be registered on the week's flag or birth registration days. "This certificate was made so attractive," reported the national GFWC magazine, "that if one mother in a neighborhood received a copy all other mothers wanted one." This was a common refrain. Connecticut's chief registrar reported that since his office had begun sending out birth certificates to parents, "there seems to be a desire among the mothers to receive these certificates." "When they have not received such a certificate and find that a neighbor has," he continued, "they write us." In Montclair, New Jersey, birth certificates were sent out with a circular that explained their value to parents and explicitly encouraged mothers to ask their friends if they had also received proof of their children's birth registration. Physicians also wrote to the Children's Bureau in search of birth certificates "suitable for framing," because their patients were asking for them.[78]

Sending out notices cost a great deal of money in printing and postage, however, and was therefore a practice that many states could not afford. Wisconsin's state registrar wrote to Julia Lathrop worried that his state would cut off funding for the practice; he asked Lathrop to write to the head of the state board of health to help him lobby for continued funds. Minnesota's chief health officer likewise explained the problem in his state in a letter to Lathrop: in order to send out birth notices he would need "an additional clerk in the office, not taking into consideration the question of postage, for there are over 50,000 births a year. . . . It would mean addressing nearly 5,000 of these [notices] a month."[79] Such extra expense and labor are why it was the State Federation of Women's Clubs in Ohio that paid for certificates to be distributed during Cleveland's baby week—the state did not supply funds for so doing. This was not the only case of a civic organization taking responsibility for the cost of printing and distribution—in Pikes Peak, Colorado, for example, the local Community Chest bore the cost.[80] The bureau also suggested to volunteers who were participating in birth registration tests that, besides assuming the cost themselves, they urge state legislatures to provide funding for sending out birth certificates. "No more useful work in the cause of complete birth registration could be done by women's organizations," the bureau's instructions explained, "than to insist that the appropriation for registration work be made sufficient to permit the registrars to send the birth notification to every mother" upon registration. Some states, however, did not begin to send out birth certificates to parents until the 1920s when they appropriated federal Sheppard-Towner funds to do so.[81] In other places, state registrars encouraged town registrars to send the names of newly registered births to local newspapers. They hoped that, like the certificates, a list of printed names in the paper would stimulate parental interest in whether their baby's birth was also registered.[82] In 1924, the Census Bureau began offering states in the birth registration area a way to make sending out certificates financially feasible. The Census Bureau supplied a "lithographed official birth certificate record" to the states and gave them the bureau's "frank," or mailing privilege. States still had to supply the labor to fill out, process, and mail the certificates, however. In Indiana, the board of health estimated that this might require an additional clerk in the office. Nevertheless, the head of the board was hopeful that they could pull it off and that it would "aid in increasing the completeness and accuracy of birth returns."[83] States also used federal Sheppard-Towner funds during the 1920s to pay for processing, printing, and mailing birth certificates to parents.[84]

The idea that parents should possess and prize the certificate, in addition to seeing that the birth was registered, caught on. In 1898, the *Ladies' Home Journal* told its readers about a "very interesting" book being made by parents of a Pennsylvania boy. It included a record of all his "firsts"—first time outside, first steps—and photographs of the boy. It was, in other words, a baby book. On the second page, his parents had glued in "a certified copy of his official birth certificate, obtained for twenty-five cents from the municipal government."[85] From the early twentieth century forward, publishers of baby books began to include a section for parents to affix their child's birth certificate in the book. Sometimes, as in the case of the book that Betty Ann Frantzich's parents purchased to commemorate her birth in 1929, a spot for the certificate was accompanied by text explaining the process and benefits of registration.[86] In other cases, the birth certificate was figured as part of the process of identifying the baby as a unique human being. In *Our Baby's First Seven Years*, first published in 1928, parents were encouraged to affix a birth certificate on the same page as they documented their child's birthmarks, the color of her hair, brow, and lashes, her complexion, and the shape of her head. Like the act of birth registration, which both entered the child into a series as a part of an aggregate and fixed her individual identity, the baby book itself served this dual function. Parents were encouraged to pour their emotions into the individual child—her first haircut, first bath, first steps—and adorn the pages with photographs of her. And yet baby books also reminded parents that their baby was expected to meet developmental goals and standards, to aspire to uniformity as a sign of wellness.[87] Affixing a birth certificate into the baby book did both. It both particularized and homogenized the child, made her part of the mass out of which statistics about development, birthrate, life expectancy, and infant mortality could be rendered. At the same time, birth registration was presented as the first act of parental devotion and duty, a protection of the child in her future life and thus a token of the kind of long-term investment that was the essence of parental love.

It is difficult to know how many parents fixed birth certificates into baby books or what they thought they were doing when they did so. But because the Children's Bureau was often the public face of birth registration, parents wrote scores of letters to the bureau seeking to obtain their children's birth certificates. In their letters, parents did not often specify why they wanted the certificate, and the bureau always sent back a boilerplate letter that explained how to obtain the certificate from their state's bureau of health, not the federal government. Nevertheless, in the outpouring of such letters we can glimpse how some parents were absorbing the message that children needed, and thus parents were responsible for, birth certificates. As one mother wrote to the bureau, "when he is older the child may need to use a birth certificate, and I would like to make sure that it has ever been issued." This mother clearly believed the message that promoters had been disseminating: registration in the present was security in the future. What is more, the letters demonstrate how even people who did not yet have their children's certificates in hand had nonetheless absorbed the standardized categories that registration required. Mrs. Clarence Davidson of Ravenna, Nebraska, for example, wrote to the Children's Bureau on 13 December 1921. She requested that the bureau send her a birth certificate for her daughter Dorothy and listed out her date of birth, the names of her mother and father, the baby's sex and birthplace, and the name of the attending physician.[88] Though Mrs. Davidson was writing to the wrong agency, she had absorbed the right message: not only did she understand that Dorothy needed a birth certificate, but also she had internalized what many of the certificate's most salient categories were.

No doubt Mrs. Davidson's desire to obtain her daughter's birth certificate would have pleased Lemuel Shattuck. Though he promoted vital registration for its ability to reveal the "laws of life and health," he too was alive to the importance of documents that could provide proof of personal identity. Indeed, alongside his work to reform Massachusetts's system of registration, Shattuck avidly traced the genealogy of his own and other prominent New England families, and in 1841 he published *A Complete System of Family Registration*, a book designed to take the place of the family Bible as a systematic register of lineage.[89] Yet the fact that Shattuck pursued these as tracks that ran parallel to vital registration shows how much had changed from the 1840s to the 1920s. Shattuck and his compatriots in the movement to establish vital registration were inspired by "life" rather than by "property"—and indeed sought actively to wrest registration away from its association with "property" and legal identification. Yet the movement to establish full registration would not be successful until it was once more sutured to property. Like Shattuck, the

Children's Bureau and many of its allies in the campaign for birth registration regarded it as an essential tool of public health—most especially a means of both gauging and preventing infant mortality. But in their appeals to parents, they stressed the ways in which birth registration acted as a kind of deed to the child's property in herself, a form of legal identification that would lay the foundation for school, work, marriage, and citizenship. In so doing, promoters of birth registration tried to make birth registration and birth certificates as objects concrete rather than abstract. By linking the object—the certificate— to the individual baby, they linked registration in the present to the future of the child.

Perhaps nothing made birth registration so concrete, however, as the way it increasingly came to function as a latch to open and close the gates of modern childhood as defined by the state. When birth certificates came to control a child's access to school and employment, for example, their meaning became quite clear. Inspired less by the abstract ideals of a statistical worldview or by the goal of public health and more by the desire to administer expanding government programs, the statesmen, administrators, and even town clerks of the twentieth century would manage to do what Shattuck and his nineteenth-century compatriots could not: touch every household and obtain information about "matters alleged to be private." But this only came to pass once individuals saw the value of having their own or their children's births registered, and that only came to pass once birth registration was integral to social policies that directly affected many citizens. The role of birth certificates in the administration of policies from infant mortality prevention and child labor law enforcement to de jure segregation showcased not only their social utility but also their power to produce rather than simply record facts. While both Shattuck and the women of the U.S. Children's Bureau equally believed that the value of birth registration lay in its ability to record objective information, whether of population aggregates or individual persons, the more birth certificates came to serve as proof of identity, the less stable their "facts" became.

PART 2

LIVING WITH BIRTH REGISTRATION

CHAPTER 4

A BASIS FOR EFFECTIVE WORK

For the U.S. Children's Bureau and its allies, birth registration was a critical tool that linked public health to child welfare and population science to social policy. The integration of birth registration with the administration of social policy made it a powerful tool because the form joined individuals to the demographic categories that administrators believed were the basis of interventions: legitimacy, race, age, nationality, and address. Not only did registration provide basic information about child life in the aggregate (the infant mortality rate), but also it allowed public health workers to deliver services more effectively. It linked knowledge to action. The bureau used the analogy of the weatherman to explain the role of birth registration in its efforts. "When we have adequate birth and death registration all over the country, the public health authorities can watch the infant mortality rate as the weather man watches his barometer, and they can pick out areas of social storm just as the weather man traces areas of ordinary storm." There was an important limit to the comparison, however: "The weather man can not change the weather, but the public-health official can change the infant-mortality rate."[1] For the advocates of better birth registration, calculating and combating infant mortality was their first sustained opportunity to demonstrate their conviction that with the proper data they could not only know the laws of life and health but also create policy on the basis of them.

In the minds of those who cared about child welfare, knowing the infant mortality rate was inseparable from acting to change it. Indeed, the rate of infant death was first crafted in the middle of the nineteenth century as a measure not of a natural but of a social law, conceptualized as a measure of community health linked to poverty, sanitation, and housing conditions. Inadequate birth registration, then, was a problem not only because it prevented public health and child welfare advocates from knowing how many babies were born and how many died but also because it prevented them from acting to ameliorate the causes of infant mortality. This was a matter of both data and identification. Quoting the pioneering child welfare reformer and head of New York City's Bureau of Child Hygiene Josephine Baker, the Children's Bureau pointed out that "the birth record is perhaps the starting point of about 75 per cent of our effective baby-saving work."[2] Beyond providing a statistical portrait, birth registration served child welfare workers as a source of information about where and to whom to direct their efforts. When a birth was registered with a municipal or state health department, the locality could send childcare instructions or a visiting nurse to the new baby's house. As the Committee on Birth Registration of the American Association for the Study and Prevention of Infant Mortality (AASPIM) put it in a 1911 report, "why should the visiting nurse or the medical inspector go groping blindly around the courts and tenements seeking babies, when a properly conducted birth registration bureau should send them on their journeys with absolute directness?" Of course, visiting nurses did not take journeys to all parts of their cities equally. While all mothers might receive a pamphlet in the mail, only some would receive a visit from a nurse. The committee explained, "The visiting nurse knows the plague spots of her particular district; she knows where poverty and overcrowding exist, where contagious diseases thrive, where dirt abounds, and where sunshine never penetrates. The mere statement of locality upon the birth certificate should bring the individual picture before her."[3]

In other words, birth registration made mothers and children visible in particular ways to the state. In addition to announcing the general fact of a birth, a properly filed birth certificate provided demographic information that would allow public health authorities to more narrowly target populations they considered at higher risk and to allocate their resources, and direct their interventions, accordingly. Reformers used birth registration to promote preventative medical practices for infants and to send both didactic materials and public health nurses into the homes of new mothers that populated the "plague spots"—ethnic enclaves in cities, Indian reservations, and heavily African American rural areas in southern states. Birth registration set these interventions in motion by providing a way for state officials and volunteers to know, locate, and try to reform the individuals who formed the basis for the "accuracy in the tables."

Using birth registration as a trigger to send out didactic materials and nurses expressed an interrelated set of convictions on the part of child welfare and public health advocates: that infant mortality was preventable if known and understood; that birth registration was integral to knowing the problem;

and that its solution required using birth registration information to deliver maternal education. By providing the means for public and private agencies to find individual mothers, birth registration allowed infant mortality and other ills of infancy to be constructed as a problem of particular kinds of people and therefore a matter of changing habits rather than of policy. The use of birth certificates to combat infant mortality and promote preventative health measures likewise illustrates how tethering birth registration to child welfare policy made visibility to the state a double-edged sword that cut across populations unevenly. For as the AASPIM terminology suggests, infant mortality prevention efforts were aimed primarily at the "plague spots" of the nation. These were not only the urban tenement districts populated by newly arrived immigrants but also the Indian reservations under control of the federal government. On the one hand, attempting to register and save all babies linked visibility to incorporation into the body politic. On the other hand, such visibility delivered uneven attention and intervention that was premised on the idea that the demographic characteristics recorded on birth registration forms differentiated babies from the start. Birth registration was both universalizing (all babies should be in the denominator) and particularizing (some babies were in the numerator).

By the time the Children's Bureau was founded in 1912, the problem of infant mortality had been flagged by statisticians and public health reformers for several decades. As early as 1845, Lemuel Shattuck used the returns from the operation of Massachusetts's new registration law to call attention to the "melancholy" fact of "great mortality among the young." Before the registration law went into effect throughout the state, Shattuck had calculated the infant mortality rate in Boston in his 1840 census of the city. But now he had statistics for the whole state for a period of three years, and they showed a disturbing pattern: nearly one-fifth of all deaths in the state were children under the age of one; the rate of infant death increased from year to year; and high rates of infant mortality visited rural areas as well as cities. Most tragic of all, Shattuck opined in a public report to the secretary of state, was that all this loss of infant life was "owing to circumstances which are mostly within the control of the people, and are partly preventable, if known and understood."[4] Concern about infant mortality sprang from the same soil as did the movement for vital registration but was also fostered by it. If creating population knowledge was always tied to the idea that population size and health were affected by human economic and political institutions, then attention to "infant mortality" was predicated on the assumption that it was controllable rather than inevitable. Specific knowledge about the amount of infant death was a product not only of such assumptions, however, but of the movement for vital registration, which allowed statists and health officials to disaggregate deaths by age and, eventually, to compare deaths to births in ways that made the perils of infancy more clear.

But the idea that infant mortality was controllable rather than inevitable, and that it was a sensitive index of a community's overall health, was a rather new idea in the 1840s and '50s. This idea would only become widely accepted by the early twentieth century. First, statists and ordinary Americans alike had to overcome their assumptions that infant death was either inevitable or desirable. Infant death was a fact of life throughout the nineteenth century, so stoic acceptance of it was emotionally prudent. Indeed, as many as 25 percent of babies born in New York City before the Civil War would die before reaching their first birthday; likewise, deaths of children under the age of five comprised nearly 40 percent of all mortality throughout much of the nineteenth century. Death was understood by most Americans in religious terms, as part of God's plan. For parents, accepting a child's death was an opportunity to demonstrate a Job-like acceptance of God's power.[5] For many statists, infant death might be framed in secular terms but many thought of it as no less inevitable. Statists believed in a "law of mortality" that dictated a certain number of deaths per year in every age category. Likewise, in the terms of Malthusian political economy, mortality operated to keep ratios between land, food, and population size in proper proportion. In this scheme, infant death was inevitable in the same way that other deaths were—they were a means of achieving equilibrium. That infants might die more readily than adults was likewise another manifestation of a general law: the strong outlive the weak.[6]

To suggest, as did proponents of public health such as Shattuck, that infant death was the result of poor sanitation or preventable disease was to remove infant mortality from the realm of religion and place it in the secular world of human accountability and control. It also made the matter public, rather than private, an occasion not just for mourning and religious reflection but for understanding and action. It was also a rejection of the idea that even in political economic terms, death was inevitable. The task instead became to differentiate between deaths that were preventable and those that were not. Indeed, doing so was part of the public health project of which accurate vital registration formed an important constituent. As we have seen, statists and public health reformers such as Shattuck were inspired by developments abroad to understand both birth and death in new ways. Infant mortality was the point at which demographic interest in the birthrate intersected with demographic interest in the death rate (as it measured both). Each was, the early statists supposed, an index of the health of a given community. Throughout the eighteenth and into the nineteenth century, statists assumed that a high birthrate was a positive indicator: a sign of prosperity, opportunity, and available land. On the other side of the spectrum, a high death rate was a negative indicator: a sign of insalubrious climatic conditions, brutal labor, war, or inadequate food supplies. Statists had long been interested in how death was distributed across age cohorts in a population, and even the earliest efforts to calculate mortality rates and life expectancy using bills of mortality paid some attention to age at death. "Infant mortality," however, emerged as a separate category during the nineteenth century and came to be regarded by public health reformers and statists on both sides of the Atlantic as a particularly sensitive index of community well-being.[7]

The disaggregation of infant deaths from deaths in general was led by sanitarians who began to document that cities had higher rates of mortality than rural areas. In decrying the insalubrity of cities, sanitarians in cities from New York to London and Paris also observed that cities were particularly dangerous for those who lived in their poorest districts. Moreover, the sanitarians' habit of disaggregating deaths by age showed them that mortality was highest among the young who lived in the most crowded, unclean, and poverty-stricken urban districts.[8] More alarming still, in cities that had been collecting vital statistics during the first half of the nineteenth century, death of children under five seemed to be on the increase. This, at least, was the conclusion of a report that New York City physician Meredith Reese presented to the American Medical Association in 1857. The problem was one of "gigantic proportions" and more troubling still as Reese believed, like most other statists, that "the general salubrity of our climate" and "the facilities for sustaining and preserving life with us, are superior to those possessed by any country on the globe." Yet statistics told the story. Children under five were more likely to die than people between the ages of five and sixty; among those from zero to five years old, those under one were twice as likely to die than those between two and five. Moreover, as Reese observed, these deaths, while not unknown among the better classes, were concentrated among the "suffering poor."[9]

Reese was hardly alone in sounding the alarm. Municipal registrars, medical professionals, and sanitarians in cities with functioning death registration also beat the drum. Nicholas Apollonio, Boston's registrar, used his reports to disaggregate death rates in cities. In 1855, for example, he pointed out that twice as many babies born to foreign parents died as those born to American parents. This wildly disproportionate infant mortality rate continued year after year, a fact Apollonio called "incredible." In 1865, he used his annual report to argue against the idea that such deaths were just part of nature. While his report compared infant mortality rates in the city based on parents' national origin, this was a proxy for poverty. "A glance at the tables in this report," he opined, "will show that the excessive mortality among young children occurs in overcrowded and badly ventilated houses." Surely "it can surprise no one, who will take the trouble to reflect, that these places furnish such abundant harvests of death."[10] Likewise, in Philadelphia, the board of health documented the rate of infant death in different wards of the city, showing that it varied widely and that the highest rates were in the poorest areas of the city. As Apollonio did in Boston, Philadelphia's health officials viewed the variability of infant death among different areas of the city as highly significant. Variation, they argued, showed that infant mortality was not a function of the law of mortality but instead the result of environmental conditions that humans could control.[11] Statists also made comparisons among cities in the United States, among states of the nation, and among nations. Here, too, they found much variability in rates of infant mortality, which confirmed the view that it was unnatural. As the author of one such comparison wrote, "it is not to be supposed that it is the primary intention of nature that the little children should perish so much more frequently in Bavaria, than in Norway or Massachusetts."[12]

If cities made people more vulnerable to death, if they made the poor particularly vulnerable, and if they made the children of the poor even more vulnerable than their parents, then infant death could serve as the best measure of overall community health. This was predicated on an understanding of infant death as largely preventable. Indeed, the notion of environmental causation and amelioration was baked into the creation of the infant mortality rate as a measure of population health. Meredith Reese explained why it made sense to wrest this species of mortality from the hands of God. "We shall find it difficult to believe," he wrote, "that the inestimable jewel of life is given by the Creator to such myriads of our race" only to be destined to die. Reese thought it more plausible that God created infants to live and that their deaths were therefore caused "by a violation of the laws of our being" rather than by divine intervention or plan.[13] Beginning in the 1860s, England's registrar-general, William Farr, began to make the case not only that a high rate of infant death was an aberration but also that, as such, this rate could be used to gauge community health. In part, this was because infant bodies were themselves so sensitive and delicate. Though not born to die, they registered environmental impurities and ill treatment with exquisite fidelity; unable to withstand the hazards of urban life, their sick and dying flesh showed civilizations what they were really made of. The General Registry Office's annual reports were eagerly consumed by American statists, and Farr's claim was soon conventional wisdom. Infant mortality, said Providence registrar Edwin Snow before the National Quarantine and Sanitary Convention in 1860, "is one of the best tests of the sanitary condition of a city."[14]

The emerging consensus that the rate of infant death was higher than it ought to be, was susceptible to human control, and was a sensitive measure of community health was accompanied by a more precise definition of "infant." It also led to a formula for measuring the "infant mortality rate" as the ratio of deaths under age one to births in a given period, usually a year. In part, this was made possible by the greater availability of birth statistics by the postbellum years. Though birth registration was still highly incomplete, it was good enough in a few states and cities that statists and public health reformers could begin to disaggregate deaths under one from deaths under five and compare them to births. Because deaths under one occurred at a much higher rate than those between ages one and five, choosing deaths under age one and comparing them to births in a year was an outgrowth of the assumption that infant mortality was a measure of how well a community handled its most vulnerable. It made the very most vulnerable among the most vulnerable into a discrete yardstick. Likewise, the decisions among statists to exclude stillbirths from the infant mortality rate reflected their assumption that infant mortality was environmental and preventable, not congenital.[15]

The construction of the infant mortality rate was a triumph for those who had been arguing for decades that vital registration would create useful and actionable public knowledge about sanitary conditions. Carving out infant mortality from death in general and asserting that it was controllable likewise folded infant death into a biopolitical discourse about population size and health. Boston registrar Nicholas Apollonio explained this thinking when he assessed his city's woefully high infant mortality rate. "On economic grounds alone," Apollonio wrote, "every healthy person, as consumer and producer, adds so much to the material wealth of the State." According to this reasoning, "the death of one such person is, to that extent, a subtraction from its wealth."

And while children were largely consumers, not producers, in the economy, without their life and growth, the nation would cease altogether. As Edward Jarvis wrote in his study of infant mortality in Massachusetts, "unless he fulfil this promise and grow to manhood, the family ceases, the state perishes, the human race comes to an end."[16] Therefore, not only did the government have a duty and power to protect the lives of its youngest citizens, but it would reap the benefits in the future.

Though medical professionals and public health advocates in the mid- and late nineteenth century had little idea of the specific causes of infant death, they inferred a causal relationship between poverty and infant death. This led in two directions simultaneously: to the habits of the poor (poor mothers in particular) and to their environment. The first efforts to reduce infant mortality largely focused on the urban environment. In his report to the American Medical Association, for example, Meredith Reese identified poor districts as "sadly deficient in the supply of light, pure air, free ventilation, cleanliness, clothing, fuel, and wholesome food" necessary to support both pregnant women and newborn babies. Boston registrar Apollonio agreed and used his annual reports to call for "rigid oversight and control" of housing: standards for ventilation, light, sanitation, and other forms of health and safety. He recognized that some people might question "how far public authorities may intervene in such a matter," but he brushed this off with the assertion that it was well established in both principle and law that "all private rights and privileges may be subordinated to the public weal."[17] Aside from housing reform, public health advocates urged other municipal infrastructure to support basic sanitation: removing garbage, providing sewer systems and clean water, and upgrading and paving streets. This approach showed that while advocates had singled out infant death as particularly problematic, they believed that reducing it required the same tactics that would improve the health of older children and adults alike. As Apollonio argued, "light, air, and cleanliness are the three great conservators of health"; thus whatever city officials could do to improve the quantity and quality of these would also reduce infant mortality. And, as Richard Meckel has shown, general sanitary reform was much more palatable and successful than tenement housing reform. Better streets and improved sewerage and garbage collection benefited everyone and gained support across the political spectrum, but housing reform ran up against entrenched property rights. What is more, even advocates of housing reform themselves were often ambivalent about how much the poor were to blame for their squalid conditions. General sanitary reform, however, did little to reduce infant mortality in cities.[18]

The initial optimism of sanitary and housing reform having been quashed, from the latter part of the nineteenth century forward, most efforts to reduce infant mortality focused more narrowly on changing the child-rearing habits of poor mothers. One of the most visible early features of the campaign against infant mortality was a widespread movement to improve the quality of milk distributed in cities. Ameliorating the urban milk supply was an outgrowth of a physician-led emphasis on improper feeding as the source of much infant illness and death. It was clear from death registrations collected by cities and states that digestive diseases caused a great deal of mortality among the very young, a fact that physicians attributed to bottle feeding. While practitioners in the burgeoning field of pediatrics began trying to perfect and prescribe the perfect "formula" to mix with cow's milk to substitute for breast milk, sanitarians joined forces with other urban charity workers and philanthropies to try to offer cleaner, unadulterated milk to city residents. They did this in part by trying to legislate standards for milk—between 1880 and 1895, for example, more than twenty cities passed ordinances regulating the content of milk sold in their markets. These regulations were largely aimed against adulteration, but toward the end of the century, advances in bacteriology made it clear that pathogens in milk remained a huge problem, even if that milk was pure. To solve this problem, many cities set up milk stations in tenement districts, particularly during the summer months when diarrheal illness and death was highest. Milk stations were mainly operated by private charities, though some municipal health departments ran their own. By 1913, there were nearly 300 milk stations operating in thirty-eight cities across the country. Milk stations offered poor mothers clean milk, often pasteurized to kill bacteria, and instructions on how to properly feed infants using milk, formula, and bottles. As with sanitary reform, however, all such efforts to improve the quality of the urban milk supply did little to reduce infant mortality.[19]

By the end of the nineteenth century, pediatricians, sanitarians, and the charitable workers who had become involved in milk stations focused more and more attention on reducing infant mortality through maternal education, especially among the poor. In part, this grew out of the work of milk stations, which were located in congested, poverty-stricken areas. Here, charity workers and municipal public health officials could see with their own eyes what the aggregated vital statistics also showed: that clean milk by itself would not solve the problem of infant mortality. Like the earliest efforts to combat infant mortality, which were grounded in a more holistic approach to infant health, the turn-of-the-century trend was to think more broadly about the factors influencing mortality rates. Yet rather than turn outward to assessing the urban environment or more broadly to combating the poverty that seemed to fate certain babies to an untimely death, most public health officials and child welfare advocates sought to penetrate more deeply into the homes and habits of the poor. In an influential text from 1906, British author George Newman put it this way: "The problem of infant mortality is not one of sanitation alone, or housing, or indeed of poverty as such, but is *mainly a question of motherhood*." If mothers could be persuaded to breast- rather than bottle-feed, to stay home with their babies rather than work outside the home, and to maintain a sanitary domestic environment, fewer babies would die before they reached their first birthday.[20]

Perhaps no development in child welfare work better exemplified the shift toward maternal education than the advent of visiting-nurse programs in major cities. The utility of visiting nurses was demonstrated by Dr. Josephine Baker, the head of the nation's first child hygiene bureau, created in 1908 as part of New York City's municipal Department of Health. To combat infant mortality, Baker determined which wards in the city had the highest rates of infant mortality and then targeted babies born in the summer months in those wards, when rates of infant mortality were highest overall. She convinced the city's education department to lend her school nurses, who were off the job for the summer. Baker's office obtained a list of new births registered each day from the municipal registrar's office and sent nurses to addresses in the wards with the worst survival rates—largely the tenement districts that were home to the city's poor, immigrant populations. Nurses were supposed to make an initial visit to each home assigned to them, instruct mothers in the basics of infant care, and encourage them to breastfeed. On follow-up visits, nurses monitored infants' health and referred the sick to clinics; they also referred mothers who could not or would not breastfeed to infant welfare stations or to physicians who would prescribe formula. During Baker's office's first summer of operation, her program succeeded in reducing infant mortality in the wards visited by nurses. The practice of paying home visits to new babies in poor districts became standard in New York City but also quickly caught on in cities such as Detroit, Indianapolis, Cincinnati, and Jersey City.[21] Over the course of the 1910s and '20s, the practice continued to grow at both the municipal and state levels.

Birth registration was essential to the success of visiting-nurse programs. Baker's department's use of birth registration to find newborns for nurses to visit led her to claim that "the birth record is perhaps the starting point of about 75 per cent of our effective baby-saving work."[22] Indeed, birth registration and infant mortality prevention were intimately bound up together. Birth registration was obviously critical to the calculation of the infant mortality rate as it was constructed by statists and public health officials—the rate of deaths per 1,000 live births in a given period. But the process was recursive. Inadequate birth registration led infant welfare reformers to press for better birth registration in order to adequately know the scope of the problem. What is more, the kinds of information that birth registration could provide for public health officials and reform organizations—including the address and nationality of parents—was integral to conceptualizing the problem and prevention of infant mortality as largely a matter of reshaping the habits and neighborhoods of the poor. In cities with large numbers of immigrants and ethnic enclaves, address and ethnicity were proxies for poverty and high infant mortality. Finally, as infant welfare work turned from larger municipal sanitation reform to maternal education, birth registration supported that individuation by providing public health workers with a way to find babies and their mothers.

Promoting birth registration as part of a broader program of child welfare went hand in hand with what Julia Lathrop called the "social arguments for the registration of births." Birth registration was not simply a way of obtaining data, a tool to reflect the reality of birth and death, but also, in the minds of child welfare reformers, a tool to intervene to shape reality. Largely this shaping took place by educating parents in what public health advocates considered proper parenting habits. Though the Children's Bureau knew from its own investigations that poverty—and specifically fathers' wages—was strongly correlated with infant mortality, the bureau placed a great deal of stock in maternal education and outreach to individual homes.[23] As Lathrop explained before the annual convention of the AASPIM in 1912, "we want to know the advent of every child, so that we may bring to his aid the assistance of doctor and nurse; so that we may put an end in this country to the preventable blindness of the newborn; so that breast feeding may be established, if possible, and the child, if its parents are handicapped, may be given the best practicable chance in the world."[24] More than a source of statistics, birth registration was a trigger to intervention in the lives of babies and their parents, a source of information about where to extend the hand of the state into the intimate lives of families. This intervention could take many forms, some of which were universal in nature, but if a family was among the urban poor, it was likely that it meant a knock on the door from a visiting nurse.

From a public health point of view, birth registration was useful for the role it could play in a wide range of universal, preventative health measures. One of these was the administration of silver nitrate eye drops at birth to prevent infantile blindness, known as ophthalmia neonatorum. The condition was transmitted to babies during birth through bacteria or virus present in the birth canal, most often caused by sexually transmitted diseases, and would result in infected eyes that could lead to blindness. In 1881, a German physician discovered that putting drops of silver nitrate into the eyes of newborn babies prevented infection. Yet according to some studies, thirty years hence, as few as one-quarter of physicians regularly administered eye drops to newborns. Physicians in the American Medical Association, advocates in the National Coalition for the Prevention of Blindness (NCPB), and child welfare advocates such as those in the Children's Bureau all considered birth registration instrumental in encouraging birth attendants to use silver nitrate drops. In 1908, the American Medical Association's Committee on Ophthalmia Neonatorum issued a report with suggestions about how to eradicate the disease. At the top of its list of recommendations was "the enactment of laws in each state or federal territory requiring the registry of births." Universal birth registration was important because, if done correctly, it presented an "educational opportunity." Advocates pointed to New York City, where the birth certificate form used by the municipal health department contained a question for birth attendants: "What preventative for ophthalmia neonatorum did you use? If none, state the reason therefor." This question was intended both to educate physicians and midwives and to promote the idea that drops should be universally administered rather than used only in cases that presented immediate symptoms.[25] Advocates for blindness prevention also pressed states to pass laws that required compulsory administration of eye drops in cases of birth "in a maternity home, a hospital, or charitable institution." They also recommended that state law require birth attendants to report any known cases of ophthalmia neonatorum to local health authorities. In the administration of these regulations, birth registration was also critical, as the NCPB believed that the best way to communicate these rules was to print them directly on the forms that attendants used to register births.[26]

The conviction that birth registration was key to shaping medical norms around blindness prevention was widespread. Charles Campbell, the general secretary of the Pennsylvania Association for the Blind, complained at length not only about the failure of the United States to achieve universal birth registration but also about the fact that in so many states, a period of ten or more days was allowed for attendants to file a certificate after birth. This meant that even if a registration form contained the language about whether silver nitrate was used, it might reach the health authorities too late to be of use. Campbell argued that states should require speedier birth reporting and include language about blindness prevention on their forms.[27] When New York State changed its vital registration law to require birth registration within thirty-six hours, it was at the behest of the NCPB.[28] Like the Children's Bureau, the NCPB encouraged women's organizations to assist their cause and recommended that they find out whether their local department of health issued birth registration forms that included the query about eye drops and reporting requirements. If not, the NCPB advised that women's clubs could "take these points up with your Health Office, interested oculists and obstetricians, and don't rest until they are all attended to."[29] In 1915, thirty states required that birth attendants report "sore eyes" to health officials, and five printed that requirement directly on the birth certificate. Nine states included on the birth certificate the question about whether eye drops had been used. By 1918, this had increased considerably: forty-one states required reporting, ten printed that requirement on the birth certificate, and nineteen included the query about eye drops.[30]

Vaccination was a second preventative public health measure that many hoped could be facilitated by better birth registration. This idea was put forward as early as 1876 by Elisha Harris, who served as New York City's sanitary superintendent and registrar of vital statistics and who helped found the American Public Health Association. During his tenure as the city's sanitary superintendent, Harris started a program of free vaccination and house-to-house visits. He complained in an 1876 article in *Public Health Papers and Reports* that no state in the nation had a comprehensive system of either vaccination or vaccination registration. Harris argued that the administration of a successful vaccination program would "depend mainly upon the public registration of all births." This was because birth registration could form the "basis of the system of notification, instruction, and following up to secure the vaccination of every child." He pointed out as well that England, Scotland, Belgium, France, and Italy all managed their vaccine programs through "the State system of birth registration."[31] Of course, a thorough system of birth registration was decades off when Harris wrote in 1876, and some forty years later, public health advocates still pointed to the potentially beneficial effects of birth registration on vaccination rates.[32] For just this reason, state health officials, such as Minnesota's H. M. Bracken, worried that anti-vaccination

forces would oppose compulsory birth registration.[33] Still, once birth registration was effective in most states, some did use the data to locate infants
and try to persuade their parents to vaccinate them. In other states, the birth
certificate sent to parents included a spot to record the dates of the baby's vac-
cines on the bottom, thus educating parents about what the state considered
necessary medical care.[34]

Birth registration also allowed public health researchers to reach populations and recruit them into studies. This was the case with a multiyear study
of rickets that the U.S. Children's Bureau conducted in collaboration with Yale
Medical School and the New Haven Department of Health. The goal of the
study was to demonstrate that rickets was an eradicable disease. Three wards
of the city were identified, "one-third being colored" and the other two-thirds
"of many nationalities." The city health department sent the birth certificate
of every newborn in each of the three wards to the study's director. Nurses
from the federal Children's Bureau then delivered the birth certificates to the
mothers personally. While there to deliver certificates, the nurses invited the
mothers to learn how to prevent rickets by bringing the babies in for an examination at the bureau's nearby clinic. In the clinic, babies were examined
and their arms were X-rayed. Mothers were told the value of cod-liver oil and
sunlight in preventing rickets. Ideally, babies returned each month for a re-
examination and another X-ray to detect any early signs of the disease. Mothers were also visited at home by bureau nurses "to show the mother how to
give the cod-liver oil and sunlight treatment." In the first year of the study,
nearly 200 mothers brought their babies for examination and continued to
cooperate with the demonstration project. Some six years later, the project
had demonstrated that the racial and income disparities in the rates of rickets
notwithstanding, cod-liver oil and sunlight were effective means of preventing
mild cases of rickets from developing into severe cases.[35] Using birth registration to find individual babies, researchers bypassed structural inequalities at
the root of health disparities and instead changed individual mothers.

Besides using birth certificates to advance preventative medical practices,
municipalities, states, and the federal government sent childcare pamphlets to
all new mothers. In most cases, birth registration was the trigger that activated
the distribution of didactic material. That is, a city or state would send its didactic literature to the mother of every baby whose birth was registered. This
practice predated the Children's Bureau campaign for birth registration; indeed, it formed part of the bureau's argument for the importance of birth registration as a tool in the fight against infant mortality. In 1898 in Milwaukee,

for example, the city registrar announced that he was initiating a "course of instruction by mail in scientific motherhood." The series of pamphlets, called *General Rules for the Management of Infants during the Hot Season*, was printed in English and German and mailed to the home of every baby as soon as their birth was registered.[36] In 1906, around the same time that Florence Kelley made her brief for a federal children's bureau that would, among other things, stimulate better birth registration, Yale professor of political economy J. Pease Norton argued the case for a national department of health. Like Kelley, he imagined that his proposed bureau would stimulate vital registration and argued that doing so would "enable wholesale education of parents by means of pamphlets and leaflets concerning the care of the child."[37]

Though Norton's imagined national health department never came to pass, the Children's Bureau, private organizations, and state and local health departments did take parental, and especially maternal, education seriously and they used birth registration to find babies and mothers. The AASPIM created a baby book and advice manual that it made available to state and local health boards to distribute. Metropolitan Life Insurance Company likewise gave its pamphlet *The Baby* to state and municipal health departments to distribute. *The Baby* had the advantage of being translated into Italian, French, German, Polish, and Yiddish. Likewise, the U.S. Children's Bureau published a series of childcare booklets authored by Mrs. Max West. Though it did not directly send these unsolicited to mothers, the bureau did allow states to do so.[38] The second book in the series, *Infant Care*, opened with the admonition that "one of the most important services to render the newborn baby is to have his birth promptly and properly registered." Between its publication in 1914 and 1921, nearly 1.5 million women received copies of *Infant Care*.[39] In some cases, the bureau's literature reached mothers of unregistered babies and stimulated them to seek registration. In 1923, for example, Mrs. R. G. Shupe of North Baltimore, Ohio, wrote the Children's Bureau to ask how she could find out if her baby's birth had been registered. She said she had seen "a place in my book 'Prenatal Care' for 'baby's registered number.'" Another mother ripped out the page promoting birth registration from her copy of West's *Infant Care* and mailed it to the Children's Bureau with the names and birth dates of her children filled in; she was requesting birth certificates for them.[40] Many states also developed their own infant care pamphlets. Indiana, for example, started issuing the *Indiana Mother's Baby Book* in 1914. Indiana's health department was led by John Hurty, a prominent eugenicist, and was home to some of the nation's strictest eugenic marriage and sterilization laws. Indiana's advice manual thus began with the admonition that only the truly healthy should marry and reproduce. It went on to provide practical advice about diet and exercise during pregnancy, advised using a physician during labor and delivery, and reminded women that they should see to it that their baby's birth was registered. The book also included a "family register" that would have pleased Lemuel Shattuck, in which the family could record all its births, not just that of the baby for whom the book had been sent (figure 4.1).[41]

Indiana was hardly alone. According to a study in the *American Journal of Public Health*, by 1916 at least twenty-three states were distributing infant care instructions, many "to each mother the birth of whose baby is registered." Doing so was considered standard best practice for public health promotion.[42] This practice expanded during the 1920s when state bureaus of maternal and child hygiene used Sheppard-Towner funds to print and mail child-rearing literature to the home of every registered baby. In 1925, for example, Michigan used federal monies to mail 98,000 copies of "a leaflet giving information on infant care" to families after a birth certificate was filed. Alabama, Arizona, Delaware, Florida, Hawaii, Idaho, Iowa, Kentucky, Maine, Maryland, Mississippi, Missouri, Montana, New Mexico, New York, Pennsylvania, South Carolina, South Dakota, Texas, Utah, Vermont, Virginia, West Virginia, Wisconsin, and Wyoming likewise used federal funds to do the same. In 1926, the City of Chicago alone delivered more than 1 million pieces of "scientific and social literature bearing on the health of babies" to mothers of newly registered infants.[43] In Hawaii and Florida, however, literature was sent only to parents known to be literate. It is unclear how the state would have known this based on the birth certificate, unless state forms included a box for the birth attendant to record that information. More likely, states used proxies such as race or address to impute literacy or illiteracy to parents, thus channeling child-rearing advice to the already more advantaged and using birth registration as a tool to reproduce inequality.

More often, however, states and municipalities used birth registration as a trigger to intervene in ways that disrupted the reproduction of local networks of knowledge and practice. Among the benefits of sending child-rearing literature to new mothers, the Children's Bureau reported, was the fact that "the health bureau thus gets in with its advice ahead of the neighbors."[44] That is, the bureau assumed that state-issued instructions were more reliable, modern, and scientific than the lore that circulated among "neighbors" about how to care for infants. Such pamphlets served as an advance guard to promote "scientific motherhood." Whereas the tenets of scientific motherhood were the

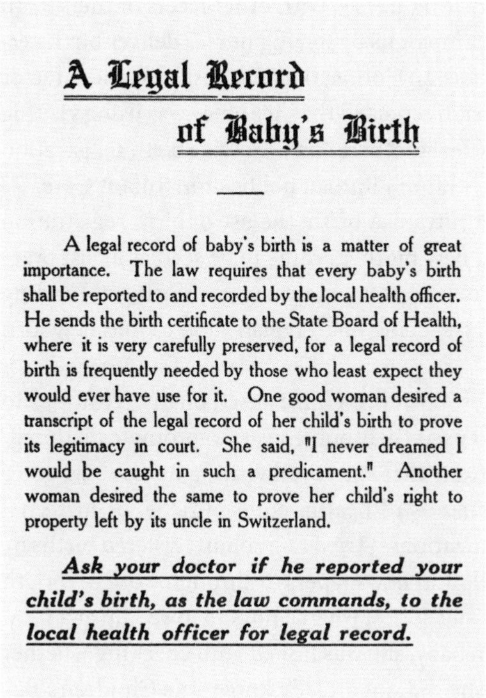

A Legal Record of Baby's Birth

A legal record of baby's birth is a matter of great importance. The law requires that every baby's birth shall be reported to and recorded by the local health officer. He sends the birth certificate to the State Board of Health, where it is very carefully preserved, for a legal record of birth is frequently needed by those who least expect they would ever have use for it. One good woman desired a transcript of the legal record of her child's birth to prove its legitimacy in court. She said, "I never dreamed I would be caught in such a predicament." Another woman desired the same to prove her child's right to property left by its uncle in Switzerland.

Ask your doctor if he reported your child's birth, as the law commands, to the local health officer for legal record.

Figure 4.1. *Indiana Mother's Baby Book* (1919)

States used birth registration to reach mothers with child-rearing advice, producing and sending pamphlets to the mothers of registered babies. At the same time, they used the pamphlets to promote birth registration as a form of protection for the child. Source: Indiana State Board of Health, *Indiana Mother's Baby Book.*

subject of scores of commercially published child-rearing manuals and filled the columns of magazines and newspapers, using birth registration to promote the practice made learning its tenets less voluntary. Unlike women who purchased books, sought out magazines, or even wrote to the Children's Bureau requesting copies of *Infant Care*, those who opened their mailbox to find the city or state childcare manual got advice whether they wanted it or not.

Better than a pamphlet, however, was what child welfare advocates considered the highest use of birth registration: targeted public health interventions on the part of visiting nurses. In Josephine Baker's demonstration of the value of visiting nurses in reducing infant mortality in New York City, the Department of Child Hygiene used birth registration to find newborns in the poorest and most deadly districts of the city. This practice became commonplace. In Chicago, a private philanthropy, the Infant Welfare Society, used birth certificates filed with the city health department to find and visit over 3,000 newborn babies a year during the 1910s.[45] Over the course of the 1910s and '20s, the practice continued to grow at both the municipal and state levels. Many localities combined the use of visiting nurses with other facets of their birth registration and infant welfare campaigns by having nurses deliver birth certificates and instructional materials. In Connecticut, for instance, the director of the state's Child Hygiene Division reported that her office was using visiting nurses associations to deliver to new mothers "an attractive birth registration card together with the federal Children's Bureau publication 'Infant Care.'"[46] Like the administration of silver nitrate at birth, the use of birth registration to help public health nurses find new mothers came to be seen as a best practice, and during the Sheppard-Towner years, many states prioritized funding home visits by public health nurses, using birth registration to find newborn babies.[47]

Nurse visits worked both ways, however. Nurses used birth certificates to find homes to visit, but they also used their home visits to promote birth registration. Many of the organizations that employed visiting nurses—whether they were municipal or state bureaus of health, child hygiene, or maternal and child health or private organizations—tried to find unregistered births by consulting church baptismal rolls and newspapers or through word of mouth in their districts. In many cities and states, when a nurse showed up at a family's home to examine a newborn baby, she was tasked with checking whether the baby had been registered if she did not already know. The Children's Bureau's Estelle Hunter laid out the ideal process for how visiting nurses would aid birth registration in her treatise *Office Administration for Organizations Supervising the Health of Mothers, Infants, and Children of Preschool Age*. Every organization using visiting nurses should have a form for each child visited and a "family folder" for information about the family as a whole. The form for each individual child should include a query about whether the birth was registered. In New Orleans, for example, the Child Welfare Association sent its nurses out with a "Child Receiving Slip" to fill out; in Bridgeport, Connecticut, this was a "First Call Slip." Both included inquiries about birth registration. In Bridgeport, for every birth marked unregistered, the nurse was to fill out a birth certificate and change the child's record when proof of registration was received. In New Orleans, Bridgeport, and Evansville, Indiana, the organizations sending out nurses encouraged them to ask about birth registration even when they were delivering birth certificates and knew the baby's birth was registered. It was still a didactic opportunity to educate the mother about the value of the certificate and how it would be used in the future and to encourage her to store it for safekeeping.[48] Frequently, if the family had older children, the nurse would inquire if they were registered and, if not, would help mothers fill out birth certificates for them.[49] In Fargo, North Dakota, for example, visiting nurses delivered birth certificates to parents but often discovered that older children in the household were unregistered. "A number of births have been found by the nurses when no report has been made to the Registrar," explained a report of the Fargo Child Health Demonstration to the American Child Health Association. Through their inquiries during home visits, nurses "have succeeded in having registered many births, several of which occurred ten and twelve years ago."[50] In Tennessee, Sheppard-Towner-funded public health nurses making house calls to newborns were instructed to "inquire as [to] the birth registration of baby" on each new call and were reminded that "it is the responsibility of the nurse to see that the baby is registered."[51]

Visiting nurses did not see all newborn babies. Whether the nurses were sent at the behest of municipal health departments, state bureaus of infant hygiene, or privately funded associations, their intervention was selective. In practice, this meant that birth registration was an essential part of a machinery that helped the state identify and target its poor and immigrant populations as in need of instruction. This was true from the beginning. When Josephine Baker began using birth certificates to identify where to send nurses, she not only singled out particular wards of New York City but also sent nurses first to women whose babies had been delivered by midwives. As the *New York Times* explained, this strategy was adopted "on the ground that families who can afford a physician need less instruction than the ones which have to do without medical care."[52] In Maryland during the 1920s, state-funded public health nurses visited all babies delivered by midwives in eleven counties but only visited babies delivered by physicians if the physicians specifically requested it. Given that, according to the state's own data, African American women were nearly three times as likely as white women to be delivered by a midwife, this policy sent a disproportionate number of nurses to African American doorsteps. Maryland tracked birth attendants by race but did not tabulate nationality among its "white" population; nevertheless, the state health department identified midwife-attended births as most prominent "among the colored population in the rural district and the foreign born population in Baltimore City." Nationally, more foreign-born than native-born women used midwives.[53] In Richmond, Virginia, and Birmingham, Alabama, the method assumed the intersection of poverty with geography; all registered births in the "poorer districts" of the city received a nurse visit.[54]

Nurses used their visits to collect data about families and make judgments about which were likely candidates for further intervention. In Rhode Island, every family that registered a newborn received a visit from staff of the state Bureau of Maternal and Child Health; this visitor was tasked not only with providing infant care instructions but also with gleaning "information concerning the health of the children, feeding sanitation, economic states, etc." Likewise, in Syracuse, New York, a public health nurse delivered birth certificates to families, and while there, the nurse "classifies the baby for future observation." Nurses grouped families into one of three categories "based on the need of supervision, as indicated by the condition of the infant, the apparent intelligence of the mother and the economic condition of the home." For "first-class" babies, no further follow-up was recommended. Second-class babies were referred to a well-baby clinic and placed on a list to receive another home visit in three to six months. For babies of the third class, a course of monthly nurse visits and "clinic service for them is regularly urged."[55]

Having nurses arrive with a birth certificate in hand was not only a way of promoting birth registration but also a way of making the nurse's intrusion more palatable. The director of Delaware's state board of health, A. T. Davis, reported that since his office had begun having nurses deliver certificates rather than mailing them out, families had become more receptive to the nurses. "This has been one of the most effective means of entering new homes," Davis wrote in the *American Journal of Public Health*. Previously, "the public health nurse was often looked upon with suspicion," but "we have found that when she presents herself at the door with a certificate she is a very welcome visitor."[56] Davis's observations hint at what other scholars have suggested about the relationship between nurses and the mothers they visited: it could be tense. As Richard Meckel argues, while mothers often welcomed practical advice about how to give their babies a better chance for survival, nurses promoted a view of the mother-child relationship that was at odds with both traditional practices that immigrants brought with them and "the realities of life in an urban immigrant slum." Nurses' instructions tended to assume that mothers were at home with their children all day, that their primary duty was childcare, and that babies had their own rooms. They discouraged many habits central to urban, working-class motherhood: using pacifiers, swaddling, feeding on irregular schedules, and leaving babies in the care of siblings.[57]

One of the practices that nurses urged on the mothers they visited was breastfeeding. Studies of infant mortality showed that breastfed babies had a better chance of survival than bottle-fed, and child welfare advocates considered that, in the words of AASPIM president Charles Richmond Henderson, the baby had a "right" to his "mother's breast." Likewise, Julia Lathrop and others viewed encouraging mothers to breastfeed as one of the main public health benefits of birth registration. This was because when visiting nurses used registration to find mothers, they could do so immediately after birth and help mothers establish breastfeeding before turning to the bottle.[58] Chicago's municipal Department of Health used its visiting nurses to advertise the benefits of breastfeeding. The nurses found babies by consulting the city registrar as well as churches, day nurseries, and the records of other institutions that came into contact with pregnant women and new babies. Beginning in 1922, the city had a nurse hand-deliver a pamphlet with information about breastfeeding; while there, the nurse made a record of whether breastfeeding was established. Similar tactics were used elsewhere. Researchers also used birth records to conduct research on breastfeeding, locating new parents and surveying them about feeding habits and correlating the information with infant morbidity and mortality.[59] Yet what many working-class, wage-earning women wanted was instruction in how to safely bottle-feed babies.[60]

Child welfare reformers also wished to promote breastfeeding to mothers of a group of babies that they knew to be particularly vulnerable: those born out of wedlock. Illegitimate babies were especially likely to be unregistered and especially likely to die before they reached the age of one. Reformers hoped both that they could increase registration of illegitimate newborns and that they could use registration as a vector for state and charitable intervention in the lives of unwed mothers and their babies. Hastings Hart, the director of the Child-Helping Department of the Russell Sage Foundation, laid out his vision for linking registration to intervention in speeches before the AASPIM and the American Public Health Association during the 1910s. Hart's plan imagined that anyone who knew of an illegitimate birth would be required to report it to a local board of health. The mother of such child would then be placed on "probation" for a year, during which time she would be under the guidance of either an institution or a visiting nurse who would serve as her "probation officer." Such officers would encourage the mother to marry the child's father "if there appears to be a genuine affection between them," to nurse her child "on the breast" for at least six months unless physically unable, and to otherwise care for the child. And, of course, if the mother was unwilling to care for her child, the officer could "bring the case before the court . . . [and] punish the mother for contempt in case such order is not obeyed."[61]

While most child welfare reformers shied away from the harshest aspects of Hart's plan, in the 1910s several states, including Maryland, North Carolina, and South Carolina, forbade the separation of mother and baby until the latter reached six months of age. The goal was to keep the two together during the "nursing period." In Minnesota, hospitals and maternity homes (where unwed mothers often went to give birth) were directed to "require their patients to nurse infants at the breast so long as they remain under the care of the institution."[62] Many other states and social service workers agreed that the reporting of illegitimate births should be used to bring mothers and children into the ambit of the state. In 1920, the Children's Bureau organized regional conferences on illegitimacy in New York and Chicago, both of which issued recommendations for the reform of state laws regarding children born out of wedlock. Among these, the New York conference urged that "the bureau of vital statistics should report all births which are not clearly legitimate to the state department having the responsibility for child welfare," and either this agency or a court should determine the paternity of the child through "case work" or "legal proceedings." If a state had no agency dedicated to overseeing child welfare, it should create one with duties that included "assisting unmarried mothers and children born out of wedlock."[63] Without thorough birth registration, however, such plans would fail.

Using birth registration to find babies and mothers put both child welfare reformers and their target populations in a bind. On the one hand, reformers used registration to sort populations according to demographic categories that they considered put babies at risk of death or ill health. At the same time, many of these target populations were more difficult to find because the births of nonwhite, rural, midwife-attended, or illegitimate babies were *less* likely to be registered in the first place. Using birth registration to target interventions thus had a contradictory effect. On one hand, reliance on documents reproduced the invisibility of those who fell outside their purview; on the other hand, documents made some communities subject to scrutiny and intervention as the result of new, bureaucratic forms of visibility that worked in concert with the campaign to universalize birth registration as part of a broader program of child welfare. These contradictions were on full display in the early twentieth-century campaign to prevent infant mortality and increase birth registration among Native American women living on federal Indian reservations.

Birth registration formed part of the federal government's effort to reform Native American mothers. During the early twentieth century, the social provisions of the Office of Indian Affairs' (OIA) assimilation programs began to target Native American health. As part of this effort, the Indian Health

Service (IHS) paired with the Children's Bureau to conduct a Save the Babies campaign on reservations. As did the Children's Bureau campaigns across the country, the efforts in Indian country focused on prenatal care, birth practices, and the reform of child and infant care. Combined with the larger effort of the health service to improve both Indian health and delivery of services, the OIA sought, once again, to improve birth registration. Like the broader campaign to promote birth registration and prevent infant mortality, the campaign on Indian reservations sought to reform mothering practices from prenatal care to childbirth and beyond. In the minds of the health officials working in the OIA, an unregistered birth was an administrative failure and a civilizational one. On federal reservations, Native American women were encouraged to register births not only as part of a general campaign against infant mortality but also as part of a broader effort to inculcate Western medicine, including changing birthing practices.

Officials in the OIA began to pay attention to health conditions among Indians at the same time that they were trying to implement the system of family registration in order to administer allotment. Traveling inspectors for the office reported high rates of tuberculosis and trachoma on reservations and among pupils in Indian boarding schools, and in 1903 the commissioner ordered a report on the state of Indian health in schools and on the agencies. The report confirmed inspectors' reports of high rates of infectious disease and led to the appointment of a new head of the medical section of the office. In 1912, Congress ordered the U.S. Public Health Service to investigate disease among Native Americans, and its report once again highlighted disproportionately high rates of smallpox, tuberculosis, and trachoma among Native Americans. In response, Congress appropriated more money for health work among Indians, and alongside allotment, education, and training in farming and housekeeping, improved health and sanitation among Indians became part of the assimilative efforts of the office.[64] While the reports generated by the Indian Office and the Public Health Service pointed to problems with the Indian medical service—namely that it was understaffed and paid too little to attract high-quality physicians—they largely blamed Indians for their own ill health. By improving Indians' knowledge of how their own practices—such as their dirty homes and indiscriminate sociability—spread disease, the office could further its civilizing mission. Commissioner Cato Sells explained this in a speech before the 1915 Congress on Indian Progress: "It is our chief duty to protect the Indian's health and to save him from premature death. Before we educate him, before we conserve his property, we should save his life."[65]

Between 1900 and 1920, the OIA doubled the number of physicians it employed, replaced many field matrons with public health nurses, and increased the number of hospitals on reservations seventeenfold. The efforts of Sells and other commissioners to expand the provision of medical care was accompanied by renewed attention to vital registration, this time with a focus not just on the legalities of allotment but also on the public health dimensions of population knowledge. As it was for the Children's Bureau, infant mortality was for the OIA the issue that connected population knowledge with public health. Beginning in 1916, Sells paired with the U.S. Children's Bureau to promote a Save the Babies campaign on reservations. In the circular letter that he sent to agency superintendents encouraging them to participate, he explained that "we must, if possible, get rid of the intolerable conditions that infest some of the Indian homes on the reservation, creating an atmosphere of death instead of life." The way to save the babies was to reform their mothers, to teach them the "simplest rules of motherhood." He implored superintendents and field matrons to inspect the homes of expectant mothers and to enlist Indian fathers to provide their wives with the tools necessary to maintain a proper home; he instructed his teachers to educate the rising generation of girls in "intelligent housekeeping" and the boys to appreciate the "sacredness of womanhood." He told his physicians that they should attend expectant mothers and that "every Indian hospital bed not necessarily occupied with those suffering from disease or injury should be available for the mother in childbirth." By 1917, at least forty-six agencies were participating in the campaign.[66]

As part of the campaign, field matrons distributed the OIA's pamphlet *Indian Babies: How to Keep Them Well*. Among the advice about prenatal care and proper infant feeding and care, the handbook admonished Indian mothers to have their babies' births registered. "Such a record may help you to prove some day that it is an American citizen," the booklet explained. "It will prove how old it is, and establish the right to vote, to marry, to make contracts, to establish claims to inheritance, etc." These were boilerplate reasons lifted from the Children's Bureau's campaign for birth registration, but the instructions about how to register a baby differed. "The superintendent, physician, or field matron will attend to this for you, if you ask them."[67] For anyone not living on a reservation or on allotted land under the control of an Indian agency, the birth attendant would have been legally required to report the birth. The unclear lines of responsibility for birth registration reflected both the fact that, even as late as 1916, federal regulations but not laws governed the collection of Native American birth reports on reservations and the fact that most Indian women did not have state-recognized medical attendance during childbirth. Thus, rather than a system in which a birth attendant could be required to report births, the OIA distributed responsibility for reporting across the employees who might learn of a birth after it had happened.

Still, the office did not confine its education about birth registration to pamphlets intended for pregnant women or new mothers. In 1916, Sells issued a circular letter admonishing field employees to register births and deaths, and in 1919 he coordinated with the U.S. Census Bureau to try to integrate Indian birth registration with that done by the states. The reforms of 1919 were spelled out in Circular No. 1506, which required that agencies record births in triplicate. One copy of the birth record would be kept at the agency, one sent to the OIA in Washington, and the third sent to the department of health in the state where the agency was located.[68] The office's new mandate integrated Indian birth registration into the regular system of registration that applied in the states. With this instruction, reports of Indian births on federal reservations would, for the first time, generate a state-issued certificate of birth rather than simply a federal record kept by an Indian agency or the OIA.

The OIA probably took this step at the behest of the Census Bureau as part of its effort to expand the birth registration area across all the states. In 1909, Walter Willcox, an eminent statistician and professor at Cornell University, drew the Census Bureau's attention to the fact that in his home state of New York, the state health department did not receive death certificates from federal Indian reservations. In response, the bureau's chief statistician, Cressy Wilbur, drew up legislation that would require "proper registration of births, deaths, and marriages occurring upon government reservations," as well as a joint resolution of Congress that called upon all agencies of the federal government to assist state authorities with vital registration. Failing that, Wilbur suggested that at the very least, the director of the Census Bureau could request assistance from the secretary of the Interior.[69] Wilbur's legislation never went anywhere, but it's likely that the changes Sells dictated in Circular No. 1506 came through the Census Bureau by way of the secretary of the Interior.

Correspondence between Indian agencies and the OIA in subsequent years suggests both that the office expected its employees to comply with the 1919 instructions and that many still failed to do so. In 1920, for example, Assistant Commissioner E. B. Meritt wrote to F. J. McKinley, the agent in charge of the Choctaws of Mississippi, taking him to task for sending in an "informal certificate of Birth" rather than using "the proper form." Meritt enclosed a copy of Circular No. 1506 with his letter and promised to send McKinley a bundle of Census Bureau–issued birth registration forms.[70] Two years later, Meritt wrote to F. T. Mann, the superintendent of the Winnebago Agency, to admonish him for failing to submit birth certificates to the State of Nebraska. Meritt explained that the Census Bureau was concerned about this because "poor registration from the agencies would in time defeat Nebraska" and push it out of the registration area of the United States.[71]

Meritt's nagging letters to agencies notwithstanding, many agents and agency physicians continued their poor record keeping. In 1928, Lewis Meriam, who had been Julia Lathrop's right-hand man at the Children's Bureau when it began its campaign for birth registration in the 1910s, issued a report called *The Problem of Indian Administration*. Commissioned by the secretary of the Interior, the report was published under the aegis of the Institute for Government Research, a predecessor to the Brookings Institution. Among the problems Meriam identified, he criticized the OIA and the agencies for "incomplete and as a rule unreliable" vital statistics. He noted that the office had issued circulars such as Circular No. 1506 but that "little has been accomplished" by them. The agencies did not coordinate vital registration with state bureaus of health, they did not know their populations, and they could not engage in true preventative medicine or public health work. "Since the record of births and deaths is incomplete," wrote Meriam, "it follows that the Service lacks vital statistics" and thus cannot "get the data essential for planning and developing an adequate health service for the Indian wards of the nation."[72] The same year that Meriam's report was published, the office issued another circular letter on birth and death registration. As in the wake of Circular No. 1506, after the publication of Circular No. 2410 bureaucrats from the OIA in Washington, D.C., wrote chastising letters to agency superintendents and physicians for their negligence in reporting births.[73]

The office did more than simply direct and chastise its agents, however. It also tried to change birth practices among Native women in ways that would yield higher rates of birth registration. Like the Children's Bureau, the OIA distributed the blame, and the responsibility, for better registration across both institutions and individuals. Throughout the United States, births attended by physicians or licensed midwives were much more likely to be reported than those that were attended by kin or neighbors. As part of the Save the Babies campaign, Sells instructed his subordinates to promote physician-attended and hospital births among Native American women, an outgrowth of which would be increased birth registration. Sells increased the number of hospitals on agencies and admonished his physicians to admit birthing mothers. "I am particularly anxious that our hospitals shall be used for mothers in childbirth," he wrote to his superintendents.[74]

Shifting childbirth from home to hospital was part of a larger decades-long campaign by the OIA to replace traditional healing with Western, allopathic medicine. This was akin to how visiting nurses and state agencies that mailed didactic pamphlets to new mothers sought to replace the advice of neighbors and countrywomen with that of medical authorities. C. C. Wainwright, the physician at the Mission-Tule Agency in California, described his work in missionary terms. He aimed "to go right into their homes, lift them up firmly out of their degradation, break up their superstitions, supplant the 'medicine man,' get them to use intelligent medicine." He added that "it takes years of constant care, vigilance, and consistency to accomplish this work."[75] Likewise, Sells bragged in 1917 that his health initiatives were reducing the influence of traditional healers, especially the medicine man. This was important because, as Sells put it, "to the extent that he has flourished his tribesmen have been nonprogressive, never reaching their possibilities, suffering for want of the hospital, physician, nurse and field matron."[76]

Indian women's use of midwives made childbirth less visible to the Anglo OIA staff on agencies, a fact they often saw as inextricable from Indian backwardness. As in the administration of the Dawes Act through registration forms, here too documentation was linked to visibility and, in turn, to civilization. IHS physician Walden Ward of the New York Agency exemplified this attitude. In explaining his low rates of birth to the commissioner of Indian Affairs in 1924, he wrote that "many of the Indians do not employ a Physician at confinement, more especially the Pagan Indians."[77] Similarly, a superintendent at the Seminole Agency bristled at the 1928 circular letter. He wrote to the commissioner that many of the Indians in his territory were "completely isolated" and "not seen"; hence "no return of births and deaths is made to the state except such cases as are attended by white physicians."[78] Lewis Meriam's 1928 report echoed this casual braiding together of Christianity, civilization, and physician-attended childbirth. In a chapter on Indian health, Meriam reported that despite the fact that the methods of Native midwives were often "cruel and brutal," many Indian women "especially in the less advanced tribes are loath to permit a white person, either physician or nurse, to attend them." In spite of such superstitions, Meriam noted an increase in physician-attended and hospital birth among "the younger generation who have been away to schools . . . the mixed bloods, and those who have lived for long periods in contact with the whites."[79] The notion that methods of childbirth were an index of civilization among Indians reinforced the assumption that underlay the collection of vital statistics as a form of public health work: this was the belief that visibility, in the form of accurate vital statistics, produced the kind of accurate scientific knowledge that allowed humans to control their destiny rather than submit to death and disease as the hand of fate. To practice traditional forms of childbirth was to remain shrouded in darkness that was both unchristian and unscientific.

The replacement of field matrons with public health nurses during the interwar years also aided both the medicalization of birth and the registration of newborns. Like field matrons, IHS nurses were supposed to impart American housekeeping and child-rearing practices to Indian women. Under the aegis of health, such practices were framed as not only civilized but also medically correct, sanitary, and life-giving.[80] On the Fort Belknap reservation in the early 1930s, the field nurse Miss Holzworth tried to visit all expectant women "at some time during pregnancy, and urge[d] hospitalization." She also made sure that such women received prenatal letters from the Montana State Board of Health, which very likely also would have urged both hospitalization and birth registration. For those women who still delivered at home, Holzworth sometimes attended them but always "secure[d] data for birth certificates."[81] The agency hospital also gave every woman who delivered a baby there a "Hospital Birth Certificate, which has a picture of the hospital on it, and is signed by the Superintendent" (figure 4.2).[82] As in other campaigns for birth registration, in those on Indian agencies superintendents and health workers believed that decorative birth certificates induced women to register births and served as a form of advertisement for the practice.

The work of field nurses across the West was similar to that of Miss Holzworth at Fort Belknap. At Fort Hall Agency in Idaho, the field nurse, Mrs. Hughes, also made it her business to find out who was pregnant and pay a visit. After a baby was born, Hughes visited the new mother at home and instructed her in infant care. If the baby had been born at home rather than in the agency hospital, Hughes would make out a birth certificate. In this, she operated much like the visiting public health nurses who scoured city wards for newborns, visiting those who were registered and registering those who were not. But according to the reports of the OIA supervisory nurse who came to inspect at Fort Hall, by 1935 over 80 percent of babies at the agency were born in the hospital, up from just over 50 percent two years earlier.[83] These numbers were fairly typical. By 1940, 80 percent of Indian babies were born

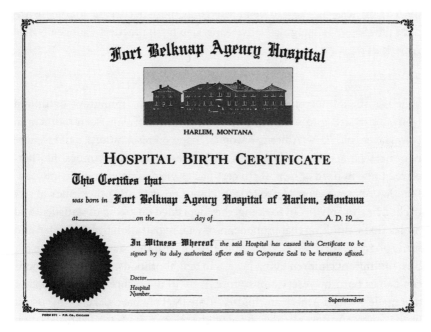

Figure 4.2. Fort Belknap Agency Hospital decorative birth certificate (ca. 1934)

As in other campaigns for birth registration, so too on Indian agencies superintendents and health workers believed that decorative birth certificates induced women to register births and served as a form of advertisement for the practice. Source: Records of the Bureau of Indian Affairs, National Archives and Records Administration, Washington, D.C.

in IHS or IHS-contracted hospitals, a rate well above the national average.[84] And, at least in the eyes of IHS medical personnel, hospital births increased the fidelity of birth registration. At Fort Hall, the agency physician assured the superintendent that "the matter of births and deaths should be free from error for the Agency Hospital" because he filled out proper forms for all the vital events that occurred there. To the extent that some births went unregistered, they were from the "rest of the agency," outside the hospital. This claim was echoed by other IHS physicians throughout the 1930s. Whatever happened in the hospital, they felt sure that they had accounted for, and for whatever happened outside it, they offered no guarantees.[85] Data collected by the National Office of Vital Statistics in 1950 affirmed agency physicians' claims. Among Native Americans, physician-attended home births or hospital births were more than twice as likely to be registered as those occurring at home without a physician.[86] Changing Native American birth practices changed Native American registration rates.

Whether their interventions targeted working-class immigrant or unwed women crowded into urban neighborhoods, African American mothers in New Haven, or Native American women living on reservations, child welfare reformers came to depend on birth certificates to find the families they perceived to be in need of help. Birth certificates yielded demographic information that reformers considered to stand in for poverty and other kinds of risk to child health and life. In so doing, they depended on a kind of statistical and probabilistic thinking that proponents of vital registration had promoted and made possible: there were "laws" of life and health that made illegitimate babies, immigrant children living in certain neighborhoods, and Native American babies born on reservations more likely to die before the age of one or that made African American children more likely to have rickets. This use of birth registration data also depended on the reforms made to vital registration systems in the nineteenth and early twentieth centuries—placing registration under the sign of "health" and requiring state boards of health to centralize the collection of registrations. Rather than using the decentralized system of clerks and parishes that had prevailed in the colonies and the early republic, by the early twentieth century visiting nurses, public health agencies, and private associations could find the records for an entire city or an entire state in one place, making the records usable in a new way.

Though many public health professionals and reformers considered problems such as infant mortality and poor child health "social" in nature, using birth registration to target interventions made the solutions, and thus recursively framed the problems, as individual in nature. Solutions offered through the data-driven use of birth registration largely sought to change the way mothers behaved toward their infants rather than remake housing, wages, or other larger structures. And though campaigns to promote birth registration promoted the practice to parents as an act of love, registration was also used to reshape families in ways that could imply that mothers unwittingly acted against their children's best interests. This was particularly true when it came to administering the legal and policy measures that used chronological age to define and protect children. In the case of child labor law, birth certificates were used to mark age in a way that was not so much integrated with parental love but used as a form of state knowledge that superseded familial knowledge and decision-making. And in the process of using birth certificates to prove eligibility for employment, child labor law helped to shift the epistemological foundation for individual identity.

CHAPTER 5

AGE OUGHT TO BE A FACT

n 1898, two decades after it had passed its first law restricting the employ-ment of children, the State of Wisconsin still found it difficult to enforce its child labor laws. Though the laws based the legality of employment on age, children's ages were nearly impossible to determine. The problem, the state's commissioner of labor explained, was twofold. First, he alleged, par-ents lied about children's ages. Second, this deception was made possible by the fact that Wisconsin suffered from "a notable lack of reliable or complete birth records." Unable to rely on documentation of children's ages, state fac-tory inspectors were forced to accept parental affidavits of age. And it was this testimony-based system that gave rise to such widespread duplicity. "Cases have even been met with," the commissioner complained, "where parents . . . have changed the records of their [children's] ages in the family Bible or other places." The Wisconsin commissioner's complaints were typical. Wherever states relied on parental affidavits of age, child labor reformers and state fac-tory inspectors complained that children's ages were misrepresented, even when affidavits were notarized.[1]

It was not only child labor reformers who worried about how to determine children's ages. As we have seen, measuring and preventing infant mortality depended upon knowing who lived and died under the age of one. Likewise, a whole host of Progressive Era reforms delimited access to rights and pro-tections by chronological age, from compulsory schooling and the juvenile court to age of consent and eligibility for benefits under workmen's compen-sation and mother's pension programs.[2] All of these reforms worked together to make chronological age into an essential means of marking the boundaries of childhood. As a result, age become an essential category of administration in the modern, bureaucratic state. Though age was a means to an end—the protection of childhood through the creation of rules around work, schooling, and sexuality—it was also a product of these same rules as they were applied in the world. This was because, as the sociologist Judith Treas has argued, "if age is the standard, there must be standards for age."[3] In other words, using age as a standard to mark the boundary between adulthood and childhood led to the creation of standards for determining age. These standards produced age as an objective, chronological fact.[4] The child labor reformers who used age to regulate employment—and who campaigned to end the use of parental affidavits of age—played an important role in transforming the birth certificate into both the standard proof of age and the epistemological foundation of individual identity.[5]

Between 1900 and 1940, reformers successfully urged both state legislatures and the federal government to eliminate affidavits of age and to rely instead on paper records and government-issued documents, ranked in order of reliability. At the top of the list was the birth certificate. As a New York State agent of the National Child Labor Committee (NCLC) explained, the birth certificate was the "most satisfactory proof of age to be obtained."[6] The solution to the problem of enforcing child labor laws was to shift the authority to authenticate a child's birth away from the people who had actually witnessed the birth—the parents. Professionally produced, birth certificates objectified a child's age and identity, making a truth that existed apart from the personal relations that created the child. The replacement of affidavits with documents represented a shift in epistemological authority, one that made age an objective fact and gave state-produced documents the status of truth. While age certification under child labor law began as a local process dependent upon personal relations, it ended as a standardized, formal, and institutionalized procedure that privileged documents and impersonal processes.

Like the use of birth registration to document and combat infant mortality, the movement to use birth certificates as proof of age was the work of reformers who sought to protect a broadly imagined "right to childhood." And like the campaign to prevent infant mortality, child labor laws created a problem of knowledge. But in this case the problem was not one of ensuring the correct numerators and denominators; rather, the problem in enforcing child labor law was one of finding and producing reliable information about specific individuals. Unlike birth certificates' use in infant mortality prevention, then, their role in establishing age privileged the legal rather than the public health benefits of registration. Opponents of child labor certainly believed that premature labor was a public health problem (and they framed their arguments against child labor partly in those terms), but they viewed the benefits of birth registration first and foremost in terms of identification. The use of birth certificates to enforce child labor law fostered a new and important role for the birth certificate as a technology to establish individual identity and to uniformly administer rights, entitlements, and protections according to chronological age.

While historians disagree about how important age and precise knowledge of age were in colonial America and during the early republic, everyone agrees that age and its proof became increasingly important during the late nineteenth and early twentieth century. While colonial-era children spent their days working, worshipping, and living alongside their parents, masters, and guardians, over the course of the nineteenth century a host of institutions and regulations worked together to construct childhood as a stage of life, to define it in opposition to adulthood, and to mark its boundaries by chronological age. Part of this transformation was political. The same contractual and consent-based ideology that underlay the American Revolution also helped make the distinction between children and adults more important legally and politically. As Holly Brewer has demonstrated, monarchical regimes relied on status to delimit individual rights, privileges, and disabilities. Republics, by contrast, idealized consent and used age as a proxy for the individual rationality that made agreements (legal, economic, or political) valid. From jury and military service to the right to make contracts for labor or marriage, "age . . . began to assume a central role in determining the exercise of public obligations and rights, replacing, as it did so, ideas both of perpetual obligation by birth and of rights associated with property ownership."[7]

As a result, in the early republic a number of legal rights, restrictions, and responsibilities hinged on a person's chronological age. Often, too, age mattered more for free, white men than it did for free white women and free people of color, for whom legal incapacities extended beyond the age of majority. The age of majority for both men and women was twenty-one, and the right to vote for propertied white men was twenty-one. The ability to marry was likewise age based and usually differed for girls and boys (the age was lower for girls). The ability to contract was limited by age, as was the ability to serve on a jury or be called for militia duty. In spite of the legal and political importance of age, chronological age mattered little socially. Most people lived out their days in multigenerational, kin-based social structures in which only broad distinctions in age mattered. Once a free boy or girl reached the age of six or seven, he or she would be expected to begin performing tasks in the household that were determined more by gender than age. The same was broadly true across many categories of difference, including for enslaved children and Native American children, who began gendered tasks around the same age. Though a concept of adolescence did not exist until the late nineteenth century, across these categories another turning point was often recognized around the age of fourteen. At this point a child might be apprenticed or given more serious gender-appropriate work.[8]

For many Americans and immigrants on the margins of literacy, imprecise knowledge of chronological age—their own and their children's—was commonplace. When asked to verify their own ages at the polling place in the nineteenth century, few white men could do so with any precision. Likewise, when, in 1900, the U.S. Census Bureau's decennial enumeration sought to record both the age and birth date of individuals, bureau demographers found not only significant discrepancies between the two but also many individuals who were unable to supply such information. Both discrepancies and missing information increased in likelihood among foreign-born, nonwhite, and illiterate men and women. While many such respondents could not give their date of birth, they offered their age in what bureau analysts called "round numbers," proof that they understood their age in approximate terms. In the absence of records, or of a need to recall precise birth dates, ordinary Americans often reckoned their own or another person's age by using "collective memory," keying it to important community events, or determining it by physical signs. One South Carolina father, for example, who wished to get his daughter a job in a textile mill during the early twentieth century, was unable to say the month or year of his daughter's birth. But to prove her of age to work, he summoned neighbors. One recalled that the girl had been born when "they were all working together on a railroad which was being built thru their town the summer after President McKinley was killed." Like time-consciousness, age- and calendar-consciousness spread both gradually and unevenly across the United States.[9]

In many colonial and antebellum settings other ways of conceptualizing age mattered as much if not more than precise chronological age. Relational age—whether a person was the eldest or youngest child, for example—might matter more than chronological age in determining the responsibilities of everyday living and the role in the household. Social age—the social role occupied by a person regardless of chronological age—might also govern rights and responsibilities. A teenage boy, for example, who supported his family in the absence of his father might be accorded both the responsibilities and privileges of an older man. Finally, people might be accorded responsibilities and privileges according to functional age, that is, their "capacity to carry out those responsibilities associated with a particular phase in the life course."¹⁰ A large, strong boy of twelve might be asked to work full-time before a small and sickly boy of fifteen would, for example. A person with debilitating injuries could remain a lifelong dependent and never assume the rights and responsibilities of adulthood. In the absence of age-stratified institutions, age norms that were relational, social, or functional served just as well, if not better, than chronological age to organize social relations and the distribution of responsibilities.

Other concepts of age intersected with categories such as gender and race because determinations of capacity and dependence were always inflected by judgments about some people's ability to ever achieve full, adult independence. During the early nineteenth century, for example, fathers could sue in court for "loss of services" when their unwed daughters were "seduced" and impregnated. This was according to the legal logic that fathers had a right to their children's labor, at least until those children reached the age of majority or married and formed households of their own. In the case of unwed daughters, however, courts recognized a father's right to his daughter's labor long after the age of majority and allowed suits for loss of services even when the pregnant daughter was as old as twenty-eight. This was because, in the case of women, lifelong dependence, rather than an age-based transition from dependence to independence, was the norm. Gender made chronological age less important than social and functional age in determining women's status.¹¹ The same was true of how race intersected with age. When northern states enacted gradual emancipation statutes, they made the age of emancipation for the children of slaves born after the statute's enactment considerably older than the age of majority for free white boys and girls. Most children of slaves were indentured until the age of twenty-eight. The terms of indenture for free white boys and girls were also age based but ended at age eighteen for girls and twenty-one for boys.¹² The extended period of indenture for African American men and women reflected the assumption that, like free white women, all Black people were naturally dependent. Thus legal norms around chronological age were modified by ideas about social and functional age, such as the idea that African Americans would always, no matter their age, perform dependent social roles in part because they would always have a lower functional age than white people. Indeed, the ability of free white women and all African Americans to achieve social, legal, and political adulthood was a rallying cry for women's rights activists and civil rights activists throughout the mid- and late nineteenth century.[13]

Concepts of age that were relational, social, and functional could be informally reckoned. When precise chronological age mattered legally or institutionally in the nineteenth century, however, the standards of proof were different. In such cases, personal judgment, oral testimony, or family records were usually considered competent proof of age. For example, colonial and state laws often made militia officers responsible for determining the age of recruits, presumably allowing them to rely on personal judgment and local knowledge.[14] In legal cases where the age of a party was a material issue—such as those involving inheritance, statutory rape, sale of intoxicants, or the validity of contracts—legal manuals and court decisions throughout the nineteenth century held that personal testimony under oath was the best proof of age. In the authoritative *Treatise on the Law of Evidence*, for example, Harvard professor Simon Greenleaf outlined rules of evidence that gave clear precedence to direct, familial testimony. In cases where a defense of infancy was involved, an underage person could prove his age "by the testimony of person acquainted with him from his birth; or by proof of his own admissions." Citing Greenleaf, nineteenth-century courts consistently preferred oral to written evidence of age. Courts explained that children's and parents' testimony as to age was preferable because, unlike a written document produced at another time and place, it was made under oath. A written document establishing age was to be admitted only when a child's parent was unable to physically attend court to offer his or her own sworn statement.[15] In those cases, courts privileged private records such as the family Bible, in which many literate families recorded births, deaths, and marriages, reasoning that the family record was "valid evidence of the information it contained about 'pedigree,' simply because the family who owned it had common access to its records and represented it as true."[16] Because most states did not have functioning vital registration systems, courts neither expected nor privileged public records such as birth certificates as proof of age.

Though chronological age had legal meaning from the colonial period through the beginning of the nineteenth century, both chronological age and its legal proof become more important over the course of the nineteenth century. As states dropped property qualifications for white male suffrage, age signified citizenship and freedom for men.[17] At the federal level, age was important to one of the largest and most comprehensive social programs of the nineteenth and early twentieth centuries: the Civil War pension system.

Created in 1862, the pension system gave financial compensation to widows and orphans of Union soldiers and to injured veterans themselves. In the beginning of the pension program, the financial compensation for veterans' disabilities was determined by elaborate formulas that monetized missing fingers and arms and other bodily injuries. Over time, the pension regulations simplified and granted veterans compensation simply for old age, which counted as its own kind of disability. Under these regulations, instead of assessing bodily injuries, pension administrators had to assess veterans' ages. Likewise, in the case of the orphaned children of deceased soldiers, pension benefits depended on age—only children under the age of sixteen were eligible. Military widows could receive a benefit for every child under sixteen. Thus at both ends of the age spectrum, youth and senescence, age and its proof were a fulcrum for pension policy.[18]

Unlike courts of law, pension regulations promulgated in the 1880s prioritized the truth value of "public records" over private ones and privileged documents in general over individual testimony. Because most people in the late nineteenth century had no "public record" of their birth, the Pension Bureau accepted a makeshift combination of other kinds of evidence: testimony of doctors or midwives who attended a child's birth, census records, army enlistment rolls, slave registers (for "colored" troops), and family Bibles (provided they were judged reliable). For white, literate families these requirements posed less of a hurdle than they did for African American widows and children, who often had to submit to whatever age pension administrators decided upon for them.[19] Though chronological age was supposed to function to streamline bureaucratic administration for the pension system, its proof remained highly variable. Thus, as with social, relational, and functional age, chronological age was modified by other social categories even as it assumed increasing importance as a gatekeeping mechanism whose very virtue seemed to be its objectivity.

The federal Pension Bureau was one of a host of institutions organized according to age. No longer able to serve on juries, act as competent witnesses, or make contracts, children also began to be cordoned off in age-stratified institutions. During the nineteenth century, destitute children were taken from poorhouses, where they lived alongside their parents, and shepherded into orphan asylums, state schools for dependent children, and religiously based foundling homes. Children were likewise removed from the institutions of the criminal justice system and, eventually, with the formation of juvenile courts, even from its procedures. The movement for common schools, begun in antebellum Massachusetts, created a separate environment for children to master basic literacy skills, a task once understood to be the province of families. Having segregated children from adults in matters of social welfare, education, and criminal justice, child welfare advocates extended the line between the two in campaigns to raise the age of consent for marriage and sexual intercourse.[20]

Though all such legal and institutional changes helped segregate childhood from adulthood, the changing relationship of children to labor was one of the most important features of modern childhood. As the advent of market economies ostensibly segregated home from work and as middle-class families began to have fewer children, they came to regard the purpose of childhood as preparation for adulthood through education, not household labor or formal apprenticeship. A developmental view of childhood, combined with a romantic notion of children as essentially innocent unless tainted by precocious contact with the world, also encouraged middle-class parents to worry that premature labor would debilitate their children. By the dawn of the Civil War, an infancy full of play followed by a childhood spent in school was the middle-class ideal.[21]

When such ideals confronted the industrialization of children's work in the years following the Civil War, "child labor" emerged as a moral problem and as the object of reform. In 1870, the first year that the Census Bureau collected information about children's paid employment, some 765,000 children between the ages of ten and fourteen were working for wages. As industrialization intensified, this number peaked at 1.75 million in 1900. National organizations to combat child labor—the NCLC and the National Consumers League—were formed at the turn of the century. And, as industrialization undermined the skilled trades, labor unions came to view competition from cheap child labor as a scourge to be eliminated.[22]

Organizations such as the NCLC framed child labor as a menace not only because it denied working children the opportunity to have a protected childhood but also because their truncated development harmed the nation as a whole. Children who left school to work at the age of twelve, thirteen, or fourteen certainly did not, the organizations argued, make for ideal citizens in a democracy. What is more, toiling long hours at a young age in a textile mill or a coal mine led to a whole class of sickly, stunted, and weak men and women, what the NCLC's Lewis Hine called "human junk." In the early twentieth century, when fears of "race suicide" were broadcast far and wide, the alleged ill health of child laborers, like the United States' high rates of infant mortality, could be framed as a national public health problem. The rhetoric of "human junk" was only barely racially coded, as fears of the physical degeneration of child laborers focused on the bodies of white children and the alleged deterioration of the sturdy race of puritans and pioneers. The children who labored today were not only the nation's future voters but also its future mothers and fathers.[23]

The earliest efforts to regulate labor by chronological age were undertaken in New England states before the Civil War, but more widespread efforts commenced in the postbellum period. From the 1870s through the late 1930s, states passed a flurry of restrictive child labor laws. Over time, laws expanded in a piecemeal fashion to cover more types of employment, to increase the minimum age for employment, to regulate the hours and conditions of labor, to increase the standards for proof of age, and to require children to meet certain educational or literacy requirements. The first child labor laws targeted employment in manufacturing. Between 1879 and 1909, for example, the number of states restricting factory work by age increased from fourteen to forty. Throughout the 1910s and '20s, many states expanded labor laws to restrict child employment in mercantile establishments and in street trades. Age limits also increased over time. In 1879, the typical age limit was ten, but in the 1890s it had increased to twelve, and after 1900, most new and revised laws put the limit at fourteen. Before the 1890s, many state rules limited children to no more than ten hours of work per day and no more than sixty per week, but by the 1920s, many states had lowered the limit to eight hours per day and no more than forty-eight per week. While most states did establish increasingly restrictive child labor laws, in those sectors that were least public and industrial in their appearance—agriculture and sweating, or "home work"—labor laws were largely ineffective in regulating children's employment.[24]

From their inception, child labor laws were resisted, or simply ignored, by many employers and working-class families. For both immigrant and native-born working-class children and their parents, age-restrictive laws contravened a household economy in which all able members of a family contributed materially to its well-being. Whether this was dictated by the necessity born of poverty or by a producerist worldview, parents and children alike assumed that work, waged or otherwise, was something that children could and should do. As historian James Schmidt has shown, working-class understandings about a child's readiness for labor typically measured a boy's or girl's perceived size and capacity as it intersected with a family's needs. In other words, they used other concepts of age—social, relational, and functional—to distribute labor. Children reared in such families expected, and wanted, to work. Even child labor reformers could sometimes admit this. NCLC agent Owen Lovejoy, investigating child labor in the Pennsylvania coalfields, reported that the youngest boys, employed to separate coal from rock, enjoyed working. "The typical breaker boy," Lovejoy wrote, "is proud of his breaker and boasts of its daily output." Not only did boys brag about their speed and acumen, but each was also "proud of the independence which personal economic value gives him in the home."[25]

Child labor laws not only violated working-class household economy but also imposed an arbitrary boundary around work by substituting contextual calculations about necessity and maturity with precise chronological age. While opponents of child labor often accused working-class parents of lying about their children's ages in order to circumvent labor law, their complaints reveal instead that reformers and working-class families understood age differently. For many working-class parents, their children's ages were not a calendrical fact. In the 1887 report of New York State's very first team of factory inspectors, the authors were shocked to find that in the manufactories they visited "very few American-born children could tell the year of their birth." Connecticut's school board officials, who issued the state's employment certificates, expressed similar outrage in 1888. "It is impossible to secure definite information as to the age of many of the children," complained board agent John Jennings. The problem, Jennings explained, was that "in too many instances the age of the children is merely a matter of speculation with the parents; they preserve no record, and their memory on the subject is worthless." It was not uncommon for enforcement officials to have to adjudicate conflicting age claims between mothers and fathers and between parents and children. Illinois factory inspector Florence Kelley made the same observations as her fellows in Connecticut and New York. "Large numbers of foreign parents," she wrote, "keep no record of births and deaths and literally do not know what to swear to in making affidavit to their children's ages."[26]

Though child labor laws regulated employment by precise chronological age, early efforts at enforcement did not necessarily disturb alternative understandings of age. Under the child labor laws enacted during the 1880s and '90s, a child's age was verified through direct parental testimony, if at all. In most states, with the exception of some in the South, child labor laws required parents to swear a child's age before "a person authorized to administer oaths." Most commonly this person was a notary public. Notarized statements of age were to be presented to employers before a young person could legally be hired. Child labor reformers dubbed this the "affidavit system." Relying on sworn parental testimony of age conformed to long-standing legal norms for proof of age, and because notarized affidavits were the product of parental testimony, they left the power to determine readiness to work—translated into the idiom of chronological age—in the hands of parents.

Investigations into child labor undertaken by an ad hoc committee of the New York state legislature in 1895—dubbed the Reinhard Committee—revealed that notarized affidavits of age bore little relationship to a child's birth date. In an attempt to expose the ineffectiveness of the affidavit system, the committee called notaries to testify and probed other witnesses about their experiences obtaining employment papers through notaries. In one case, a newspaper reporter, John McLean, had approached several notaries on the Lower East Side of Manhattan with the story that he wanted to get an employment certificate for his eleven-year-old son who, he claimed, was big enough to pass for fourteen. On one occasion, McLean enlisted a twelve-year-old boy, Benjamin Siren, to act as his son and brought him to the office of Magnus Levy, a notary. When Levy asked Benjamin how old he was, he replied that he was twelve. According to McLean, Levy told him that "he will have to be 14; he could not be legally employed unless he was 14 years old," at which point McLean offered to swear that the boy was in fact fourteen. Levy replied, "If you swear he is 14 it is nothing to me; you ought to know his age." On the stand, Levy affirmed much of McLean's story but reported that he did not find it suspicious that Benjamin's alleged father had changed the boy's age. "He said it was a mistake" was Levy's reasoning. Pressed by the committee's attorney, Levy averred that, based on the father's claims and on the boy's appearance, he would "guess" the boy really was fourteen.[27]

Like most of the notaries the Reinhard Committee interviewed, Levy hid behind what the committee regarded as a technicality: in taking an affidavit of a child's age for employment, the notary was not certifying that the child was any particular age but only that a parent had taken an *oath* that his or her child was a particular age. The actual age of the child was, most notaries claimed, not their business—liability for the truth or falsity of the claim lay with the parent. Said notary Jacob Denenholz, "I do not set up my impression as against the oath of a man on the question of the child's age; I don't know the child's age, I was not at the christening." Notaries' testimony revealed that they regarded their role as formal rather than substantive—they executed a process rather than ascertaining the truth.[28]

Though child labor opponents such as Lovejoy, Kelley, and the Reinhard

Committee blamed parents and notaries for their duplicity, those tasked with enforcing child labor laws also often took a casual attitude toward age verification. Records from late nineteenth-century Connecticut reveal that factory inspectors often dispensed with affidavits and relied on their own judgments—or on children's own testimony—when confirming age. Connecticut youth were required by law to have state-issued certificates proving their age in order to work, but inspectors repeatedly found children working without these papers. Instead of requiring that such children obtain formal verification of their ages, state agents often assessed age on the spot. After an 1887 visit to a manufactory in Norwalk, agent H. J. Curtis reported that a boy working there without a certificate "did not look very *young*." At a silk manufacturer in South Coventry, agent C. E. Ward noted that though he had received reports of underage employment, "in personal investigation I see that none looked to me less than even 16 years." Presumably Curtis and Ward, like many working-class parents and employers, relied on physical signs of maturity to adjudge the propriety of youthful employment.[29] Looking at the physical maturity of boys who seemed able to perform the work they had been given, Connecticut's factory inspectors made functional age a proxy for chronological age.

Whether parents actually lied or not, the affidavit system did not fundamentally alter their calculations about when to send their children to work. Instead, the system made statements of chronological age into a bureaucratic hurdle, one that rendered age a product of the testimonial process rather than an immutable, biologically based fact. For child labor reformers, who believed that childhood was universal and age biological, this was a travesty. As decades of reformist protest against the affidavit system attest, the problem of enforcing child labor laws was as much epistemological as administrative. How could the truth about age be ascertained? Who could certify the age of a child—and under what conditions? As notary Denenholz correctly pointed out to his inquisitors, parents, not notaries, were present at their children's births. But parents, reformers came to believe, could not be trusted to tell the truth. As a pro forma process, affidavits, they alleged, formed a shaky foundation upon which to build child labor law.

Between 1900 and 1940, child labor reformers dismantled the affidavit system. Frustrated with its flaws, child labor reformers lobbied state legislatures and the federal government to change the rules of age certification for employment. Rather than using the affidavit system, reformers urged a shift to reliance on "documentary evidence" to establish a child's date of birth. Documents represented an entirely different system for generating the truth about age. Affidavits were the result of eyewitness, oral testimony and operated on the assumption that those who witnessed the event in question—the birth of a child—were in the best position to recall its details. They permitted indeterminacy about age and working-class family calculations to persist in spite of age-restrictive legal requirements. Documents, on the other hand, were generated and tended by institutions who claimed a different authority over events—*not* being a party to the birth, their remove made them disinterested, neutral, objective. Documents, reformers hoped, would tell the truth about chronological age and fix it as something concrete, absolute, and independent of family calculations.

In a pattern typical of other Progressive Era reforms, child labor reformers initiated legislative reform of age verification in the states and then federalized the new standards. Passed in 1903, New York's amended child labor law became a model both for other states and for the federal government. In 1903 the Child Labor Committee (which later spawned the National Child Labor Committee) was formed in New York City to advocate for the expansion and improvement of child labor law. Headed by Robert Hunter, a former resident of Hull House and now the head of the University Settlement in New York City, the Child Labor Committee gathered a coalition of reformers, trade unionists, and ministers for this purpose. In concert with the state Department of Labor, the Child Labor Committee drafted new legislation and presented it to the state legislature. In addition to restricting child labor in the previously unregulated mercantile and street trades, and requiring licensure of newsboys, the 1903 bill changed the procedure for the issuance of employment certificates to children.[30]

New York reformers used the new law to express not only their preference for documents over affidavits but, more specifically, their preference for the birth certificate above all other documents. The law abolished certificates based on affidavits alone. Instead, parental affidavits had to be corroborated by documentary evidence: a signed school record, a passport, or a baptismal certificate. A birth certificate, by contrast, was considered prima facie evidence of age and required no corroboration by oath. In the absence of a birth certificate, parents would swear their oaths before board of health employees, not notaries. "Under the new law," explained the *New York Times*, "the parent's word is not recognized as proving age. For every certificate issued there is filed some official or religious paper as evidence of age."[31]

After New York's new law was passed, other states followed suit. By 1907,

Figure 5.1. *When You Go Out to Work* (1919)

Handbooks such as this one, issued by the Massachusetts Child Labor Committee, introduced children to the fact that they would be required to obtain a certificate in order to work. Proving one's age was the centerpiece of the certification process. The long line makes it clear that the experience is a bureaucratic one. Source: Massachusetts Child Labor Committee, *When You Go Out to Work* (Boston: Massachusetts Child Labor Committee, 1919).

eighteen states had passed legislation requiring "documentary proof" of birth and eliminating notaries' role. Just eight years later, thirty-one states and the District of Columbia required documentary proof of age for employment, while the remaining fourteen states with child labor laws still relied on parental affidavits. By 1917, thirty-nine states and the District of Columbia had what most reformers considered to be "a reasonably satisfactory certificating system"—one requiring documents over affidavits (figure 5.1).[32]

Child labor opponents also made documentary proof of age central to federal child labor law. In 1916 and 1919, opponents of child labor were successful in pressing the U.S. Congress to pass laws regulating child labor. The 1916 Keating-Owen Act forbade interstate commerce in products manufactured by children in factories under the age of fourteen or in mines or quarries under the age of sixteen. The U.S. Children's Bureau was given the authority to enforce the law by issuing federal employment certificates, the chief purpose of which was to authenticate the age of child workers. The task of administering the federal certificate system was given to the Chicago-based reformer Grace Abbott, who became the head of the bureau's newly created Child Labor Division.

Before the provisions of the Keating-Owen Act went into effect on 1 September 1917, Abbott convened a series of meetings with representatives from the Children's Bureau, the Department of Labor, state factory inspection departments, and the NCLC to promulgate the federal standards for employment certificates. In her notes on these meetings, Abbott wrote that all parties agreed that the "provision for proof of age was all important," and indeed, the bulk of the planning for the new law revolved around what kinds of proof of age should be required under federal law. In the end, the requirements largely conformed to the ideals promoted by the NCLC and embodied in New York's 1903 law. This was no accident, as the board of the NCLC was urged by Florence Kelley to take an active role in developing the "rules and regulations regarding birth registration, physical examination and other technical details" of the new federal law. Like the New York law, the final federal regulations also specified a precise, hierarchical list of documents with minimal room for interpretation by local officials. The federal protocol specified that every child seeking an age certificate must appear in person with a child or guardian and with "documentary evidence of age."[33]

Once again, first preference was given to the birth certificate. If no birth certificate was available, inspectors were authorized to accept a baptismal certificate, showing date of birth and place of baptism; "a bona fide contemporary record of the date of the child's birth, comprising a part of the family record of births in the Bible[;] or other documentary evidence" such as immigration records showing arrival in the United States, a passport, or a life insurance policy. Parental affidavits and school records would only be accepted in conjunction with a public health or school physician's certificate certifying the "physical age" of the child. Inspectors were instructed that they must proceed down the list of documents in rank order. Where states' own laws for evidence of age met those of the federal government's, the Children's Bureau empowered state officials to issue federal certificates. In states that did not have adequate requirements for documentary proof of age, however—North Carolina, South Carolina, Georgia, Virginia, and Mississippi—the bureau directly issued the certificates. Before the law was declared unconstitutional in 1918, over 19,000 children in these five states had received federal certificates. Under the terms of the 1919 Child Labor Tax Law, which imposed a tax on all employers who did not comply with federal child labor restrictions, the federal certification system worked the same way, and with the same standards, as it had under the 1916 law.[34]

Though both the Keating-Owen Act and the Child Labor Tax Law were declared unconstitutional, federal standards for child labor—and for evidence of age for employment certificates—remained an ideal for most child labor reformers. While opponents of child labor spent much of the 1920s campaigning (unsuccessfully) for a constitutional amendment that would permit Congress to regulate child labor, during the New Deal reformers again had the chance to urge the federal government to issue standards for employment of the young. Under both the 1933 National Recovery Act, which issued a series of codes for different industries (and which was declared unconstitutional in 1935), and the Fair Labor Standards Act of 1938, reformers fought hard to make federal standards for proof of age adhere to those contained in the defunct 1916 and 1919 laws. Under the Fair Labor Standards Act, the Children's Bureau, as it had under the 1916 law, again determined which states could issue their own age certificates and helped those that did not conform to federal standards to establish the requisite document-based protocol. By 1940, the documentary protocol for proof of age was once again the national standard.[35]

Though child labor reformers were largely successful in convincing legislatures to enact laws requiring documentary evidence of age for employment, they quickly came to believe that not all documents were created equal. Increasingly, opponents of child labor vested more authority in one document above all others: the government-issued birth certificate. Unlike most other forms of documentary proof—baptismal records, family Bible entries, passport or other immigration papers, school records, or life insurance policies—birth certificates, reformers believed, were unassailable. Because they were produced and superintended by disinterested government officials, reformers believed they were free from the taint of either personal influence or "interest." Birth certificates, explained one child labor reformer, "being official, are usually to be depended upon." By preferring the birth certificate to all other documents, not only did child labor reformers make it clear that they considered state-generated information more empirically stable than all other kinds, but also they helped promulgate the notion that the birth certificate was the foundational document for establishing personal identity, including age.[36] From the beginning of the American campaign to promote laws for vital registration, proponents had argued that birth certificates would make individuals "able to prove, in a legal way, their age and place of birth." But as the first large-scale statutory and administrative incorporation of birth certificates as identity documents, the campaign against child labor was the first chance that reformers had to put this claim to the test.

In their objections to other kinds of documentary proof, child labor reformers revealed their preference for official, state-generated information and their belief that knowledge could best be established through uniform rules and procedures. Though most child labor opponents considered church records as a sound source of information about children's ages, they also worried—and sometimes knew—that such records were not, as one reformer put it, "above suspicion." One problem was simply that it was often unclear to the state and local officials who issued employment certificates how "official" church records were required to be. Laws usually specified that baptismal records had to be "duly attested," but what did this mean? Signed by the priest? Stamped and sealed? Moreover, different churches all had different forms and seals, making the records profoundly dissimilar and thus hard to authenticate at a glance. Sometimes, complained Children's Bureau issuing agent Mary Moran, baptismal records "are on official paper and sometimes they are not." How could she tell which were authentic? The lack of uniformity was more than simply annoying; it was epistemologically destabilizing. More troubling, however, was that some baptismal records were fake. U.S. Department of Labor agents who investigated child labor in Maine, Rhode Island, New Jersey, and Massachusetts reported that forged and altered baptismal certificates were common. Likewise, in May 1918, Children's Bureau agents discovered that Providence, Rhode Island, resident Benedetto Santurri made a business of selling forged birth and baptismal certificates to fellow Italians. For a fee of fifteen dollars, paid in installments, an American-born child of Italian immigrants could obtain a baptismal certificate certifying her birth in Italy.[37]

Besides baptismal records, which in some parts of the country were the most commonly used evidence of birth, many children also produced family Bibles to serve as record proof of age. But what was true of baptismal certificates—that they were both disturbingly inconsistent and easily forgeable—proved even more troubling in the case of Bible records. The problem, moreover, with Bible records was that they, like affidavits, were produced by the very people whom reformers suspected of exploiting underage workers: their parents. As one Children's Bureau official wrote, because "this record is in the possession of the family interested, alterations are frequently made." Under the federal child labor law of 1916, family Bibles were the single greatest source of age evidence used in the southern states where the Children's Bureau administered federal employment certificates. Bureau officials were vexed about how to handle such records. In some families, "the Bibles were excellent records" carefully kept by family members who entered births and deaths "at the time the event occurred." But in a great many other instances, bureau agents found reason to doubt their veracity. They told stories of Bibles with pages cut, dates erased and rewritten, and entries on which "the ink was hardly dry." Such experiences led the bureau to conclude that "accepting the Bible record often leads to fraud and misrepresentation." Obvious fraud aside, the greatest problem with Bible records was that there was often simply no way to tell if they were honest and reliable. Agents were left scratching their heads. Many Bibles had missing publication dates, entries made entirely in pencil and not ink, entries "so badly written as to be illegible," or entries written by multiple hands. Bureau agents also confronted how the migratory patterns of many southern workers—who left family farms to work in textile mills— complicated the possibility of keeping family records intact. Instead of a Bible, some families presented issuing officers with what they claimed were transcripts of their Bible records, copied by "neighbors who could write when the family left the mountains." Such circumstances meant that in a great many cases, bureau agents "could find no internal evidence whatever" to guide their decision about whether a particular Bible was reliable. In more than one case, bureau employees traveled to a family's "old homestead" in search of original Bible entries. As the bureau's concerns indicate, the problem was not simply fraud or manipulation but more serious: the nonstandard character of the Bible record and the lack of "internal evidence" to certify a particular Bible's information as either true or false.[38]

When they relied on baptismal records and family Bibles to ascertain age, officials charged with issuing employment certificates made recourse to traditional sources of birth information. But across the country, child labor laws requiring documentary evidence of age also typically provided that children might establish their age by using novel kinds of information: school records, immigration records, and life insurance policies. Though such evidence was "documentary" and came in the form of papers produced by agencies outside a child's family, the empirical basis for each was usually the unsworn claim of the child's parent at some time in the relatively recent past. In the end, most reformers concluded that these were all little better than a parental affidavit.[39]

More and more, opponents of child labor identified the trouble with adequate child labor law enforcement as a problem of inadequate birth registration. Reflecting on the Children's Bureau's experience enforcing the federal child labor law of 1916, one official wrote that "age ought to be a fact which could be quickly and finally established; but as vital statistics have not been kept in a large part of the United States, much time must be spent in the search for proof of age, and in many instances unimpeachable evidence can not be obtained." In noting the connection between adequate birth registration and child labor law enforcement, the bureau was voicing a position that had circulated among child labor opponents for decades.[40] In her 1905 book, *Some Ethical Gains through Legislation*, Florence Kelley identified both birth registration and child labor law enforcement using documentary proof of age as tasks that a federal children's bureau should undertake. As she introduced the Children's Bureau in the pages of the NCLC's *Child Labor Bulletin*, bureau chief Julia Lathrop explained that her agency wished to help "awaken America to its responsibility for publicly recording the birthdays of its children." Among the benefits of registration, Lathrop cited the government's ability to ensure that "no parent shall be tempted to make a false statement as to a child's age." Unlike the Census Bureau, which regarded birth registration as important mainly for statistical purposes, the Children's Bureau regarded the token of registration—the birth certificate—as a vital form of both statistical data *and* identity documentation.[41]

The problem, of course, at it had been for Civil War pension administrators, was that birth registration in many states was spotty at best, and among foreign-born children, birth certificates could be hard to obtain even where they did exist. In the five southern states where the Children's Bureau administered employment certificates under the Keating-Owen law, birth certificates were used to verify age in only 150 of a total 19,696 cases—less than 1 percent. Likewise, a Children's Bureau investigation found that though Maryland's state laws expressed a clear preference for the birth certificate to serve as proof of age for employment, even as late as 1918 officials could not reasonably expect that children born in the state fourteen years hence would have had their births registered (Maryland entered the birth registration area in 1916). This was particularly true in the eastern counties of the state where "colored children" made up most of the employment certificate seekers but where births were often unattended and unregistered and baptisms likewise unrecorded. In these counties, only 14 percent of children could present birth certificates to prove their ages; nearly three-quarters of all employment certificates were instead based on Bible records or parental affidavits.[42] Throughout the states (even those included in the birth registration area), a birth was more likely to be registered if it took place in a city, if it was attended by a doctor, and if the mother was native born and white.[43]

The Children's Bureau did not design child labor law enforcement to increase birth registration, but the two campaigns reinforced each other. Comparing the effectiveness of child labor law enforcement in Chicago and New York City, the Field Work Committee of the NCLC noted that though both states had the same documentary protocol, enforcement was much more effective in New York than in Chicago because New York had been registering births for decades, whereas effective registration in Chicago had only been in force for three years. Not only did good child labor law enforcement depend on good birth registration, but also the relationship was mutually reinforcing. Requiring birth certificates for employment in New York "stimulates the health authorities to get the completest possible registration of births," claimed the NCLC.[44] State health officials seemed to agree. In 1917, when the Children's Bureau was designing the proof-of-age standards it would use to enforce the Keating-Owen Act, the secretary of the Kentucky State Board of Health wrote to Julia Lathrop, suggesting that in all states "having birth registration under the model law" (that is, all the states in the Census Bureau's birth registration area) the bureau should require children to provide a birth certificate as the only acceptable proof of age. "Nothing else," the secretary's letter concluded, "would help birth registration so much." Lathrop agreed. Child labor enforcement that rested on the use of birth certificates would, Lathrop replied to the secretary, "help all campaigns for registration."[45] Writing to Minnesota State Bureau of Health chief H. M. Bracken, Lathrop explained that "the recent passage of the Federal Child Labor Law" placed "new emphasis" on the problem of inadequate birth registration. She went on to say that "those who urged the passage of the law are now urging the necessity of uniform complete birth registration as the basis for its effective application."[46] The women's organizations that got involved in helping the Children's Bureau with its birth registration campaigns also identified child labor law enforcement, in addition to infant mortality prevention, as a benefit of universal birth registration. "The knowledge of exact age," explained the *Bulletin of the Illinois Federation of Women's Clubs* to members, "makes possible the enforcement of laws regulating school attendance, child labor law, marriage, voting, military service and age of consent."[47]

The campaign that brought all forty-eight states into the birth registration area was complete five years before the 1938 Fair Labor Standards Act once again made birth certificates prima facie evidence of age for employment. This made a clear difference in the enforcement of child labor laws. In 1936, when the NCLC submitted its materials for a Senate hearing on the child labor provisions of the Fair Labor Standards Act, the committee homed in on this point. NCLC testimony pointed out that under the proposed federal child labor bills, it would be even easier for the federal government to issue employment certificates than it had been when the Keating-Owen Act was in force.

"In the last 20 years," the NCLC wrote, "it has become possible in practically all parts of the country to obtain better evidence of age with less expenditure of time and effort." Because so many states had improved their birth registration practices, "birth records should be available to a larger number of the children" than previously. In North Carolina, for example, under the Keating-Owen Act, Children's Bureau officials had been able to secure birth certificates for less than 1 percent of all children. But in 1935, state officials reported that 15 percent of all employment certificates utilized birth certificates as proof of age.[48]

In theory, many more than 15 percent of North Carolina's working children should have been able to produce birth certificates in 1935 because the state had entered the birth registration area in 1917. That so few did might reveal the reluctance of both working-class families and the low-level state officials issuing employment certificates to treat the birth certificate as an especially authoritative document. Indeed, even as the Children's Bureau pursued legislative reform to make both birth registration and documentary proof of age compulsory across the states, its research revealed that labor law enforcers often strayed from the documentary protocol. A survey conducted in New York State in 1914, for example, showed significant discrepancies in practice. In large cities such as New York and Buffalo, state officials issuing employment certificates kept a copy of the city's birth registry in their office and largely managed to certify age, even for foreign-born children, based on birth certificates. In smaller towns and cities, however, it was common for certificating officers to accept baptismal certificates, passports, and other "lesser" proofs of age without first investigating whether an applicant's birth registration was available. "Thus birth certificates as evidence of age are made practically unavailable for the very children for whose benefit in large part these communities maintain their system of birth registration," complained the Children's Bureau. Worse still, in some towns, certificating officers still operated entirely on the affidavit system, despite the fact that it was explicitly illegal. A similar situation prevailed in Wisconsin. Children living in Milwaukee nearly always had their ages verified by birth certificates before being issued employment certificates, but children living in Oshkosh and Kenosha could bring in a baptismal certificate and never have their birth registration checked, while children living in Marinette routinely received permits based on parental affidavit alone.[49]

While opponents of child labor vested the birth certificate with a special power to tell the truth about people, these findings made it clear that ordinary

Americans, including those who enforced the labor laws, did not. Researchers for the Children's Bureau often interpreted such deviation from the law's documentary protocol as evidence that a state's labor laws were ineffectively administered. No doubt true, this assessment nonetheless ignores how profoundly the laws requiring documentary proof of age sought to alter both the culture of age in working-class communities and the evidentiary authority of families and the spoken word. That it took so long for the veneration of the birth certificate to permeate the United States is a measure of how profound the proposed changes were. Well into the twentieth century, working-class families, employers, and some enforcement officials continued to blur the distinction between age and size. Writing to the U.S. Children's Bureau in 1918, a Mississippi man explained that though he knew his son was not of legal age to work, he pleaded that he be allowed to since the boy was "Over Grown to his age" and "can do as much work as I can." Defending himself against a suit for violation of child labor standards, a Wisconsin employer explained that the allegedly underage boy "was 5 feet 11 ¼ inches in height, weighed 163 pounds, and had every appearance of being at least 20 years of age."[50] Why should chronological age dictate, or documents be required to prove, what the evidence of the senses so clearly could ascertain? This Mississippian held fast to a concept of functional age as more important than chronological age; his son's size made him functionally able to perform the duties of a breadwinning man.

The notion that bureaucrats and outsiders could find documents to contravene a parent's own word was, for many, a bitter pill to swallow. By the time that the Keating-Owen Act took effect in 1917, parents, children, and enforcement officials in northern and midwestern states had at least a decade's experience with a documentary system of age verification. But many southern states still required only parental affidavits of age. Thus for many southern families the new federal proof-of-age standards came as a shock. In Georgia, Children's Bureau officials denied an employment certificate to a boy whose life insurance policy listed him as younger than his mother claimed him to be. The boy's mother was indignant. She wrote to the bureau promising to sue the agency "to test whether a mother's word will not hold in court." Likewise, an obviously frustrated father from Tarboro, North Carolina, J. A. Rideout, wrote to the Children's Bureau asking why it would "accept evidence obtained from people who don't know only what they was told" when he, unlike such outsiders, "am in a position to *know*" his son's date of birth and age. Contrasting the secondhand knowledge lodged in documentary records with his own firsthand knowledge, Rideout had trouble believing that the former would carry greater weight than the latter.[51]

What parents such as Rideout failed to understand—but what they quickly learned—was how profoundly state and federal laws altered their autonomy over their children. Birth registration not only made age absolute but shifted authority from families to documents and from oral to documentary forms of knowledge. Just as the architects of land allotment in the Office of Indian Affairs used birth registration to impose Anglo-American family structures on Native Americans, so too the use of birth certificates to administer child labor law intervened in the family structures and political economy of working-class families. In both cases, birth registration was part of a shift in epistemological authority, where state-imposed categories were reckoned according to state-produced documents.

As soon as it began promoting birth registration, the Children's Bureau received scores of letters every year from mothers and fathers who wished to know whether their children's births had been registered. Some parents wished to secure evidence of birth to use as proof of age for employment. In 1921, for example, Mrs. Louis Bergeron of Chicago wrote to the bureau asking for "information concerning the Birth Registration of my two boys." She reported that the Catholic church in which they had been baptized "is burn to the ground" and she could locate no other record of the boys' birth dates. The boys, she explained, "need to work for we are poor people and eight children's in the family."[52]

Bergeron clearly understood that she needed to supply state employment officials with some documentary evidence of her boys' ages. "They all claim for those paper," she wrote, "because they are law." And, she noted, "I am under the law." In 1923, Mrs. Lelah H. Garel of Grand Rapids, Michigan, likewise wrote the bureau seeking a birth certificate for her daughter. The girl, Garel explained, was ready to leave school for work and needed the certificate to prove her age. Like Bergeron, Garel was "under the law" and understood what its priorities were. Indeed, Garel's letter to the bureau indicated her absorption of many of the basic categories of the birth certificate: she listed her daughter's full name and exact birth date, her and her husband's names, and the name of the attending physician at the birth.[53]

That parents such as Bergeron and Garel wrote the Children's Bureau seeking help in locating birth certificates—and that they tied the matter to employment—is a measure of how much had changed since Wisconsin's com-missioner of labor had complained that he was helpless to enforce child labor law because proof of age rested on testimony, not documents. When he wrote in 1898, age verification was almost entirely in the hands of parents through-out the nation. Though Wisconsin's laws, like many at the time, required par-ents to swear affidavits of age for their working children, parents were not required to supply any external or "objective" evidence to corroborate their oaths. And unless a labor law enforcer could himself supply contradictory documentary evidence, such affidavits were impossible to disprove. In 1921, by contrast, when Bergeron wrote to the U.S. Children's Bureau, it was she who was helpless to prove her own children's ages. The Illinois law requiring docu-mentary evidence of age had been in effect for eighteen years. Significantly, Bergeron did not claim ignorance of her children's birth dates or ages; rather, her problem was that she lacked the authority to make her own knowledge, however accurate it might have been, recognizable by the state. She was "under the law" and she needed paper.

Though the transference of authority from oral to written statements, and from families to the state, is a hallmark of "modernization," this transforma-tion was rocky. In the case of age verification, documentary evidence gained epistemological authority only as the result of a multidecade campaign by opponents of child labor to change labor and vital statics registration laws, practices at the local level, cultural assumptions about age, and standards for producing empirical truth about age. Moreover, there is scattered evidence suggesting that as the twentieth century wore on, the documentary regime became a fact of life for many working-class parents and children. In 1915, the Massachusetts State Child Labor Committee reported that when young boys were found selling newspapers on the streets without the proper employment certificates, they were quick to give the excuse of "Waiting for my birth cer-tificate." Even as the boys circumvented the state's laws, they were well aware of its requirement for documentary proof of age.[54]

Though child labor reformers initially regarded many kinds of documents as similar or equal in their evidentiary value, their experiences enforcing laws and investigating the practice of issuing employment certificates convinced them that not all documents deserved the same credence. Affidavits, bap-tismal records, family Bibles, school records, and life insurance policies all lacked the stable empirical foundation that the shift to documentary proof had been intended to supply. By contrast, reformers believed, "public birth records" could remove all taint of interest, and any possibility of mutability, from the process of age verification. The information they contained was normally supplied by those outside the family—birth attendants such as doctors and midwives—and the time horizon connecting the registration of a birth to a child's employment was sufficiently broad to remove all incentives to lie. Just as important, birth certificates recorded and presented information in a uniform manner, one that made the knowledge they contained stable and easy to authenticate. "The public birth record," wrote the Children's Bureau in 1916, "affords absolutely unimpeachable and uniform proof." Indeed, according to the standards for truth adhered to by the bureau, a birth certificate's proofs were unimpeachable *because* they were uniform.[55] Ostensibly marking singular individuality and unique identity, birth certificates also became mechanisms for managing populations as faceless masses.

Simultaneous with the campaign to make child labor law rest on documentary proof of age, many states and localities began to require pupils to present proof of age for school enrollment. Compulsory schooling was the other side of the coin of what Florence Kelley called the "statutory prolongation of childhood," and like child labor, schooling was also age based. In their study of truancy in Chicago, Edith Abbott and Sophonisba Breckenridge noted that inadequate birth registration was the system's Achilles heel. "No system can be devised" to keep children in school until the statutory age of fourteen "until birth registration is really compulsory and every child's age is a matter of public record." A child who was enrolled in school at five years old instead of seven to relieve his widowed mother of childcare so that she could enter the workforce would be erroneously released at twelve instead of fourteen to himself go out and work.[56] Like child labor law, the requirement that pupils present proof of age to enter, and not just exit, school had the effect of stimulating the demand for birth registration in cities and states. When Illinois public schools started requiring a birth certificate to enter school in 1925, the demand for birth certificates skyrocketed. In particular, parents sought to register children who had been born "5, 6, 7 years ago—evidently to meet school requirements." Requests for such "delayed" registrations tripled after the 1925 law.[57] William Guilfoy, the registrar of records of New York City, complained as early as 1911 about "the increased burdens" his office faced "by reason of the compulsory issuance of birth certificates for school and employment purposes." Compared with just ten years earlier, New York City's Bureau of Vital Statistics was performing 500 percent more searches to verify marriages, births, and deaths, most of these, as Guilfoy indicated, stemming from demands for age verification.[58] Reformers seeking to end child marriage and

Figure 5.2. "The Government Demands Proof" (1925)

The increased demand for proof of age and identity was met by birth certificates. This illustration shows a mother with her children as she tries to get one or both of them into school. The piece of paper—presumably a birth certificate—held by the school official literally stands between the children and school. The illustration's caption explains that "school authorities now require all new pupils to produce birth certificates before they can be enrolled." The accompanying newspaper article noted that the "government demands proof" not just for school but also for passports, to work, to vote, and to marry. Source: "Providing Birth Certificates in State," *Sun*, 23 August 1925.

raise the age of consent likewise hoped to make birth certificates into tools of law enforcement. "In a multitude of ways," wrote the U.S. Census Bureau's Cressy Wilbur in 1916, "the state is entering into the daily life of the people and requiring records of births and marriages and deaths for the interest of the individual" (figure 5.2).[59]

The utility of birth certificates to prove age was also demonstrated by the World War I draft.[60] The Selective Service Act of May 1917, which required the registration of all male citizens between the ages of twenty-one and thirty (later extended to eighteen and forty-five), "brings home the need of birth records to every community and to almost every family in the United States," claimed one publication. Formed in 1917, the American Protective League sought to assist the U.S. government's war efforts by, among other things, patrolling communities and looking for "slackers," those men of draft age who

Figure 5.3. "How Can We Prove It?" (1917)

Proof of age was important not just for child labor law enforcement but also for the age requirements of the World War I draft. Source: *Illinois Health News* 3 (July 1917).

failed to register. In urban areas, the American Protective League stormed into entertainment venues where they believed they would find men of draft age and demanded to see customers' registration cards. These so-called slacker raids sent many unregistered men to prison until they either registered or proved they were not of draft age. As the historian Christopher Capozzola has noted, in such raids, freedom depended on a man's ability to "demonstrate a state-sanctioned identity, age, and classification status to the satisfaction of authorities by showing his card."[61] As birth certificates had been the answer to the fraudulent employment of underage children, they were also the answer to the "slacker" problem. "Many slackers are claiming to be either under age or over age," wrote Dr. W. A. Evans, the health columnist for the *Chicago Daily Tribune*. They did this "knowing the difficulty the boards will have in disproving their statements."[62] The Illinois State Board of Health captured this predicament in an editorial cartoon in its *Health News*: two men, identical in appearance, appeared before the draft registration board, but one claimed to be thirty-three and the other only eighteen. The board's commissioners were helpless in the face of such claims. The caption pointed out that if Illinois had had a functioning vital registration law "years ago," this "embarrassing situation" could have been avoided (figure 5.3).

In reality, there was often little officials could do to dispute registrants' age claims. In 1918, the adjutant general of New Jersey wrote to E. H. Crowder, the provost marshal general of the army, asking what to do about men who were over the draft age but could not prove this fact, "as most states do not have a record of births going back 45 or 50 years." Crowder replied that "there appears to be nothing" his office could do in the matter.[63] Only in states and cities with long-standing, functional vital registration systems could reliable proof of draft age be proffered. New York City's registrar, for example, reported that his office aided federal officials in rooting out slackers who gave draft boards the wrong birth date.[64]

In the draft as in compulsory schooling, misstatements made for one purpose caused problems elsewhere, as a person used proof of age from one bureaucratic system to establish age in another. In several cases that appeared before local draft boards, for example, registrants presented allegedly false proof of age based on statements made years earlier to their employers. The adjutant general of Alabama wrote to Provost Marshal General Crowder that he had a number of cases from "industrial centers in the state" in which the registrant was under twenty-one but "had represented his age to be 21 at some previous time in order to secure employment in some industrial plant." This earlier age fraud, probably in the form of an affidavit to secure an employment certificate, might now mean the underage registration of a young man for the draft. On the other end of the spectrum, a case in Nebraska involved a man who claimed to be thirty-seven, and thus over draft age, even though he had registered with the draft board as twenty-eight. He subsequently said that he had lied about his age because he had "contemplated applying for a position in the railroad service, where the age limit for acceptance of new employees is 35 years." It's unclear if he presented fraudulent papers to the draft board or if he hoped to use his draft registration as proof of age in subsequent employment applications. Either way, lack of birth registration permitted this indeterminacy. In order to establish his true age, the man submitted the testimony of a neighbor who said that she knew him to be more than thirty-five because her house was built thirty-six years ago, and "prior to the time the house was built the said William Joseph Heming played in the neighborhood as a child." Taking a page from the playbook of child labor reformers, the army refused to accept the affidavits, saying, "We have found that we absolutely cannot accept the affidavits of relatives or friends, nor can we accept family records." The only acceptable proof of age in case of dispute was "a certified copy of some record established prior to the entrance of this country into war."[65]

Papers, not people, told the truth. While the army held this as a general proposition, local draft boards often applied more scrutiny to African Americans than to whites. Like child labor reformers who assumed that shiftless working-class parents were more likely to lie, officials from southern draft boards assumed that African Americans would try to avoid the draft. They also knew that African Americans were less likely to have documentation of their age. In June 1917, the sheriff of Jones County, Georgia, wrote to the adjutant general of his state about "several negro's [sic] in the community" who claimed to be either older or younger than draft age, "and we are not able to prove otherwise." The sheriff noted that he believed they were lying, "and so do the white people of the community." He wanted to arrest them and "let them make the proof." What is more, the sheriff explained that he had no problem verifying the ages of local whites because "we have the voting registration to guide us." Disfranchised African Americans, on the other hand, had their tenuous citizenship follow them when it came to draft registration. Georgia, having made it impossible for its Black citizens to register to vote, now wanted to use Black men's lack of documentation as presumptive proof of their draft fraud and hold them in jail until they could produce the papers that the state had denied them in the first place. This roundup was forestalled, however, by the captain of the U.S. Cavalry, who explained to the sheriff that arrests could proceed if there was "reasonable ground," but the burden of proof would then be on the U.S. government to "prove that allegation" of fraud.[66]

The World War I draft was a particularly striking example of a more general phenomenon: the knot tying together chronological age, citizenship, and documentation was tightening in the early twentieth century. It would only grow denser with time. The more protections and entitlements that states and the federal government offered, the more important both age and documentation became to the basic functioning of social institutions. In such a system, documentary invisibility or illegibility—such as that of Georgia's disfranchised African Americans—was a barrier to receiving the benefits and entitlements of citizenship. Remarking on the importance of birth certificates to modern citizenship, Census Bureau employee Robert Lenhart observed in 1940 that "each step we take toward the goal of social and economic security for everyone makes more precious each individual's proof of his rights to such benefits." Chronological age was often the administrative gate that opened and closed access to such benefits. By legally making the birth certificate the threshold of modern age-based citizenship, child labor law led the way, transforming the epistemological grounds for rights and protections, inclusions and exclusions.[67] But age was not the only fact that birth certificates established. From the administration of child labor laws through the rest of the twentieth century, states and the federal government would trust in the truths created by birth registration. Just as child protectionists and other government officials would use the birth certificate to fix age, the architects and administrators of Jim Crow segregation would rely on registration to construct race and administer white supremacy.

CHAPTER 6

ADJUSTING THE COLOR PROBLEM

I n 1936, after just one year of marriage, Cyril Sunseri sued to have his marriage to his wife, Verna Cassagne, annulled by a civil court in New Orleans. According to Sunseri, Cassagne was "a person of color" and their marriage had been illegal under Louisiana's miscegenation statute. By seeking annulment rather than divorce, Sunseri was asking the court to declare that his marriage to Cassagne had never been valid. The court thus had to determine whether Cassagne possessed even "a trace of negro blood." Sunseri alleged that Cassagne's great-great-grandmother Fanny Ducre was a "full-blooded negress," while Cassagne insisted that Ducre was an Indian. Both parties to the suit brought witnesses to testify in support of their claims, but Sunseri also adduced a trail of documentary evidence marking Ducre and her descendants as "colored." These documents included Verna Cassagne's own birth certificate, which, despite the fact that she had been born on a "white" maternity ward, marked her as colored. In the end, the oral testimony of relatives and friends—that Cassagne and her mother "have always been considered as being of the white race by their acquaintance in the City of New Orleans"—could not win out over the documentary trail: Cassagne, the trial and appeals courts found, was Black, not white. The marriage was annulled.[1]

Cassagne's fate demonstrates the power of vital statistics documents in determining racial classification and administering the racial state. Although *Sunseri v. Cassagne* involved a great deal of testimony about the (white) racial reputation of Verna Cassagne, her fate was ultimately determined by the bureaucratic document filed when she was born: her birth certificate. By the 1930s, the power of birth certificates to determine the facts of a person's identity (name, parentage, exact age, sex, and race) was well established. Though scholars have often portrayed the courtroom determination of racial identity as a matter of racial reputation and association, Cassagne's case demonstrates that by the twentieth century, bureaucratic forms of knowledge could supplement and even replace local knowledge about racial identity.[2]

Before the twentieth century, all states and localities that registered births included information about the race or color of a child's parents on the form. This was, as we have seen, considered a basic fact of both personal identity and population knowledge. But increased use of birth certificates as instruments of identification coincided with the administrative use of blood quantum to distribute (and block) access to the goods of citizenship. This was true both in federal Indian policy and state-based Jim Crow segregation. This made vital documents attractive to the architects of a racial order who sought not only to enforce segregation but also to impose a Black-white order on the racially ambiguous, racially mixed communities scattered throughout the South.[3]

The power of birth registration went far beyond the simple ability to administer segregation and other blood-based policies, however. The assumption of state officials who used birth certificates to sort people according to race was that such documents provided a disinterested, epistemologically stable source of information. But as was the case with age, racial classification through birth registration worked less to record and stabilize the truth than to help produce it. Because state bureaus of vital statistics could racially classify individuals on their birth documents, they were able to redefine the racial landscape. In Jim Crow–era Virginia, state officials did this by denying babies and their parents access to the racial category of "Indian" and foreclosing all the state and federal recognition that entailed.

From the beginning of vital statistics registration reform in the antebellum era, almost every city and state that collected birth registrations required that certificates indicate the "race or color" of the parents or the child.[4] Like other aspects of vital registration, however, the administration of racial classification through birth registration was easier said than done. One part of the problem was that midwives, doctors, clerks, and parents failed to report race. In 1850 Connecticut's secretary of state complained that "color" was often left blank on birth certificates. A decade later at a meeting of Philadelphia's medical society, local physicians lamented that there were no accurate statistics on "colored births" because, as one of their group reported, "the colour in every instance [of birth] has not been designated."[5] Likewise, throughout the second half of the nineteenth century, Michigan officials complained not just that certificates were returned with the "wrong" sort of racial classification but also that too many were returned with no race or color recorded at all. "This imperfection in the returns is to be regretted," the state registrar chided in 1879, "because it detracts so much from the value of the statistics."[6]

Part of the problem was obviously that racial categories had no stable content. While statisticians or state registrars might have agreed among themselves about a discrete set of possible answers to the "race or color" question—white, colored, mulatto, quadroon, octoroon, Indian, Japanese, Chinese, or Mongolian—returns on birth certificates made it clear that birth attendants did not share the same understanding of racial categories. Virginia's registrar complained that his state's midwives would indicate a baby's "color" with terms "such as 'brunette,' 'blond,' 'light skinned,' 'dark,' etc." This wasn't just a southern complaint. In his 1874 annual report, Michigan's state registrar reprimanded local officials for their dereliction in matters of race. "The color should be stated as Black, Mulatto, Indian, White and Indian, etc., and not as African or Colored," he grumped. Five years later, he was still complaining that birth certificates were being filed with terms that were not "in conformity to the suggestions in the blanks and circulars of the State Department." He singled out answers such as "dark" and "light" for scorn as "terms [that] have no definite meaning."[7] Nor was this simply a problem that plagued the early days of registration; errors or omissions in recording race lasted well into the twentieth century, at least according to state registrars.[8] As late as 1946, field reports from Census Bureau agents complained of similar problems. In Ohio, one bureau agent reported, "Colored people insist they are colored, light born, or Afro-American but not 'Black' as shown on birth certificates." Likewise in Tennessee, African American parents sometimes insisted on putting "light brown" in the box for race.[9] States and the federal government tried to make racial categories more uniform. In 1920, Minnesota's state registrar provided detailed instructions to clerks on how to record race, including the fact that *B* for Black should encompass "all degrees of negro descent, as mulatto, quadroon, etc."[10] The Census Bureau attempted to help standardize racial categories in its *Physician's Handbook on Birth and Death Registration*, first issued in 1939. "Racial origin should be described by stating to what people or race each parent belongs," the handbook instructed, "as *white, Indian, Negro, Chinese,* etc." And in spite of the last category—Chinese—the handbook reminded doctors not to use terms such as "American" or "Canadian" because these "express citizenship rather than a race or people."[11]

But the problem was more than just a misunderstanding. Racial categories such as "mulatto" and "quadroon" required not just a commitment to the social fiction of "blood" but also a precise knowledge of marriage patterns going back generations. In a discussion of vital statistics related to race, Columbia University economist and racial theorist W. Z. Ripley complained that census racial categories of Black, mulatto, quadroon, and octoroon were "worthless" because "such a query is often impossible of exact answer." For Ripley this was because ascertaining precise blood quantum "is a severe tax upon the genealogical resources of the average southern negro family."[12] A seemingly simple query on a form, "color or race" traced histories and called forth answers that were unintended or unknowable. The result was that racial categories were muddled, and the effort to use vital statistics to bring clarity to the study of racial science only compounded the problem. "Perfect accuracy could not be attained," confessed the *Medical and Surgical Reporter* in 1869, for under the category "mulatto," "every shade of color and degree of intermixture from the mulatto to the octaroon, would be reported."[13] So much for the hope that birth statistics could help settle the pressing questions about the relationship between racial mixture and racial health.

In the case of Native Americans, the standard Census Bureau–issued certificates of birth were also ill equipped to reckon "blood." Though the Census Bureau's standard certificates included blanks to indicate the race or nativity of a baby's parents, they did not have blanks to indicate tribal membership or degree of "blood." Federal officials repeatedly reminded superintendents and agency physicians to include this information on birth certificates. In May of 1928, for example, Assistant Commissioner for Indian Affairs E. B. Meritt wrote to J. A. Buntin, the superintendent of the Kiowa Agency, asking him to "kindly give the birth and death reports of your jurisdiction more careful attention." Meritt noted that Buntin omitted information from the birth certificates he sent to the office, including "the tribe and degree of blood" of both parents on the birth certificate. According to another letter on the matter, such information was "often omitted" by superintendents.[14] Indeed, the office frequently sent back birth certificates to the agencies requesting tribe and degree of blood.[15] In response to one such letter, the superintendent of the Carson Agency in Nevada sent back missing tribal and blood quantum information, noting for example that a baby born 19 December 1927 was "¾ Washoe Indian," while another born in March of that year was "full blood."[16] In order to record this on birth certificates, agency employees had to write fractional information on the forms' blanks for "race or color." That agents frequently failed to notate blood or tribal membership is not surprising, because the forms were created for general use, not for the administration of federal policies that differentiated among Indians based on a fictional quantum of blood. By contrast, when the office designed forms for its own use, it differentiated births in the precise fractional terms that mattered to its own record keeping and administration.

As the correspondence from the Office of Indian Affairs indicates, the failure to classify births according to race and the problems posed by racial ambiguity were more than a statistical annoyance. As the nineteenth century turned into the twentieth, accurate racial classification of births became important not simply to test theories of racial fitness but also to sort individuals according to the terms supplied both by state segregation and miscegenation laws and by federal legislation distributing land and other goods to Native Americans. The instability of racial classification collided with the bureaucratic imperative to classify people on forms, to literally put them in a box. On the one hand, early twentieth-century racial science held fast to the idea that race was a biological reality, while on the other hand, even proponents acknowledged that there was no scientific test to establish race. Racial ambiguity thus became an administrative problem that administrators of race-based policies tried to solve through recourse to genealogy, a knowledge of ancestry. This made birth certificates pivotal to the racial state.

Laws mandating race-specific privileges and penalties (regardless of status) were hardly new in the post–Civil War era, but many states revised such laws to make them more expansive and stringent. By the early twentieth century, sixteen states already had laws expressly requiring school segregation, while in six other states segregation was permitted but not required. Across the South, states mandated segregation on rail- and streetcars and in public accommodations such as hotels, saloons, and cemeteries. Twenty-six states and territories prohibited marriage between whites and other races. Many states also revised their definitions of "negro" or "colored" to include a much wider array of persons, reducing the blood quantum from one-fourth or one-eighth to one-sixteenth, for example.[17] For Native Americans, citizenship and access to land also depended on precise racial identity reckoned in fractions of "blood." Under the terms of the Dawes Act, individual allotments were held in trust for a period of twenty-five years, after which they became fee-simple patents that individuals could dispose of as they wished. Passed in 1906, the Burke Act modified the terms of allotment in ways that made blood quantum into a system for determining control of property and citizenship. The act provided that Indians who received an allotment would not become citizens until their trust period ended. At the same time, the act made the trust period more flexible: it gave the president the power to extend the period beyond twenty-five years for individuals but also to release any Indian deemed "competent and capable of managing his or her affairs" from the trust period early. As the act was made into policy by the Office of Indian Affairs, blood quantum became what historian Rose Stremlau calls a "filing system for human beings" to determine competency.[18]

During the 1910s, the commissioners of the office were eager to have as many Indians as possible declared competent, given fee-simple title, and thrust out of wardship into citizenship. To expedite the process, the office settled on a simple formula: anyone with less than one-half Indian "blood" would be given a patent before the trust period ended; anyone with one-half or more Indian blood would have to undergo a competency hearing. Though the so-called Five Civilized Tribes, who had reservations in Oklahoma, were governed by separate agreements with the U.S. government, there too the administration of Indian property was reduced to a blood quantum formula. In 1908, Congress "removed all restrictions (including those on homestead and the lands of minors) from the allotments of intermarried whites, freedmen, and mixed-blood Indians with less than half Indian blood." Those with one-half to three-quarters Indian blood could sell their surplus lands but not their homesteads. Finally, an order from the commissioner of Indian Affairs in 1919 removed all restrictions from allottees with one-half Indian blood.[19]

The reckoning of Native American blood that accompanied allotment functioned within and supported the system of racial segregation. As states redefined what it meant to be "Black," usually downward to ever-decreasing fractions including the infamous "one drop" rule, the allotment procedures of the Office of Indian Affairs differently registered Indians who were also of African descent. Among tribes who had held slaves—the Five Civilized Tribes—commissioners from the Office of Indian Affairs forced descendants of former slaves, no matter their degree of Indian "blood," to register on "freedman's rolls" rather than the "Indian rolls" that recorded quantum for purposes of allotment. Within a Jim Crow racial order, Black "blood" trumped both white and Indian ancestry. Just as anyone with African American ancestors could never be "white" according to the state laws governing access to schools, marriage, and other rights, so too no one with African ancestry could be fully "Indian" for the purposes of federal allotment and enrollment policy. When it came to land alienation, "freedmen" (no matter their actual ancestry) were allowed to sell land before those with one-half or more Indian blood.[20]

Allotment ended in 1934 with the passage of the Indian Reorganization

Act, but this did not end the federal government's investment in using blood quantum to administer policy. The act not only stopped the privatization of Indian land but also prohibited the alienation of previously allotted land, allowed the return of surplus lands to Indian tribes, enabled the secretary of the Interior to purchase land to enlarge reservations, and created a process through which tribes could formally organize for self-governance. It also provided educational loans to tribal members and called for preferential hiring of Native Americans in the Indian Service. At the same time, the act made blood quantum into the federal legal standard for defining an Indian. For purposes of gaining access to federal resources, an Indian was a member of a recognized tribe under federal jurisdiction, a descendant of such a person, or any person with one-half or more Indian "blood."[21] Unlike the logic of hypodescent that animated the legal structures of white supremacy, in which even one "drop" of Black "blood" made a person Black, Native Americans instead had to meet a minimum threshold in order to qualify as Indian. Narrow, blood-based definitions of Indian status reduced federal obligations to Indians by reducing the number of people to whom the government owed land, annuities, or other entitlements.[22]

Before the twentieth century, race was rarely a matter of documentation. Rather, race was treated by white Americans as self-evident: you knew a person's race by looking at them. Of course, race was frequently far from self-evident. Because antebellum state laws regulated rights and freedoms according to race, individual racial status was frequently contested in the courtroom. When pre–Civil War courts had to adjudicate identity, they relied on racial performance to settle matters. For a man, whiteness was demonstrated through participation in civic rituals: voting, militia mustering, and jury duty. For a woman, her whiteness was a function of adherence to codes of respectable womanhood, sexual purity most important among them. This was not simply a matter of juries using performative clues to reckon race because documentation was unavailable; judges and juries often ignored or overruled documentary evidence of ancestry. As Ariela Gross has argued, whites had an ideological commitment to race as performance. Rather than destabilizing race, the reliance on performative clues bolstered "racial common sense," the notion that race was something you could "tell by looking." And when performative criteria were used to establish racial classification, this brought communities into courtrooms to testify about the behaviors and associations of their neighbors. "This common sense of race," Gross writes, "kept the power to decide racial identity in local communities." Paradoxically, whites' commitment to the stability of racial identity led them to rely on reputation rather than documentation of ancestry. By contrast, an individual's status—whether free or slave—*was* a matter of documentation through evidence of ancestry, wills, bills of sale, and other legal instruments. Documentation, in other words, was more important for establishing freedom than it was for determining racial identity.[23]

In the postbellum era, the tools used to establish status—free or slave—were applied to race, which became a matter of bureaucratic and legal administration rather than just reputation or association. Though many courtroom battles over racial identification continued to turn on questions of racial performance and, more important in the era of segregation, racial association, outside the courtroom the routine administration of segregation also relied on documentation of ancestry and identity. Like the reformers of the U.S. Children's Bureau who believed that documentary proof of age was the best form of administration of child labor laws, some white supremacists put their faith in documents as the best proof of race. The use of documents to establish racial identity in a society structured by de jure segregation was part and parcel of the bureaucratization and modernization of white supremacy, the creation of what Peggy Pascoe has called a "racial state." Though racial classification and hierarchy were always creatures of the state, this shifted in the postbellum era as more legal and administrative power devolved from planter heads of household to the state, which at the same time was expanding its regulatory reach through the creation of new agencies such as boards of health.[24] The creation of systems of vital registration across the South also gave state functionaries, from registrars to clerks of court, the quasi-judicial power to determine race.

Just as the creation of systems of vital registration accompanied the creation and administration of the Dawes Act in Indian country, the enforcement of racial segregation accompanied the efforts of both federal agencies and civic organizations to improve birth and death certification. In 1912, for example, the *Atlanta Constitution* reported that members of the local chapter of the Daughters of the American Revolution were working to help pass a bill for compulsory birth registration in the state. Daughters of the American Revolution member Mrs. William Lawson explained that knowing one's genealogy was more than a matter of personal interest. In the South, it was particularly important, "owing to our large negro population." She described traveling in Latin America and seeing "the fearful mixture of races." Knowing that Georgians would like to put a stop to such racial mixing, she predicted that "the time will come when the need to prove your Anglo-Saxon descent will become imperative."[25] Likewise in 1917, Kentucky physician and public health reformer W. L. Heiser urged the men and women of his state to enforce compulsory birth registration lest "our grandchildren and great-grandchildren will be marrying persons having Negro blood in their veins."[26] Lawson and Heiser were correct: being able to prove one's whiteness was critical in order to access a whole host of race-based rights and privileges, and vital registration would be instrumental in the effort to maintain racial purity in the postbellum South.

Nowhere were the ideological links between vital registration and administration of the racial state made more apparent than in Virginia. In 1912 the state reformed its floundering registration system by creating a state board of health. The board included a Bureau of Vital Statistics (BVS) and a state registrar to enforce a new vital statistics registration law. The job of enforcement was given to Assistant Registrar Walter Plecker. Plecker became state registrar in 1914 and served in the post until 1946. During those years he used his position not only to collect and broadcast racial statistics but also to engage in racial purification through racial classification. Plecker and his efforts to police interracial marriages and to deny recognition to Virginia's Indigenous peoples are notorious. Yet the foundational role of vital documents and birth certificates in his machinations is less well understood. In Walter Plecker's hands, racial purity was the product of properly recorded births.

Plecker made common cause with fellow Virginians John Powell and Ernest Cox, founders of the Anglo-Saxon Clubs of America, to urge his state to pass the antimiscegenation Racial Integrity Act (RIA), which it did in 1924. The act defined "white," "Negro," and "Indian" not only for purposes of marriage but also for "school attendance and for all other purposes." In the original version of the RIA, Powell and Plecker included a provision that would have required every Virginian to have a racial registration document. This provision was stripped from the final bill, but the final act forbade marriages between whites and nonwhites except those possessing "one-sixteenth or less of the blood of the American Indian and . . . no other non-Caucasic blood." In 1930, the act was amended to "define a colored person as one with any ascertainable negro blood." This was the so-called one-drop rule. The RIA also directed the state registrar to prepare "registration certificates" to record the racial history of any person born in Virginia before 1912 who lacked a birth certificate. Writing in favor of the act, Plecker argued that though his office was already the "greatest force in the state today combating this condition [racially mixed marriages]," it would have the power to act with greater clarity and force under the terms of the RIA.[27]

Like Virginia, Georgia reformed its vital statistics laws in the 1910s, and it soon linked improvements in registration to improved racial classification in the service of racial purity. In 1927, Georgia's legislature adopted a racial integrity act that was very similar to Virginia's. In the run-up to the bill's passage, its sponsor, Assemblyman James C. Davis, explained that his bill included a racial registration provision so that the many Georgians who did not have their births registered could "apply to the local registrar . . . and present satisfactory proof, and be registered under the terms of the act." Such registration would fix both the applicant's age and race. Other supporters of the bill were pleased that it would substitute a one-drop definition of Blackness for the current standard, which defined as white anyone with one-eighth or less of "negro blood." By contrast, the new one-drop rule, combined with better state record keeping, promised to "keep all mulattoes and their descendants out of the white class forever; the permanent record of their antecedents will prevent their ever graduating from the colored to the white class."[28] For the architects of racial purity, vital registration was a critical tool—only by correctly recording the past could the future be secured.

While several states linked segregation, racial classification, and the reform of vital statistics collection, Virginia's Plecker is the best-known example of relentless bureaucratic dedication to ensuring the "correct" racial classification on vital statistics documents.[29] Plecker's renown not only is due to the fact that he was the public face of Virginia's now infamous RIA but also owes to the fact that, unlike many other state registrars who labored to enforce racial classification, Plecker both publicized his work and left records. Plecker was a staunch eugenicist, white supremacist, and colonizationist who promoted the beliefs of authors such as Madison Grant and Lothrop Stoddard whenever he could. Like these contemporaries, Plecker believed that whiteness was imperiled not only by immigration but, closer to home, by miscegenation and racial passing. In a speech before the American Public Health Association in 1924, entitled "Virginia's Attempt to Adjust the Color Problem," Plecker outlined his views. "The white race in this land is the foundation upon which rests its civilization," he explained, "and is responsible for the leading position which we occupy amongst the nations of the world." It had been a grave error to bring Africans to the New World, Plecker argued, because Europeans and

Africans were "materially divergent . . . in morals, mental powers, and cultural fitness." Whites would be brought down by contact with Blacks, while Blacks could never be raised to the level of whites; racial amalgamation would therefore produce an inferior race and threaten the downfall of the nation itself. Plecker believed not just that the negro and white races should remain separate, but also that in the Southeast, those who claimed to be "Indian" were really descendants of African Americans who were trying to, as he put it, "pass over" into the white race. Indeed, he believed that there were no true Indians in Virginia at all, and that anyone who claimed the mantle was simply trying to cover up Black blood going back generations. Plecker granted that though some in Virginia might be descended from the state's original inhabitants, all such were also at least partially descended from illegitimate unions between white men and Black female slaves and thus had to be classified as "negro" under the terms of the RIA.[30] Plecker therefore saw his job not only as making certain that all those with "negro" blood were identified as Black in order ensure white racial purity but also as stamping out "Indian" as a possible racial category in Virginia.

As soon as the RIA was law, Plecker set to work. As Plecker explained in a letter to Powell, he was "impressed with the immensity and importance of the job which the legislature has given me to do." Likewise, Plecker's employer, the Virginia State Board of Health, immediately recognized that the work of the state's BVS was "enlarged" by the RIA.[31] Plecker began with an information campaign. In July 1924, Plecker issued instructions to state registrars for enforcing the terms of the new law. In the case of anyone seeking a racial registration certificate, Plecker admonished local registrars that they "must be sure that there is no trace of colored blood in any one offering to register as a white person." Likewise, registrars must take "equal care" when registering new births or when issuing a marriage license. Plecker's instructions reminded registrars that the state's documentary records might be of service in these tasks: the state had marriage records dating back to 1853 and birth and death records covering the years between 1853 and 1896, so registrars need not accept either racial self-identification or racial reputation in order to classify a baby's race, make a new racial registration, or decide the legality of a marriage.[32] Likewise, in a form letter to the state's doctors—who, as birth attendants, might fill out birth certificates—Plecker detailed the requirements of the new state law and reminded doctors that they had an important role to play in carrying it out. "You are requested to use care not to report births of children of 'Mixed' or 'Issue' parents as whites," Plecker wrote. In order to avoid the "serious problem" of racial misidentification, Plecker told physicians that if they did not know a child's race, "use an interrogation mark (?) and write to us privately." Plecker wrote a similar form letter to county clerks, the men and women who might file birth certificates or might use them to see that the marriage licenses they issued did not violate the RIA's miscegenation provisions.[33]

Plecker and his allies also took it upon themselves to spread the word about the dangers of racial mixing and the promise of the legislative solution provided by Virginia's RIA. Plecker wrote to registrars in surrounding states urging them to pass their own RIA so that families could not move from another state to Virginia in an effort to illegitimately register themselves and their offspring as white. He corresponded with legislators in states from Ohio to Massachusetts and with U.S. senators, advising them on the main features of Virginia's law and its bureaucratic administration through his office. He took his show on the road, speaking before the Southern Medical Association and the American Public Health Association. He offered up the services of his compatriots John Powell and Major Cox to come and speak to state legislatures on the subject. Like the Census Bureau and Children's Bureau officials who promoted uniform state laws for vital statistics collection, Plecker dreamed of a day when every state in the nation would possess a uniform law for racial purity.[34]

But Plecker also believed that the success of the law did not depend on state officials alone. In the *Virginia Health Bulletin*, Plecker explained that "the Bureau of Vital Statistics, Clerks who issue marriage licenses and the school authorities are the barriers placed by this law between the danger and the safety of the Commonwealth. The task of the Bureau of Vital Statistics is a great one." But he also urged ordinary citizens to do their part by making sure that all births in their family were registered and by taking advantage of the law's allowance for retroactive registration. Not only would thorough birth registration make administration of the RIA easier, but also the revenue generated by the twenty-five-cent registration fees would provide a windfall to the BVS. The bureau would in turn use the money to purchase new filing equipment, print new forms, hire a new clerk to process forms under the RIA, and—most important—index the state's nineteenth-century birth, death, and marriage records. "If these can be properly indexed they will afford an invaluable source of reference for establishing color in many cases," Plecker explained.[35] For just as W. Z. Ripley had recognized in his complaint many decades earlier, racial classification was as much about the past as about the present, and it therefore required genealogical knowledge—information that, if families were unable or untrusted to supply, the state's own records could provide.

For Plecker, ensuring accurate registration of vital events meant investigating families' histories. Or at least some families' histories. To that end, Plecker and his clerks scoured registration records as they came in and took great pains to map the genealogies of families they believed were trying to pass as white or Indian when they were actually "negro." Like the racial regime of allotment in the federal Office of Indian Affairs, Plecker, too, used African ancestry to override "white" or "Indian" blood. Plecker identified several areas of the state where he believed that "families of mixed blood" tried to pass themselves off as white, Native American, or a mixture of the two. With the help of local clerks of court, registrars, and commissioners of revenue, the BVS focused its attention on Amherst, Rockbridge, and Augusta Counties as sites of centuries-old racial mixing. In communications with the public, Plecker warned that perhaps as many as 20,000 "near white people" resided in these areas, sometimes sending their children to white schools and marrying white people. Though such families were able at times to get their offspring registered at birth as white or Indian, Plecker believed that all of them were properly classed as "negro" because of their descent. In order to protect the integrity of the white race, Plecker and his clerks in the BVS compiled a list of surnames from families they believed were racially mixed and carefully checked any birth, marriage, and death records that were sent to their office under these names. Plecker also distributed this list of surnames, organized by county, to all the state's registrars, physicians, health officers, nurses, school superintendents, and clerks of court, urging them to "report all known or suspicious cases" to him along with "names, ages, parents, and as much other information as possible."[36]

Plecker asked for "as much other information as possible" because he intended to exhaustively document the racial genealogy of Virginia's "mixed blood" families. As Plecker explained in a letter to a fellow physician, because there was no blood test for race, the only proof was "by genealogical records."[37] Plecker used a combination of records to establish family trees for the surnames he considered suspect. He had birth and death records covering the period 1853–96 and marriage records beginning in 1853, all of which listed the race of registered parties. During the 1930s, Virginia was one of the states where the Works Progress Administration indexed vital registration documents, which boosted RIA enforcement by making old records easier to search. Plecker was also delighted to discover the work of the pathbreaking

African American historian Carter G. Woodson who, in 1925, published the book *Free Negro Heads of Families in the United States in 1830* under the auspices of the Association for the Study of Negro Life and History. Plecker distributed information from Woodson's book to clerks in Virginia counties, asking them to "look them over and tell us all of the names that now figure as Indian or white" but who were listed by Woodson as "free negroes" in 1830. "We believe that this will be of great value to us in establishing the fact that many of these people were in 1830 considered free negroes, who are now claiming to be pure Indian and white blood." Plecker and his clerks also used other state and federal records that, while not vital registration documents, categorized enumerated persons by race. These included tax rolls stretching back to 1785, federal census records, and rolls of eligible voters created during Reconstruction by the "army of occupation." This latter record Plecker considered particularly damning since it was an act of self-identification intended to grant a privilege. "Practically all of these people who are now calling themselves Indians rushed in to register themselves as negroes in order to become voters," he explained. It was only now, when being a "negro" was tied to a prohibition rather than a privilege, that such families wanted to be considered "Indian."[38]

Plecker used this array of records to construct genealogies of suspect families, which he kept on file in his office. In an annual report, Plecker crowed that while his bureau was established "only in view of securing and compiling birth and death statistics," under the RIA he was "making it of equal or even greater value as a clearing house for assembling of the family and genealogical records of the population." He was assisted in this by Eva Kelley, a clerk in his office who, according to a visitor to the BVS from the U.S. Census Bureau, "devotes practically full time to research into family histories." She compiled family trees and searched them when the surnames of "mixed blood" families came across her desk on registration documents. Plecker praised Kelley as "a racial genealogical expert never equaled," bragging that she could trace "the racial pedigree of practically all of our pseudo-Indians, family by family, back to the free negro list of 1830." This was the date of Woodson's lists of free negroes, not by coincidence. On the eve of his retirement, Plecker claimed that Kelley's files were "unequalled" in any other state or nation in the world. Without a blush, Plecker told John Collier, the federal commissioner of Indian Affairs, that even "Hitler's genealogical study of the Jews is not more complete."[39]

Like the administrators and agents of the Children's Bureau who used birth certificates to transform age into a documentary fact, Plecker also believed that documents could supplant informal knowledge—in this case physical appearance or racial reputation—with a more objective and durable truth. However people might look, whatever they might say about themselves, and however they might be regarded by their neighbors, the documentary record would tell the truth about a person's lineage. In *Connor v. Shields*, the first case to come before state courts under the RIA, the court had to decide whether James Connor and Dorothy Johns could be married. The Amherst County clerk of court had denied their application for a marriage license on the grounds that James Connor was white and Dorothy Johns was not. In writing to another local clerk about the case, Plecker explained that "I had all of the Amherst county birth records and we showed conclusively that she was descended from the Amherst family of Johns, all of who are listed in the old records as of colored descent." Plecker wrote to the commonwealth attorney trying the case to offer "certified copies of these birth and death certificates" as evidence. Judge Holt, who presided in the case, accepted the records Plecker provided rather than the testimony of Johns's family members, but he clearly saw the damage that using documents to dislodge racial reputation could cause. Just as replacing testimony with documentary proof of age had been, this move was legally innovative, epistemologically radical, and socially disruptive. Judge Holt, newspapers reported, felt that this new regime would "cause untold trouble" by disrupting centuries of racial reputation with a stringent new definition of race and its proof.[40]

"Old records" were critical to Plecker's efforts to create and maintain racial purity because, just like opponents of child labor who believed that a document from the past was more reliable than a claim in the present, Plecker believed that the state's older documents were necessary to verify new acts of registration. But whereas opponents of child labor believed that parents had an incentive to lie when they brought their children to an employer's office, Plecker believed that parents had an incentive to lie at the moment of registration itself: mixed-race parents would want their children to pass as Indian or white and so would try to file false birth certificates. In his testimony before a Rockbridge County court in another marriage case, *Sorrells v. Shields*, Plecker explained this view. After presenting the court with a register of births from the mid-nineteenth century, Plecker testified that "I consider these old records more accurate as to some of these people than some of the more recent ones." This was because "the birth certificates that are coming in now from persons whose record in the past shows they were colored ancestry are coming in now from mid-wives as white."[41] While midwives in the present might accept the false claims of parents, documentation of ancestors as nonwhite was unassailable. By using supporting documentation to vet racial claims on new registrations, Plecker believed that he could preserve the effectiveness of vital documents as a tool in the administration of white supremacy. Plecker's office therefore used this genealogical method both to create racially valid vital registration documents in the present and to use other kinds of official records to "correct" past registration.

As in the case of age verification, the epistemological supremacy of documents over testimony to establish race was new, and courts did not always recognize the legal status of state records. This frustrated Plecker to no end, and in railing against it, he expressed his view that documents were the superior means to establish legal fact. In a 1938 letter regarding a miscegenation case being tried in the courts, Plecker complained that judges sometimes ignored the "old records" in favor of testimony from local residents who would claim that alleged violators of the RIA had always been known as white or Indian. "Living witnesses seem to have more influence over the court than dead ones," he noted. This was in spite of the fact that "the dead ones were duly appointed officials and making statements under oath." These "dead" witnesses were, of course, the old records themselves. Plecker explained that under Virginia's old system of birth registration, records were entered by commissioners of revenue who went house to house assessing properties for taxes and inquiring about any new births, which they recorded by race in neat columns. Each commissioner swore an oath to execute his duties to the "best of his skill," and by statute the records that commissioners gave to clerks were considered prima facie evidence of the facts contained therein. The statute that created the BVS gave it legal custody of these documents, and thus Plecker believed that there was an unbroken line of legal authority that connected the original creation of the records with his office and his use of them to corroborate present vital registration.[42]

The relationship between documents and authority was particularly fraught because the state's interpretation of its registration laws essentially allowed low-level state agents—registrars of vital statistics, county clerks, and even midwives and doctors—to call into question the racial identity of anyone using a vital statistics form. Because such officers had to fill in the "race" or "color" of a corpse, newborn baby, or applicant for marriage, they became, as Peggy Pascoe has written, "the gatekeepers of white supremacy."[43] While registrars, clerks, and medical providers could accept a person's racial self-identification, they could also question it. Once the question of a person's racial identity was raised, she would have to provide affirmative proof of her race—a task that could array her own claims against whatever Plecker and other state officials could dig up from the "old records." This was true even before the RIA was passed. Indeed, as Plecker noted in an annual report, the 1912 law establishing vital registration under the Virginia State Department of Health both required vital documents to record race and defined a person as white only if she had fifteen-sixteenths or more of "white blood." This meant that from the beginning, the BVS had to act "in a judicial, as well as a clerical capacity, in numerous instances when the color [of a person] became a question of dispute." Indeed, Plecker reported to a state senator that he changed several birth certificates from white to colored in a single "mountain county" after securing "additional information" about the families in question.[44]

The judicial capacity of registration officials expanded under the RIA. Just after the new law took effect, A. T. Shields, the clerk of court in Rockbridge County who would later go on to deny a marriage license to Dorothy Johns and James Connor, wrote to the Virginia attorney general, John Saunders, seeking clarification about his duties. As clerk of court, he issued marriage licenses. Would the applicants for a license be required to swear an affidavit that they were both white? Saunders replied to Shields that no affidavits were necessary in ordinary cases, but the law specified that when a clerk had a "reasonable cause" to believe one party was not white, he could ask for "satisfactory proof." The standard of proof was whatever "will satisfy his [the clerk's] own mind upon the point." As Saunders explained, "the law makes the officer issuing the license the judge of the question." As the prosecutor, judge, and jury, the clerk could "require such evidence, either written or oral, as he may deem necessary."[45] While Saunders's interpretation did not require clerks such as Shields to demand documentary proof, clerks, registrars, and birth attendants worked in tandem with the BVS, where Plecker interpreted "satisfactory proof" in documentary terms and employed his genealogical methods to establish racial lineage going back generations.

The BVS's genealogical method was evident in its correspondence with the state's doctors and midwives, particularly those who practiced in the areas of the state that Plecker considered racially suspect. In August 1924, for example, Plecker wrote to Dr. Robert Glasgow in Lexington, Virginia, to inquire about a birth he had registered in March of the same year. The baby's surname (Beverly), the surname of the midwife who attended the birth (Hartless), and the place of birth (Amherst County) all suggested to Plecker that the baby might be improperly classed as white. Plecker explained to Glasgow that the baby's surname "is that of a numerous family of mixed races living in that County," and he went on to explain that the family "are probably a mixture of three Cherokee Indians of North Carolina passing back home from a visit to Washington" who remained in Virginia "and mated with white women, their children afterwards mating with negroes" in a pattern that continued over generations. The midwife's surname was also "one which appears frequently among these people," adding further suspicion to the case. Plecker pleaded with Glasgow to "take the proper steps to see that these people are not classed as white unless they are known absolutely to be such."[46]

Plecker sent similarly threatening letters to midwives. In correspondence with midwife Josie Hartless (who delivered the Beverly baby in question), Plecker questioned her classification of a baby from the Floyd family as white. He asked Hartless whether the baby's father, Orie Lee Floyd, was "from the same connection as the Irish-Creek and Amherst County people of that name." If so, Plecker explained, "even though he may be white in appearance," in actuality his family history told another story, one of mixed blood. This meant that neither he nor his baby can "be considered white." And in case Hartless had any mind to protect her neighbors in their self-identification as white, Plecker reminder her that the BVS was enforcing the RIA and that "under the new law it is a penitentiary offence to make a willfully false statement as to color."[47]

From his post at the BVS, Plecker imagined that he could use the registration machinery of the state to create and enforce racial purity. For this to work, doctors and midwives would have to put the correct race on their reports. As his letters indicate, Plecker believed that some birth attendants misreported race, intentionally or not. Not only did Plecker chide doctors and midwives that they might go to jail if they falsely registered mixed-race babies as white, but he also used other tools at his disposal. His office received and filed birth certificates and also controlled their distribution. Plecker therefore refused to issue new birth certificates when he believed that the racial identification on them was wrong. In a letter to Dr. Vaden, Plecker explained that he would not issue a birth certificate for the baby of Joseph Hartless and Nora Ogden until Vaden could confirm that Joseph was actually white. Plecker suspected him of racial impurity because he was, like the other births that Plecker flagged, from a suspect lineage, as indicated by his surname and his place of residence, Amherst County.[48]

When appealing to birth attendants or refusing to issue certificates failed him, Plecker sometimes appealed directly to suspect families themselves. Plecker's October 1929 letter to Pal Beverly showcases this tactic and reveals his relentless genealogical pursuits. Pal Beverly claimed that he was white, but Plecker did not believe him. In order to try to settle the question, Plecker wrote to Beverly asking him to name his father, grandfather, and great-grandfather. Beverly refused, so Plecker marshalled the state's documentary record to prove to Beverly that he was not in fact white. Beverly's marriage license listed his parents' names, Adolphus and Leander Beverly. Likewise, Leander Beverly's death certificate listed her husband as Adolphus. The marriage license for Adolphus and Leander "gives him as colored." That same marriage license named Adolphus's father as Frederick Beverly. Frederick, Plecker reported, was born before the state started recording births in 1853, but tax records from the nineteenth century listed him as a "free negro." Several other Beverlys were also listed as "free negro" in the same record books. Plecker also claimed that "further evidence in our office" showed that Frederick's mother—Pal's grandmother—was Betty Buck, a slave who had been freed by her owner along with her mulatto sons (Frederick among them) and sent to live in Amherst. This genealogy, "secured from our old records, from tax books, from U.S. census reports, and from the positive knowledge of old persons now living," was proof enough for Plecker. "I am notifying you," he admonished Pal Beverly, "that you can have no other rating in our office under the Act of 1924 than that of a mulatto or colored man." Plecker closed by reminding Beverly that it was a crime to register himself or any family members as white or to aid and abet Amherst County midwives in so doing.[49]

In cases such as that of Pal Beverly and his children, the "old records" supported Plecker's claim that the family failed the one-drop test established by the RIA. But in cases in which a family or some of its members had previously been registered as white or Indian, the situation was more difficult. The BVS wanted to stop such families from registering new children as white, and it did not want to issue "white" birth, death, or marriage certificates to families it believed had been registered as "white" under old rules but who would be "colored" under the RIA. When birth certificates had been filed many years earlier under a different set of rules for racial classification, Plecker's office could not refuse to issue the certificates it believed incorrectly identified persons as "white" or "Indian" when they were actually mixed with "negro" blood. In those cases, the BVS issued the certificate but appended a letter of "warning" to those "believed to be incorrectly recorded as to color or race" (figure 6.1). This letter at length cited from histories of Virginia alleging to show that there were no pure-blood Indians in the state going back as far as the 1840s; all were mixed with "negro" blood. Therefore, the bearer of the certificate to which the letter was appended, though he or she may be listed as "Indian, Mixed Indian, Mixed, Melungeon, Issue, [or] Free Issue," should be regarded as "negro or colored." Lest there be any confusion, the letter ended by stating that the information contained therein "is intended to apply to the individual whose birth is reported on the [attached] certificate."[50] Plecker usually also gave detailed genealogical information on the back of the certificate, citing "old records" that showed that the bearer's ancestors had been registered as colored in previous state documents. Beyond publicly declaring that the BVS did not consider the bearer of the birth certificate to be either white or Indian, Plecker also made certain that his office's genealogical evidence was bound into its own permanent volumes of birth records. This practice ensured that in the future, whenever a clerk searched for a birth record that Plecker believed deserved reclassification, she would find the genealogical evidence that prior generations of BVS clerks had assembled.[51]

Though he was unable to change the faces of the older birth certificates whose racial identification he believed was fraudulent, Plecker's rearguard solution raised legal problems. The probative value of a birth certificate lay in its *inability* to be changed or altered from the day it had been made. Plecker clearly believed that stemming the tide of racial passing, and hence racial amalgamation, was a matter of critical importance. Yet he knew that his appendices, though they did not alter the faces of the certificates, were on shaky legal ground. The BVS was challenged about the practice in the 1940s by several families. In one case, siblings Lenard and Cora Branham hired a lawyer to write to Plecker's office on their behalf, demanding that he issue their birth certificates as "Indian" without appended commentary on the back. The certificates that had been issued by the BVS explained that the office "does not accept the racial classification 'Indian' on this certificate as correct" because, as the note went on, Lenard and Cora's parents had been married "under a colored license" and their grandparents "are colored and descendants of . . . free negroes." J. R. Tucker, the attorney for the Branham siblings, argued that the state laws governing vital registration required Plecker's office to issue a certified copy of a birth certificate on demand but did not authorize him to editorialize or act in a judicial capacity. "I find no where in the law any provision which authorizes the Registrar to constitute himself judge and jury for the purpose of determining the race of a child born and authorizing him to alter the record as filed." In his reply to the Branhams' attorney, Plecker refused to

WARNING.—To be attached to the backs of birth or death certificates of those believed to be incorrectly recorded as to color or race.

Howe in his History of Virginia, 1845, Pages 349-350 says of the Mattaponi and Pamunkey Indians of King William County: "Their Indian character is nearly extinct by intermixture with the whites and negroes."

Encyclopaedia Britannica, Eleventh Edition, Volume 14, Pages 460 and 464, says of Chickahominy Indians, "No pure bloods left, considerable negro admixture," and of the Pamunkeys, "All mixed-bloods; some negro mixture."

The Handbook of American Indians (Bulletin 30), Bureau of American Ethnology, under the heading "Croatan Indians," says: "The theory of descent from the colony may be regarded as baseless, but the name itself serves as a convenient label for a people who combine in themselves the blood of the wasted native tribes, the early colonists or forest rovers, the runaway slaves or other negroes, and probably also of stray seamen of the Latin races from coasting vessels in the West Indian or Brazilian trade.

Across the line in South Carolina are found a people, evidently of similar origin, designated "Redbones." In portions of western North Carolina and eastern Tennessee are found the so-called "Melungeons" (probably from French melange, "mixed") or "Portuguese," apparently an offshoot from Croatan proper, and in Delaware are found the "Moors." All of these are local designations for people of mixed race with an Indian nucleus differing in no way from the present mixed-blood remnants known as Pamunkey, Chickahominy, and Nansemond Indians in Virginia, excepting in the more complete loss of their identity. In general, the physical features and complexion of the persons of this mixed stock incline more to the Indian than to the white or negro."

The same under "Mixed-bloods," says; "The Pamunkey, Chickahominy, Marshpee, Narraganset, and Gay Head remnants have much negro blood, and conversely there is no doubt that many of the broken coast tribes have been completely absorbed into the negro race."

In 1843, 144 freeholders of King William County in a petition to the legislature to abolish the two Indian reservations of that county, B. 1207, State Library, say: "There are two parcels or tracts of land situated within the said County, on which a number of persons are now living, all of whom by the laws of Virginia, would be deemed and taken to be free mulattoes, in any Court of Justice; as it is believed they all have one-fourth or more of negro blood; and as proof of this, they would rely on the generally admitted fact, that not one individual can be found among them, of whose grandfathers and grandmothers, one or more is or was not a negro; which proportion of negro blood constitutes a free mulatto—see R. C. Vol. 1st page." These conclusions are confirmed by responsibe citizens now living in that county December 1927.

A. H. Estabrook and Ivan E. McDougle in their book, "Mongrel Virginians," 1926, describe a group of mixed breeds centering in Amherst County and extending to the Irish Creek valley in Rockbridge, and to other surrounding counties, known locally as "Issue" or "Free Issue." They say, Page 15: "These freed negroes mated with them-selves or the half-breed Indians in the County."

Therefore:—In consideration of the above and other similar evidence relating to all, or practically all groups claiming to be "Indians," the Virginia Bureau of Vital Statistics accepts the belief that there are no descendants of Virginia Indians claiming or reputed to be Indians, who are unmixed with negro blood, and in accordance with the requirements of the Vital Statistics and Racial Integrity laws that births and deaths be correctly recorded as to race, classifies as negro or colored, persons either or both of whose parents are recorded on the birth or death certificate or marriage license, or who are themselves recorded as Indian, Mixed Indian, Mixed, Melungeon, Issue, Free Issue, or other similar non-white terms.

The Bureau of Vital Statistics has consented to accept an interrogation mark (?) as indication that the writer of the certificate considered the individual as probably of colored origin, but preferred not stating the fact, to appear in the local record.

This warning will apply also to any who may be incorrectly recorded as white, when known to be of negro, Malay, Mongolian, West Indian, East Indian, Mexican, Filipino or other non-white mixture.

The above statement of information now available, is given for the guidance of those to follow us in this work, and is intended to apply to the individual whose birth is reported on the certificate Vol.   No.   to which this is attached.

Figure 6.1. "Warning.—To be attached to the backs of birth or death certificates of those believed to be incorrectly recorded as to color or race" (ca. 1930)

This was an all-purpose statement that the Virginia Bureau of Vital Statistics attached to the backs of birth certificates it believed contained an incorrect racial designation. The bureau claimed that a history of racial mixing between Indians and Black Americans demonstrated that there were no real Indians in the state of Virginia. Source: Courtesy of the Library of Virginia.

remove the explanatory note. He argued that "the law does not permit us to give the truth on the certificates but seems to compel me as State Registrar to certify to what I know to be absolutely false."[52] In other words, the BVS was not allowed to change the faces of the certificates it issued, yet it was also duty bound to enforce the RIA by making proper racial classifications. Appending a note to the back was Plecker's path through the loophole.

But the Branhams' attorney was correct: Plecker had no legal authority to change the certificates, even by appendix. In 1942, the Virginia attorney general's office advised Plecker as much and the U.S. Census Bureau agreed with the state on this point. "If a certificate with the facts on the back is refused," Plecker complained to a friend, his office was compelled to give a copy of the original without commentary. "That removes our last defense against those whose certificates have already been filed and accepted, and we are now compelled to declare them Indian or white as the case may be." The only hope, he concluded, was to get the legislature to amend the law to positively authorize the BVS to issue such statements, thus clearing up the legal ambiguity in favor of correcting racial misclassification on certificates issued before the RIA took effect. "In reality," Plecker admitted, "I have been doing a good deal of bluffing." He admitted to his friend that while he had been publicly declaring that the RIA required him to see that all vital documents contained correct racial classification, and thus he was duty bound to find a solution for older documents that contained misclassification, he had known "all the while that it could not be legally sustained." The flare-up over the Branhams' birth certificates and the attorney general's subsequent opinion was "the first time my hand has absolutely been called."[53] In 1944, the Virginia legislature gave Plecker the grant of positive authority he required when it passed House Bill 55. The law required the state registrar to "enter upon the backs of the original certificate and certified copy" any information he had regarding "the true race of the person or person named in the original certificate."[54] Now when Plecker acted as judge and jury, it was no bluff.

With the 1944 legislation in place, the chain linking documentary authority to racial classification was complete. Under the RIA, Plecker and his clerks could use genealogical methods to ensure that all new registrations adhered to the one-drop rule, and under the terms of House Bill 55, he and his clerks could with impunity use the same methods to reclass "fraudulent" registration from the past. Now all documents under the purview of the BVS would be true because they were subject to genealogical controls. In reality, however, when race was contested on vital documents, registrars such as Plecker never relied solely on documentary evidence to establish race. But their power as registrars meant that they could transform racial reputation into documentary fact at will.

Though Walter Plecker maintained that there was no scientific test that could prove a person's race, when his own documentary trail went cold, he often made recourse to other markers of race besides the genealogical record. For example, as a eugenicist who believed in Mendel's law of inheritance, Plecker maintained that nonwhite "blood" might show itself in some members of a family even if most appeared to be white. In a 1935 letter, Plecker sought to track the racial identity of members of the Ogden family, the children of which had recently been expelled from a white school on suspicion of being colored. He wrote to Lizzie Ware, a local registrar in Amherst County, asking her to have Mrs. Ogden fill out forms detailing her ancestry, but he also asked Ware to describe the appearance of the Ogdens. "Do any of the family have any negro characteristics," he wondered, explaining that "frequently these show in one member of the family and not in another."[55] Because Plecker was disposed to believe that "near-whites" were trying to pass as white and would use documents to do so, he was prepared to believe appearances when it served his cause.

He was also prepared to transform racial reputation into fact when it served the cause of racial purity. In 1940, Plecker's office received a petition from citizens of Pittsylvania County asking that children of the King family be barred from attending white schools because, as the petition maintained, they were actually mixed race. In a letter to the county school board chairman, Plecker explained that his office could find a birth certificate for only one of the children. But he urged the chairman to use his own eyes, and local knowledge, to classify the children as colored. "It is quite simple," he explained, "for a local community to handle such cases as they have the children before them for inspection and are usually familiar with all the facts and the parentage of the children." In other words, if the children looked mixed race, or if people in the community believed that one or both of their parents were nonwhite, they could be excluded from white schools based on reputation rather than documentation. Plecker went further, however, and reported that the BVS would enter the citizens' petition into their own records, and "upon that information we will designate any of these children found in our records as colored regardless of the statement of the attendant who reported these births." With this, Plecker transformed the racial reputation of the Kings—whom their white neighbors regarded as mixed race—into a documentary fact that would henceforth be prima facie true.[56]

The role of rumor and reputation in the "correction" of vital statistics documents is evident in Louisiana as well as in Virginia. As in Virginia, the practice of changing a person's racial designation on birth, death, and marriage certificates was common in Louisiana. Indeed, as Plecker wrote to the state's head of public health statistics, "your office is the only one in the Country, or, I may say, in the world, which seems in sympathy with our efforts." Louisiana law empowered registrars to amend vital documents, and this, coupled with a court ruling that there must be "no doubt" about race in suits to change state documents, gave registrars a powerful set of tools for policing racial lines.[57] As far as records show, registrars without exception turned Louisianans from white to colored. The city records office in New Orleans and the state board of health's BVS both maintained "flag lists" of surnames that they believed belonged to families that were likely to try to illegitimately pass themselves off as white. Naomi Drake, who in 1949 became a supervisor and deputy registrar of vital statistics in Louisiana's BVS, led the charge, and during her tenure the bureau challenged the original racial classification on more than 4,000 birth certificates and 1,000 death certificates. Drake was fired in 1965, but as late as 1977, the state bureau employed two full-time clerks whose sole duties were to investigate racial classification.[58]

Once changed by a registrar or her deputy, the changed certificate, rather than the one originally filed, became prima facie true. In the case of *Soulet v. City of New Orleans* (1957), Estelle Soulet, née Rodi, sued to have the race on her father's death certificate changed from colored to white. When Steve Rodi died in 1953, the attending physician filed a death certificate that classified him as white, and the preparation and burial of his body were performed by professionals who testified that they do "not perform such services for Negroes." Several months after Steve Rodi's death, officials in the New Orleans BVS "obtained evidence which convinced them that Rodi was in fact a Negro and not white," and they changed his racial classification accordingly. Because such changes were permitted under Louisiana's vital statistics laws, Rodi's new designation as colored became prima facie true. Thus in Soulet's suit on behalf of her father, it was not the state that bore the burden of proving the justness of its change but Soulet, who bore the burden of proving that there was "no doubt" that her father was actually white. Of course, the state was able to produce enough collateral documentation of Rodi's relatives to introduce doubt about his race. Soulet's plea to revert to the original classification was denied.[59]

Soulet made it clear that documents had more power than racial reputation or self-authentication, but they also made it abundantly clear that the privileged epistemological status of vital registration documents made the truth a function of power. For while documentary evidence of race was supposed to be superior to reputation or other kinds of evidence, in practice genres of evidence blurred together. In deciding to change Steve Rodi's race from white to "negro," for example, both Naomi Drake and Anthony Ciaccio, the state registrar of vital statistics, testified that they had each spent time in Pointe à la Hache, Louisiana, where Steve Rodi and many of his relatives came from. There, Drake testified, she had not only "checked various records" but also "interviewed numerous people." Ciaccio reported that he had "made several trips to Pointe-a-la-Hache, interviewed numerous people," and became convinced that Rodi was not white.[60] Thus what became prima facie truth because of its appearance on a vital records document was established in part through local reputation. But unlike Estelle Soulet, state officials such as Drake and Ciaccio had the power to turn reputation into documentation. And once racial reputation had become documentation, Louisiana's rule that there must be "no doubt" in suits for a change of racial classification meant that birth certificates were essentially protected by a standard higher than that used in criminal courts, where reasonable doubt was exculpatory.[61]

Whether state registrars acted with legal authority or not, the consequences of using vital documents to adjudicate racial identification were profound. In Virginia, two of the most important institutions that birth certificates helped to segregate were education and marriage. But the power of birth registration went far beyond the simple ability to administer segregation. Because Plecker was empowered not just to provide information to institutions about what existing birth registration documents said but also to alter documents in accordance with his office's genealogical research, the BVS possessed the ability to redefine the racial landscape of Virginia by denying access to the racial category of "Indian."

Documentary control of education worked in several ways. First, the Virginia state superintendent of public instruction recommended to all school districts that they ask pupils to provide proof of birth registration in order to enroll in school.[62] As more towns, cities, and counties complied, the racial identification on the certificates functioned as a gate that funneled children into either white or colored schools. Second, Plecker sought to ensure that no children "incorrectly" registered as white or Indian before the RIA took effect were permitted to attend white schools, and he used genealogy to scrub the record, and the schools, clean. Just as Plecker used his list of surnames in certain counties to warn local clerks, registrars, and birth attendants not to falsely register these families as white, so too he warned school authorities not to allow children from such families to attend white schools.[63] In addition to providing general letters of warning, however, Plecker's office also wrote in specific cases to school authorities. When the BVS discovered nonwhite "blood" in a family line, Plecker wrote, "we write to the Clerk and School Superintendent giving them they [sic] information which we have."[64] In one such case, Plecker wrote to a superintendent in Lexington warning him that the Tyree children, who had been allowed to attend the white school, were actually part of a "large group of mixed breeds of negro extraction." Plecker also wrote directly to Mrs. Tyree to tell her that she could neither receive birth certificates for her children marking them as white nor enroll them in white schools.[65]

Third, the BVS responded to requests for information from local school authorities and used its documents as evidence in contested cases. Plecker encouraged schools to bring questionable cases to his attention, at which point his genealogical machinery would produce the evidence required. "We have usually been able," Plecker reported, "to furnish district superintendents the facts sought by them" and thus prevent "near-white families of negro descent" from entering white schools. This assistance even extended to school officials in neighboring states where Virginians and their children had moved.[66] Sometimes it was not school authorities but others in the community who sought Plecker's assistance in ensuring complete school segregation. Such had been the case in Pittsylvania County, where the group of fifteen residents had petitioned the BVS to help them keep the children of the King family out of their white public school.[67]

BVS vigilance paid off as families who sought to enroll children in "white" schools were denied entrance. This was not just a matter of sorting new enrollees into the right schools, but it also involved reshuffling the racial deck according to the racial definitions of the RIA and the genealogical information provided by the BVS. Indeed, as soon as the law took effect, some children who had been attending white schools "for several years" were suspended "pending an investigation as to whether they were white or colored."[68] In 1925, Plecker responded to a letter from Kate Robinson "begging that your children be allowed to go to the white schools." He explained that because of what he believed was her racial heritage, it was not possible.[69] In Richmond, several families who identified as Chickahominy Indians and whose children had been allowed to attend white schools were kicked out.[70] In the case of Pal Beverly, whom, as we have seen, Plecker had directly admonished for trying to pass as white, the BVS's research into his family's racial lineage had embold- ened local officials to be "firm in opposing their admittance into the white public schools."[71] In 1930, Mascott Hamilton wrote to Plecker, infuriated that the BVS had marked his family as colored and that his children were now being forced to attend a segregated colored school. "I am glad," Plecker replied and refused to reclassify the family. In some families, one branch might be recognized as white and another classed as colored. Such was the case with the Ogdens of Amherst County. While Warren Ogden's children were suspended from the white schools, their cousins in Richmond and Lynchburg continued to attend segregated schools as whites.[72]

Such inconsistency points to the importance of local authorities in law enforcement. As with interracial marriage, the enforcement of school seg- regation according to the racial definitions of the RIA depended not only on accurate birth registration but also on the discretion of local authorities to call into question the racial identity of families previously registered as white. Like clerks of court who issued marriage licenses and thus could act in a ju- dicial capacity to demand evidence of racial purity, local school authorities had it in their power to call people's racial identity into question and demand documentary proof of whiteness. Skeptical school authorities seldom made decisions themselves but invoked the document-based authority of the BVS. Their power lay in their capacity to express doubt and demand verification. In one case from 1925, Clarence Jennings, the superintendent of schools in James City, Charles City, and New Kent Counties, was confronted by W. A. T. Jones, who wanted his children to attend a state school for Indians rather than local colored schools. In order to do so, the Jones children would need to be classified as "mixed Indian" rather than colored on their birth certificates. Jennings referred the matter to the BVS to decide, explaining that "neither the School Board nor I care to pass upon the race of a man where there is a Bureau established, you might say, for this purpose."[73] Jennings had it in his power to transfer the Jones children directly to the Indian school without consulting the BVS, but he used his power instead to doubt their claim and invoke the regulatory power of Plecker's documentary regime, a regime in which, as Jennings correctly assessed, vital registration and racial detection were inextricable.

Plecker regarded school segregation not only as an end in itself but also as instrumental to another of the state's top priorities: the enforcement of miscegenation law. As he explained in a letter to an attorney, the problem was not simply that colored and white children might sit side by side in the classroom. Rather, if children with any "negro" blood were "permitted to attend white schools they naturally form white attachments, with the result of afterwards intermarrying into the white race, thus establishing a line of mixed breeds to give trouble to every one."[74] It was a slippery slope from shared schooling to racial amalgamation, and birth certificates helped create friction on the slope. Birth registration was useful to the enforcement of miscegenation law in three ways. First, accurate birth registration ensured the prevention of intermarriage in the future. When Plecker reminded birth attendants and local registrars about their duty to properly record race on new registrations, he told them that if they had any doubt about the race of either of the parents, and hence of the child, they should consult the local clerk of court. The clerk was responsible for issuing marriage licenses in the future and thus would be materially interested in settling any racial ambiguity. In his annual report for 1926, Plecker also averred that he aimed to prevent miscegenation by "securing proper and exact registration which he can prove in courts when called upon so to do."[75]

Besides providing a form of preventative gatekeeping, birth records had a second important function: they could be used to prove that one of the applicants for a marriage license was nonwhite while the other was white. In *Connor v. Shields*, this was exactly what Plecker did to argue that Dorothy Johns had "negro" blood in her veins. Plecker used similar tactics to contest the marriage of Benjamin Beverly to Dollie Garrett and of Cecil Spitler to Ella Anna Clark, all of whom declared themselves white on their applications for a marriage license.[76] In such cases, the BVS could adduce either the birth certificate of one of the applicants or use the genealogical method and provide evidence that an ancestor of an applicant was considered nonwhite in a past act of registration. In the case of Spitler and Clark, Plecker wrote to the clerk of court who had issued them a marriage license and explained that Clark was a descendent of persons "shown in our old records to be of negro descent." Thus, he reminded the clerk, "if Cecil Spitler is a white man, the marriage is illegal and should be annulled."[77]

Vital statistics documents were used to determine racial classification in contested marriages even outside Virginia, in states where interracial marriage was legal. In 1925, New York high society was scandalized by the marriage of a wealthy young man, Leonard Rhinelander, to a chambermaid, Alice Jones. After a New York newspaper published an article claiming that Alice was the son of a "colored man," Leonard sued for annulment of the marriage. Though interracial marriages were legal in New York State, he argued that Alice had represented herself as white and the marriage had been based on a fraud. During the trial Alice and her attorney did not deny she was part "colored," but Leonard's attorney claimed that Leonard had no knowledge of her race until confronted by his own family with her birth certificate, which marked her as colored. Once this had been entered into evidence, Alice had little choice but to contest Leonard's claims on other grounds. Instead of defending her whiteness, she contested Leonard's claim that he had been ignorant of her race before their marriage. The jury found in her favor.[78] In this case, racial misrepresentation—established by the truths revealed on Jones's birth certificate—could have invalidated an otherwise legal marriage.

Third, when parents registered the birth of a child, it could trigger the BVS to inquire about the legality of their marriage. This might be because, as in the case of Lawrence Sperka and Ida Hartless, one of the parents had a surname that the BVS considered suspect. In October 1930, Plecker penned a letter to Sperka about the birth certificate he had recently filed on behalf of his newborn. Plecker explained that the baby's mother might be from a "mixed blood" group of Hartlesses who congregated around Buena Vista and Irish Creek. His letter included a questionnaire for the couple to fill out that would establish her genealogy. "In order to establish the legality of your marriage," Plecker wrote, "will you please advise as to which family your wife belongs." He warned Sperka that "if [she belongs] to the family of mixed breeds, your marriage is not legal."[79]

While a suspect last name might trigger an inquiry, so too could a parent's racial self-identification on a child's birth certificate. If, for example, a new registration listed one parent as white and the other as Indian, it was a flag for the BVS to call the legality of the marriage into question. Mrs. Ruth Rogers found herself in this predicament when she registered the birth of her child in 1943. On the certificate, she was identified as "Indian" while her husband was listed as "white." Plecker wrote to Rogers and explained that Virginia did not recognize the term "Indian," and he demanded that she send in her marriage license or her birth certificate to settle her true racial identity. If she really was identified as "Indian" or otherwise nonwhite on either of these, Plecker warned, her marriage was illegal because "it is not legal for a white person and an Indian to marry in Virginia nor to live in marriage relations." In his letter, Plecker intimated that Rogers might have been born outside Virginia, in North Carolina, but reminded her that no matter where she'd been born and whether that state recognized her as "Indian," Virginia would not; nor would it recognize her marriage to a white person no matter where the marriage had been contracted.[80] Because the BVS used birth certificates to trigger investigations into marriage, parents who obeyed the law's requirement to register their children's births might find their marriage declared illegal and their children officially marked as not only colored but also illegitimate.[81] In 1940, Plecker wrote to a commonwealth attorney about the birth registration of a child born to a "mulatto" woman and a white man. The physician who signed the registration confirmed the racial identity of the parents as listed on the certificate. "That being true," Plecker wrote, "they were married illegally and under the laws of Virginia they are not legally married." Plecker ended his letter to the state's lawyer with the hope that "you may take such action as you may deem necessary."[82]

Though Plecker regarded the prevention of interracial marriage and schooling as the heart of his efforts to preserve racial purity, he used birth records to help segregate other civil and state institutions: cemeteries, hospitals, and public welfare agencies. Many such institutions, while they might avow a policy of segregation, did not always use the same kind of formal identification requirements as schools and marriage-licensing county clerks. In these instances, Plecker and his clerks at the BVS were usually chasing down instances of racial passing or mixing that had already taken place. In a letter to the superintendent of the whites-only Riverview Cemetery, Plecker admonished him for burying William H. Moon on the grounds. Moon, Plecker explained, is colored, a fact established by his birth record. Whether this sort of racial mixing was legal at the cemetery or not, Plecker reminded the superintendent that "to a white owner of a lot, it might prove embarrassing to meet with negroes visiting at one of their graves on the adjoining lot." Plecker also explained that he had helped make similar corrections in other cases of "passing" in death.[83]

The BVS also corresponded with hospitals to help ensure that they remained segregated by race, a practice that was common throughout the United States until at least 1965.[84] In one case, a local registrar of vital statistics wrote to the BVS because a hospital in her area did not know whether to put Ethel Mae Brame in the colored ward or admit her to the whites-only ward. In another case, Plecker wrote to a physician who had filed a birth certificate that identified one of the child's parents as "Indian." Plecker explained that his family was really "mixed negro" and could not be identified as Indian; likewise, they ought never have been allowed into the hospital where the child was born. "I presume that you do not desire to mix negroes with white patients."[85] In addition to preventing the kind of racial mixing and familiarity that might, like common schooling, lead to "attachments," preventing "mixed negro" families from entering white cemeteries and hospitals ensured that such families would not be able to establish a local racial reputation as white in defiance of the documentary record. In one case, Plecker described a family that was "aggressive" in trying to be classified as white. "The fact that the mother secured admittance into the white ward of Memorial Hospital is evidence of this fact," he lamented.[86] Because the mother gave birth to a child on the "white ward," it was only logical that the birth attendants there would agree to register the child as white. Plecker worried that this sort of passing was how the contemporary documentary record could be made to lie even when the old records told a different story.

Plecker also corresponded with officials from public welfare and selective service boards in Virginia and surrounding states. Often this was at their behest. In most instances, it was not clear why public welfare officials wanted to know the racial identity of the children who came under their aegis, but in all cases Plecker was willing to use whatever documents he had to settle the matter.[87] Some records, however, do indicate just what was at stake. Mrs. Nancy Hundley of the Cumberland County Public Welfare Board wrote to the BVS to ask how she should classify the children of Mattie Murray, a "feebleminded white woman who seems to have given birth to one or two mulatto children." Plecker replied that if Murray had "association with negroes," then the answer was quite obvious. He also recommended that she be placed "in the State Colony" and "sterilized." These measures—the state's colony for the feebleminded and sterilization—were part and parcel of the larger project to which the RIA also belonged. Indeed, the same year that the Virginia legislature passed the RIA, it also enacted an involuntary sterilization law designed to stop anyone the state deemed feebleminded, insane, or criminally inclined from reproducing.[88] As in the case of a birth registration that might lead to the negation of a marriage and the transformation of its offspring into bastards, in Murray's case the matter of racial classification on a birth certificate also turned out to be a powerful instrument in the administration of a racial state.

Besides denying Black Virginians the ability to marry, attend schools, and enter other institutions of their choosing, Plecker's use of birth registration to police racial lines imposed a Black-white binary on a complex history of intermarriage and kinship between descendants of Africans, Native Americans, and whites from the colonial era forward. The end result was the erasure of many of Virginia's Native inhabitants who had to fight against the documentary record in order to receive state and federal tribal recognition. That fight began as soon as did Plecker's efforts to enforce the RIA, when leaders of the Mattaponis and Pamunkeys publicly rebuked their classification as "negroid" by the BVS.[89] Over the next several decades, Native Virginians collected evidence of their racial reputation as "Indian" as well as the documents that had registered their children as such before the RIA.[90] And, in a campaign that stretched into the twenty-first century, they also amassed evidence of Plecker's efforts to remove them from the documentary record. Eventually, members of the Pamunkey, Chickahominy, Eastern Chickahominy, Upper Mattaponi, Rappahannock, Nansemond, and Monacan were able to convince the State of Virginia and the federal government to recognize them as sovereign nations.[91]

In spite of the fact that Walter Plecker invested his entire career in the epistemological power of documents, evidence of their fundamental instability was all around him. For one thing, documents were made by humans, and parents and birth attendants could enter the "wrong" race on a baby's birth certificate. In these cases, Plecker might have the "old records" available to justify appending a change to the racial classification, but much as this corrective sought to set the record straight, it also called attention to the fact that the originals could lie. Likewise, Plecker eschewed racial reputation when it led to what he considered the false designation of "mixed" babies as "white," but he happily employed it to reverse course, turning reputation into documentation and "white" babies into "mixed" ones. It is tempting to see this as a lesson in white supremacists' inconsistent dedication to truth and their willingness to bend institutions to their own ends, but that lesson is only part of the story. In matters of age as well as in matters of race, the truths recorded on birth certificates were products of the documentary process. Birth certificates did not invent categories such as "age" and "race," but birth certificates gave special power to state-produced knowledge in the context of social reforms—against child labor and racial heterogeneity—that sought to displace local and testamentary forms of establishing truth. In this, they joined the use of birth certificates to reform motherhood undertaken by child welfare reformers. That too was a project about knowledge that sought not only to know who was being born, where, and to whom but also to displace certain kinds of childbirth and child-rearing practices with those of scientific motherhood. For all of these, birth certificates were a technology that identified and sorted people, making them visible in terms of categories congruent with the administration of policies meant to promote the health of the social body. What reformers did not anticipate, however, was the ways that privileging the function of birth certificates as a form of identification would come into conflict with their function as a tool of public health and social welfare. The more that governments relied on birth certificates to tell them who people were, the more these functions clashed.

PART 3

CONTESTING BIRTH REGISTRATION

CHAPTER 7

CONTROVERSY AS TO THE METHOD

n January 1957, Harold Bartness, a clerk of court in Elbow Lake, Minnesota, wrote to his state's Division of Vital Statistics (DVS) seeking advice. He wasn't sure what to do about a person who wanted to get a delayed registration of birth. The person in question had been born before 1900 but never had his birth registered. Now he wished to establish the facts of his birth for "proof of age for social security benefits." Minnesota had a procedure for registering births many years after the fact, and Bartness knew how to create a belated birth registration in ordinary cases, but this one was tricky. The birth had been illegitimate and "this person has been going under a name other than that of the natural father." In response, a DVS clerk explained that Bartness should issue a birth certificate that included only the mother's name, not that of the father. Moreover, since this was an illegitimate birth, the DVS would want to review all the evidence used to retroactively establish the facts of birth, "because there is a possibility that we may make a special statement on the certificate concerning the evidence." Finally, explained the clerk, the DVS would not send Bartness a copy of the birth certificate once it was filed because state law provided that "illegitimate birth certificates shall be on file only with the State Registrar."[1]

This case combined two of the thorniest problems facing those responsible for registering births in the middle of the twentieth century: the recording of illegitimate births and the creation of delayed, or retroactive, birth certificates. The fact that Minnesota's DVS did not want to include paternity information on the birth certificate of Bartness's petitioner and the fact that it would keep a copy of the birth certificate on file only in the state's central office were the result of decades-long campaigns to reform both the manner in which out-of-wedlock births were recorded and the ways in which information about birth status could be used. As legislators, child welfare advocates, and state registrars sought to protect illegitimate children from the revelations contained on their birth certificates, they developed procedures that sought to balance different categories of fact.

The increased use of birth certificates as proof of identity in administration led to protections for illegitimate children and to procedures for delayed registration. Programs such as social security—for which Bartness's petitioner wanted his birth certificate—multiplied the demand for age verification among adults over the age of fifty when the program was created in 1935; these adults were very unlikely to have had their births registered when they were born. Such programs always allowed applicants to use an alternative proof of identity, but many, such as Bartness's petitioner, wanted to obtain a birth certificate anyway. Bartness reported that he had suggested "using other documents & forego [sic] a delayed certificate, but the party indicates a desire to put it on record."[2] Like the government agencies that demanded them, ordinary Americans had come to believe that birth certificates were especially authoritative documents, and thus they wanted the facts "on record" and asked for retroactive certificates in droves. Demand for delayed birth certificates spiked during the 1930s and '40s as the advent of social security and the United States' participation in World War II increased the demand for proof of age and of citizenship.

Though the problems created by illegitimate and previously unregistered births seldom intersected as neatly as they did in Bartness's case, they both grew out of the increased social and legal value of birth certificates. Progressive Era reform of child labor law administration had succeeded in transforming the birth certificate into a foundational and privileged token of identity. This definitive role for birth certificates increased demand for birth registration and created tensions between the public health, or statistical, nature of birth records and their legal character. Whereas the nineteenth- and early twentieth-century campaign for better birth registration had been undertaken by statisticians and public health reformers, the reformers who used the birth certificate to certify facts of identity made it a central tool in the administration of a state that placed its faith in documents and distributed rights and protections according to categories such as citizenship, age, and kinship. In other words, the "facts" that the birth certificate could establish for the purpose of administering and enforcing laws against child labor, truancy, under-age marriage, and statutory rape or for protecting illegitimate children were less medical and statistical than they were legal and social.

Opponents of child labor had been sure that basing age verification on the state-produced birth certificate would replace fraud with truth and uncertainty with certainty. For reformers, the veracity of the birth certificate was based on its conditions of production. The first of these was its relation to time: it was created within a legally specified number of days after birth. And this limited time horizon ensured that the facts of birth would be accurate, subject neither to the depredations of memory nor to the motivation to misrepresent a child's identity for gain. The second condition was the birth certificate's relation to authority: the document was created by the birth attendant, received by the local registrar, and filed permanently with the state. It was not a product of the family. Because it was made by the state rather than recorded by families, wrote the U.S. Children's Bureau in 1916, "there can be no falsification which may defraud the child of years of school, and the official record of one State is accepted, of course, in all others."[3]

But what had seemed to be the virtue of the birth certificate—its neutrality and uniformity—began to crumble under the increased legal and social demands that belief in these virtues spawned. The more reliable that birth certificates came to seem, the more widespread birth registration became; the more legal and administrative uses to which birth certificates were put, the less stable their truths became. Two mid-twentieth-century examples illustrate how challenges to the epistemological stability of the birth certificate were a result of its social utility; these were the campaign to remove illegitimacy information from the certificate and the onslaught of requests for post hoc, or delayed, birth registration. Both pitted the instrumental use of the birth certificate as a form of legal identification against its value as a technology for recording the "vital statistics" so important to public health and social welfare. These examples also show how birth registration changed in response to public pressure. Far from being a neutral recorder of facts, the birth certificate was a contested document.

As soon as the U.S. Children's Bureau launched its campaign for full birth registration in 1914, it began to pay special attention to the problems surrounding the registration of illegitimate births. While all births in the United States were vastly underreported, child welfare reformers and vital statisticians believed that out-of-wedlock births were especially likely to escape notice. Boston's registrar complained about this problem in 1888, just two years after he had begun to try to calculate how many illegitimate births occurred in the city each year. He suspected that many such births escaped his notice or were misrepresented as legitimate. "It is not strange, however," he mused, "that there should be a wish, in many cases, to conceal the character of these births."[4] Indeed, the town clerks and local registrars responsible for collecting birth returns sometimes learned of cases of concealment. J. A. Duclos, a doctor and the registrar for Henderson, Minnesota, learned of one such case in April 1915. A girl who worked in a store near his office was visibly pregnant. After staying away from the store for a few weeks, the girl returned to work but was no longer pregnant. The girl's mother, meanwhile, "was seen taking the train at 6 am, with a baby in her arms. . . . Now the birth of this child has not been reported." When Duclos wrote to the state board of health, the baby's whereabouts were not known and, as he complained, "that baby may have been dead for all I know." The state board of health wrote the girl's father admonishing him to report the birth because it had taken place in his house. But the board also offered that he could file the certificate directly with the state rather than with the local registrar to avoid "publicity." Some months later, the board received an anonymously filed certificate with information about the child's legitimacy left blank.[5] Thus, although the girl in Henderson had been obviously pregnant, the girl's parents attempted to conceal the baby's birth: no doctor attended the birth, the baby was quickly taken out of town, and the birth was not initially reported.

From the point of view of those interested in child welfare, the problems with cases such as these were statistical, social, and legal. Underreporting of illegitimate births was a statistical problem insofar as it meant that communities could never know how many births really occurred, illegitimate or otherwise. In 1915, only sixteen states and twenty cities recorded the number of illegitimate births that occurred therein, and these statistics were considered largely unreliable. But as John Anderson, the health officer of Spokane, Washington, wrote, "an illegitimate child is the same as a legitimate child so far as the value of vital statistics is concerned."[6] The registration of illegitimate births would provide more than just good statistics, however. If, as the Children's Bureau argued, birth registration was "an aid in protecting the lives and rights of children," this was doubly so for children born out of wedlock. Just as the bureau had become interested in birth registration as a result of its attempt to discover the extent and causes of infant mortality, so too it became interested in registering and protecting illegitimate children because they were vastly overrepresented in the numbers of infant deaths. In its first community study of infant mortality, the bureau found that babies born out of wedlock died at an alarmingly higher rate than those born to married mothers.[7]

Child welfare reformers and vital statisticians alike linked the especial vulnerability of illegitimate children to their registration. "It is really more important that the birth of an illegitimate child should be recorded than of a legitimate child," explained H. M. Bracken of the Minnesota Department of Health, "for its birth certificate is, in a certain sense, a protection of the life of the child." Illegitimate children were as much as three times as likely to die in infancy, and even if they lived, they were often abandoned or placed out by their mothers. According to studies that Chicago's Juvenile Protective Association undertook in 1914, unregistered children "are often treated as chattels instead of as human beings, and . . . they are frequently lost, sold, or abandoned." Of the 3,000 illegitimate children born in Chicago's hospitals in 1914, for example, the Juvenile Protective Association found that one-third "were lost so absolutely that it was impossible to find any trace of them—even whether they were living or dead." And such numbers did not begin to account for the illegitimate children born to unattended mothers or in the city's unlicensed maternity homes.[8] Like the baby whose disappearance came to J. A. Duclos's attention, many other illegitimate children were unregistered, untracked, and disposed of in an unregulated manner. An illegitimate child might be abandoned in a city's foundling home, sold for adoption in the thriving black market for white babies, or privately placed in a home by a pregnant woman's doctor or by her caseworker at a maternity home. The precarious early lives of illegitimate children were a product of the stigma attached to being born out of wedlock. This led women to hide their babies' births, seek to rid themselves of the evidence of their criminal sexual activity, assume false names when they delivered babies in maternity homes and hospitals, and refuse to register the babies.[9]

Underreporting could prove to be a legal problem for the illegitimate child in subsequent years when she needed a birth certificate to establish her citizenship, age, or parentage. A case in South Dakota dramatized the issue. Mr. F. Tielebein wrote to the U.S. Children's Bureau in 1922 on behalf of his niece Dorothy, the illegitimate offspring of an incestuous union between his brother Walter and his sister Annie. "Grandparents where [sic] ashamed of the case and did not have the child registered," explained Tielebein. Now, however, some thirty years later, Walter was dead and a struggle was being waged over the disposition of his estate. Tielebein believed that Dorothy was entitled to some of the property as Walter's offspring. But because her birth had never been registered, Walter's paternity was not established and she had no legal claim to any portion of his "legacy."[10] The Tielebein family drama was proof that, in the words of a state registrar from Mississippi, the record of an illegitimate birth could "afford protection to children that might otherwise be deprived of their rights."[11]

Child welfare reformers wanted to do more, however, than simply ensure that all illegitimate births were recorded. They also wanted to change the *way* that out-of-wedlock births were recorded, and here their public health goals were at odds with their social goals. From a public health point of view, it was essential that all births be recorded. State and social service agencies wanted information about aggregate numbers of illegitimate births and knowledge of which particular children in a community were born to unmarried parents. (Recall that child welfare officers wanted to use birth registration to target unwed mothers and their babies for interventions.) But from a social point of view, reformers wanted to reduce the stigma attached to illegitimate children in order to lessen their early vulnerability and because they believed that it was unjust to make children suffer for the sins of their parents. In this, American child welfare reformers were inspired by legal reforms pioneered in Norway that sought to assist illegitimate children by removing the legal distinction between children born in and out of wedlock. The so-called Castberg law held that all children were the legitimate offspring of their parents and were entitled to support and inheritance rights. The state would initiate paternity proceedings so that fathers could be held to account for maintenance until their offspring reached majority.[12]

Most American reformers interested in protecting illegitimate children found the Castberg law too radical, but they did support legal reforms that would both materially support illegitimate children and reduce their social shame. When it came to the latter, reformers sought to change how birth status was recorded on birth certificates. The Children's Bureau organized a series of regional conferences on illegitimacy in 1920, at which the discussion of how and what to record in cases of illegitimacy took center stage. "There is much controversy as to the method by which these births shall be so recorded as best to safeguard the child's legal status and property rights and at the same time protect him against any stigma," wrote the Children's Bureau's Emma Lundberg and Katharine Lenroot. In almost every state, a child's birth certificate would indicate whether she was legitimate or illegitimate. In most states, the certificate also recorded the names of both parents. In a handful of others, however, state law actually prohibited the birth record from including the name of the father of a child born out of wedlock. In either case, a child who had to use her birth certificate to prove her name, age, or citizenship would have to advertise her illegitimacy. "How should the child be protected," asked the Children's Bureau, "in the case of transcripts of his birth record for school enrollment, working papers, and similar purposes?"[13]

Most of the registrars, lawyers, social workers, and medical professionals who attended the 1920 conferences agreed that records of illegitimate births should be confidential, "open to inspection only upon order of court." Transcripts of birth records used "for school and work purposes should omit the names of parents."[14] In other words, many child welfare advocates agreed both that birth records should be closed to public inspection and that information about a child's birth status should be scrubbed from the public face of the birth certificate. In public at least, reformers wanted the state's legal distinction between illegitimate and legitimate children to be erased. In recommending that birth records be made confidential, reformers took inspiration not only from the Castberg law but also from Minnesota's 1917 Children's Code. Among the states, Minnesota was the first in the nation to make birth records confidential and to issue only partial transcripts of birth records that made no reference to birth status.[15]

Between the 1910s and the 1940s, the standard certificate of birth issued by the U.S. Census Bureau continued to include a statement of legitimacy (figure 7.1). During the 1920s, however, several states did adopt laws akin to Minnesota's that treated birth records as confidential and that eliminated information about birth status from copies of birth records used for proof of age and other routine verifications. In these states, the full birth record was available only to the child, to his or her parents, or by court order. In a handful of other states, state health officers used their discretionary power to adopt office procedures that ensured that birth certificates of illegitimate children were only issued "once careful inquiry has been made as to the use to which they are to be put." But in still other states, vital records were considered, by statute, as public records that should be available to any person who paid the required fee for their inspection and reproduction.[16] What was the virtue of the birth certificate was also its vice. Child welfare reformers were sure that the "public birth record" afforded children the best protection against premature labor, marriage, and other violations of childhood, but the fact that the information contained therein was "public" also hurt the most vulnerable among them: children born to unmarried mothers.

Adopting a shortened form of the birth certificate for purposes of identification balanced the public health and social goals of child welfare reformers. By making birth certificates confidential, public health officials could continue to collect information about aggregate numbers of illegitimate children

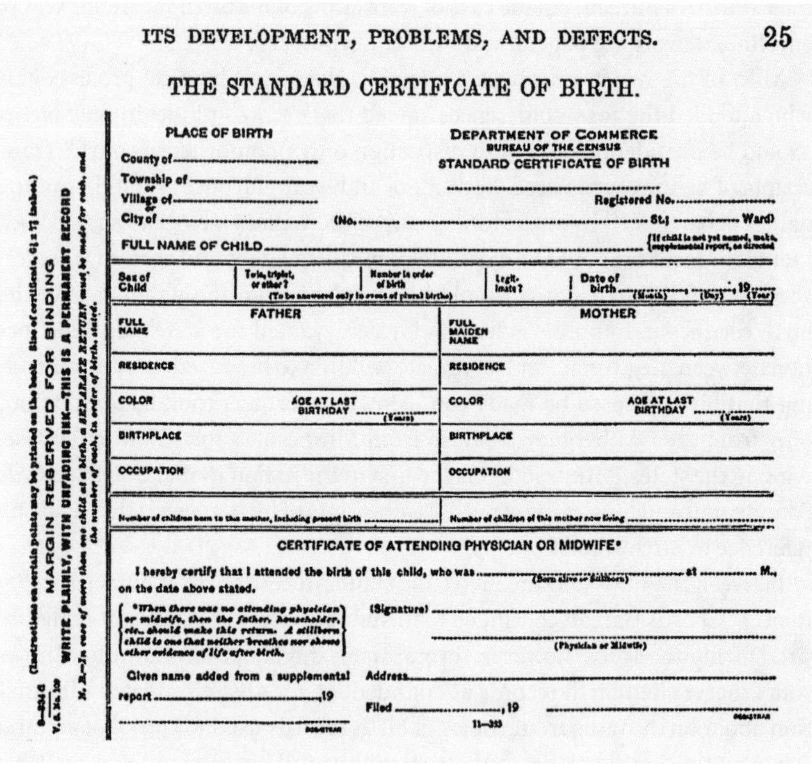

ITS DEVELOPMENT, PROBLEMS, AND DEFECTS. 25

THE STANDARD CERTIFICATE OF BIRTH.

8—2346
V. S. No. 109

(Instructions on certain points may be printed on the back. Size of certificate, 6½ x 7½ inches.)

MARGIN RESERVED FOR BINDING

WRITE PLAINLY, WITH UNFADING INK—THIS IS A PERMANENT RECORD

N. B.—In case of more than one child at a birth, a SEPARATE RETURN must be made for each, and the number of each, in order of birth, stated.

PLACE OF BIRTH

County of

Township of
or
Village of
or
City of (No. St.; Ward)

DEPARTMENT OF COMMERCE
BUREAU OF THE CENSUS
STANDARD CERTIFICATE OF BIRTH

Registered No.

FULL NAME OF CHILD (If child is not yet named, make supplemental report, as directed)

Sex of Child | Twin, triplet, or other? | Number in order of birth | Legitimate? | Date of birth (Month) (Day), 19 (Year)

(To be answered only in event of plural births)

FATHER	MOTHER
FULL NAME	FULL MAIDEN NAME
RESIDENCE	RESIDENCE
COLOR — AGE AT LAST BIRTHDAY (Years)	COLOR — AGE AT LAST BIRTHDAY (Years)
BIRTHPLACE	BIRTHPLACE
OCCUPATION	OCCUPATION
Number of children born to this mother, including present birth	Number of children of this mother now living

CERTIFICATE OF ATTENDING PHYSICIAN OR MIDWIFE*

I hereby certify that I attended the birth of this child, who was (Born alive or Stillborn) at M., on the date above stated.

*When there was no attending physician or midwife, then the father, householder, etc., should make this return. A stillborn child is one that neither breathes nor shows other evidence of life after birth.

(Signature)

(Physician or Midwife)

Given name added from a supplemental report , 19

REGISTRAR

Address

Filed , 19

11—355

REGISTRAR

Figure 7.1. The standard certificate of birth (1916)

The standard birth certificate, issued by the U.S. Census Bureau and used by most states, included information about legitimacy on its face, indicated with a "yes" or "no" in the box just to the left of the date of birth. Source: Wilbur, *Federal Registration Service.*

without exposing particular children to the "most distressing revelations."[17] Though this compromise was met with near-unanimous approval among social workers and child welfare advocates, some registrars of vital statistics worried that it changed the nature of the birth certificate. Where it had once been regarded as a particularly trustworthy document because it was a literal transcript of the facts of birth as they were recorded at the time of birth, now it was a partial transcript, so altered to accommodate the intersection between the state's need for identification and the child's need for protection. Stewart Thompson, Florida's chief vital statistician, expressed such concerns in his correspondence with Gerda Pierson, Minnesota's head of vital statistics. He told Pierson that he found Minnesota's partial transcript "not proper" because "when a certified copy is desired, the State Registrar is supposed to certify that it is a true and correct copy of the original." But if registrars left off information such as legitimacy, then the record they issued "is not a true certification."[18] In amending certificates through omission, Thompson believed that registrars risked sacrificing both the credibility and the probative value of birth certificates on the altar of the social good. Changing the content altered the relations of time and authority that proponents of birth certificates so valued. When the birth certificate was a true transcript, it replicated the moment of original recording, the moments just after the birth of the child. But when registrars created a partial transcript, they exchanged their authority for that of the birth certificate's original filer and they created a document that reflected the needs of the present moment rather than the facts as recorded in the past. This, registrars worried, would undermine the legal authority of the document.

But partial transcripts were only one kind of solution (or problem). In addition to making birth status confidential, during the 1920s and '30s some states also began to allow changes to the birth certificates of children whose parents married after they were born. Most state laws declared that a child born out of wedlock became legitimate if and when the child's parents subsequently married. The customary way of noting this on a child's birth certificate had been simply to make amendatory changes directly on the face of the birth record. "The usual procedure consists of crossing out 'No' and inserting 'Yes'" where the standard certificate asked if the birth was legitimate. In this way, the certificate showed the child's history, her move from illegitimate to legitimate. From the point of view of child welfare advocates who wanted to protect illegitimate children from the sins of their parents, this was inadequate. Instead, reformers urged that states adopt laws such as the one passed in Illinois in 1931. The Illinois law provided that when an illegitimate child's parents married, an entirely new birth certificate would be issued for the child, showing that the child had been legitimate at the time of birth. By 1938, at least ten states had similar legislation on the books, and in many others parents who requested new birth certificates for their children were granted them "since the law specifically states that the birth is legitimated by marriage."[19]

Issuing legitimated children new birth certificates that showed they had been born to married parents went hand in hand with another reform urged by child welfare advocates: issuing new birth certificates to adopted children. Like illegitimacy, adoption was regarded as an embarrassing circumstance that should be kept confidential so as not to haunt the child with the ghost of its past. Moreover, making adopted status confidential was, quite often, another means of concealing illegitimacy, because children born out of wedlock comprised the vast majority of adoptees. Learning—or having it publicized—that one was adopted was as good as learning that one was a bastard. In 1929, the U.S. Children's Bureau first proposed that adopted children be issued new birth records showing that they had been born to their adoptive parents; their original birth records would be placed under seal and open to inspection or reproduction only at the request of the adoptive parents or the child herself or by court order. This procedure, explained the Children's Bureau's Mary Ruth Colby, would spare the child "the embarrassment of explaining why his own name and the names of his parents are not the same as the names on his birth record." By 1941, thirty-five states had passed such laws.[20]

While many child welfare advocates were happy about such changes, registrars of vital statistics were less sanguine. Their concerns, like those of Florida's Thompson, centered on how such changes affected the truth value of the birth record. When the American Public Health Association's (APHA) Committee on Registration of Births out of Wedlock took up this issue, its members cautioned against issuing new birth certificates in cases of legitimation by marriage. "From a strictly legal point of view," read one committee report, "a certificate must show the facts as they are at the time of birth." When states changed certificates to read that a child was born to married parents, when in fact the child was born to unmarried parents, they compromised the legal integrity of birth certificates. Essentially, the certificates told a lie about the past to tell a truth about the present. The lie was necessary, advocates of such changes explained, because of the social nature of birth records. "The old order has given way to the new," wrote two registrars from Illinois, "and although formerly the statements of the child or its parents as to name, age, and relationship were accepted," nowadays "the presentation of a duly authenticated birth certificate has become an almost universal prerequisite for admittance to school or employment, or for foreign travel." And while this was but a "small barrier" to the legitimate child, for the illegitimate child it carried a heavy penalty.

In order to protect both the legitimated child and the integrity of birth certificates as legal documents, the APHA approved a resolution in 1935 that called for the removal of birth status—legitimate or illegitimate—from *all* birth certificates. "Only in this way," reasoned the APHA committee, "could the stigma of illegitimacy be removed from the child born out of wedlock who is later legitimized through the marriage of his parents."[21] While the increased social use of birth certificates was based on their legal value as prima facie evidence, the same evidentiary value threatened to bring social ruin to some users of birth certificates, and for the APHA, the only solution to this problem was to create a new structure of *legal* facts in which birth status did not exist. This solution would ensure that the critical relations of time and authority would be restored. The APHA's proposal signaled, to some, that the legal character of the birth certificate—its use as identification—had trumped its public health value. And for many of those interested in how birth certificates were used, this made the APHA's proposal quite controversial.

Shortly after the APHA made its proposal public, staff of the Census Bureau and Children's Bureau surveyed social work and public health professionals to gauge their opinion about the idea of no longer recording birth status. According to the results of the surveys, many agreed with the APHA's position. Margaret MacGunigal, the director of the Children's Bureau of North Dakota, wrote that she agreed that birth status should be eliminated, because "every child born must have parents. . . . I do not believe a child can be illegitimate," and "wholly aside from injustice, sentiment, stigma to the child, or other superficial reasons, I profoundly believe that we should have uniform birth reporting regulations" that treat all children as equally "legitimate." MacGunigal, like some others involved in child welfare, rejected the legal theory behind distinctions of birth status—that illegitimate children were filius nullius, children without parents. J. V. Deporte, the director of New York City's DVS and the chairman of the APHA committee that made the recommendation, put the matter this way: "There may be illegitimate parents, but there can be no illegitimate children." Though less radical in their total rejection of the concept of illegitimacy, other respondents agreed with MacGunigal and the APHA. "I see no reason why the information that a child is born out of wedlock is necessary in the registration of his birth," wrote Lavinia Keys from the South Carolina Department of Public Welfare. "Certainly from a social point of view," she continued, "it can do a great deal of harm."[22] For some, the logical conclusion of the effort to protect illegitimate children from the social harm that would come from the use of birth certificates to establish identity was to simply cease to collect birth status information altogether.

The U.S. Census Bureau's DVS and much of the Children's Bureau's staff were alarmed by the APHA's proposal. Officials from the Census Bureau believed that the APHA's position privileged the legal uses of birth certificates over their statistical and public health value. Taking inspiration from the minority report of the APHA's Committee on Registration of Births out of Wedlock, officials from both bureaus quickly mobilized a campaign against the recommendation. The minority report had stressed that collecting information about legitimacy as part of birth registration was an invaluable source of "obtaining statistics as to the extent of illegitimacy." Ironically, this was the position taken some twenty years earlier by child welfare advocates, who wanted not only to register all births and have accurate birth statistics but, even more pointedly, to make certain that illegitimate births in particular were registered and tracked as such so as to afford protection. As the minority report pointed out, "such statistics are of great value in planning community programs for services for the protection of children born out of wedlock."[23] This was precisely because an earlier generation of reformers had made birth certificates the trigger for intervention; were the information on births status to be eliminated, so would the trigger. Luetta Magruder, the superintendent of charities in Ohio, explained that it was "valuable to know statistics on the subject. We cannot combat increase of illegitimacy or plan successfully to handle situations without knowledge of extent of groups most largely affected." Many who supported the minority report also rejected the notion that all children were legitimate. C. C. Carstens, the executive director of the Child Welfare League of America, wrote that "as long as we have the institution of marriage we shall have children born in or out of wedlock." In his view, it was naïve to think that a birth registration form could change that. Still others, such as Gerda Pierson of the Minnesota DVS, worried that if illegitimacy were removed from all birth records, legitimate children would be unable to prove their inheritance rights.[24]

The minority report and its supporters stressed, moreover, that many states already protected birth status information from public disclosure by sealing the records of illegitimate births and issuing short-form birth certificates when necessary to prove citizenship, age, or name. This bifurcation of the birth certificate into its public and private parts was done in order to protect illegitimate children, but it was also part of a growing recognition that birth certificates served many purposes and, as a result, had many faces. Mary Frances Smith of the Children's Bureau of Philadelphia expressed this view in a letter to Agnes Hanna of the U.S. Children's Bureau. "The two-fold purpose of the birth certificate has to be recognized," she wrote. "It is to be used for statistical purposes, and also for informational purposes." From the point of view of statistics, information about illegitimacy was important, whereas "from the point of view of the use of the birth certificate for school, proof of age, etc., it would seem very wise that this information should not be included."[25]

The APHA's recommendation that states stop collecting information about illegitimacy was adopted by some states, but not all, likely due to the fact that both the Census Bureau and the Children's Bureau opposed the move.[26] Nevertheless, the federal government took steps to recognize what Mary Frances Smith had called the "two-fold" nature of the birth certificate. At a minimum, the Census Bureau committee responsible for designing the standard birth certificate recommended in 1938 that "vital facts" not necessary for "legal identification" be put somewhere other than the face of the birth certificate. In meetings between the Children's Bureau and the Census Bureau, administrators from the two agencies attempted to work out ways to "preserve the integrity of the birth certificate [and] at the same time satisfy the social pressures arising because of illegitimacy and adoption." More substantially, the Census Bureau addressed the problem by developing new technologies for converting the "informational" character of the birth record into a document for the verification of identity. One of these was a form that could be used by federal agencies to request the confidential verification of birth. When the U.S. Armed Forces, the State Department (for passports), the Social Security Agency, or another federal bureaucracy needed to verify the name, age, or place of birth of an individual, it could directly request that information from the state DVS rather than requiring the individual to furnish a birth certificate. "The reason for the confidential verification," explained the Census Bureau's Halbert Dunn, "is to protect the illegitimate child."[27] Thus, even in states that did not issue short-form birth certificates or protect birth records as confidential, federal agencies could avoid asking for—and thus avoid seeing—information about birth status.

In addition to trying to amend the way the federal government used state birth records, during the 1940s officials from the Census Bureau, the Children's Bureau, and the American Association of Registration Executives encouraged states to adopt a short-form birth certificate that they called a birth card—a laminated, wallet-sized version of the birth record that would omit birth status (figure 7.2). Here was a portable identity document that an individual could carry with him to supply the facts of his identity, except, of course, for his parentage. Because parentage would be omitted from *all* birth cards, those of legitimate and illegitimate persons would appear identical. "A child who is asked to show a birth record to get a work permit," argued Helen C. Huffman of the U.S. Public Health Service, "should not have to show a paper revealing that he was born out of wedlock." Many state registrars were enthusiastic about the birth cards. Tennessee's state registrar, Don Peterson, reported that he promoted them "to the work permit offices, big manufacturers, and others

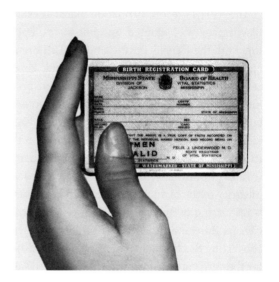

Figure 7.2. Birth card (1946)

The hand holding the birth card was meant to show its "convenient" size, made to fit in a wallet as a source of ready identification. Source: Huffman, "First Protection," 34.

who routinely require proof of age." He also reported that "people who have Birth Cards are proud of them and show them around." Mississippi's state registrar likewise raved about the cards. "It is one of the nicest things I have ever done in my office," gushed Richard Whitfield, who also reported that he carried his own card "with me all the time. It's the most useful thing I ever saw for cashing checks, and other needs for identification." Indeed, in some states, birth cards issued to adults contained a photograph on the back so that they could better serve as identification. At a point when not all states yet issued driver's licenses, this form of pocket credential could prove useful.[28]

By 1950, seventeen states issued birth cards as an alternative to birth certificates, though their use varied widely among states. While in North Carolina, as many as 75 percent of requests for copies of certified birth records were met by issuing a birth card, in states such as Tennessee and California this number was less than 1 percent. In states that used the birth card, "the determining factor in most instances for issuance of birth cards rather than regular photostatic copies was the question of legitimacy." Surveys undertaken by the American Association of Registration Executives uncovered not only the uneven use of the birth card among the states but also some of the reasons for it. The virtue of the birth card—that it was a partial transcript—meant that it was not accepted by some federal, state, or local agencies as proof of identity. Many individuals, moreover, shied away from getting a birth card rather than a certified copy of their birth certificate precisely because the birth card did *not* contain information about legitimacy and was therefore "stigmatized" by its association with illegitimacy.[29] Not only were partial transcripts considered less trustworthy, but also they reproduced the problem they were designed to solve: revealing, albeit indirectly, the facts of birth status.

Finally, in 1949 the Census Bureau issued a revised standard certificate of live birth that attempted to resolve the tensions between the statistical, social, and legal uses of the birth record. The new certificate was bifurcated into its public and private dimensions. While the certificate retained boxes for most of the information traditionally collected on birth records—place of birth, information about the child's parents, sex, and date of birth—it moved information about legitimacy to a new section that was designated "for health and medical use only." Information collected in this section would not, by definition, become part of the official transcript and thus would not be reproduced. Information contained there could, however, be used to collect aggregate statistics. In this way, the legal integrity of the birth certificate and its value as a form of identification could be preserved without compromising either the social status of those born out of wedlock or the state's desire to track information about its illegitimate population. And, by relegating legitimacy to the realm of "health and medical" information, the Census Bureau's form allowed Americans to preserve the status distinction between children born in and out of wedlock while also erasing it as an obvious basis for discrimination in the law.[30] A social and legal category became a matter of health.

Figuring out how to balance the state's desire to know how many illegitimate children were born each year and which specific children were illegitimate with its desire to protect those same children from stigma was not the only challenge to the integrity of birth certificates during the mid-twentieth century. The problem of delayed registration, though it met very different social goals than the recording of birth status, similarly troubled the relations of time and authority that made birth certificates trustworthy and similarly created tension between the legal and public health functions of birth registration.

As soon as states began to systematically register births and centralize the collection and certification of birth records, they put those whose births had never been registered at a disadvantage. Thus many individuals, confronted with a sudden awareness of their inability to prove their citizenship, age, or family relations, sought to have their births registered many years after the fact. Registrars called this "delayed registration." Systematic vital registration also meant that that states suddenly became aware of, and wished to correct, the unevenness of their population records and thus, at least initially, they freely offered delayed registration to anyone who wished to benefit from having a birth certificate. But beginning in the 1930s, delayed registration became both an administrative and epistemological problem for vital statistics offices at the local, state, and federal levels. The creation of age-based social security pensions in the 1930s and the demand for verification of citizenship during World War II multiplied requests for delayed registrations and stretched state bureaus of vital statistics to the breaking point. Administratively, they could not handle the increased workload, and the strain led the federal government to contemplate, for the first time, creating a national population registry. But epistemologically, delayed registration in the 1930s and '40s created troubling questions about the purpose and veracity of birth certificates because registration after the fact muddied the relations of time and authority that were supposed to make the facts of identity on a birth certificate stable and true. That, of course, was a problem. Reformers had taught the public to trust birth certificates, but the more people needed them, the less stable their truths became.

Between the 1880s and the 1930s, state officials were keen to have people register births even well after the fact. For them, any public demand for registration was a sign that their constituents were beginning to understand the legal value of birth certificates. As early as 1853, Boston's city registrar boasted that the citizenry expressed a great deal of interest in his work, evinced by the fact that "we have often been delayed by parents insisting upon instituting inquiries respecting the Registration of children" who they feared had not been registered in the past. Fifty years later, shortly after Minnesota created a statewide vital registration system, local officials reported unregistered births from the field. "I have just met a man," wrote the town clerk from Hillsdale to the state board of health in 1903, "who has lived in an out of the way place or corner" and who "has just returned to me several Births in his family[;] some go back to 1885." In such cases, state officials advised town clerks to simply record the information presented to them on a standard birth certificate and send it in to the state office.[31]

States went beyond simply accepting delayed certificates and actively promoted the practice among the population. Upon the initiation of its first vital registration law in 1912, Virginia's Bureau of Vital Statistics offered to register any and all births that had occurred before the new law had taken effect, a practice replicated in many other states.[32] The U.S. Census Bureau also encouraged states to promote delayed registration. In a letter to the state registrar of Minnesota, the bureau's director encouraged him to register citizens born before the state had started collecting vital statistics "so that the birth record of every individual . . . may be found in the Family Bible of Minnesota." And in some states, members of hereditary societies such as the Native Sons of Minnesota undertook their own campaigns to register all those born before vital statistics collection began.[33]

This changed with the passage of the Social Security Act in 1935. Both old-age assistance grants to the states and the federal old-age pension created new entitlements that depended, like access to employment under child labor laws, on a recipient's precise chronological age. Officials of the Bureau of Old-Age Insurance (BOAI) were well aware that this age-based scheme would create tremendous administrative problems because so few citizens would be able to produce a birth certificate to establish their age. They proposed a rule of "next best evidence" and adhered to the documentary hierarchy established by child labor law: though officials preferred the birth certificate, they would also accept church records, baptismal records, doctors' records, or affidavits of "persons who have direct knowledge of the birth." In cases where an applicant could not produce any of these records, he could be permitted to present Bible or family records or "business, fraternal, school, governmental, or other similar records" that might establish his age. Unfortunately, assessing such evidence would require exercising a great deal of "discretionary power" on the part of federal claims adjudicators and low-level clerks in state aid offices. And in fact, once old-age pensions were being administered on the ground, field representatives from the BOAI encountered a "great deal of difficulty . . . in the interpretation and application of the regulations regarding proof of age." In the first few years of the act alone, more than 25,000 people claimed a different date of birth at the time of application for benefits than they had claimed at the time they enrolled in social security.[34] Indeed, the BOAI's mandate that applicants provide proof of age created such distress and confusion that members of Congress, responding to aggrieved constituents, repeatedly introduced bills that sought to change the terms of the BOAI's proof-of-age requirements. Only one of these, which required the BOAI to accept U.S. Census Bureau enumerations as evidence, was enacted.[35]

Though the BOAI accepted proof of age other than birth certificates, old-age pensions nonetheless created an unprecedented demand for such documents. As early as 1935, Gerda Pierson, the head of the Minnesota DVS, complained to the Census Bureau that state old-age pension programs had "resulted in much additional work." Births registered before 1900 were not indexed, and the records were held by clerks of the county court, not centrally by the state. Clerks of court were "constantly besieged" with requests for certificates. Applicants frequently could not say where or exactly when they were born, nor could they state with any certainty whether their births were registered, making the search for the record "time consuming" to say the least. By 1937, the demand was even worse. One clerk of court in Mankato, Minnesota, reported that he was "just about to give up in dispair [sic]" over the "overwhelming" problem of searching past records.[36] In response to the need for birth records created by social security, many states began to apply Works Progress Administration funds to the problem. Where early records were unindexed, states employed Works Progress Administration clerks to index them. Where early records were spotty, states used Works Progress Administration clerks to collate and index other records of birth, especially local church records.[37] Like Walter Plecker in Virginia, who collated all the "old records" he could find, the federal government helped states and communities centralize other kinds of records that could be used to verify facts of identity and, under the right circumstances, be transformed into the data on a birth certificate.

Even with better indexes, though, the simple fact remained that most of those eligible for state and federal old-age pensions had never had their births registered. "The greatest problem" for those seeking social security benefits, reported the Baltimore *Sun*, "is that of establishing the date of their birth." On the eve of World War II, 60 million Americans did not have birth certificates. Many of these unregistered Americans began to apply for delayed certificates—the Census Bureau reported that social security created a 300–400 percent increase in the demand for delayed registration.[38] Where states had once been happy to register long-unrecorded births, they now saw it as a burden that created not only new administrative problems but also epistemological ones. Delayed registration destroyed the conditions of time and authority that made birth certificates trustworthy, and the exigencies of social security added a pecuniary motive for fraud: as in the case of child labor, a family stood to gain money if one of its members could be proved to be a particular age. Mississippi's state registrar, Richard Whitfield, laid out the dimensions of the problem in a 1938 letter to his peers. "Within the near future," he wrote, "there will be such a demand from Social Security, and many other government agencies for proof of birth in millions of cases." But because most states have been registering births for only the past twenty-five or thirty years, much of this demand would have to be met by delayed registration.

"All state departments," Whitfield continued, "realize they are taking great chances in registering births that occurred some years ago, especially when the applicants have in mind some ulterior motive or motives."[39] At regional and national meetings of vital statistics officers, delayed registration began to assume a prominent place on the agenda as states scrambled not only to meet the demand for post hoc birth certificates but also to figure out on what evidentiary basis to issue them.[40]

By the beginning of World War II, standards for delayed certificates remained in disarray. What had been a problem under the demands of social security legislation became, with the beginning of war, a "birth certificate epidemic."[41] In order to work in the war industries—at any plant that had a defense contract—federal regulations required that an employee present proof of U.S. citizenship. For the first time, U.S. citizens en masse needed to be able to prove their citizenship, yet there was no national mechanism for doing so. The simplest way to do this, of course, was with a birth certificate. Army and navy regulations issued in 1941 required that military contractors and subcontractors demand either a birth certificate or a delayed birth certificate from prospective employees before accepting other documentary evidence of American birth.[42] The requirement immediately overwhelmed state health departments. In 1936, Minnesota's Bureau of Vital Statistics issued 2,968 certified copies of birth and death records. In 1941, that number increased to 21,192, and in 1942 the number increased again to 41,192. This rapid uptick was common. By September 1941, bureaus of vital statistics were reporting that their work had increased by anywhere from 50 to over 2,000 percent under the national defense requirement. The federal government, meanwhile, was receiving upward of 7,000 requests daily from people seeking assistance in proving their citizenship. In order to meet the demand for delayed registrations, state bureaus fell behind on registering new births, employed Works Progress Administration clerks to assist with office work, and ceased to perform some of their other regular functions. After a trip to visit the vital statistics offices in Missouri, Kansas, Oklahoma, Texas, and Louisiana, a field agent of the Census Bureau reported that "every available clerk, every piece of equipment and every square foot of office space has been sequestered from other work and turned to the delayed birth business."[43] Racketeers operating in the private marketplace were, meanwhile, only too happy to step into the breach and provide job seekers with counterfeit birth certificates.[44]

Officials in the army, navy, and Census Bureau feared that the backlog of delayed registrations in the states would hamper the war effort by making it too difficult to fill jobs in defense plants. Forty-three million Americans eligible for defense employment—those between the ages of eighteen and sixty-five—had no birth certificate. Just as troubling to many, foreign-born naturalized citizens would have an easier time getting defense jobs than would the native born because the former had easy access to their citizenship papers. "You can go and ask for a job, without your birth certificate, and be refused," complained an official in the army's manpower division, "whereas an alien with naturalization papers will walk right in and start to work immediately." An American without a birth certificate was, in the words of the head of the Census Bureau's DVS, "worse off than an alien"—essentially a stranger in his own land.[45]

The federal government tackled the "birth certificate epidemic" in a number of ways. In July 1941, the Census Bureau issued a manual designed to establish uniform procedures for delayed registration of births. It outlined what kinds of evidence were acceptable to establish the facts of birth and also provided the form that states should use in making delayed registrations. The manual was endorsed by the army and navy, both of which encouraged state registrars to adopt its procedures.[46] At the behest of the army, members of Congress, meanwhile, introduced legislation that would establish, for the first time, a national vital statistics registration service. Under the proposal, the Census Bureau would have the authority and responsibility to provide birth certificates for anyone whose birth had not been previously registered. The procedures for so doing were identical to those outlined by the Census-issued manual. In addition, the legislation changed the legal status of census enumeration records. Unlike state-issued birth certificates, census enumerations had no legal status as evidence of birth or identity, and the bills would have allowed the bureau to use them as the basis for a delayed birth certificate.[47] Officials in the army's manpower branch reasoned that since the citizenship requirement asked that a person prove his country, not his state, of birth, it was a federal matter. "This is a national problem," declared Major Smith at a meeting of the Office of Defense, Health, and Welfare Services' Health and Medical Committee. "National action is necessary," he continued, "and that unequivocally demands a federal statute which will offer every citizen immediate means of securing birth certification." Officials in the Census Bureau were inclined to agree. Halbert Dunn, the head of the bureau's DVS, argued that the inability of the states to efficiently process delayed registration and do so on a sound evidentiary basis was only the latest offense in a long history of inefficient and error-laden vital registration. A member of the bureau's advisory board, Haven Emerson, asserted that registration was a "right" of citizens and argued that "if the [state] health departments cannot run their offices of vital statistics in a way to insure this indispensable right of the people, they should give up that duty."[48]

The Bureau of the Budget recommended against the legislation and, without the backing of the executive branch, congressional support for the bills withered. But the dream of national vital registration was far from dead. The Office of Defense, Health, and Welfare Services appointed the Committee on Vital Records to study the crisis facing state bureaus of vital statistics and to make recommendations for strengthening and standardizing the collection of vital records across the states. Lowell Reed, the dean of the school of public health at Johns Hopkins, was appointed the chairman. The Reed Committee, as it came to be known, entertained the idea of "permanent population registration such as is found in certain European countries."[49] In the eyes of the Reed Committee and its allies in the Census Bureau, the virtues of population registration were manifold. On the most basic level, it would avoid the crushing problem facing states, employers, and individual citizens during wartime: lack of individual identification and proof of citizenship. Population registration could, moreover, be more effective than even birth registration because, the committee hoped, it would be linked both to the issuance of an individual number for each citizen and to fingerprints. These documents would not, like birth certificates, be even potentially fungible for purposes of fraud.[50] Finally, a population registration would more narrowly serve the purposes for which it was designed. The wartime deluge of delayed birth registration, remarked a Census Bureau fieldworker, "has converted bureaus of vital statistics, to a large extent, from service to public health to centers of information for proof of citizenship."[51] Birth registration had not, in other words, been created for the purpose of establishing citizenship, and birth certificates did nothing to ensure the patriotic loyalty of their bearers. National population registration would detach the legal functions of the birth certificate—its use as a document to establish the facts of identity—from its public health and social welfare functions and lodge the former in a different document and a different administrative schema.

Like the contest over how to record and represent illegitimacy, the onslaught of delayed registration due to social security and wartime proof of citizenship had, in particular, brought to the fore this conflict between the legal and public health functions of the birth certificate. William Woodward, the chief health officer of the District of Columbia, explained the problem in a letter to the president of the Association of State and Territorial Health Officers. "In cases of delayed registration of birth," he wrote, "the question as to the time, place, and circumstances of birth are only secondary. The real object . . . is to establish the civic status of the petitioner and his rights, privileges, and duties as they are determined by his age, sex, and parentage." These facts, Woodward believed, were "matters not of medicine and health but of law."[52] Normally, when a birth was registered at the time that it happened, the legal and health functions of the birth certificate were aligned. But when registration happened long after the fact, the legal functions of the registration eclipsed the health ones. Indeed, delayed registration served no public health purpose whatsoever.

The divergent functions of the birth certificate were both reflected in and ramified by the chaos that reigned in the states when it came to filing delayed registrations. Unlike the procedure for filing a certificate at the time of birth, the procedure for filing a delayed birth certificate varied widely from state to state. In some states, delayed certificates were issued based simply on the affidavit of "a person older than the registrant who has, and had, knowledge of the facts at the time of birth." This procedure turned testimony into documentary fact. Other states required that applicants obtain the signature of the birth attendant, if possible. Still others asked for documentary evidence to corroborate affidavits. And in some states, delayed registration was taken out of the hands of state bureaus of vital statistics and handled entirely by the court system, where judges might accept affidavits or require documentary evidence as they saw fit. Indeed, because of the variability in procedure, and because of the distance in time between the event (the birth) and its record (the delayed certificate), the U.S. State Department had long rejected delayed certificates as acceptable proof of citizenship in applications for U.S. passports.[53]

In addition to procedures, the certificates themselves also varied from state to state. Where some states made it clear that the certificate was a delayed filing, and even abstracted the evidence on which the certificate had been made, others made no such indication.[54] Registrars were divided over which procedure was best. At a regional conference of state registrars, some attendees argued that "it is the duty of the court" to decide on the authenticity of evidence presented for delayed registration. Courts, after all, were experienced in taking testimony, handling evidence, and adjudicating claims. But other state registrars disagreed, arguing that they must have the discretion to accept or reject the evidence in order "to be reasonably assured that the records on file in their offices are authentic."[55] The disagreement hinged on the question of whether delayed certificates, because they were produced under radically different conditions, varied so much from standard certificates of birth that they belonged to another regime of knowledge and, hence, to another administrative jurisdiction. Where the movement to centralize vital registration under the aegis of state boards of health had been a major innovation in the nineteenth century, and signaled the suturing of registration to public health rather than legal identification, the clamor for delayed registration strained that relationship, tugging registration back to identification rather than health.

Officials from the Census Bureau worried that the divergent standards in the states would undermine the legal validity of birth certificates. As far as they were concerned, affidavits were useless; in order to protect the integrity of the facts contained in delayed birth certificates, applicants should provide several pieces of documentary evidence that were at least five years old and that corroborated one another. Beginning in 1938, bureau officials began to draft a new model vital statistics law for the states that included uniform procedures for delayed registration. The law, wrote the director of the bureau, was a response to "the increased use of these records by federal and State agencies in establishing and adjudicating claims under various provisions of the Social Security Act and other social legislation." No states passed the model law before or during the war, and it was not until 1942 that a final version was approved by the National Conference of Uniform Law Commissioners and the American Bar Association. The experience of World War II, of course, only amplified the problem and highlighted the need, in the eyes of many state registrars and vital statisticians, for epistemological and procedural uniformity across the states. Reflecting on his experience as the chief of the Bureau of Statistics in Illinois during the early 1940s, O. K. Sagen commented that "the war taught people a bad thing. The war taught them that just as long as you get a birth certificate it doesn't matter how you got it or how good it is."[56]

The new model law not only provided a set of uniform procedures for delayed registrations but also included a provision for how to record and represent illegitimacy. A decade before the Census Bureau dropped birth status to the "health and medical" section of the standard certificate of birth, it wrote into the model law the practice of concealing birth status on transcripts of birth certificates. Thus what had become the practice in many, but not all, states became the official recommendation of the U.S. government: states would collect birth status information but not report it, or information from which it might be deduced, on transcripts of birth certificates unless ordered to do so by a court.[57] In specifying procedures for delayed and out-of-wedlock births, the proposed model law sought to find a balance between the legal and public health functions of the modern birth certificate.

The new model law did more, however, than simply provide a uniform set of procedures for the nettlesome problems that accompanied the increased use of birth certificates by public health practitioners and government agencies. As it was envisioned by those who helped to craft it, the revised model law was part of an effort to construct a different underlying rationale for state vital statistics collection. Whereas the practice had been justified as a proper exercise of state police power in protecting the public health, the new law, argued the attorneys who helped to draft it, recognized that "these certificates have now become of great legal importance" and are accepted as "prima facie evidence" of the information—such as age, name, and citizenship—that they contain.[58] Where state registrars had often justified their work in terms of linking the "population movements" of birth and death to epidemiological problems such as infant mortality and disease, the retroactive registration of births among the adult population could serve no such purpose. In the "expression of legislative intent" included in the language of the new model law, the bill's authors wrote that creation of the vital statistics documents (birth, death, and marriage certificates) that the law licensed "shall serve not only to aid the public health and social policies of the State, but concurrently, to protect and preserve legal evidence in support of personal and property rights of the citizens to which the facts underlying such data of vital statistics may give rise."[59] In other words, while the collection of vital statistics information created aggregate data that was useful for public health, the new model law explicitly acknowledged that such data collection *simultaneously* generated information about individuals that was routinely used by them, in public, to prove the basic facts of their identity. Indeed, under no other theory of the law's purpose would it make sense to both collect *and* conceal information about birth status or to allow post hoc registration of births.

By acknowledging the new uses to which birth certificates were being put, the draft model law explicitly enshrined the changes begun by the use of birth registration to enforce child labor law. But it also sought to fight them. By creating strict standards for delayed registration and specifying how information about the "stigmas" of adoption and illegitimacy should be handled, the law attempted to insulate state registrars from political pressure. After the war ended, Arthur Hedrick, the state registrar of Maryland, complained that during the war states passed "crazy bills" with low standards for delayed birth certificates; he also knew, however, that there had been little other choice because "the people needed birth certificates to get jobs" and "the registrars were out to help their constituents." In other words, faced with overwhelming political pressure to grease the wheels of the war industry and without any statutory guidance, registrars had little choice but to give the people what they wanted, which was a ticket to a job. The new model law, they hoped, could help insulate them in the future from the influence of what Illinois's O. K. Sagen called a "social pressure group."[60]

The more useful birth certificates became, the more pressure registrars were under to alter them to meet the demands of different constituencies. By passing the new model law, state registrars also preserved their autonomy. The war had taught state registrars that if they did not provide high-quality delayed registration efficiently, "the Federal Government may seize that failure as an excuse for enlarging its own jurisdiction over state [vital registration] affairs" such that state bureaus would end up as little more than "mere covers for a federal bureau."[61]

The administrative and epistemological utility of birth certificates turned out to be both a blessing and a curse. As state-produced documents, birth certificates seemed to establish the facts of identity both efficiently and authoritatively. Unlike almost every kind of substitute for it, a birth certificate offered its users uniformity and verifiability. Yet as these assets led policy administrators to rely on them to attest to facts such as age and citizenship, those who were disadvantaged—either by what their birth certificates revealed about them or by not having been registered in the first place—posed a problem that led to a fundamental change in how birth certificates were conceptualized. Not only did states change their laws around *how* to register nonmarital births or issue delayed registrations, but also the federal government realized that birth certificates were being asked to do fundamentally different kinds of things. This led to the flirtation with a national registration system to establish citizenship and to a new model law with a new justification for registration as both statistical *and* legal. The compromises that states crafted around birth status and delayed registration and the new model law were hardly the last word, however. World War II not only heightened attention to the problem of unregistered Americans generally, but new requirements for proof of birth posed particular problems for nonwhite Americans. Not only were nonwhites less likely to be registered at birth, but when they were, the practice of using birth registration to administer racial classification put state documents in the service of white supremacy. By the middle of the twentieth century, Black Americans began to challenge the link between documentation and discrimination in ways that, like the effort to end the recording of birth status, would fundamentally change how states categorized and cataloged their populations.

CHAPTER 8

WE ARE SIMPLY ALL AMERICANS

For Walter Plecker and his program of racial purification, the surge in demand for delayed birth registrations during World War II was both a hardship and an opportunity. On the one hand, like vital registration offices everywhere, the Virginia Bureau of Vital Statistics (BVS) was overwhelmed by new work during the war. The skyrocketing number of requests for certificates made it more difficult, Plecker believed, for the clerks to maintain their customary vigilance about racial passing. He did, however, catch one case, a birth certificate on which the child was identified, mistakenly he believed, as white. Plecker sent the certificate back to the attending physician and explained that the child's family was one of those that was near-white and trying to pass. "In the terrible rush of war work, we have not been able to watch them, and many certificates such as this have slipped by without being caught," he lamented.[1] Decades of careful scrutiny dedicated to ensuring the accuracy of new birth registrations and to "correcting" mistaken registrations of the past might go down the tubes as clerks rushed to process, but not check, the birth certificates that they had to produce on an unprecedented scale. This was the hardship.

On the other hand, the same high demand for proof of age and citizenship presented an opportunity. Existing certificates could be checked for accurate racial classification and, if necessary, issued with corrections appended on the rear face. The demand for delayed birth certificates also meant that the BVS had a whole new, previously unregistered population to scrutinize for racial classification. These were adults, some of whom had been outside Virginia for decades, some of whom may have been regarded as white where they lived. For Plecker, it was just these cases that were an especial sort of prize, since it was these would-be racial interlopers that posed the starkest threat to white purity. Like other states, Virginia also had to scramble to create new legislation for standards and procedures pertaining to delayed birth registration.

In Virginia, the legislature specified that applicants for a delayed birth certificate could submit evidence of their birth to the state registrar, but if he deemed the evidence unsatisfactory, a local judge could adjudicate the matter and "set forth the date and place of the person's birth as so proven, together with the sex, height, weight, color of hair and eyes, and any distinguishing physical mark or characteristic of the person." Importantly, race was left out of the "distinguishing" physical marks that courts were allowed to determine. This was by design. The original bill establishing procedures for delayed registration would have allowed the courts to determine race in addition to date and place of birth. But Plecker argued to the bill's author, Mr. Campbell, that "judges were not in position to establish that fact as well as is the Bureau of Vital Statistics, with all of our records and experience." Campbell was persuaded by this line of argument and removed race from the bill. In the bill that passed, only the BVS had the power to make that determination, ensuring that the genealogical method and the use of documentary evidence would prevail over the vagaries of local racial reputation. Plecker believed that this preserved the intent of the Racial Integrity Act (RIA), which had made the BVS into the state's paramount authority on the race of its citizens.[2]

As requests for birth certificates—both existing and delayed—poured in, Plecker and his clerks used their power to purify the population. Wartime demand for birth certificates allowed the RIA to extend its reach far beyond Virginia's borders. Applicants born in Virginia but residing in Maryland, Tennessee, North Carolina, Kentucky, Michigan, Indiana, Ohio, New York, New Jersey, and Pennsylvania all had their birth certificates "corrected" or rejected by the BVS during the war.[3] In August 1944, for example, Plecker wrote to Solomon Collins of Niagara Falls, New York. Collins had sent in an application for a delayed birth registration, which Plecker refused to issue "until the question of your pedigree is established." As he explained to Collins, the BVS would not issue any certificates "as long as we have any doubt as to the correctness of any part of them." In Collins's case, the information about his grandparents was contradictory. Plecker suspected that they had come to Virginia via North Carolina and Tennessee, but "since we do not have access to the North Carolina and Tennessee records, we cannot trace your ancestry and cannot accept a birth certificate without such knowledge."[4] In other words, unless Collins could provide positive proof that his ancestors were all "pure" white, or unless Plecker himself could prove this through Virginia's "old records," he would not issue Collins a birth certificate of any kind. Plecker, in effect, denied Collins the ability to establish his citizenship, let alone his race.

In other cases, Plecker was willing to issue a birth certificate but only if the applicant agreed to be identified as "colored." William Cleveland from Muncie, Indiana, had sent in a request for his wife's birth certificate, but Plecker wrote that because his wife's family was known to be mixed race in spite of many having registered successfully as "white," he could only issue her birth certificate with "the racial pedigree noted on the back."[5] Plecker had always hoped that all states would pass their own RIAs, but even in the absence of a uniform legal definition of race across the country, he could use his office to impose RIA standards on Virginia-born residents of other states, effectively making them "colored" whether or not they would be considered as such in their adopted states. And when applicants refused to accept a birth certificate on the terms proffered by Plecker—that they be identified as Black—he effectively denied them equal access to citizenship.

Plecker's use of delayed registration to police racial lines was not the only way that birth certificates enforced white supremacy in the mid-twentieth-century United States. Whenever employers demanded that job candidates submit birth certificates as a condition of employment, African Americans were at a disadvantage. This was not only because employers could use racial classification to discriminate by refusing to interview and hire candidates labeled as nonwhite but also because African Americans were less likely to have birth certificates in the first place. The inability of Black job seekers to establish their official identity made them ineligible to apply for many jobs and stymied their ability to seek rights including schooling and voting.

By the middle of the twentieth century, the unmistakable role of birth certificates in maintaining white supremacy led civil rights organizations to launch a multipronged attack on the problem. In one phase, activists tried to simply increase African American and Native American access to birth registration to prevent the administrative denial of identity. This dovetailed with targeted federal campaigns to achieve full birth registration among both African Americans and Native Americans. On the other hand, African American activists also challenged racial classification on vital documents. Like those who argued for removing birth status from registration documents, local advocates in cities such as New York and Chicago, and national organizations such as the NAACP, argued that race served no purpose other than to stigmatize nonwhites. This campaign was successful, and by 1968 the standard certificate of live birth issued by the U.S. Census Bureau had moved "race/color" to the confidential, medical section of the certificate (where it remains today). This was the same compromise procedure used several decades earlier in the case of illegitimacy, and as in that earlier case, it represented a conflict between the legal and the statistical uses of birth certificates. Where race now appeared to many, like birth status once had, as a "stigma" that the state should not participate in perpetuating on its own forms of legal identification, others fervently believed that race, like illegitimacy, was an important social fact, the knowledge of which was essential to combat the ill effects of structural racism. Likewise, as in the case of illegitimacy, the campaign to end racial identification showed that the more imbricated in all forms of public administration that birth certificates became, the more their basic categories were subject to contestation and revision.

Even after the army reversed its requirement that potential workers in war industry plants provide birth certificates as proof of citizenship, employers across the country hewed to the new standard. Thus, being denied a birth certificate, or being issued one as "colored," might affect a person's ability to find work. Here the issue was less proof of age, as in the case of child labor laws, and more the entwined proof of citizenship and race. The issue was suggested by a correspondence between Plecker and Clayton Pugh of Amherst, Virginia. Pugh had requested his birth certificate from the BVS. Upon being issued one that identified him as "negro," he returned it, contesting his racial designation. Plecker sent him back the same one, this time with "a statement on the back referring to the evidence showing that your mother is of negro descent." Plecker closed his letter to Pugh by saying, "There are plenty of jobs open for colored people. You need have no trouble about that."[6] Pugh had obviously been worried that if Plecker forced him to present an employer with a birth certificate identifying him as "colored," he would be denied a job or denied the specific job he sought.

Pugh's concerns about his employment prospects had merit, and the experiences of countless African Americans like him eventually led civil rights organizations to try to curtail the administrative power of birth certificates. Employment discrimination was widespread, and during World War II it was tied to the practice of using birth certificates to establish the facts of identity. African Americans had experienced disproportionately high rates of unemployment during the Great Depression and naturally hoped that with the increased production and economic activity of the war years, that would change. But it did not. African Americans were less likely to be hired or, when hired, were given unskilled jobs with less pay. The 1940 census showed that whereas only 21.5 percent of white workers were employed in unskilled, service, or agricultural labor, 64.5 percent of all African Americans were employed in these sectors. Such disparity continued into the war years and reflected not just previous patterns of employment but also discrimination in the training programs created to fill the unmet demand for wartime production. In the earliest years of the war, vocational training programs placed some 15,455 workers—only fifty of whom were nonwhite. Major wartime employers such as aviation companies made it clear they would consider African Americans only for janitorial jobs regardless of training.[7]

Given that there was an acute manpower shortage in many key industries, these disparities in employment could only be explained by discrimination. In February 1941, A. Philip Randolph, the head of the International Brotherhood of Sleeping Car Porters, called together leaders from the NAACP, the YMCA, the National Council of Negro Women, the Urban League, and the Council of Churches of Christ in America to discuss the problem. Led by Randolph, the group settled on a tactic that became known as the March on Washington Movement. The idea was to put pressure on the federal government to end employment discrimination by holding mass meetings in urban areas and, barring an adequate response to those, organizing 10,000 African Americans to march in the nation's capital. March on Washington Movement chapters organized in cities across the nation, held local demonstrations, and vowed to send thousands to the D.C. march, scheduled for 1 July 1941. But the march was never held. On 25 July 1941, President Roosevelt issued Executive Order 8802, which prohibited discrimination in defense industries. The order also created a Fair Employment Practice Committee (FEPC) to hear complaints and make redress. In 1943, a second executive order transformed the FEPC into an independent agency with twelve regional offices. By the end of the 1940s, ten states and twenty-eight cities had enacted bans on employment discrimination. By 1960, seven more states had joined the original ten.[8]

Birth certificates played a role both in employment discrimination and its prohibition. As the case of Clayton Pugh suggests, employers demanded proof of name, age, and citizenship, and they often asked that prospective employees establish these facts with a birth certificate. In Pugh's case, his family seems to have been known and registered as white; thus the requirement for a birth certificate would have changed his employment prospects. As soon as national civil rights organizations such as the NAACP become involved in the March on Washington Movement, and as soon as offices of the FEPC were established, complaints of discrimination involving birth certificates began to roll in. One of these was from Charles Norris, who wrote to the NAACP in 1941. Norris, born in Virginia, was a resident of Paterson, New Jersey. He reported to the NAACP that he had been accepted into a vocational training program run by the State Employment Service and designed to funnel its graduates into jobs at a local aviation company. After being accepted, Norris was directed to bring his social security card and his birth certificate to an interview at the Edison Vocational School. After the interview and the presentation of his documents, Norris's place in the program was withdrawn. Allegedly this was because he already had a job, but he reported that since unemployment was not a condition for the training program, he could only conclude that "the final refusal to accept my application is based on the fact that through my birth certificate, my identity as a Negro was disclosed."[9] Likewise, Donald McRaven of Minneapolis complained to the FEPC that after he signed a contract for employment, his offer was rescinded when his birth certificate revealed that he was not white. While it was unclear whether Norris had a racial reputation as white in New Jersey, the Chicago regional office of the FEPC described McRaven "as an individual, who appears to be white."[10] In both cases, the requirement for documentary proof of identity functioned in the service of racial discrimination, now officially illegal.

Birth certificates excluded African Americans from jobs not just because they marked an applicant's race but also because employers frequently required birth certificates as a condition of employment. This was certainly true for young people once documentary proof of age was required across all states, and it was also true for adults seeking employment in many industries. During the 1930s, in order to work in an aircraft plant, for example, employees had to have their names verified by birth certificate.[11] Moreover, once employers started giving out pensions, and once they were obligated to have employees register for social security as part of their employment, proof of age for adults became as important as it was for adolescents. And just as in the case of child labor, it was employers and employees in southern states in particular who found it hardest to comply with requirements for documentary proof of age. "What will be considered to be 'satisfactory evidence' [of age] for white and colored employees in the States of Virginia, North Carolina, South Carolina, Georgia and Kentucky[?]," Vance Terrell of the Imperial Tobacco Company asked the Social Security Board in 1936.[12] Reports from the Works Progress Administration during the Depression era likewise noted that it was hardest for African Americans to obtain social security and other benefits, because they lacked proof of birth. "A great many [African American] persons complain they are refused WPA employment, general relief, and social security benefits because they cannot produce credentials to substantiate their age, marriage, and residential claims," wrote one Works Progress Administration field agent to his superiors in Washington.[13]

Lack of documentation continued to dog African Americans during the period when the War Department required that anyone working in a plant with a government contract provide documentary proof of citizenship. In a series of letters to William Hastie, the civilian aide to the secretary of war, Sidney Williams, the executive secretary of the Cleveland branch of the Urban League, explained the problem. "The birth certificate problem I find is hounding Negro workers here in Cleveland just as it did in St. Louis," he reported. Williams estimated that more than 70 percent of African Americans living and working in the North "were born in southern states before these states adopted the practice of issuing birth certificates." Thus the demand for documentation of birth put African American applicants "at a sever[e] disadvantage." Williams reminded Hastie that "southern-born Negro workers are suffering because of state governments over which they had absolutely no control." Indeed, "if they could have voted, this would have changed the picture slightly."[14] Civil rights organizations such as the NAACP and the Urban League argued not only that southern states had been slow to register births but also that they were particularly neglectful when it came to registering Black babies. "Southern cities are notoriously lax in registering Negro babies," claimed a press release from the Associated Negro Press.[15] As these complaints suggested, lax birth registration was a function of politics, not just poor administration. Disfranchised and undocumented, African American workers fleeing racist home rule and seeking economic opportunity in northern war industries found that their states' exclusion of them followed them northward. In response, local branches of the Urban League advertised that they could help African Americans navigate the process of receiving a delayed birth certificate.[16]

Like African Americans, Native Americans were disproportionately represented among the millions of unregistered Americans. In spite of efforts such as the Save the Babies campaign run by the Office of Indian Affairs (OIA), Native Americans on reservations remained, like other nonwhite and rural populations, less likely to have their births registered throughout the twentieth century. In 1940, only 68 percent of Indian babies had their births registered; by 1950, 85 percent of Indian births were registered nationally, compared to 93.4 percent of nonwhite births as a whole and 98.5 percent of white births.[17] Unlike many African Americans, however, Native Americans often had recourse to other government-issued documents to establish their identity. Correspondence with the Bureau of Indian Affairs (BIA) shows that Indians sought proof of identity for the same reasons as any other Americans. More often than not, however, the BIA supplied that information from allotment rolls and censuses, not vital registration documents. During the World War I draft, for example, draft boards and individual Native Americans had used tribal rolls to establish eligibility for service.[18] After social security was established, Native Americans used federal records to access those benefits. In 1939, a group of allotted Pottawatomie Indians met and "decided to ask the Commissioner of Indian Affairs to furnish the business committee with a copy of the allotment roll. . . . It is felt that this would be a great help to our old people in receiving Old Age Assistance, as birth certificates are impossible to procure."[19] The Pottawatomie clearly understood the importance that federal records had for them and acted as a group to gain access to them. Most evidence suggests, however, that individuals sought documentary evidence of their identity on a case-by-case basis. Chickasaw member Ada Phillips Trout Heaston, for example, wrote to the BIA in the 1940s seeking her birth information. "Will you please tell me how get a Birth Certificate," she asked. She explained that she had her "papers from Muskogee," meaning her enrollment papers, but she wondered, "Is this official & will it ans [sic] for Birth Certificate every place?" Now living in Los Angeles, Heaston was trying to get an old-age pension. The OIA wrote Heaston back explaining that the tribal roll was "official and accepted as proof of age by all state departments of public welfare for use in establishing eligibility for old age assistance."[20]

During World War II, Indians used allotment rolls and tribal censuses to establish age and citizenship to serve in the military and work in the war industries.[21] These records were considered valid in spite of the fact that for decades the OIA had acknowledged that its tribal censuses were incomplete and haphazard and in spite of the fact that the roll recorded the person's age in years on a particular date but did not record a birth date. Still, this was acceptable to state and federal agencies because, like a birth certificate, the roll was a creature of the state. A 1945 article in the Registrar, a publication of the Census Bureau, recognized this. "The Indian does have . . . an Indian Census roll record," the article explained, and "nine times out of ten a certification of this record is used, accompanied by a form letter, and these are always acceptable to the Army, Navy, and other agencies." The record created from the roll could give many of the same facts as a birth certificate—name, surname, sex, tribe, date of birth or age, "degree of Indian blood," and family relationships (mother and father)—as well as things not supplied by the birth certificate such as marital status.[22] On some agencies, however, superintendents used tribal documents to help Native Americans obtain state-issued delayed birth certificates in order to find work in defense industries.[23] Like African Americans, Indians also needed proof of birth and citizenship, but unlike many born during the first half of the twentieth century, they had access to government-issued documents even when they had no birth certificate on file.

The War Department did eventually relax its rules for proof of citizenship, but employers did not always follow suit. At an October 1942 meeting of the Metropolitan Council on Fair Employment Practice in New York City, representatives from organizations such as the NAACP, the Urban League, and the American Jewish Congress discussed "the difficulties experienced by Negroes and other groups of native-born American citizens unable to obtain birth certificates." These difficulties persisted because "very few companies" were accepting the War Department's "alternate procedure."[24] As employers continued to ask applicants for birth certificates, these requirements disproportionately excluded African Americans. "Many employers are using the birth certificates as a convenient excuse for not employing Negroes," lamented the Cleveland *Call and Post*. Even after Executive Order 8802 and the establishment of the FEPC, the *Atlanta Daily World* reported that Cleveland manufacturers were finding ways to evade the orders. "Smart anti-Negro employers had their personnel managers send in orders for Negro men between 45 and 60 years old." When the men showed up to apply for work, managers told them that they would be employed only if they could present a birth certificate. But, the paper noted, "since most of the colored population is from the south where there are few birth records of Negroes of that age," almost no men were actually hired. The employers, meanwhile, "use this as 'proof' of their willingness to hire colored."[25] E. W. Bailey of Norwich, New York, described a similar strategy in a 1942 letter to the NAACP. Bailey opened his letter by asking, "Why is it just about impossible for a Race member to secure employment in Defense work?" He immediately connected this to the requirement for birth certificates. "Why do they not tell applicants when first contact is made," he went on, "that a Certificate of Birth or Affidavit is required instead of the dangling method which is used?"[26] The "dangling method" accords with the report on Ohio factories in the *Atlanta Daily World*. Employers "dangled" jobs before African Americans and then denied them for a bureaucratic reason: lack of proper documentation. The NAACP likewise reported on the case of a woman in Detroit who, after being hired at the Hudson Naval Arsenal, was denied her job once her employer discovered that she was "colored." Officially, however, "the 'excuse' given was that she had no birth certificate."[27] Thelma Cleage of Springfield, Ohio, reported a similar story to a regional office of the federal FEPC in Ohio.[28]

Not only were African Americans less likely than whites to have their birth registered in the first place, but also obtaining a delayed birth certificate could be more difficult for African Americans than for those presumed to be white. In his *Pittsburgh Courier* column, George Schuyler of the NAACP reported a dispatch he'd received from FP, "a colored man of San Diego." Here, in a major center of naval operations and war production, FP reported that "it is getting increasingly harder to get delayed certificates for colored people from States in the South." Texas was reputed to be the "worst offender."[29] While FP did not say what made it "increasingly harder," even the routine backlog created by the wartime demand for delayed birth certificates would have hit African Americans more squarely than it did whites. African Americans were both more likely to need a delayed certificate and more likely to face an ironclad requirement to present a birth certificate to an employer. Thus, whether or not southern registrars intentionally made it harder for African Americans to obtain delayed registration—and we know that some such as Plecker did— even seemingly ordinary bureaucratic procedures on both the production and consumption side of birth registration acted to keep African Americans from fully participating in the wartime economic boom.

There is evidence that increased demand for birth certificates as a condition of employment affected other minority groups as well. American Jews, for example, had long adopted anglicized surnames to avoid discrimination in employment and higher education. For the first several decades of the twentieth century, this was done informally rather than legally. During the 1940s, however, the number of legal name changes among American Jews skyrocketed. This was in no small part because of the increasingly common requirement that official documentation, such as a birth certificate, accompany applications for a variety of things, including employment. In this case, American Jews needed to have official documents that matched their informal, anglicized names. Thus they flooded courts with requests for legal name changes that would produce new birth certificates with their new names.[30] Unlike African Americans, Jews could use legal procedures to pass, at least on paper. For those who did not avail themselves of this option, American Jewish advocacy organizations worked with the NAACP, the Urban League, and others to help usher in the federal and state FEPCs.

The civil rights organizations that pressured the federal government to create the FEPC, and who worked to pass similar measures in states and municipalities, clearly recognized the role that documentation of identity could play in discrimination. While the federal FEPC adjudicated complaints about discrimination, the state FEPCs promulgated clear rules about what constituted discriminatory hiring practices. Among other things, state rules specified what kinds of questions employers could ask and what kinds of identification they could seek as part of the hiring process. In Massachusetts, for example, employers were forbidden from asking applicants for "a photograph, birth certificate, discharge papers and other such personal documents as disclosed information concerning race, color, religion or national origin." Most other state FEPCs adopted similar rules and published guides for employers, directing them to the questions and proof of identification that they could and could not require during the hiring process.[31] As such laws took effect in states, corporations incorporated fair employment practices into their hiring procedures. In Michigan, for example, after the state adopted an antidiscrimination law in 1955, the Chrysler Corporation's manuals for supervisors clearly reminded them that they could not seek a birth certificate from a job applicant until *after* he had been hired.[32]

As the experience of World War II–era employment discrimination suggests, the increasingly common requirement on the part of institutions that people present birth certificates to verify their identity helped maintain white supremacy. This was the case not just when institutions used positive racial identification to sort people for the purpose of unequally distributing resources such as jobs or schooling but also when birth certificates were entirely absent. This was true for African Americans seeking employment during the war years—when not having a birth certificate could become a disqualification— and it was true when civil rights organizations sought to breach other barriers as well. In 1939, for example, the Young Men's Civic Club of Savannah, Georgia, wrote to the NAACP for help. At the time, a fellow Savannahian, Walter White, was the national president of the NAACP. The Young Men's Civic Club had been founded in 1938, organized by African American longshoremen who worked on the city's docks.[33] As the club described itself to the NAACP, it was "organized for the sole purpose of getting more Negroes to become registered voters" in Savannah. In just four months, the club had increased the number of African American voters from 600 to 1,000. But now its efforts were being stonewalled. Suddenly the registrar began to demand "such forms as birth certificates, insurance policies, and the old Family Bible" as proof of age to vote. As the club's letter pointed out, "birth certificates have only been issued to Negroes about 17 years ago." The club helped registrants to find these documents—and to answer the detailed questions posed by registrars—but found that registrars simply made the requirements more stringent. "As we neared the 400 mark . . . the qualifications became more exact, they wanted only birth certificates." Of course, even when registrants could produce birth certificates, registrars found other ways to disqualify them.[34] Nonetheless, many Black Georgians could not produce birth certificates, and this apparently neutral requirement helped form the edifice of disfranchisement.

The Young Men's Civic Club was a pioneer in the effort to boost Black voter rolls, but even when national organizations such as the NAACP and the Student Nonviolent Coordinating Committee fanned out across southern states in the mid-1960s, birth certificates were still used to keep African Americans from voting. The field reports from an NAACP summer voter registration project in Mississippi, for example, noted that the Jones County registrar "demonstrated a high degree of ingenuity in requiring Negro applicants to furnish birth certificates to prove age, real property deeds to prove residency." In one case, a sixty-seven-year-old woman who could prove her residency with her electric bill was turned away for want of a birth certificate.[35] There's little doubt that she appeared too young to vote. Congress of Racial Equality (CORE) fieldworker Ronnie Sigal described teaching African Americans in St. Helena Parish, Louisiana, to fill out voter registration forms. Each applicant had to prove that she was twenty-one years of age. "A great grandmother might come to register, but if she didn't have a birth certificate stating she was 21, she was refused."[36] As in Savannah, so too in Jones County and St. Helena Parish documentary requirements formed an allegedly race-neutral barrier.

Public officials also used birth certificates to slow down school integration. Progressives in the U.S. Children's Bureau and state registrars across the country had viewed the requirement for children to present birth certificates to enroll in school as a way to both protect children and promote vital registration. Now that such requirements were integrated into the administrative machinery of school districts, the requirement could be strategically deployed as it was in the cases of employment and voting. In Louisiana, the legislature adopted a new law after the Supreme Court's 1954 *Brown v. Board of Education* decision. According to a report by the Associated Negro Press, the new law required that a student applying to attend a new school "must furnish proof of his date of birth, place of birth, sex, and race."[37] All of these were, of course, items reported on a birth certificate, and the requirement to provide documentation of them in the wake of *Brown* was clearly an attempt to turn the stream of integration into a trickle. Such efforts were not isolated. Field reports from Mississippi to the national office of the Student Nonviolent Coordinating Committee in 1965 described efforts at school integration. In Panola County, African American children attempting to register at a "white school" were "turned away for not having proper birth certificates." In Holmes County, 289 African American children registered to attend a formerly all-white school. Roughly one-third were turned away for lack of documentation— forty-five for not having a birth certificate and another forty-seven for not having proof of legal guardianship.[38] In Winston County, Mississippi, when a delegation of African American parents sought to learn the requirements to apply for a school transfer, the superintendent of schools refused to tell them "what kinds of inoculation records would be needed or if we would have to produce permanent record birth certificates."[39]

Compared to the violent intimidation faced by many African Americans who sought to vote or attend white schools, a registrar's or school official's request for a birth certificate might seem a mild affront. Yet the presence of these accounts of administrative discrimination alongside those of overt violence demonstrates that documentation and violence are not opposed but exist on a continuum. And as birth certificates came to play an unmistakable role in enforcing state-sanctioned segregation, prosecuting antimiscegenation laws, and bolstering disfranchisement, birth registration became a civil rights issue. Civil rights organizations came to see registration as a path to the entitlements of equal citizenship, and they saw it as within their purview to assist their constituents with the process.

The importance of documentation to strategies of segregation not only resulted in rules such as those created under state FEPCs—which banned employers from requiring birth certificates as part of an application for employment—but also meant that civil rights organizations had to confront the role documentation played in denying access to other state and federal entitlements. Even as agencies of the federal government targeted African American communities, civil rights organizations began to incorporate birth registration into their work. On the most basic level, they understood that lack of documentation hampered African American efforts to gain access to the polling place, the integrated school, and other entitlements. The Coordinating Council of New Orleans ran a voter registration drive in 1963. Irvin S.

Daniel, the director of voter education in charge of the drive, reported that more than 800 people applied for registration. "Most of the Negro applicants were turned away for insufficient identification; yet these applicants have presented such documents as driver's license, marriage license, birth certificates, credit cards, charge plates, bank book, personal mail, rent receipts, etc."[40] The fact that Daniel had his registrants show up with such documents illustrates how civil rights organizations were preparing ordinary people to fight back against documentation's role in preserving white supremacy. Likewise, at the CORE annual meeting in 1962, the Education Workshop advised CORE chapters on how to conduct local school integration campaigns. It was important to make sure parents were organized and prepared for the obstacles that white schools would throw up as parents tried to register their children for transfers. "Be sure parents committed to the transfer know the procedure, and have all the necessary documents and information (birth certificates, etc.)," CORE leadership told those gathered.[41] As CORE's advice suggests, part of the work that civil rights organizations had to do at the local level was assist African Americans in securing documentation, whether that meant obtaining delayed registration or ordering a copy of an original birth certificate. In the summer of 1967, for example, a branch of the NAACP in Autauga County, Alabama, reported helping Mrs. Rosa Motley secure her birth certificate in order to apply for social security. This was after the NAACP had also filed complaints of discrimination against "Pensions and Security offices" in fourteen Alabama counties.[42]

Civil rights organizations' efforts to assist their constituencies with registration dovetailed with efforts on the part of federal agencies that worked throughout the 1940s to improve birth registration among nonwhites. The Census Bureau, for example, encouraged African Americans to register births as a path to full citizenship and enlisted Black institutions to help deliver the message. In 1945, the Children's Bureau and the Census Bureau cooperated to make the annual May 1 celebration of Child Health Day into a promotion of birth registration. In their material explaining the campaign, the two bureaus argued that it was especially important to target "Negro and Spanish-speaking groups" in the South and Southwest because these populations were disproportionately underregistered.[43] In internal memos, Census Bureau staff discussed the best ways to reach African Americans, whom they characterized as more likely to be rural, illiterate, and suspicious of official record keeping. Staff member Elisabeth Clayton recommended getting local race leaders to participate—"namely minister, school teacher, Lawyer, physician and midwives." Clayton also recommended reaching out to the NAACP, which she characterized as "a very active body of Colored leaders organized to help the negro where ever possible." She felt sure the NAACP would help, "since one of our biggest registration problems is with the Colored people in the South."[44]

As field agents from the Census Bureau traveled throughout the South and Southwest organizing events for May Day 1945, they attempted to put Clayton's suggestions in place. Evelyn Halpin described her trip to Alabama and reported that while there, she gave speeches to "colored public health nurses" and prepared "in cooperation with the Negro public health education consultant, a letter to accompany literature to colored leaders."[45] Katharine Lenroot, the chief of the Children's Bureau, also sent a letter to "Negro Leaders" imploring them to aid their states' health departments in the campaign for complete birth registration.[46] In 1946, the Census Bureau created a pamphlet for distribution to African American midwives. Entitled *A Birth Certificate for Baby*, it explained the importance of birth registration for the individual child and the steps that a midwife would have to take to register a birth (figure 8.1).[47] Some of this outreach was effective. The National Medical Association, the premier organization of Black doctors, printed an article about the May Day campaign and the importance of birth registration in its journal.[48] The *Atlanta Daily World* likewise reproduced a letter from the Georgia Congress of Colored Parents and Teachers on 1 May 1945 that urged parents to see that their children were registered. The advantages of birth registration were framed by the congress in terms of both public health and citizenship. While a birth certificate is not used to "check up on people," the letter explained, it does entitle each person "to all the privileges and protections of citizenship."[49]

The Census Bureau also worked with the OIA to try to bolster Native American birth registration. This was not a new idea. Throughout the 1930s, employees in the Census Bureau's Division of Vital Statistics recommended coordination with the OIA to improve registration of Indians both on and off the reservation.[50] But nothing seems to have come of these suggestions until the 1940s, when the bureau and the OIA partnered to improve Indian birth registration. In 1940, the Division of Vital Statistics in the Census Bureau sent out a field agent to speak at an annual meeting of reservation staff from the Southwest, supplied the agencies with Census Bureau–issued materials promoting birth registration, and commissioned the superintendent of the Pueblo Indian Agency in New Mexico to write an account of how he, unlike most southwestern agencies, succeeded in registering vital events among reservation Indians. In 1942, the OIA sent yet another circular letter to its

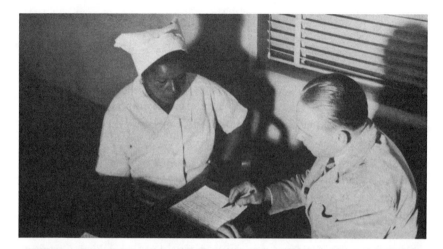

Figure 8.1. *A Birth Certificate for Baby* (1946)

The U.S. Census Bureau's pamphlet promoting birth registration to African Americans emphasized interactions with the state. A midwife brings her certificate to the registrar, and a young boy brings his to enroll in school. Source: Records of the U.S. Census Bureau, National Archives and Records Administration, Washington, D.C.

superintendents imploring them to follow state rules for reporting births and deaths.[51]

That same year, the Census Bureau sent three different fieldworkers to the southwestern states with Navajo reservations. The Navajo had the lowest rates of registration among all minority groups. Field agents met with state officials, reservation officials, and representatives from the Interior Department.[52] The next year, the New Mexico BVS announced a campaign to promote birth registration among Indians. The campaign was run by a visiting nurse of the Indian Health Service who also served as a field agent for the New Mexico State Department of Health. Her approach was to try to reach parents through their children. She delivered talks at Indian schools and gave children pamphlets about the benefits of birth registration. "It is felt that the children can be depended on to talk over the situation at home, and to assure their parents of the importance of filing vital records with the State Bureau of Vital Statistics."[53]

Finally, as part of the 1945 May Day campaign that also promoted registration among African Americans, the Census Bureau worked with the State of New Mexico and the OIA to promote registration among Indians, and the Navajo in particular. Though the OIA instructed all its personnel to participate in the May Day campaign and promote birth registration on the agencies, in meetings between OIA officials and those from the Census Bureau, the OIA defended rates of Indian registration. OIA representatives were willing to concede only that the Navajo were particularly bad, and they reminded Census Bureau officials that though some agency staff were dilatory in filing birth reports, state health officials were often uninterested in Indian registration. Everyone present could agree, however, that reaching the Navajo would require something more than distributing the usual pamphlets. Darcy McNickle, the head of the OIA, recommended enlisting the support of tribal councils and producing promotional materials in the Navajo language. The Census Bureau recommended that babies be registered when they were entered on the tribal roll and that the number of registrars be expanded.[54]

In 1946 and 1947, the National Office of Vital Statistics (NOVS), in collaboration with several other federal agencies and the State of New Mexico, rolled out promotional materials in the Navajo language. Some of these were what the NOVS newsletter, the *Registrar*, described as "humorous stories" published in the Navajo-language newspapers sponsored by the agency. The stories appropriated the "manner and style of the Coyote cycle of Navajo mythology" to promote birth registration. In the sample story printed in the *Registrar*, called "Why Old Man Coyote's Children Didn't Go to School," Coyote is a layabout who lives "way out among the junipers and pinons," sitting under a tree and singing songs while his four wives work hard and give birth to four new children each year. Coyote prizes his isolation and his independence and ignores a cousin who warns him that unless he registers his children's births, they won't have a school to go to when they get old enough. Sure enough, when the time comes to put his thirty older children in school, Coyote marches them down into the town only to be told that the school is full and he must wait until a new school is built to house all his children.[55] Coyote's failure to register his children's births, then, not only was a result of his laziness but also showed that he did not grasp the basics of rational planning, could not understand cause and effect inside a system of linear time, and did not have either abstract or concrete conceptions of population, public health, or the common good. His lack of work, his marital patterns, and his neglect of vital registration all went hand in hand.

In addition to the ersatz Coyote stories, NOVS made a pamphlet and a film in Navajo. Both had the title *A Birth Certificate Tells the Facts*, or *Áwéé binaltsoos beedáhazingo adenchsin*. The film was, the NOVS boasted, narrated by a Navajo tribal councilman and was the first ever "talking picture" in Navajo. It was meant to help address the fact that three-quarters of Navajo did not speak English and were illiterate in any language.[56] The pamphlet was bilingual and illustrated with photographs of Navajo people. The first page showed a mother holding her baby in a traditional cradleboard with the caption "Of course you love your baby. Do you know how much it needs a right name and a certificate as soon as it is born?" In an effort that had begun some sixty years earlier with the advent of allotment, the campaign for birth registration among the Navajo was in part an effort to convince them to adopt Western naming practices. Throughout the pamphlet, the concept of the "right name" is used. "As soon as your baby is born, give it a right name" and make sure that is the same name you tell the doctor and the registrar. The pamphlet also stressed that though birth registration may not seem important to the baby, it would help in the future. Echoing the Coyote story, the pamphlet explained that the birth certificate would help the child go to school. Not only will the school need to know "the permanent name of your child," but also "Washington needs to know how many" schools to build. When the child grows up, he may leave the reservation for a job, and he will need to show his name, "what people he comes from, and how old he is." When he is older, the certificate may help him get his social security or his pension or help his dependents get veterans' benefits. The pamphlet closed with a photo of a Navajo couple staring lovingly down at their baby, swaddled and held in his mother's arms. "Make his life easier," the text urged, "by giving him a right name, and getting a certificate for him, as soon as he is born."[57] Though the pamphlet presented birth registration as an act of parental love, it could not hide the fact that registration was entirely about interfacing with the state, which came with a white face.

Photographs in the pamphlet showing Navajos reporting a birth to a registrar, attending school, using the bank, and collecting a pension or veterans' benefits all embodied the government in the person of an Anglo.

Though such campaigns had some success, success was also hard to measure. Between 1940 and 1950, registration among the Navajo doubled. Even so, it hovered around 50 percent. But as the federal government had to admit, it did not actually know what percentage of Navajo babies were registered. That was because, as J. Nixon Hadley, a statistician for the Indian Health Service, explained, birth registration completeness was measured by matching an existing birth certificate with a card filled out during a test period for an infant under the age of one. In the case of the Navajo, this meant that measures of birth registration "represent the degree of success in matching names between two records for an illiterate and non-record-conscious people whose culture allows for easy change of name."[58] Testing methods could not account for these cultural differences. Even more to the point, Hadley wrote in another article, the federal government did not really know how many "Indians" there were in the United States to begin with—"no clear-cut definition of 'Indian' is readily available." The Census Bureau's own definitions were not stable over time, and tribal membership lay largely within the control of tribal councils. Myriad treaties and laws defined "Indian" in particular ways for purposes of specific agreements.[59] The problem was circular: improving nonwhite registration led straight back to the problem of racial classification in the first place.

Ensuring better registration was only one piece of the puzzle, however. While organizations such as the Census Bureau had their own, largely statistical, reasons for wanting to improve registration among Native Americans and Black Americans, civil rights organizations applied multiple strategies to untie the knot tying documentation to discrimination. Even as they took on the task of helping ensure that more African Americans had their births registered, and even as they helped those already registered to obtain proof of birth, advocates also continued to promote the idea, born of the FEPC, that birth certificates should not be used as a gatekeeping device in the first place. Walter White, the journalist and longtime head of the NAACP, reported favorably in 1952 about Brandeis University's policy for admissions. Brandeis, White wrote, was a place where "students of every race, religion or place of birth could come, on merit and merit alone, to study." Brandeis made admission by "merit alone" because its application forms "scrupulously exclude questions not only of race and religion but those about birthplace, birth certificate, change of name, language spoken at home, mother's maiden name, nationality, birthplace of parents or name of pastor."[60] As White's list suggested, birth certificates were among the most efficient tools by which institutions could determine race and ethnicity—with the exception of language spoken at home, change of name, or name of pastor, most of the potentially discriminating data that Brandeis avoided were condensed on the birth certificate. To allow applicants to be considered without a birth certificate, and without asking the proxy questions that would substitute for it, was, in White's mind, to allow meritocracy to trump status. Because they recorded and disseminated information that could be used to discriminate, birth certificates were instruments of status rather than integration and merit.

As they had with the FEPC, civil rights organizations after the war also sought to create public rules about the use of birth certificates to create gates in and out of institutions. The 1964 Civil Rights Act was an opportunity to create national standards for school integration that might overcome the state and local use of myriad tactics of delay and obstruction, including schools' demands for specific kinds of documentation. Civil rights organizations successfully argued for the inclusion of schools in the "public accommodations" covered by the 1964 Civil Rights Act. The act gave the U.S. Justice Department the power to bring suits against school districts, and it resulted in federal rules governing integration plans used by districts under both voluntary and court-ordered desegregation.[61] In 1966, the U.S. Department of Health, Education, and Welfare created a series of rules for communities seeking to implement "school choice" plans. These federal rules made it clear that a student could not be denied admission to school or denied a transfer under school choice because she lacked a birth certificate. In its "Notice of School Desegregation Plan under Title VI of the Civil Rights Act of 1964," the Department of Health, Education, and Welfare supplied school districts with text that they were legally required to publicly post before implementing school choice plans. Section 13 of the notice limited how schools could assign students to new schools. "No choice of school will be denied because of failure at the time of choice to provide any health record, birth certificate, or other document," it read.[62] Just as requiring a birth certificate for employment became prohibited under the state FEPCs, some twenty years later the same conditions were applied to school registration in an effort to disable one of the tools used by school districts to limit integration.

If one tactic in the fight against discrimination was limiting the role that birth certificates could play in gatekeeping access to fundamental institutions of citizenship, a more radical strategy was confronting the role of birth registration in maintaining the fiction of race itself. Beginning in the 1950s, both local and national civil rights organizations challenged the use of birth certificates to establish racial identity. Like the child welfare advocates who had argued that birth status did not belong on birth certificates, civil rights leaders argued that racial identification should be eliminated. Though never as coordinated and large-scale as their campaigns against segregation and discrimination in employment (and thus harder to find in the documentary record), civil rights organizations nonetheless chipped away at racial identification by confronting the practice where it originated: at the municipal and state levels, where boards of health controlled vital registration practices.

In July 1950, the *Chicago Defender* reported that a physician from Harrisburg, Pennsylvania, Leonard Z. Johnson, had decided to write "human" in the box for "race." Johnson, an African American and the son of a Howard University professor and prominent minister from Washington, D.C., wrote a letter to his state department of health explaining his decision. "I have decided that hereafter I will sign all such certificates" with the race marked only as "human" because "it is my opinion that all such statistics are not necessary, and, in fact, are detrimental to the solution of the racial problem in this country."[63] In Johnson's view, recording an infant's race served no legitimate or statistical purpose but did serve to make life more difficult for ordinary African Americans. This was a radical move. For while some ethnic or racial groups had successfully lobbied to change their categorization in the U.S. Census— Mexican Americans, for example, ended their separate enumeration and were counted as white beginning in 1940—none had suggested that the state abandon racial classification altogether.[64] In 1951, another African American physician called attention to the matter. Dr. A. Maceo Mercer of Chicago asked the Chicago health department "for a statement of the law regarding 'What is a Negro' in the state of Illinois." Mercer, described later by the NAACP as a "conscientious objector to indications of race on public records," was presumably not asking for a Virginia-style set of rules about blood quantum but rather asking so as to reveal the absurdity of using a medical form to populate a category—race—that had no biological reality. Indeed, according to the *Journal of the National Medical Association*, Mercer told the health department that if state law required him to designate race on birth certificates, "he would never deliver another baby." Mercer also refused to "correct" the birth certificate returned to him by the state because he had written "human" in the box for race. Mercer later addressed his protests to the Illinois State Department of Health and the U.S. Public Health Service. At the state level, a bill to remove race from the state's birth certificates had passed the house but failed in the senate. The head of the state Department of Health, Dr. Roland Cross, did not support removing race from birth certificates. He claimed, first, that the Census Bureau created the certificates and he had no control over their content and, second, that recording race was integral to correlating "health data" with conditions of "the minority races."[65]

Though Johnson's and Mercer's protests were reported as the work of lone individuals, the National Medical Association supported their actions and believed that racial designation served no legitimate public health purpose.[66] National civil rights organizations soon reached similar conclusions. In a 1952 meeting of the NAACP's National Medical Committee, the gathered physicians discussed "the necessity of racial identification on birth certificates." Like Johnson and Mercer, many on the committee believed that race did not belong. Minutes from the meeting reported that "it was the general opinion of the group that a statement of race had negligible scientific value and only served to lend a social stigma to an individual." One of those present, Dr. W. Montague Cobb, pointed out that race was a social fiction— "anthropologists had proven there was no biological difference between Negroes and whites"—and thus racial designation had no place on a birth certificate. Still, despite the "general opinion" against racial categorization on birth certificates, some committee members had qualms. Their arguments were not unlike the arguments of those who had wanted to preserve a record of birth status. Dr. Ernest Boas, for example, was reluctant to give up the possibility that racial classification on birth records was "of value in compiling statistical data regarding incidence of TB and other diseases among particular groups." Was it worth giving up the ability to aggregate data linking race and disease? As had been the case when child welfare advocates debated removing illegitimacy from the face of birth certificates, here too the public health value of vital registration butted up against the use of registration documents as forms of identification that could reveal stigmatizing information about individuals.

Others on the committee cautioned that advocating for the removal of racial designations from birth records might be politically premature. One physician pointed out that were the NAACP to adopt this position it would occasion "great controversy" because it was "such a departure from an accepted convention." Likewise, another worried that it would paint the NAACP as "radical with extremists [sic] views." Was it worth the political cost, particularly when the political landscape was changing? Dr. Herbert Marshall argued that at present it might be a disadvantage to be marked as "negro," but "in future generations the term Negro will bear less and less stigma." Why subject the committee and the NAACP to ridicule and controversy over the terms of birth certificates when the progress of history might alter "the connotation of Negro" all on its own? Such cautionary notes notwithstanding, the committee decided to go on record "as being opposed to racial identification on birth certificates."[67]

Though the documentary record does not make clear what the NAACP's National Medical Committee did to broadcast its view that racial identification had no place on birth records, within a decade of its resolution, local chapters and lawyers had some success at the municipal level. In 1959, for example, the Legal Redress Committee of the St. Paul, Minnesota, branch filed suit against the St. Paul Bureau of Public Health for "inclusion of term black, as racial designation on birth certificate." The committee reported that the suit resulted in a change from "black" to "negro" on the particular birth certificate in question, but that "problem regarding policy on this issue remains to be settled."[68] Three years earlier, Mrs. Shelton B. Granger of Minneapolis, Minnesota, had refused to fill out her and her husband's races on her son's birth certificate. Though there is no evidence that she did so in coordination with the same NAACP chapter that filed suit against her Twin Cities neighbor, her actions prompted rebuke from the state Bureau of Public Health.[69]

In 1960, the action shifted to New York City. Attorney Newton Greenberg assisted Mr. and Mrs. Gregory Simms in challenging their racial designation on their daughter's birth certificate. In his challenge to the New York City Department of Health, Greenberg sought the advice of NAACP chief counsel Robert L. Carter. The Simmses requested that their daughter's birth certificate be changed to reflect the race of the father (item 9) as "ruddy" and the race of the mother (item 14) as "fair." A hospital official had filled them in as "negro" and "white," respectively.[70] In correspondence with the Department of Health, Greenberg challenged the department's authority to determine the Simmses' races as "negro" and "white" rather than "ruddy" and "fair." He averred that if the primary purpose of including the race of parents was identification, then "ruddy" and "fair" would be more accurate than "negro" and "white." The department insisted that in order for Mr. and Mrs. Simms to change their racial identification on their daughter's birth certificate, they would have to submit "appropriate proof of the true ethnological background of the parents," namely "certified copies of their own birth records" showing their race at birth. Moreover, the department explained that racial identification on birth records was not primarily for identification, as Greenberg and Simms assumed. Rather, it served a public health purpose. Carl Erhardt, the director of the Bureau of Records and Statistics for the City of New York, wrote to Greenberg that the purpose was to obtain "ethnological" data that would be used for "compilation of statistical facts extremely important in planning the department's public health program." Like those on the NAACP's National Medical Committee who expressed skepticism, Erhardt connected racial identification on birth records to ameliorative public health policy. "Mortality and natality date for various ethnic and other groups are frequently used," he went on, "to show which groups are at a disadvantage" and thus which might need "special attention and help" from public agencies. With that, Erhardt dismissed the Simmses and Greenberg as mistaking the true purpose of racial classification and thus illegitimately questioning the department's authority to collect and record race.[71]

Though Erhardt mounted a firm defense of racial classification on vital documents, he and other registration officials knew that the trickle of protests against the practice would only grow in strength. As early as 1956, the American Association of Registration Executives and the NOVS began discussing the matter behind the scenes. Led by Jerome Brower, the deputy director of the Minnesota State Department of Health, the American Association of Registration Executives asked the NOVS to conduct a survey to see how many municipalities or states included "color" or "race" on the face of birth certificates. The answer was that they all did—hardly surprising given that it was also part of the Census Bureau's standard certificate of live birth. The NOVS also prepared a report defending the use of race in vital statistics. The report analyzed a single issue of the *Journal of Negro Education* from 1949 and argued that "examination of the issue as a whole demonstrates the reliance placed by the contributors on tabulations of vital statistics classified by race," most of which "derived originally from race items on birth and death certificates."[72] In other words, even the leading African American intellectuals relied on race classification to understand racial problems. This argument, developed in 1956, was essentially the same as that presented by New York City four years later.

Its defense of racial identification as benign and palliative notwithstanding, New York City did eliminate race from the face of its birth records. The policy, announced by Dr. Leona Baumgartner, took effect on 1 January 1961. As states and cities across the country had done with birth status, New York City's policy stripped race from the front of its birth certificates but recorded it on the rear face with "medical" and "confidential" information and where it would not be reproduced as part of a certified copy. The official rationale for continuing to record race was, as Erhardt had suggested, to help direct public policy. According to Shad Polier, the chairman of the American Jewish Congress's Commission on Law and Social Action, the change was the result of pressure from the Urban League, the NAACP, and the American Jewish Congress.[73] No doubt Greenberg's letters with Erhardt played a role as well. Though Greenberg acted only on behalf of the Simmses and without official sponsorship from of any of these organizations, his letters made clear that the Department of Health had no statutory basis for engaging in racial classification.

In November 1961, the American Public Health Association annual meeting hosted a panel discussion on racial identification on vital documents, prompted in large part by New York City's decision. As part of this panel, Carl Erhardt, who had not long before fended off the Simmses and their attorney, explained the New York City Department of Health's action in terms that revealed that the decision was at once principled, political, and administrative. On principle, Erhardt argued that eliminating race from vital statistics documents was consistent with the State Commission against Discrimination's guidelines, which required "justification of the need for stating race or color on any state form where such an item is included." The City of New York had similar policies, and together state and city regulations suggested that the inclusion of race on vital registration forms had to serve a real, nondiscriminatory purpose. But, as Erhardt pointed out, "the major private purposes for which copies of birth records are needed do not seem to require any statement of color or race in most areas."[74] Thus there was in fact little justification for a practice that seemed on its face to violate principle. Though Erhardt did not say so, this principle was political: state policies against discrimination were the result of political agitation going back to the March on Washington Movement, the creation of federal and state FEPCs, and the court battle against school desegregation that established antidiscrimination norms in employment, schooling, housing, and beyond.

Beyond the politics that produced the city's and state's official nondiscrimination policies, Erhardt also detailed more immediate skirmishes. Without naming the Simmses, he alluded to a number of parents who had recently tried to enter racial designations such as "pink" or "human," as well as a number who refused to enter any race at all. Moreover, he claimed that the Puerto Ricans of the city refused to be identified as either white or Black, so hospitals often wrote "Puerto Rican" for race or color, which the city subsequently coded as white. Still, Erhardt pointed out that Puerto Ricans themselves were divided on the issue, with some apparently preferring to be identified as white and some insisting on identification by national origin. All of this pointed to what Erhardt called "administrative factors" in the health department's decision to remove racial identification. When parents refused to cooperate with racial classification, or when some Puerto Ricans might choose "white" while others might choose another category, this disrupted the smooth functioning of the vital registration system and created potential conflict between the different constituencies involved. If parents refused to name an acceptable race on the form, would the Department of Health then require the hospital or attending physician to fill out the category? Erhardt worried that "such action would lead to considerable controversy between hospital authorities, attending physicians, Department of Health, and parents." Like with Plecker's adjudication of racial status in Virginia, dissenters from existing categories raised the possibility that divination of race might be taken away from those being identified and handed instead to physicians and city bureaucrats. This clearly made the Department of Health uncomfortable. In order to avoid disrupting the "cordial relations" that ensured high rates of birth registration in the city, better to just eliminate the source of controversy by making race medical and confidential.[75]

The Department of Health was also trying to avoid what it considered worse political outcomes—a lawsuit or action by the state legislature. These quietly simmering controversies had so far, Erhardt explained, involved only individuals, but it seemed likely that "active group representations" might be on the horizon, by which he presumably meant agitation by civil rights organizations. And though he did not say so, newspaper and documentary records indicate that such groups had already started to press the matter with the city. Erhardt's comments before the American Public Health Association suggest that he and the Department of Health saw the writing on the wall. He told conference attendees that he sensed it was only a matter of time before activists would move the issue squarely onto the political stage. Already, the New York legislature had considered, but not passed, a bill to remove race from marriage licenses, and the Massachusetts house had taken up, but not passed, a bill to remove race from birth certificates. Erhardt and the department feared that if they did not act soon, the legislature would. Worrying that the legislature would cave to political pressure to remove race entirely, the department decided to act preemptively in order to preserve race for statistical purposes in the medical/confidential section. "Thus," Erhardt concluded his presentation, "fears that information on race or color will be used to the detriment of the individual are alleviated and political or other pressures that might force complete elimination of the item are relieved." Erhardt pointed explicitly to the example of illegitimacy as a model for how to strike the balance between protection of individual privacy, the social good of equal treatment, and the state's desire to use population statistics for public health and welfare programs. But in New York, unlike in most of the rest of the nation, the state legislature had decades earlier acted to eliminate any collection of birth status, even in the medical section of the birth certificate. This was what the department wanted to avoid in the case of race.[76]

The Baltimore *Sun* endorsed the move, expressing relief that New York City did not "do what some extremists ask and abolish all record of race in births and deaths."[77] But Lester Granger, head of the Urban League, recognized that while Baumgartner's stance was an improvement, he declared that it was "still a violation of principle."[78] The *New York Amsterdam News* similarly congratulated Baumgartner for the new policy and said it "took courage." At the same time, the *News* said that it wasn't "really true" that it was necessary for public health and social work to record race for statistical purposes. This was a dodge that would probably be eliminated in due course. As soon as other cities and states followed New York City's example, "race as a matter of record, will disappear from the records of true Americanism." This was a way station on the road to the true destination, a time when "we are simply all Americans!"[79] The *News* editorial suggested that, like ending segregation and employment discrimination, removing race from birth certificates was a way of dismantling the legacy of slavery and Jim Crow and moving Americans toward full equality.

Not everyone agreed that removing race from birth records was a step in the right direction. While civil rights organizations and the Black press heralded the change, the preservation of racial categories in any form, even as part of statistics gathering, remained controversial. In part, this controversy reflected the fact that racial classification on birth certificates was a species of a larger set of questions about universalism, particularism, and civil rights in the post–World War II United States. As the United States positioned itself as the bulwark of universal human rights against totalitarian, fascist, and communist regimes, the government was pushed at home to dismantle Jim Crow laws and create a color-blind legal order. In fields such as anthropology, which had long trucked in the delineation of difference, scholars also began to insist that all humans were the same everywhere.[80] This was what Dr. A. Maceo Mercer of Chicago had insisted on when he filled in "human" on the birth certificates of the babies he delivered. Yet this kind of universalism did not satisfy everyone. Even as many civil rights activists—and legislation such as the 1964 Civil Rights Act—sought to create color-blind institutions, leaders such as the National Urban League's Whitney Young began to argue that true justice required the sort of quantitative, race-conscious, ameliorative action that would ultimately result in affirmative action.[81]

Though their reasoning differed in its particulars, most dissenters agreed that New York's birth certificate policy prematurely denied that race was a salient social fact in 1960s America. The conservative columnist for the *Los Angeles Times*, Morrie Ryskind, called the gesture "silly and childish" because it would do nothing to stop racial identification, while it suggested, at the same time, that being nonwhite was a "shameful secret" rather than something to be proud of.[82] Howard University sociologist G. Franklin Edwards also criticized the move as a naïve political gesture but from a slightly different angle. He believed that eliminating race from vital documents would actually make it more difficult to document patterns of discrimination in health and social policy by "undermining the factual basis from which inequities could be questioned." He pointed to the 1959 report of the U.S. Civil Rights Commission, which had complained that it was hard to assess the pace of desegregation in those parts of the country "where race had been removed from the school records."[83] In a private meeting, the executive committee of the NAACP discussed a similar concern with how lack of race-based data could obscure discrimination; the organization's general counsel urged it to reconsider its opposition to racial identification.[84] Leona Baumgartner reported, meanwhile, that she received a "mixed reaction" from health commissioners in other cities alongside a number of "really vicious" letters denouncing the policy change. Among those municipal health commissioners who did not support Baumgartner, New Orleans's Dr. Walter Gardiner took his complaints public. He vowed that no one born in New York City would be able to marry in New Orleans so long as he was around to enforce Louisiana's miscegenation law, which required that marriage licenses be granted only after the applicants could submit birth certificates to prove their race.[85] Gardiner's dissent acted to shore up white supremacy while Edwards's was meant to help collect data to undermine it, but both shared a belief with Ryskind that race continued to structure the world whether racial liberals wanted it to or not.

Though people from across the political spectrum lamented it, New York City's compromise solution became a model for the nation. The same year that the change took effect in New York City, the State of New York announced it would follow suit. And ten years after Dr. A. Maceo Mercer had protested his state's use of racial classification on birth documents, Illinois announced a similar change for its birth certificates. Even a state legislator in far-flung Alaska took note. James Fisher, a representative from Anchorage, wrote the national American Civil Liberties Union that after learning of New York City's move, he had "begun an inquiry into the reason for entering race on birth certificates in the State of Alaska."[86] Still, the move raised concerns among registrars and public health officials who sought to catch up with and control the direction of change. Hazel Aune from the National Vital Statistics Division of the U.S. Public Health Service worried that as states and municipalities started to individually make changes to registration documents, the carefully crafted system of national uniformity would crumble. (Aune's concerns ignored the fact that across the states there was no stable definition of "white" and "Black" to begin with.) At a meeting of the American Public Health Association, Aune pleaded with state registrars to wait for the next revision of the standard certificate of live birth rather than make changes piecemeal.[87]

Planning for the new standard certificate began in 1962, and the new form was implemented in 1968 (figure 8.2). In 1963, the Public Health Conference on Records and Statistics formed a study group to advise the National Center for Health Statistics (NCHS) on the form and content of revisions. The study group surveyed over 1,000 people and organizations about possible revisions, including to racial identification. Fifty-six percent of all those who responded approved of the proposed relocation of race to the medical/confidential section of the birth certificate. The percentage was slightly lower when state registrars' responses were disaggregated from the total pool—only 48 percent welcomed the change. In 1964, at a meeting of the Public Health Conference on Records and Statistics, the federal Public Health Service proposed moving "color or race from the top portion of the certificate to the lower portion" on the U.S. standard certificate of birth.[88] This would effectively nationalize the New York City model. The proposed revisions were also discussed at national meeting of the American Association for Vital Records and Public Health Statistics in 1965 and endorsed by a number of other national organizations including the National Urban League, the American Statistical Association, the American Public Health Association, the American Sociological Association, and the Association of State and Territorial Health Officers. In 1966, the Eleventh National Meeting of the Public Health Conference on Records and Statistics devoted two workshops to discussing the proposed new standard certificate; conference proceedings reported that the proposal to move race to

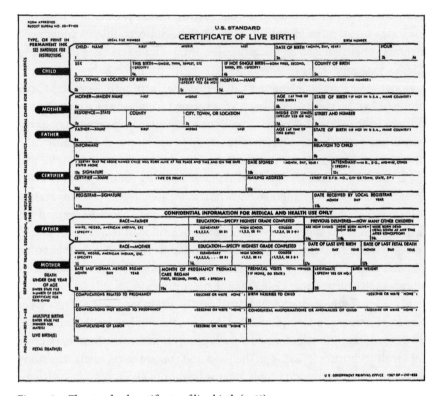

Figure 8.2. The standard certificate of live birth (1968)

The 1968 revision of the standard certificate moved the "race" of the child's mother and father to the section that includes "confidential information for medical and health use only." It joined birth status, or legitimacy, as a piece of "confidential" information that had been removed from the public face of the birth certificate. Source: Grover, *1968 Revision.*

the confidential section of the birth certificate was "accepted without objection."[89] The next year, the U.S. Census Bureau released the new certificate in preparation for use in 1968.[90] The NCHS also issued manuals for hospitals and physicians instructing them how to fill out the new certificates.[91] By 1968, the NCHS reported that thirty-eight states had adopted either the new standard certificate or the practice of recording race only in the "restricted sections" of their birth certificates.[92]

Of course, the end of legal identification of race only came to those born after the new standard certificate was adopted. Because of this, some states made the change retroactive as well. In 1969, for example, Massachusetts made it possible for a person born before 1968 to obtain a new birth certificate stripped of all references to race.[93] In 1978, California removed race or color from certified copies of all birth certificates and, in 1989, enabled individuals to have their original birth certificates sealed if the original "contained a term which, in the individual's opinion, was a slur or otherwise offensive."[94] Likewise, in Virginia in 1979 the state declared that birth certificates filed before 1960 would henceforth be issued without racial designation.[95] Even Louisiana eventually came around. In 1979 the state legislature directed the state registrar to exclude race from certified copies of birth certificates.[96] In all these instances, registrars performed a sleight of hand like the one they had objected to when it came to illegitimate births: they agreed to issue certified copies of certificates that were different in some measurable way from those that were originally filed.

The bifurcation of the birth certificate—into a public-facing section, which would become the basis for the portable identity document required for so many institutions of American life, and a private-facing "health and medical" section used only to gather public health and population statistics—made it a document that could solve thorny political and philosophical problems in ways that few other instruments of governmental policy could. The line separating the facts of identification from "health and welfare" meant that the state could regard its population, at least on its paper forms, as both universal and particular. Through the dotted line of the bureaucratic form, the state could know, but not show, the race of its citizens, on one hand committing to making every baby born a deracinated "human" and, on the other hand, locating the population into groups defined by particular histories.

While states and municipalities acted over the course of several decades to remove race from vital documents, this hardly ended racial classification or spelled the end of a role for documentary evidence of racial identity. As states and cities ceased to publish racial classification on vital documents, health officials still recorded the race of those who were born, married, and died so that vital events and other measures of personal and social health could be sorted by race. After 1989, most states followed elaborate formulae provided by the NCHS to determine the racial classification of newborn infants. And though the NCHS classifications were kept off the face of certificates, they were recorded on the long-form birth certificate and might be referenced later. Like the "corrections" made by Plecker and Davis, an NCHS formula could often produce a racial classification that was quite distant from an individual's racial self-identification.[97] Recent studies comparing the racial classification of infants who died under the age of one, for example, found that Native American infants were almost always racially misclassified, usually as white, at birth. While such misclassifications do not form the basis for racial identification, they skew infant mortality rates and underrepresent the health hazards faced by Native American children.[98]

Beyond recording race under the "health" section of vital registration documents, state policies continued to "file" humans according to race and continued to rely on documents to establish racial identity. The legacy of the Indian Reorganization Act (IRA) of 1934, for example, meant that Native American nations were often vested in the vexed process of defining membership according to rules about blood quantum. Though the IRA offered a legal definition of "Indian" based on blood quantum, it also restored a degree of tribal sovereignty by allowing the organization of tribal councils that could, in turn, establish their own criteria for membership. In spite of the fact that Indians may have relied less on birth certificates than other Americans, and in spite of the fact that much of what the federal government wanted to know about them was imperfectly recorded on those records, Native American nations, like civil rights organizations, saw the importance of such documents both to their own members and to their internal administration. Like allotment policy itself, the determination of membership often turned on questions of blood quantum and descent. Tribal councils faced the task of deciding who could be enrolled, who would be purged, and how new applicants for enrollment would be judged. All of these questions involved the issue of proof. Under what terms would descent and degree of blood be established? Tribal councils had the authority to determine this themselves.

The meeting minutes of the executive committee of the Minnesota Chippewa provide an example of this process at work. In 1941, when the committee met to consider establishing rules for enrollment, they discussed whether to include all descendants of the Chippewa, whether to create a blood quantum cutoff, and how to corroborate descent. A proposal created by a subcommittee on enrollment provided that all descendants of Chippewa enrolled according to the terms of an 1889 treaty with the U.S. government were eligible for enrollment in the present. This was no matter whether they had been born on or off the reservations and no matter the blood quantum. Making descent the rule, rather than descent in combination with blood quantum, helped address the concern among some Chippewa that the IRA's rule of one-half blood quantum was too strict. The proposal also provided that applicants for enrollment "must file a birth certificate and other supporting evidence so that it will be possible for the tribe and the agency to definitely establish the fact that they are rightfully entitled to enrollment." Though committee members disagreed about whether they should create a blood quantum standard in addition to requiring proof of descent, no one questioned that descent and its proof were the main administrative apparatus governing enrollment in the future. The Minnesota Chippewa agreed, in the end, that they would admit all those who could prove lineal descent from signers of the 1889 treaty. The BIA, however, recommended that the secretary of the Interior reject their constitution because it did not include a blood quantum minimum in addition to proof of descent. For this reason, the Minnesota Chippewa had no constitution until the 1960s, when they agreed to include a blood quantum requirement.[99]

The Cheyenne-Arapaho of Oklahoma, by contrast, included a blood quantum minimum in their very first constitution, adopted in 1937. The constitution's enrollment rules specified lineal descent from someone on the original tribal roll plus a minimum of one-fourth Cheyenne-Arapaho "blood." The constitution also provided that "the burden of proof as to quantum of blood of the Cheyenne-Arapaho Tribes of Oklahoma will be on the claimant for enrollment in each case." In 1959, the tribe amended the enrollment rules to require that "all applications for membership for enrollment of persons born after June 26, 1936, shall be supported by a copy of a birth certificate or other record such as is recognized by State and Federal recorders." After they passed this amendment in 1959, the Cheyenne-Arapaho spent the next several years trying to reconcile the membership lists with the birth certificates they had on file. Members of the tribal council were given lists of enrollees in their districts and asked to check that each person born after 1936 had a birth certificate on file in the tribal office. In specific cases, the enrollment committee also recommended adopting new members who had previously been rejected or purged from the roles. In these cases, "they have been screened and have birth certificates to prove eligibility."[100] As a part of tribal self-governance, birth certificates could be a useful administrative tool.

There is evidence that many nations considered them essential to the enrollment process. Like the Cheyenne River Sioux who used racial designations on birth certificates to reject applicants for enrollment, other Indian nations insisted that applicants' birth records show they met basic criteria. Many sent back applicants who had no birth records.[101] Multiple records of tribal council meetings also show that applicants who had previously been rejected reapplied after having their birth certificates changed.[102] Though the council minutes do not specify how the certificates were changed, it's likely that these changes were meant to show proper lineal descent, by including previously unacknowledged paternity, for instance, or by correcting the racial designation or blood quantum shown on the original certificate.

Having members provide birth certificates as part of enrollment, and having the tribal office keep such certificates on file, made tribal administration easier overall. Besides streamlining enrollment, birth certificates saved labor in other areas. This is demonstrated by a discussion that took place at a meeting of the advisory committee of the Navajo Tribal Council in early 1950. In a discussion of how the upcoming federal census would be conducted in Navajo country, the conversation quickly turned to the importance of accurate population knowledge and accurate vital registration. Wilbur Morgan, a tribal member who headed the Navajo Welfare Office, reported that his office spent a great deal of time making out birth affidavits for Navajo so that they could enroll in school, obtain social security or other pensions, get veterans' benefits, and so on. In the absence of birth records, the office often spent weeks chasing down information and people who could swear to the facts of the case.[103] On the one hand, the fact that Morgan's office made birth affidavits for the Navajo, and that these were accepted by state and federal agencies and private employers, shows that the Navajo were served even without birth registration. On the other hand, Morgan and members of the advisory committee agreed that making out birth affidavits delayed Navajo access to benefits and created more work for the tribal offices. They wanted this to change.

The federal government, for its part, also had to create mechanisms by which it could establish who met the blood-quantum-based definition of "Indian" for purposes of federal programs under the IRA. Particularly in the early years after the IRA was passed, BIA officials were aware that there would often be little documentation to establish blood quantum for individuals. This was particularly the case among those who fell into the third category of the IRA's definition of "Indian": those who were not a member of a federally recognized tribe or the descendant of a member but who wished to be recognized as "Indian" based on blood quantum alone. The BIA recognized that screening such applicants was an "administrative problem of some complexity." This was not only because there was, according to the BIA, no "scientific proof" of Indian blood but also because there was no legal standard of proof either. The bureau had no expectation that applicants would submit birth certificates showing their degree of blood. Instead, the bureau created a hierarchy of documentation that descended from tribal rolls and affidavits to physical inspection by an anthropologist.[104] The bureau strongly preferred evidence from either tribal rolls or physical anthropologists to affidavits, however, since it felt that applicants would all claim blood quantum of one-half "for the purpose of complying with the legal requirement." The problem, however, was that many tribal rolls had not included blood quantum information because it was membership and descent, not blood, that made one an Indian in the IRA's definition.[105] Like opponents of child labor who had suspected that parents would lie in order to have their children work, BIA bureaucrats mistrusted Indians to tell the truth about themselves and their relatives. Yet the bureau had little other reliable documentation to substitute for oral testimony and self-identification.

After the IRA was passed, the BIA issued instructions for how to establish the blood quantum of individuals, and it issued letters to individuals that served, in lieu of other documents, as evidence of their blood quantum for purposes of accessing federal entitlements. Though the date is unclear, at some point after the 1930s the BIA began to issue a document that is still in use, the federal Certificate of Degree of Indian Blood (CDIB). The CDIB was created for the purpose of federal programs, but the federal government also contracts out the issuance of CDIBs to many Indian nations, and several nations require that applicants obtain a CDIB as part of the enrollment process.[106] In the present, CDIBs are issued based on an applicant's ability to prove lineal descent from an enrolled member of a federally recognized Indian nation. The BIA's instructions specify that applicants must provide birth certificates that show their relationship to their parents or, if their parents were not enrolled, that show the relationship of their parents to any enrolled grandparents.[107] Like Walter Plecker's efforts to prove that the "Indians" of Virginia were really "Negroes" trying to pass over into whiteness, the logic of both tribal enrollment and the CDIB depends on the ability of governments to establish lineage through documents. Of course as Thomas Cromwell's 1538 edict establishing parish records acknowledged, establishing lineage for the transmission of estates was among the very first reasons that churches and governments began to record births. Thanks to state and federal policies that allocated access to citizenship along racial lines, in the United States racial identity became, like any other form of wealth, a property to pass along.

As polities designed to serve their members, Indian nations had to provide their citizens with proof of birth and age so that they could navigate state and federal bureaucracies. They also had to balance their duty to preserve the integrity of the tribe with their desire not to allow it to wither away by making enrollment requirements overly strict. Requirements such as lineal descent, blood quantum, and residence or birth on tribal land were, in one combination or another, criteria that most tribes adopted. Birth certificates were an efficient administrative tool for reckoning these qualifications. Yet they were also part of a colonial legacy, promoted as a central tool in allotment policies designed to remake Indian families, destroy tribal relations, and acculturate Native Americans to Euro-American norms of property and kinship. That birth certificates later became an administrative tool for tribal sovereignty is but a particular example of a larger pattern: to be known by the state is at once a marker of citizenship and a sign of subordination. This paradox confronted not just the tribal councils who had to draw up membership criteria and enforce standards of proof but also reformers who wanted to establish that race was a fiction while documenting the effects of racial discrimination. How to see the latter without investing in the former?

Including race on birth certificates in the first place had been part of the larger quest on the part of statists, demographers, legislators, and government administrators to know the population in order to govern it. Such population knowledge was always bound up with colonialism and racial science as early modern kings and their advisors sought to figure out how much land their populations could conquer and how fast they could reproduce compared to Native inhabitants. When the United States broke away from England, it lacked the institutional structures necessary to answer these questions definitely, but over time the new states, together with an expanding federal bureaucracy, built the infrastructure not only to aggregate the population, but also to subdivide it into categories of race, nativity, region, legitimacy, age, and others. This same birth registration infrastructure also provided policy makers the ability to locate particular individuals within these larger categories, to identify them as members of a race, as born to certain kinds of parents—white, Black, Irish, Chinese, married, unmarried—or as over or under a certain age. As the modern state built more and more policies that depended on its ability to know these facts about its population and each and every person in it, birth certificates became an indispensable tool, an authoritative and seemingly efficient way to fix identity while also creating aggregate knowledge.

The case of the rise and (partial) fall of racial classification on the face of birth certificates demonstrates, however, that such documents were never the neutral and stable providers of epistemological certainty and "accuracy in the tables" that dreamers from Lemuel Shattuck forward hoped that they would be. Though it took more than a century, the states built the capacity to register all births; veracity, however, remained chimerical. Indeed, the more widespread and integral to basic functioning birth certificates became, the more the people who used them contested them. Though ordinary Americans came to believe that birth certificates represented them, they did not always like what they saw.

FROM BIBLES TO BATHROOMS

n July 2019, the State of North Carolina reached a settlement in a lawsuit brought, in part, to contest its infamous "bathroom bill." Passed in 2016, House Bill 2 required persons in state buildings to use the bathroom that corresponded to the sex on their birth certificates. Though it was perhaps the most notorious example, House Bill 2 was part of a wave of state legislation that curtailed the use of bathrooms and locker rooms by transgender people by stipulating that biological sex rather than gender identity would dictate access to sex-segregated facilities.[1] North Carolina's effort to use birth certificates to fix bathroom access reveals the otherwise hidden political work that documents do to stabilize gender. While such proposals relied on assumptions about the naturalness and immutability of gender, North Carolina's legislators were equally invested in the epistemological stability of birth certificates. Like the child labor reformers of the first half of the twentieth century, the authors and supporters of House Bill 2 believed that birth certificates tell the truth about people. And like child labor reformers and others who came to see birth certificates as particularly reliable sources of identification, likewise in the case of bathroom bills, the objectivity of the birth certificate was a function of its relation to time and authority. The sex marked on a form in the past, at birth, was true, and this truth was made durable by public authorities rather than private feelings. The bathroom bills also share a history with the efforts of Walter Plecker and other registrars who believed that birth certificates could be used to fix and accurately represent the biological truth of race. Whatever the racial reputation or performance of a person, states invested time, money, and enforcement power in the belief that birth certificates recorded the correct racial history of families and individuals. Bathroom bills likewise assumed that birth certificates could preserve a stable sex apart from gender self-identification, performance, or reputation. Whatever gender a person might express, legislators assumed, their birth certificate fixed their sex. In other words, legislators' faith in documents is the product of the history this book describes.

Yet, as we have seen, birth certificates, like gender expression, are mutable. Before 1900, there was no standard certificate of birth in the United States, and even now, states are not required to adopt the standard certificate issued by the federal government. Beyond the possibility for variation in the categories and data collected through registration, the certificate's categories have changed over time to meet the demands and desires of both citizens and the state. This is abundantly clear from the ways that birth status and race were removed from birth certificates. In both cases, registration documents were changed only with direct pressure from affected constituencies who were able to argue that the revelation of bastardy or race was discriminatory. Likewise, in both cases, this pitted the identificatory functions of birth certificates against their data collection functions. These conflicts required states and the federal government to come up with ways to balance their desire to sort people into categories with people's own desire to refuse such categorization.

The history of the changing face of the birth certificate should remind us that despite the faith our institutions place in documents, the epistemological grounding of citizenship is slippery. Not only are birth certificates the product of historical contest and negotiation, but also the sexual designations listed on birth certificates, like names, are changeable by law in most states. Since 1977, the model law has included a provision to allow transgender people to change the sex on their birth certificate.[2] Like the birth certificate of an adoptee, which shows that she is the biological child of her adoptive parents, the new birth certificate of a transgender person can show that they were born as the gender with which they identify rather than the sex assigned to them at birth. However, most states that have adopted this provision of the model law, or some version of it, require individuals to undergo gender reassignment surgery in order to get a new birth certificate. In other states, no specific standard is specified, but a court order and medical certification are often required. Only a handful of states explicitly refuse to correct gender markers, and their number is dwindling thanks to successful court challenges.[3] Thus, though not all states offer gender marker correction, and though most that do still require sex change surgery, the model law has recognized that, as in cases such as illegitimacy, adoption, and race, altering or removing information on birth certificates can serve an important social function, equal to that served by the legal, probative value assigned to the certificate as a source of stable empirical information about an individual's identity.

Still, most trans people do not undergo gender reassignment surgery, and trans activists have begun to argue that requiring this is harmful and discriminatory; they also press states to make gender correction an administrative process rather than a court procedure. More than 40 percent of trans people report experiencing discrimination, harassment, and even assault when presenting identification documents that did not match their gender expression. Nationally, only a small minority of trans people have birth certificates that have been changed to match their gender identity, and likewise only a small minority have undergone the surgical procedures that many states require.[4] Thus even with the model law's allowances for gender correction, most trans people live with identification that does not match their gender expression. This not only results in harassment and discrimination but enables the logic of regulatory legislation such as North Carolina's "bathroom bill," which assumes that, state laws notwithstanding, birth certificates will reliably reveal a person's assigned sex at birth.

As was the case with the debate about whether and how to remove racial classification from birth certificates, trans activists disagree about how best to confront the role of birth certificates in regulating gender identification. Though many of the LGBTQ organizations that bring court cases and attempt to reform laws around identification simply seek to make it easier to correct birth certificates, some trans advocates argue, as civil rights organizations did in the case of race, that sexual classification should simply be removed from birth certificates. In this view, the state has no business registering and regulating sex, especially because doing so always acts to create insiders and outsiders and "unfairly distributes life chances." Simply being able to change the sex on a birth certificate from female to male or male to female, they argue, does nothing to disrupt the gender binary that is at the root of transphobia in the first place. Indeed, these and other reforms to legal recognition "would prop up the current system of legal sex classification and coercion and would continue to harm the most powerless trans* people."[5] Instead, such abolitionists argue that state-based sex classification should go the way of state-based racial classification: to the graveyard or perhaps just to the "health and medical" section of the long-form birth certificate.[6] And while no states as yet have taken this step, a handful have begun to or will soon offer gender-neutral driver's licenses.[7]

Unsurprisingly, the same people who back legislation such as North Carolina's "bathroom bill" also oppose altering birth certificates and other identification documents. Against the winds of change, Arkansas in 2017 attempted to pass a bill eliminating the state's provisions for gender correction on birth certificates. This bill passed the state house but died in the state senate.[8] Making it impossible to change one's gender on a birth certificate is rooted in the idea that sex is biological, binary, and properly expressed in a linear and fixed fashion by either male or female gender identity. It is not a choice. As such it is easily and permanently fixed at birth by a baby's chromosomal makeup, made manifest in their genitals, and marked for all time on their birth certificate. However, as we have seen, birth certificates, while intended to fix the truth about people, are mutable. Whether and how gender will be recorded or changed on them is not a matter of biology but, like whether and how we record birth status and race, a matter of politics.

While some may lament the empirical instability that this history of birth certificates reveals, it also shows us a via media between those who think of state-based documentation as a form of surveillance and those who think of it as a source of rights and inclusion. Because being known by the state is a sine qua non of citizenship, and because birth certificates are the foundation of official identity, they will always function both to include and to exclude. They are linked both to provision of social goods such as employment protections and social welfare and to exclusion from such provisions. Yet the history this book tells also demonstrates that states do not have the final say in whether and how their citizens are documented. Nonstate actors, from the General Federation of Women's Clubs to the NAACP and the Congress of Racial Equality, helped to achieve full registration in the United States, ensuring that registration spread beyond the capacity, or willingness, of states to provide people with the documents they needed to access their rights. And in changing the categories of identification on birth certificates, states responded to pressure groups who argued that birth certificates discriminated through classification. The picture is less top-down than some theorists might have it and probably less so than many policy makers would prefer. But in a democracy, that is just. If our documents are meant to say who we are, then we ought to have a say in our documents.

ACKNOWLEDGMENTS

When I was a new graduate student in 1997, researching my master's thesis on better baby contests, I came across the U.S. Children's Bureau's 1914 pamphlet promoting birth registration. I thought it was interesting that at one time this completely quotidian document was not something that ordinary people could take for granted. I became a historian because I liked uncovering the weird and interesting origins of the things and practices that are so commonplace we don't even notice them. As a Foucault-reading child of 1990s academia, I knew that this was exactly where power buried its tendrils. So I filed this pamphlet, and my reaction to it, away in my head. I wrote my MA thesis, wrote my dissertation, wrote my first book, and then, more than a decade later, finally had the chance to come back to find out more about this odd fact. Luckily for me, the story turned out to be even more interesting and complex than I had first imagined.

As much fun and satisfaction as I derived from researching and writing this book, it's also fair to say that it was written during the most difficult years of my life (let's hope). My mother developed dementia and died, I got divorced, Donald Trump was elected and incited an insurrection to overturn the results of the 2020 election, and the coronavirus and the struggle for racial justice in the United States upended the functioning of basic institutions and made everyday life exhausting. I finished revising this book while my children's schools were shuttered and I snatched pieces of time between their, and my, video calls and meetings. On many days, my "office" was wherever I could turn on noise-canceling headphones and find ten minutes of concentration.

John Donne famously said that no man is an island, and it turns out that no woman is either. It gives me great pleasure to be able to acknowledge the support of many people and institutions. Before my children were old enough to attend public school, regular access to the loving childcare provided by Dancy Bateman and Meredith Lownes was as vital to my professional success as any grant or publication. Once my children were in school, I relied on the support not only of their teachers but also of school-based aftercare programs to help me survive as a working mother. During COVID, Jasper Dabbs and Alice Gold were incredible companions for my daughter.

I received generous financial support for research and writing from the

National Endowment for the Humanities, the American Council of Learned Societies, and the Weinberg College of Arts and Sciences at Northwestern University. I also received but did not accept support from the Kluge Fellowship at the Library of Congress, the University of Connecticut Humanities Center, and the Kaplan Humanities Institute at Northwestern University. Without the time and money supplied by these institutions, I would never have completed this book.

Through the Leopold Fellows program of the Chabraja Center for Historical Studies at Northwestern University, I had the help of outstanding undergraduate research assistants Fiona Maxwell, Ailyn Gonzalez, Jessica Cardenas Lewis, and Alexa Herzog. I also had the help of graduate research assistants Lillian Hoodes and Hope McCaffrey thanks to funds supplied by the History Department at Northwestern. Research for this book was conducted in collections held by the National Archives in College Park, Maryland, and Washington, D.C.; the Library of Congress; the Library of Virginia; the University of Virginia Special Collections; the Indiana State Archives; the Massachusetts Historical Society; the Herbert Hoover Presidential Library; the South Carolina State Historical Society; the Connecticut State Archives; the Minnesota Historical Society; the Chicago History Museum; the University of Chicago Library; and the University of California, Los Angeles, Biomedical Library. Librarians and archivists working in all of these places helped both me and my research assistants figure out how to find and use their extraordinary collections.

So many people have taken time out of their own busy lives to give me feedback on part or all of this book. I presented early versions of various chapters to audiences at Northwestern University: the U.S. History Working Group; the Chabraja Center for Historical Studies Faculty Works in Progress seminar; the Comparative Historical Social Science Workshop; and the American Political Development Working Group. Many other institutions also provided me the opportunity to try out my ideas: the Newberry Library's labor history seminar; the University of Pennsylvania's Mellon Sawyer Seminar on Race across Time and Place; the Northwestern University–University of Wisconsin Nineteenth Century U.S. History Working Group; the Organization of American Historians; the Society for the History of Children and Youth; and the Workshop on the Comparative History of Civil Registration at Cambridge University. For commentary at these venues, I need to particularly thank Abigail Trollinger, Michelle Bezark, Janice Reiff, James Schmidt, Margo Anderson, and Barbara Welke.

A long list of friends and professional interlocutors have been pressed into duty to read a chapter, or three, of this book. For helpful comments and occasional cheerleading, I want to shout out Michael Allen, Kevin Boyle, Gerry Cadava, Margaret Jacobs, Sarah Pearsall, Helen Tilley, Corrine Field, Susan Burch, Doug Kiel, Rose Stremlau, Daniel Immerwahr, Leslie Harris, and Jo-anna Grisinger. Some colleagues were pressed into duty to read the entire manuscript, some of it more than once. I don't know how to adequately thank Kate Masur, Amy Stanley, Keith Woodhouse, Laura Edwards, Brian Balogh, Sarah Igo, Michelle Bezark, and Dan Bouk for reading and commenting on the first draft of the whole thing. These folks participated in a manuscript workshop, funded generously by the History Department at Northwestern, and their comments pushed me to reorganize the book in ways that made its arguments and narrative arc so much better. Sarah Igo's suggestions on this front were particularly helpful. Thanks to Laura Hein, who was the chair-person of my department at the time, for funding these workshops designed to help associate professors writing second books. Her successor, Deborah Cohen, helped me protect my time and energy to finish this book during the pandemic, and I owe her a great debt of gratitude. Debbie Gershenowitz, my editor at the University of North Carolina Press, supported this project with great confidence and made the process of publication painless. I don't know what I would do without these friends and professional interlocutors. Of course, all the mistakes are mine alone.

Life isn't all research and writing, and the things that sustain the body and the heart also sustain the mind. During the years I was researching and writing this book, I gave birth to my daughter, Jane, and witnessed the evolution of her bright spirit. She joined her funny, brilliant older sibling, Kira, to make my family complete. The kids' dad, Michael Kramer, juggled co-parenting sched-ules so that I could make research trips and find time to work. Kate Masur, Amy Stanley, and Helen Tilley are both my work wives and true friends. For friendship that has nothing to do with this book but that keeps me whole, love goes out to Ingrid Ordal Plunkett, Tamara Cohen Daley, Jill Bowdon, Naomi Crummey, Clare Stacey, Carrie Risatti, and Julie Siegel. My father, David Pearson, and my brother, Matthew Pearson, were rock solid through sickness, death, and divorce. I also have to thank the Hoyle Brothers for play-ing every Friday's Honky-Tonk Happy Hour at the Empty Bottle in Chicago. There is no band I'd rather dance to. Many years into this project, I met Dave Abatangelo. He taught me to play pool, he agreed to go dancing with me, he seemed to take it as given that I could do hard things, and he showed me that I could also write in a completely different voice. He has promised to throw me a party when this book is finally published, and I cannot wait.

NOTES

CHBU-CF
  Central Files, RG 102, Records of the U.S. Children's Bureau, National Archives
  and Records Administration, College Park, Maryland
CHBU-CF-CL
  Central Files Relating to Child Labor, 1914–40, RG 102, Records of the U.S.
  Children's Bureau, National Archives and Records Administration, College Park,
  Maryland
EGAP
  Edith and Grace Abbott Papers, Hanna Holborn Gray Special Collections Research
  Center, University of Chicago Library, Chicago
ISB-DICH-PFC
  Indiana State Board of Health, Division of Infant and Child Hygiene, Policy Files
  and Correspondence, Indiana State Archives, Indianapolis
JPP
  Papers of John Powell, Special Collections, University of Virginia Library,
  Charlottesville
LSP
  Lemuel Shattuck Papers, Massachusetts Historical Society, Boston
MLK Center
  Martin Luther King Jr. Center for Nonviolent Social Change, Inc.,
  Atlanta, Georgia
MN-SBH-CMR
  Minnesota State Health Department, Correspondence and Miscellaneous Records,
  Minnesota State Archives, Minnesota Historical Society, St. Paul
MN-VSD-SF
  Minnesota State Health Department, Vital Statistics Division, Subject Files,
  Minnesota State Archives, Minnesota Historical Society, St. Paul
NARA-DC
  National Archives and Records Administration, Washington, D.C.
NARA-MD
  National Archives and Records Administration, College Park, Maryland
PNAACP
  Papers of the NAACP, Library of Congress, Manuscripts Division,
  Washington, D.C.
RCCR-CC
  Rockbridge County Court Records, Clerks' Records, Clerk's Correspondence,
  Library of Virginia, Richmond
SSB-MF
  Records of the Social Security Board, Central File, Master File, 1935–47, RG 47,
  Records of the Social Security Administration, National Archives and Records
  Administration, College Park, Maryland
WWP
  Walter F. Willcox Papers, Library of Congress, Manuscripts Division,
  Washington, D.C.

INTRODUCTION

1. Craig Robertson, *Passport in America*.
2. United Nations Children's Fund, *Every Child's Birth Right*, 18.
3. Wendy Hunter, *Undocumented Nationals*, 1; Brennan Center for Justice, *Citizens without Proof*, 2.
4. Amy Blank Wilson, "It Takes ID," 111–32; Rapoport, "Want to Vote?," 63; Haley Hoff, "Get Real," 379–400; LeBrón et al., "Restrictive ID Policies," 255–60.
5. Finnegan, "Deportation Machine."
6. Mackenzie, "To Know a Citizen," 117–31.
7. Caplan and Torpey, introduction, 1–2, 7–8.
8. On family records, see Weil, *Family Trees*, 31–35. On ways to establish age before birth certificates were common, see Landrum, "From Family Bibles," 124–27; Pearson, "'Age Ought to Be a Fact,'" 1150–51; and Field, "'If You Have the Right,'" 76–77. On proof of name and citizenship before birth certificates were common, see Craig Robertson, *Passport in America*.
9. Hunter and Brill, "'Documents Please,'" 191–228. Edward Higgs also cautions against seeing documentary identification as a necessary outcome of modernization. Rather, it is an outcome of policy choices. Higgs, *Identifying the English*, 209–10.
10. Shattuck, *Report*, 284.
11. USDL, *Cotton Textile Industry*, 192.
12. Minor, "Proof-of-Age Records," 127.
13. Plecker to Josie Hartless, 15 August 1924, box 1, RCCR-CC.
14. For scholarship that discusses parts of this history, see Gutman, *Birth and Death Registration*; Rule et al., "Documentary Identification," 222–34; Hetzel, *History and Organization*; Watner, "Compulsory Birth and Death Certificate," 70–86; Brumberg, Dozor, and Golombek, "History of the Birth Certificate," 407–11; Landrum, "From Family Bibles"; Pearson, "'Age Ought to Be a Fact'"; Critical Genealogies Collaboratory, "Standard Forms of Power," 641–56; and Koopman, *How We Became Our Data*, 35–65. The best and most comprehensive account of this history is a dissertation that I became aware of while I was writing this book. See Landrum, "State's Big Family Bible."
15. Burns, "Notaries, Truth, and Consequences."
16. Cohn, *Colonialism*, esp. chap. 4. For histories of information gathering, including both population counting and identity documentation, see Foucault, *History of Sexuality*; Groebner, *Who Are You?*; Schweber, *Disciplining Statistics*; Higgs, *Identifying the English*; Higgs, *Information State in England*; Caplan and Torpey, *Documenting Individual Identity*; Curtis, *Politics of Population*; Patriarca, *Numbers and Nationhood*; and Dandeker, *Surveillance, Power and Modernity*. For the link between knowledge production and colonial governance, see Burns, *Into the Archive*. For histories of population counting and documentation in the United States, see Gutman, *Birth and Death Registration*; Cassedy, *Demography in Early America*; Margo J. Anderson, *American Census*; Craig Robertson, *Passport in America*; Prewitt, *What Is Your Race?*; and Schor, *Counting Americans*. On the importance of documentation in histories of race and immigration, see Pascoe, *What Comes Naturally*; Ngai, *Impossible Subjects*; and Lee, *At America's Gates*.
17. Foucault, *History of Sexuality*; Critical Genealogies Collaboratory, "Standard

Forms of Power"; Cohn, *Colonialism*, 3; Scott, *Seeing Like a State*, 2–3, 80–83. See also Dandeker, *Surveillance, Power and Modernity*.

18. Novak, "Myth."

19. For interest in demography and population knowledge, see Cassedy, *Demography in Early America*; Derek S. Hoff, *State and the Stork*; and Hannah, *Governmentality*. Important revisionist interpretations of the U.S. state in the nineteenth century include Novak, *People's Welfare*; John, *Spreading the News*; Balogh, *Government out of Sight*; Rockwell, *Indian Affairs*; Pearson, *Rights of the Defenseless*; and Pearson, "New Birth of Regulation." This list is not exhaustive.

20. Wilbur, "Chief Statistician," 94.

21. Clemens, "Lineages."

22. Brewer, *By Birth or Consent*; Chudacoff, *How Old Are You?* See also Mintz, "Reflections on Age," 91–94; James D. Schmidt, "Ends of Innocence"; and James D. Schmidt, *Industrial Violence*, 167–75.

23. I am indebted to Caitlin Rosenthal (*Accounting for Slavery*, 6) for calling my attention to this phrase. The phrase itself comes from Zakim, "Paperwork"; on taming chance, see Hacking, *Taming of Chance*.

24. Rosenthal, *Accounting for Slavery*, 50–83; Gitelman, *Paper Knowledge*, 24–49; Zakim, *Accounting for Capitalism*, 9–46.

25. CHBU, *Birth Registration*, 17. See also Landrum, "State's Big Family Bible," 74.

26. Poovey, *History of the Modern Fact*, 58–59.

27. John, "Recasting the Information Infrastructure," 55–106.

28. On credit reporting bureaus, see Lauer, *Creditworthy*.

29. Harris, "General Sanitary Laws," 477. Shane Landrum ("State's Big Family Bible," 65–96) provides a detailed account of the ways that vital statistics collection used the same "modern information technologies" as those created for "streamlining business operations and maximizing profits in a booming capitalist economy" (65–66).

30. Rule et al., "Documentary Identification," 223; Weber quoted in Dandeker, *Surveillance, Power and Modernity*, 9; Scott, *Seeing Like a State*, 78.

31. Watner, "Compulsory Birth and Death Certificate," 83; Abumrad, "Girl Who Doesn't Exist." See also Westover, *Educated*. Westover's parents, Mormon fundamentalists, also refused to register her birth because it was part of the rule of man rather than the kingdom of God.

32. Breckenridge and Szreter, "Recognition and Registration," 12, 16. See also Hunter and Brill, "'Documents Please,'" for the ways that birth registration is linked mostly with the creation of a social welfare rather than a surveillance state.

33. Igo, *Known Citizen*, chap. 2; Bouk, *How Our Days*, 224–27.

34. Tamar Lewin, "Out of Grief Grows Desire for Birth Certificates for Stillborn Babies," *New York Times*, 22 May 2007.

CHAPTER 1

1. Shattuck, *Report*, 284, 9.

2. "To the Citizens of Boston," *Boston Transcript*, 11 June 1846, vol. 1, LSP.

3. Shattuck, *Report*, 284, 285, 286.

4. Foucault, *History of Sexuality*, 139, 136.

5. For birthing practices in colonial North America, including the gradual introduction of male physicians, see Scholten, "'On the Importance'"; Wertz and Wertz, *Lying-In*; and Leavitt, *Brought to Bed*.

6. Wulf, "Bible, King, and Common Law," 467–502.

7. Wulf, 477–78; Barnhill, "'Keep Sacred the Memory,'" 60–65; Benes, "Family Representations and Remembrances," 13–59; Simons, "New England Family Record," 91–113.

8. Weil, *Family Trees*, 32–34; Landrum, "State's Big Family Bible," 1–3, 21–22.

9. Brown Arithmetic Book, Library of Virginia.

10. Wulf, "Bible, King, and Common Law," 482–86.

11. Brown Arithmetic Book, Library of Virginia.

12. Rosenthal, *Accounting for Slavery*, 12, 16, 31, 50–60, 121, 134–47.

13. Karin Wulf points out that genealogical knowledge was mobilized in freedom suits and contests of manumission under age-based gradual emancipation laws passed in some northern states after the Revolution. The evidence in such cases seems to have been oral rather than written testimony. Wulf, "Bible, King, and Common Law," 496–99.

14. Douglass, *Narrative of the Life*, 1–2.

15. Watson, *Narrative of Henry Watson*, 5.

16. Love, *Life and Adventures*, 7.

17. Edge, "Vital Registration in Europe," 347–48, 354–59. On Protestant practice, see Looijesteijn and Van Leeuwen, "Establishing and Registering Identity," 214–19.

18. Glass, *Numbering the People*, 15–16.

19. Glass, 15; Szreter, "Right of Registration," 72.

20. Szreter, "Registration of Identities," 70–71, 73–75, Cromwell quote on 71.

21. Records [photostats] 1724–1851, Christ Church (Boston, Mass.), Massachusetts Historical Society.

22. Register of baptisms, 1861–79, box 22, St. Michael's Church Records, South Carolina Historical Society.

23. Freeman Diary, Massachusetts Historical Society.

24. Shattuck, "Ecclesiastical Register," 285. Historians agree that "church registers were unsystematic and unreliable." Weil, *Family Trees*, 31.

25. Quoted in Cassedy, *Demography in Early America*, 15; *Act for Registering Births, Christenings, and Burials*.

26. Kuczynski, "Registration Laws," 1–9; Cassedy, *Demography in Early America*, 29.

27. Kuczynski, "Registration Laws," 1–6; Glass, *Numbering the People*, 118–29; Gutman, *Birth and Death Registration*, 20–21; Cassedy, *Demography in Early America*, 29–30.

28. Cooper, *Statutes at Large*, 120–21; Kuczynski, *West Indian and American Territories*.

29. Gutman, *Birth and Death Registration*, 24.

30. Porter, *Rise of Statistical Thinking*, 19; Glass, *Numbering the People*, 13; Rusnock, *Vital Accounts*, 37–38.

31. Bashford and Chaplin, *New Worlds*, 23.

32. McCormick, "Governing Model Populations," 180.

33. Petty, *Essays on Mankind*.

34. Though her interest is more in the concern about the politics of overpopulation

following Malthus, Alison Bashford calls this the linking of the "bio" and the "geo," fertility and soil, in population thought. Bashford, *Global Population*.

35. Bashford and Chaplin, *New Worlds*, 32–33. See also McCormick, "Governing Model Populations."

36. McCormick, "Statistics," 578–81.

37. Klepp, *Revolutionary Conceptions*; Bashford and Chaplin, *New Worlds*, 33.

38. Franklin, "Benjamin Franklin," 107–12; Chaplin, *Benjamin Franklin's Political Arithmetic*.

39. Chaplin, *Benjamin Franklin's Political Arithmetic*, 35–38.

40. Bashford and Chaplin, *New Worlds*, 240; McCormick, "Statistics," 585.

41. Bashford and Chaplin, *New Worlds*, 43–51, 240.

42. Hacking, "Biopower," 279–95.

43. Patricia Cline Cohen, *Calculating People*; Robert C. Davis, "Beginnings."

44. Porter, *Rise of Statistical Thinking*, 23–27, 56–57; Headrick, *When Information Came of Age*, 9–11.

45. American Statistical Association, *Constitution and By-laws*, 20–23.

46. Tucker, *Progress of the United States*, iv, 14.

47. Hacking, *Taming of Chance*, 105.

48. Hacking, 107–8; Porter, *Rise of Statistical Thinking*, 51–54.

49. Editor, "Nature and History," 320, 332.

50. Shattuck to Adolphe Quetelet, 27 August 1849, box 1, folder July–December 1849, LSP.

51. JHG, "Fourth Annual Report," 246.

52. Duffy, *Healers*, 189–92.

53. Shattuck, *Letter*, 27; Griscom, *Sanitary Condition*, 3, 6–11, 23, 46–49. Shattuck and Griscom were frequent correspondents. See Cassedy, "Roots of American Sanitary Reform."

54. For Shattuck's study of Prussian medical police, see Shattuck to Dr. Rothenburg, 21 August 1849, box 1, folder July–December 1849; and [illegible] of Prussian Legation at Washington, D.C., to Shattuck, 31 August 1851, oversize box 1, folder 1846–51. For examples of his correspondence with other foreign statistical and medical authorities, see Shattuck to T. H. Lister, 20 February 1839; and T. R. Edmonds to Shattuck, 29 June 1839, both in box 1, folder January–June 1839; and Adolphe Quetelet to Shattuck, 1 February 1840, box 1, folder 1840. All in LSP.

55. "Second Annual Report of the Legislature," 190.

56. "American Intelligence and Editorial," 112.

57. Eyler, *Victorian Social Medicine*, 43. See also Higgs, *Information State in England*.

58. Editor, "Nature and History," 333.

59. Secretary of the Commonwealth, *Instructions Concerning the Registration*, 30; Farr to Shattuck, 5 November 1846, box 1, folder 1846, LSP. For more on Farr, see Eyler, *Victorian Social Medicine*. For more praise of other countries' systems—and implicit or explicit criticism of the U.S. state systems—see EJ, "Report of the Births," 147–50.

60. Shattuck, *Letter*, 31.

61. "Second Annual Report of the Legislature," 190.

62. Gutman, *Birth and Death Registration*, 24–31.

63. EJ, "Report of the Births," 153.

64. Shattuck, *Letter*, 27–28, 32, 34–35.

65. Gutman, *Birth and Death Registration*, 73–83; "Massachusetts Medical Society," *Boston Daily Advertiser*, 30 May 1861; "News and Miscellany," 344; Shattuck, *Letter*, 35.

66. "Medical General Convention," 6; "Meeting of the American Medical Association," 434; "American Medical Association," *New Jersey Medical Reporter*, 294; "American Medical Association," *Medical Examiner*, 364; "American Medical Association," *North American and United States Gazette*, 19 May 1858; "Minutes of the Eleventh Annual Meeting," 378–79.

67. Robert C. Davis, "Beginnings," 171; Snow, *Report on Registration*.

68. Duffy, *Sanitarians*, 94.

69. Sutton to Shattuck, 3 December 1850, box 1, folder May–August 1850, LSP; "Registration," *Western Journal of Medicine and Surgery*, 547–48; B., "Vital Statistics," 453; "Vital Statistics of Kentucky," 293; Richard D. Arnold to Dr. Jas. M. Green, 18 April 1850, in Arnold, *Letters*, 39; Billings, "Registration of Vital Statistics," 49.

70. "Proceedings of a Conference," 11; Duffy, *Sanitarians*, 94; Duffy, *Healers*, 180–88.

71. Faust, *This Republic of Suffering*, 111–16.

72. Connecticut State Librarian, *Report* (1862), 12.

73. Billings, "Registration of Vital Statistics," 49–51.

74. Landrum, "State's Big Family Bible," 35.

75. "Proceedings of a Conference," 16.

76. Roberton to Shattuck, 17 November 1849, box 1, LSP.

77. Nott to Shattuck, 29 May 1853, box 2, LSP.

78. Margo J. Anderson, *American Census*, 29–31, quote on 29 (originally from the *Southern Literary Messenger*).

79. "Vital Statistics of Philadelphia," *North American and United States Gazette*, 19 July 1848.

80. *Report of the City Registrar* (1863), 10–11.

81. Richard Mayo Smith, "Outline of Statistics," 22.

82. Billings, "Original Lectures," 563.

83. "Vital Statistics," *Medical and Surgical Reporter*, 194.

84. Biographical information on Allen is from "Inauguration of the City Government," 2 January 1865; "City and Vicinity," 23 January 1865; and letter to the editor, 12 October 1866, all in *Lowell Daily Citizen and News*.

85. Nathan Allen, "Vital Statistics of Massachusetts," *Lowell Daily Citizen and News*, 10 October 1866. See also Nathan Allen, "Vital Statistics of Massachusetts," *New York Observer*, 4 October 1866; "Are the Yankees Dying Out?," *Cleveland Daily Herald*, 12 October 1866; "Radicalism in Massachusetts Doomed," *Columbian Register*, 27 October 1866; "Vital Statistics of Massachusetts"; "Are the Yankees Dying Out?," *Daily Evening Bulletin*, 4 December 1866; and "Yankees in Massachusetts," *Congregationalist*, 1 February 1867.

86. "Decrease of Population in Massachusetts," *New York Observer*, 11 April 1867.

87. *Annual Report of the Secretary of State of the State of Michigan* (1870), 34–38. As was common, Striker's report and its findings were digested in a variety of magazines and newspapers. "Registration Report of Michigan," 519–20.

88. U.S. Census Office, *Compendium*, 1405.

89. Prevost, "Controversy and Demarcation"; Hodgson, "Ideological Currents"; Hannah, *Governmentality*, 181–86; Ross, *Origins of American Social Science*, 146–7.

90. "American Public Health Association"; "Conference of Boards of Public Health," 210–28; "Meeting of the American Public Health Association," 449; Harris, "Report of the Committee," 432.

91. Michael, "National Board of Health," 125–26; Duffy, *Sanitarians*, 162–68; Cox, "Report upon the Necessity," 522–32.

92. Board minutes, 4 April 1879, vol. 1, no. 4, box 1; 5 April 1879, vol. 1, no. 5, box 1; and 17 December 1879, vol. 1 [unboxed], pp. 154–55, all in Minutes of the Board; and Billings to E. M. Snow, 9 February 1880; and to Thas. Wood, 5 March 1880, both in vol. 2, Copies of Letters Sent. All in Records of the National Board of Health, RG 90, NARA-MD.

93. "Proceedings of a Conference," 5–11.

94. "Proceedings of a Conference," 5–11.

95. Harris, "Report of the Committee," 434.

96. "Report of Dr. Billings on Vital Statistics," 8–10, in board minutes, 22 June 1882, vol. 4, no. 2, box 1, Minutes of the Board, Records of the National Board of Health, RG 90, NARA-MD; Billings, "Registration of Vital Statistics," 33–49; Duffy, *Sanitarians*, 171–72.

97. Holt, *Bureau of the Census*, 127–28; "Thirty-Third Congress," *North American and United States Gazette*, 14 December 1854; U.S. Congress, "Printing of Mortality Statistics," 45–46; "Minutes of the Eleventh Annual Meeting," 378.

98. "The Census of 1880," *Milwaukee Daily Sentinel*, 3 July 1879.

99. Wright, "Studies in Statistics," 64.

100. Mayo Smith, "Permanent Census Bureau," 589–600; Willcox, "Difficulty," 459–74; Wilbur, "Notes on Recent Progress," 269–79; Cressy Wilbur to Paulus Irving, 2 January 1897, Virginia State Board of Health, Library of Virginia.

101. USCB, *Report of the Director of the Census*, 9; U.S. Census Office, *Legislative Requirement for Registration*, 8.

102. USCB, *Report of the Director of the Census*, 9.

103. USCB, 9–10; U.S. Census Office, *Legislative Requirement for Registration*; USCB, *Legal Importance of Registration*; USCB, *Registration of Births and Deaths*; Willcox to Cressy Wilbur, 18 September 1907, box 23, folder "General Correspondence, Cressy L. Wilbur, 1904–7," WWP.

104. USCB, *Registration of Births and Deaths*, 30; Wilbur, *Federal Registration Service*, 21–22.

105. Wilbur to Walter Willcox, 15 June 1908, box 23, folder "Correspondence, Cressy Wilbur, 1908–11," WWP.

106. Walter Willcox to Wilbur, 13 September 1907; and Wilbur to Willcox, 16 September 1907, both in box 23, folder "Correspondence, Cressy Wilbur, 1904–7," WWP.

107. U.S. Department of Commerce, Bureau of the Census, "Vital Statistics Records Available in State Offices," box 118, Census-ROADSS.

CHAPTER 2

1. "Infantile Mortality," *St. Louis Globe-Democrat*, 14 July 1879.

2. Foucault, *History of Sexuality*; Scott, *Seeing Like a State*.

3. "Annual Meeting of the Medical Society," 132–34.

4. "Some Funny Answers," *Milwaukee Sentinel*, 1 May 1898.

5. "Investigation Made by Miss Gertrude Barnes," 387–90; *Cleveland Year Book*, 193.

6. Fuller, *History of Morrison and Todd Counties*, 176; Bracken to Hoffman, 27 July 1911; and Hoffman to Bracken, [received 12 September 1911], both in box 2, MN-SBH-CMR. See also Sherbon and Moore, *Maternity and Infant Care*.

7. G. W. Smith to Bracken, 4 May 1903, box 20, MN-SBH-CMR.

8. "Midwife Inspection," 291–92.

9. Bradley and Williamson, *Rural Children*, 30–31, 69–70.

10. White House Conference on Child Health and Protection, *Obstetric Education*, 211.

11. Physician, "Half a Century Behind Is Atlanta on Statistics," *Atlanta Constitution*, 3 October 1909.

12. *Annual Report of the Commissioner of Health to the Governor of Virginia*, 105.

13. Dart, *Maternity and Child Care*, 22–27.

14. Litoff, *American Midwives*, 78.

15. "Investigation Made by Miss Gertrude Barnes," 388.

16. AASPIM, *Transactions of the Second Annual Meeting*, 253.

17. Sherbon and Moore, *Maternity and Infant Care*, 27.

18. Dart, *Maternity and Child Care*, 41.

19. Litoff, *American Midwives*, 99, 107.

20. "Official Notice to All Registrars of Vital Statistics [. . .] and Persons in Charge of Cemeteries," box 24, folder "General Correspondence, CL Wilbur, 1915–23," WWP.

21. Smith to H. M. Bracken, 4 May 1903, box 20, MN-SBH-CMR.

22. Balfe, "Birth Registration in Connecticut," 777–78.

23. Dempsey, *Infant Mortality*, 17.

24. Weekly report, 11 May 1929, box 374, file 4-2-1-2-1, CHBU-CF.

25. Billings, "Registration of Vital Statistics," 33–49.

26. Wertz and Wertz, *Lying-In*, 212–15.

27. "Health Maryland," 2139.

28. "Midwifery—Practice," 2687.

29. Wertz and Wertz, *Lying-In*, 214.

30. CHBU, *Promotion of the Welfare* (1926), 45.

31. Hughes, *Infant Mortality*, 35. See also Steele, *Maternity and Infant Care*.

32. Felix J. Underwood, "Relation of Midwife to the State Board of Health," in White House Conference on Child Health and Protection, *Obstetric Education*, 218–26.

33. Rude, *Midwife Problem*, 13.

34. Duffy, *Healers*, 294.

35. "Annual Meeting of the Medical Society," 132–34.

36. "Real Man without a Country," *Boston Globe*, 6 January 1910.

37. Landrum makes the point that the legal requirement that attendants report births "created an infrastructure of state power outside the formal structures of government, enlisting professionals in the routine work of the state." Landrum, "State's Big Family Bible," 46.

38. Connecticut State Librarian, *Report* (1854), 6; Indiana State Board of Health, [*Fifth*] *Annual Report*, 43.

39. Indiana State Board of Health, [*Tenth*] *Annual Report*, 290.

40. Gitelman, *Paper Knowledge*, 30–31; Bouk, *How Our Days*, 70–77.

41. "Money for Doctors," *Butte Weekly Miner*, 15 December 1898; "Out of Self Respect," *Sun*, 13 May 1906; Petrie, "Practical Workings," 506–9; Grubbs, "Public Health Administration," 1479–545.

42. "Scores of Doctors in Danger," *Milwaukee Journal*, 28 March 1898.

43. Price, "Vital Statistics," 364–65.

44. Trask, *Vital Statistics*, 22.

45. Hurty to W. A. Bailey, 8 July 1908, series 11, Letter Press Books, 1907–8, box 4, Hurty Papers, Indiana State Archives.

46. J. N. Hurty, "The Bookkeeping of Humanity," chairman's address, Section on Preventative Medicine and Public Health, at the St. Louis Meeting of the American Medical Association, 7–10 June 1910, typescript, box 3a, folder 13, Vital Statistics Writings, 1910–21, Hurty Papers, Indiana State Archives.

47. Monger, "Why Births and Deaths," 140.

48. Duffy, *Healers*, 294.

49. Bracken to W. A. Jones, 20 December 1910, box 26, MN-SBH-CMR.

50. AASPIM, *Transactions of the Eighth Annual Meeting*, 138.

51. "State Laws and Regulations Pertaining to Public Health: Wisconsin," 979; CHBU, *Proceedings of the Third Annual Conference*, 102.

52. O. C. Pierson, "The Duty of Physicians and the Enforcement of the Law in Minnesota in Relation to Reporting Births," n.d. [ca. 1914–15], typescript, box 1, folder "Field Trip Reports, 1914–15," MN-VSD-SF.

53. *Ohio v. Boone*, No. 12846, 1911 Ohio LEXIS 97.

54. Walter Willcox to Cressy Wilbur, 28 September 1911, box 23, folder "General Correspondence, CL Wilbur, 1908–11," WWP; "State Laws and Regulations Pertaining to Public Health: Ohio," 1272.

55. Feezer, "Collection of Birth Reports," 908.

56. O. C. Pierson, "Report on Trip to Little Fork Township, Jamieson Township," [ca. 1911]; O. C. Pierson, "Report on Trip to Rosemount Township, Dakota County, to Collect Returns," [ca. 1911]; O. C. Pierson, "Report on Trip to East Grand Forks [. . .]," n.d.; and O. C. Pierson, "Report on Trip to Odessa [. . .]," 5 November 1914, all in box 1, folder "Field Trip Reports, 1914–15," MN-VSD-SF; E. F. Hunt to H. M. Bracken, 4 April 1904; and Hoper to Bracken, 1 July 1903, both in box 20, unlabeled folder, MN-SBH-CMR.

57. O. C. Pierson, "Report on Trip to Odessa [. . .]," 5 November 1914, box 1, folder "Field Trip Reports, 1914–15," Minnesota State Health Department, Vital Statistics Division, Subject Files.

58. Gladys Casady, "Result of a Special Survey Made by the Field Agent of Records of Births and Deaths in Possession of Certain Local Registrars," box 1, folder "Field Trip Reports, 1931–38," Minnesota State Health Department, Vital Statistics Division, Subject Files.

59. *Act Concerning the Registration of Births, Marriages, and Deaths*.

60. Graves to Sir [auditor of public accounts], 1 February 1854, box 53; and Lands to Sir, 20 January 1854, box 54, both in Auditor of Public Accounts, Library of Virginia.

61. Fox, "Public Health Administration," 3663.

62. Elizabeth Moore, *Maternity and Infant Care*, 45. See also Sherbon and Moore, *Maternity and Infant Care*, 73.

63. EJ, "Report of the Births," 149–50.

64. Warner, *Instructions Concerning the Registration*, 15, 27. Italics in original.

65. Bracken to Dear Sir, 30 June 1903; [Polk County Clerk] to Bracken, n.d.; S. D. Beyer to Bracken, 3 July 1903; E. O. Larson to Bracken, 5 July 1903; and Charles Swanson to Bracken, 6 July 1903, all in box 20, MN-SBH-CMR.

66. "Securing Birth Reports," 233.

67. Hurty to W. A. Bailey, 8 July 1908, series 11, Letter Press Books, 1907–9, box 4, Hurty Papers, Indiana State Archives.

68. Cressy Wilbur to Walter Willcox, 29 February 1916, box 24, folder "General Correspondence, Cressy L. Wilbur, 1915–23," WWP.

69. Guilfoy, "Enforcement of Registration," 99.

70. O. C. Pierson, "Report on Trip to Study Vital Statistics Registration Methods at Washington and Harrisburg," n.d., box 1, folder "Field Trip Reports, 1914–15," MN-VSD-SF.

71. "Vital Statistics Investigation [in Albert Lea]," 17–20 September 1917, box 1, folder "Field Trip Reports, 1917–30," MN-VSD-SF.

72. [Report on trip to] Princeton, 30 October 1922, box 1, folder "Field Trip Reports, 1917–30," MN-VSD-SF.

73. [Report on trip to] Winona-Pleasant Hill Township, 17–20 October 1922, box 1, folder "Field Trip Reports, 1917–30," MN-VSD-SF.

74. "Summary of the Transactions," 410; "Annual Report of the City Inspector," 222–27.

75. "Proposed State Board of Health," 339–40.

76. Chapin, *Report on State Public Health Work*.

77. Cressy Wilbur to Walter Willcox, 16 February 1916, box 24, folder "General Correspondence, Cressy Wilbur, 1915–23," WWP.

78. Prucha, *Great Father*, 110–19; Cahill, *Federal Fathers and Mothers*, 8–10.

79. Rowse, "Population Knowledge," 18–23.

80. Francis A. Walker, *Statistical Atlas*; Hannah, *Governmentality*.

81. USOIA, *Annual Report* (1877), 490; Jobe, "Native Americans."

82. Shoemaker, "Census as Civilizer," 8.

83. USOIA, *Annual Report of the Commissioner* (1870), 84.

84. USOIA, *Annual Report* (1880), xxxviii, 97.

85. USOIA, *Annual Report* (1881), 105; USOIA, *Annual Report* (1882), 91.

86. USOIA, *Annual Report* (1874), 243.

87. USOIA, 45–46.

88. USOIA, *Annual Report* (1887), xxxviii. See also Hoy, "Uncertain Counts," 729–50.

89. See USOIA, *Annual Report* (1878), 124; and USOIA, *Annual Report* (1881), 109, 116.

90. USOIA, *Annual Report* (1877), 516–17; USOIA, *Annual Report* (1878), 124.

91. USOIA, *Annual Report* (1882), 64.

92. Meriam, *Problem of Indian Administration*, 171.

93. Prucha, *Great Father*, 196.

94. Hoxie, *Final Promise*, chaps. 1–2; Stremlau, "'To Domesticate and Civilize,'" 265–86; Cahill, *Federal Mothers and Fathers*, chap. 1.

95. USOIA, *Annual Report* (1877), 494, 519.

96. Rowse, "Population Knowledge," 15–42.

97. Prucha, *Great Father*, 226.

98. Hoxie, *Final Promise*, 39; *Proceedings of the Fifth Annual Meeting of the Lake Mohonk Conference*, 2.

99. *Proceedings of the Eighteenth Annual Meeting of the Lake Mohonk Conference*, 16, 11. The phrase "mighty pulverizing engine" is actually a minor variation on a Teddy Roosevelt speech defending the Dawes Act.

100. Cahill, *Federal Mothers and Fathers*, 6; Stremlau, "'To Domesticate and Civilize.'"

101. Harmon, "Tribal Enrollment Councils." Harmon does not discuss documentation per se but says that during the allotment process on the Colville reservation in Washington State, agency personnel believed that part of their duty was to teach Colville Indians about "standard American methods of fact-finding," including asking applicants for corroboration of their claims (185).

102. The best description of the documentary process of allotment is from Stremlau, *Sustaining the Cherokee Family*, 112–25.

103. Alice Fletcher, "The Registration of Indian Families," in *Proceedings of the Eighteenth Annual Meeting of the Lake Mohonk Conference*, 73–75.

104. Stremlau, *Sustaining the Cherokee Family*, 112–16, 129–36.

105. Board of Indian Commissioners, *Thirty-First Annual Report*, 8.

106. Board of Indian Commissioners, 47, 59, 66.

107. Board of Indian Commissioners, 8, 14–15, 17, 47–49, 65–66, 75.

108. *Proceedings of the Eighteenth Annual Meeting of the Lake Mohonk Conference*, 17–18; Board of Indian Commissioners, *Thirty-Second Annual Report*, 8–9, 16; U.S. Congress, Senate, *An Act to Provide for the Registration*.

109. USOIA, *Annual Report* (1901), 42–46.

110. "Report of Superintendent in Charge of Mohave," in USOIA, *Annual Report* (1905), pt. 1, 162.

111. Acting Secretary of the Interior to Commissioner of Indian Affairs, 20 November 1907, Shawnee box 4, folder 88842-1907 Shawnee 033, BIA-CCF.

112. USOIA, *Annual Report* (1905), pt. 2, pp. 12, 16.

113. Jacobs, *White Mother*, 155–57.

114. Untitled manuscript [article for *Kentucky Women's Clubs Magazine*, signed by E. R. Goodwin and sent to Mrs. Lafon Rike, 22 October 1915], box 75, file 8-2-1-7, CHBU-CF.

CHAPTER 3

1. CHBU, *[Second] Annual Report of the Chief*, 5; CHBU, *Birth Registration*, 7.

2. CHBU, *Birth Registration*, 5–6.

3. Derek S. Hoff, *State and the Stork*, 44–60; Brosco, "Early History," 478–85; Meckel, *Save the Babies*.

4. AASPIM, *Transactions of the First Annual Meeting*, 6, 12–14.

5. AASPIM, 14.

6. Kelley, *Some Ethical Gains*, 99–100; Wald quote in Lindenmeyer, *"A Right to Childhood,"* 10.

7. On the legislative history of the creation of the bureau and the politics surrounding it, see Lindenmeyer, *"A Right to Childhood,"* 15–17. The creation of the bureau is usually interpreted as a form of maternalist politics growing out of the increasing political influence of female reformers such as Kelley, Wald, Jane Addams, and others. See also Ladd-Taylor, *Mother-Work,* chap. 3; and Skocpol, *Protecting Soldiers and Mothers.*

8. CHBU, [*First*] *Annual Report of the Chief,* 7–10.

9. Estelle Hunter to Miss Titzell, 17 September 1918, box 142, file 12-8-3-1, CHBU-CF; CHBU, *Outline of a Birth Registration Test.*

10. Landrum covers much of the same ground, interpreting the Children's Bureau's campaign and the work of the GFWC as an example of maternalism. See Landrum, "State's Big Family Bible," 97–129. See also Goldin, *Babies Made Us Modern,* chap. 3.

11. Meriam, "Auditing the Birth Account," 178.

12. General Federation of Women's Clubs, *Twelfth Biennial Convention,* 257, 572–73; CHBU, [*First*] *Annual Report of the Chief,* 10, 12.

13. "Women's Clubs to Check Birth Registration," 71.

14. General Federation of Women's Clubs, *Twelfth Biennial Convention,* 286, 307, 309, 346; Blair et al., "Public Health," 24; Sage, "Report of the Child Health Committee," 24; Minnesota Federation of Women's Clubs, *Annual Report,* 26, 29, 55; Brown and Spafford, "Report on Birth Registration," 29–30.

15. Eva Perry Moore, "Committee on Resolutions," 50; Frances Haldeman Sidwell, "Report of the Vice-President," 55; Violet Jayne Schmidt, "Report of the Vice-President," 51; Sophie Chantal Hart, "North Atlantic Section," 613.

16. "Progress Made in Birth Registration Test in Cooperation with General and State Federations of Women's Clubs and the Association of Collegiate Alumnae and Other Women's Organizations," 1 July 1915, box 75, file 8-2-1-7, CHBU-CF.

17. AASPIM, *Transactions of the Eighth Annual Meeting,* 148, 151; Kansas State Board of Health, [*Ninth*] *Biennial Report,* 89–90; State Council of Child Welfare, Women's Committee, New Jersey State Council of Defense, "About the Birth Registration Test," reports from the field, July 1919, box 142, files 12-8-3-1 to 12-8-3-3, CHBU-CF; Talbot, *Post-war Activities,* 27; Ada Schweitzer, "Count Babies," typescript article sent to the League of Women Voters, 31 May 1923, box 4, folder 2, ISB-DICH-PFC; Mary Dempsey to Robert Woodbury, 17 March 1924, box 185, file 4-2-1-2 (1 of 2), CHBU-CF.

18. CHBU, *Birth-Registration Test,* 5–8; "Birth Registration," undated manuscript [sent by Julia Lathrop to the chairman of the Iowa Department of Women and Children]; and birth registration test form, n.d., both in box 142, files 12-8-3-1 to 12-8-3-3, CHBU-CF.

19. Bracken to Mrs. F. L. Barrows, 10 December 1914; to Lathrop, 16, 30 December 1914; and to Marcley, 30 December 1914; Lathrop to Bracken, 21 December 1914; Marcley to Bracken, 4, 23 January 1915; and to Chairman [form letter], 14 January 1915; and Lewis Meriam to Bracken, 8 February 1915, all in box 26, no folder, MN-SBH-CMR; Bracken to Mrs. W. T. Cole, 5 February 1916, box 9, folder 72 Vital Statistics 1916, MN-SBH-CMR.

20. CHBU, *Birth-Registration Test,* 4; Hunter to Miss Titzell, memorandum, 17 September 1918, box 142, files 12-8-3-1 to 12-8-3-3, CHBU-CF.

21. Bracken to Webster, 10 December 1914; Webster to Bracken, 12 December 1914; Barrows to Bracken, 13 December 1914; and "[Illegible] Find Many Births Not Recorded; Webster Errs," newspaper clipping, 13 December 1914, all in box 26, no folder, MN-SBH-CMR.

22. Bracken to Webster, 10 December 1914; Webster to Bracken, 12 December 1914; Barrows to Bracken, 13 December 1914; "[Illegible] Find Many Births Not Recorded; Webster Errs," newspaper clipping, 13 December 1914; and C. H. Schroeder to Bracken, 19 January 1915, all in box 26, no folder, MN-SBH-CMR; Bracken to Lathrop, 17 November 1916, box 2, folder "U.S. Department of Labor, Children's Bureau," MN-SBH-CMR.

23. CHBU, *Birth-Registration Test*, 4.

24. General Federation of Women's Clubs, *Twelfth Biennial Convention*, 574.

25. Untitled manuscript [article for *Kentucky Women's Clubs Magazine*, signed by E. R. Goodwin and sent to Mrs. Lafon Rike, 22 October 1915], box 75, file 8-2-1-7, CHBU-CF.

26. CHBU, *Birth-Registration Test*, 4.

27. Meriam, "Auditing the Birth Account," 178.

28. "Letters and Extracts from Letters of Women Taking Part in the Investigation of Birth Registration," box 75, file 8-2-1-7, CHBU-CF.

29. "Birth Registration," undated and unsigned manuscript, box 142, files 12-8-3-1 to 12-8-3-3, CHBU-CF.

30. CHBU, *Baby-Week Campaigns*, 7, 24; William Davis to Dear Doctor, n.d. [ca. 1917], box 9, folder 72 Vital Statistics 1917, MN-SBH-CMR.

31. Goodwin, "Methods of Popularizing Birth Registration," 149–51; Hammond et al., "Departments of Work," 55; CHBU, *Baby-Week Campaigns*, rev. ed., 42, 44, 123–24, 126, 128, 130–31.

32. Meanes and Turner, "Committee," 1755–56.

33. CHBU, *Baby-Week Campaigns*, 35–43.

34. Mrs. Andrew Wilson, "Child Welfare Work," 141.

35. Indiana State Board of Health, [*Thirty-Fifth*] *Annual Report*, 161; Mrs. James Goodrich et al. to My Dear County Chairman, 16 July 1919, box 2, folder 3, ISB-DICH-PFC; CHBU newsletter, 2 January 1920, box 45, scrapbook 41, EGAP.

36. Feezer, "Collection of Birth Reports," 908.

37. Meckel, *Save the Babies*, 204–12; Lindenmeyer, *"Right to Childhood,"* 76–90.

38. CHBU, *Promotion of the Welfare* (1923), 20.

39. Radio Talk II, "What the Sheppard-Towner Act Is Doing for Mothers and Babies," transcript of a radio broadcast, 10 October 1922, box 40, "Radio Talks, Scrap Book, Department of Commerce and Labor," EGAP.

40. U.S. Congress, Senate, Committee on Commerce, *Federal Cooperation with States*, 346, 299, 305, 218, 323, 393, 388; Blanche Haines to William Davis, 18 June 1926, box 266, file 4-2-1-2-1, CHBU-CF.

41. CHBU, *Promotion of the Welfare* (1923), 15.

42. Blanche Haines to William Davis, 1 December 1927, box 266, file 4-2-1-2-1, CHBU-CF.

43. CHBU, *Promotion of the Welfare* (1929), 59.

44. CHBU, *Promotion of the Welfare* (1924), 24; CHBU, *Promotion of the Welfare* (1925), 25, 34, 58; CHBU, *Promotion of the Welfare* (1926), 29, 42, 67.

45. G. S. Luckett to William Davis, 31 January 1927; and Blanche Haines to William Davis, 8 February 1927, both in box 266, file 4-2-1-2-1, CHBU-CF.

46. Jones to CHBU, report, n.d. [ca. 1928], box 266, file 4-2-1-2-1, CHBU-CF.

47. Jones to CHBU.

48. Jones to CHBU, report, [received 20 November 1928], box 266, file 4-2-1-2-1, CHBU-CF.

49. Jones to CHBU, report, [received 15 October 1928], box 266, file 4-2-1-2-1, CHBU-CF.

50. On fairs etc., see Jones to CHBU, report, [received 15 October 1928]; "Birth Registration Booth Goes Over Big at Las Vegas," *Santa Fe New Mexican*, 2 October 1928; and "Blue Ribbon Babies," *Lincoln County News*, 12 October 1928, all in box 266, file 4-2-1-2-1, CHBU-CF. Shane Landrum makes the excellent point that the midwives reached by bureau agents such as Jones and Whipper were themselves "a crucial link between newborn American citizens and the expanding federal state." Landrum, "State's Big Family Bible," 132. His discussion of the bureau's work with midwives in the 1920s can be found in chapter 4.

51. Abbott to Hoover, 8 February 1923, box 4, folder "Children's Bureau, 1923–24," ACHA.

52. Second Monthly Report to Board of Directors, 15 May 1923; Report to Directors, 15 July 1923; Report to Directors, 15 September 1923; Acting General Executive's Report of Division Activities for January and February 1925; Report to the Executive Committee of the American Child Health Association, by General Executive, 15 May–14 October 1925; and Estimated Budget for Three Years, American Child Health Association, 1926–27, all in box 43, folder "Reports to Directors"; "Recent Progress in Child Health," *Child Health Magazine*, January 1925, box 35, folder "Publications and Printed Matter, Miscellaneous, 1925"; Quarterly Report of the General Executive to Executive Committee, 26 February 1926, box 31, folder "Publications and Printed Matter, Annual and Quarterly Reports, 1926." All in ACHA.

53. Ella Crandall to Christian Herter, 12 December 1923, folder "Reports, Statements, etc., 1923"; and "Work of the ACHA for January," n.d., folder "Reports, Statements, etc., 1924–25," both in box 44, ACHA.

54. Fargo Public School History Record, n.d.; Report of the Fargo Child Health Demonstration for the Month of September [1923]; and Report of the Fargo Child Health Demonstration for August 1923, all in box 7, folder "Demonstrations, Fargo, N.D.," ACHA; Dempsey to Robert Woodbury, 14 March, 17 April 1924; and Woodbury to Dempsey, 11 April 1924, all in box 185, file 4-2-1-2 (1 of 2), CHBU-CF.

55. Report to the Executive Committee of the American Child Health Association, 24 April 1924, box 12, folder "Financial, E. M. Flesh Files, Minutes of Meetings, 1923–24," ACHA; "Facts and Recommendations from a Health Survey of 86 Cities," *American City Magazine*, November 1925, box 7, folder "Demonstrations, Programs, Surveys, 1923–26," ACHA.

56. William H. Davis, "Report of Committee," 1015.

57. Dublin et al., "Growth," 606.

58. "How a Life Insurance Company Helps," 576; Dublin, "Present Status," 543–44; W. Thurber Fales to John A. Ferrell, 31 May 1933, box 4, folder "APHA Correspondence, August 1932–33," MS C 316, Dublin Papers, National Library of Medicine.

59. William Davis to Dear Doctor, [1926], box 266, file 4-2-1-2-1, CHBU-CF.

60. Minutes of the Committee to Aid the Completion of the Registration Area before 1930, 19 February 1927; and Progress Report, 9 February 1927, both in box 266, file 4-2-1-2-1, CHBU-CF.

61. William H. Davis, "1926 Progress Report," 275–76.

62. Minutes of the Committee to Aid the Completion of the Registration Area before 1930, 15 March 1926; and General Plan of Work of the Committee to Aid the Completion of the Registration Area before 1930, [ca. 1926], both in box 266, file 4-2-1-2-1, CHBU-CF.

63. Davis to Abbott, 2 August 1926, box 266, file 4-2-1-2-1, CHBU-CF.

64. Cook to H. S. Cumming, 1 July 1926, box 266, file 4-2-1-2-1, CHBU-CF.

65. Minutes of the Committee to Aid the Completion of the Registration Area before 1930, 19 February 1927, box 266, file 4-2-1-2-1, CHBU-CF.

66. Progress Report of Registration Promotion, 2 October 1926, box 266, file 4-2-1-2-1, CHBU-CF; "P.T.A. Is Help in Health Work," *Aberdeen Daily News*, 23 November 1927; "Below Appoints Freda Kramer to Welfare Board," *Aberdeen Daily News*, 24 September 1930.

67. Minutes of the Committee to Aid the Completion of the Registration Area before 1930, 19 February 1927, box 266, file 4-2-1-2-1, CHBU-CF.

68. Minutes of the Committee.

69. General Outline of Registration Promotion Campaign Being Conducted by Dr. Batt, Special Agent, Bureau of the Census, [ca. 1926]; and Minutes of the Committee to Aid the Completion of the Registration Area before 1930, 19 February 1927, both in box 266, file 4-2-1-2-1, CHBU-CF.

70. Minutes of the Committee to Aid the Completion of the Registration Area before 1930, 19 February 1927; W. H. Lackey to William Davis, 30 November 1927; Blanche Haines to Davis, 1 December 1927; Marie T. Phelan, daily report, 5 May 1928; and Marie T. Phelan, weekly report, 11–16 June, 7 July 1928, all in box 266, file 4-2-1-2-1, CHBU-CF.

71. *Annual Report of the Commissioner of Health to the Governor of Virginia*, 28, 74–76, 79; press article, North Carolina Board of Health, 1914, box 26, no folder, MN-SBH-CMR; Special Press Material on Birth Registration I–III, February 1917, box 75, file 8-2-1-7, CHBU-CF; "Why Registered Babies," press release, 1918, box 43, scrapbook, vol. 1, EGAP; Howard, "Division of Vital Statistics," 43; "Can You Prove Your Right to Vote?," press release, 9 August 1920, file 10,341, box 118, CHBU-CF; L. E. Ross [state registrar of California] to Robert Woodbury, box 185, file 4-2-1-2, CHBU-CF; Routzahn, "Education and Publicity," 1035; Report to the Executive Committee of the American Child Health Association by the Acting General Executive, 15 May 1925, box 44, folder "Reports, Statements, etc., 1924–25," ACHA; General Outline of a Registration Promotion Campaign Being Conducted by Dr. Batt, Special Agent, Bureau of the Census, n.d. [1926], box 266, file 4-2-1-2-1 (3 of 3), CHBU-CF. For another discussion of publicity around birth registration, see Landrum, "State's Big Family Bible," 55–60.

72. See, e.g., "Record Your Baby's Birth," *Chicago Defender*, 10 October 1914; *Nurse Instruction for Civil Service Examinations*, 8; Bradley, *Care of the Baby*, 8; Dickinson, *Children Well and Happy*, 35; CHBU, *Child-Welfare Programs*; "Care of Your Baby"; U.S. Bureau of Naturalization, *Suggestions for Americanization Work*, 7; Marion Edwards to CHBU, 5 March 1923; and Mrs. B. M. Anderson to CHBU, 13 February 1921, both in box 185, file 4-2-1-2, CHBU-CF; American Child Health Association, *Expectant Mother*, 20; Ada Schweitzer, "Abstract of Lectures for Mother's Classes," box 17, folder 10, ISB-DICH-PFC; and Marie T. Phelan, daily report, 5 May 1928, box 266, file 4-2-1-2-1 (2 of 3), CHBU-CF. See also Landrum, "State's Big Family Bible," 101.

73. Routzahn, "Education and Publicity," 1035.

74. For descriptions of the movie, see *Bulletin, Chicago School of Sanitary Instruction*, 5 October 1912, 157–59; "Moving Picture and Public Health," 903–4; and "Tommy's Birth Certificate," 18–19. For evidence of the movie's use and distribution, see CHBU, *Baby Week-Campaigns*, rev. ed., 124; and National Motion Pictures Company, "The Error of Omission," press release, [1920], box 2, folder 8, ISB-DICH-PFC.

75. Early adopters include New York City and the State of Virginia. J. T. Walsh to Robert Woodbury, 14 July 1924, box 185, file 4-2-1-2 (2 of 2), CHBU-CF; *Virginia Health Bulletin*, March 1918, 20.

76. Special Press Material on Birth Registration III, February 1917, box 75, file 8-2-1-7, CHBU-CF.

77. L. W. Hutchcroft to Julia Lathrop, 17 April 1916, box 126, file 11,115, CHBU-CF.

78. Zimmerman, "Civics and Baby Week," 18; William C. Welling to Robert Woodbury, 11 June 1924, box 185, file 4-2-1-2 (2 of 2), CHBU-CF; CHBU, *Infant Mortality, Montclair*, 25; L. A. Wheelwright to CHBU, 22 January 1936, box 490, file 4-2-1-2, CHBU-CF.

79. L. W. Hutchcroft to Lathrop, 11 April 1916, box 126, file 11115, CHBU-CF; H. M. Bracken to Lathrop, 21 September 1916, box 2, folder "U.S. Children's Bureau," MN-SBH-CMR.

80. Mrs. George H. Robinson to Ethel Waters, files 4-2-0-1 to 4-2-0-5-2; and Charles I. Madison to CHBU, 22 March 1924, file 4-2-1-2 (2 of 2), both in box 185, CHBU-CF.

81. CHBU, *Birth-Registration Test*, 4; Blanche Haines to Grace Abbott, 15 December 1924, CHBU-CF.

82. William H. Davis, "Check for the Registration," 762–63; Feezer, "Collection of Birth Reports," 907; CHBU, *Outline*, 13; Rawlings, "Symposium," 1010; A. T. Davis, "Aids in Securing," 28.

83. Minutes, 16 April 1924, Indiana State Board of Health, Minutes of the Executive Board, Indiana State Archives.

84. CHBU, *Promotion of the Welfare* (1925), 29–30, 39, 41, 52–53.

85. Webster, "Boy's Life in Photographs," 6.

86. *Our Baby's Book*.

87. On baby books, see Goldin, *Babies Made Us Modern*, chap. 4.

88. Edith L. May to CHBU, 11 August 1923; and Mrs. Clarence Davidson to CHBU, 13 December 1921, both in box 185, folder 4-2-1-2, CHBU-CF.

89. Shattuck, *Complete System*.

CHAPTER 4

1. CHBU, *Birth Registration*, 10.

2. AASPIM, *Transactions of the Fourth Annual Meeting*, quoted in CHBU, [*Second*] *Annual Report*, 10.

3. AASPIM, *Transactions of the Second Annual Meeting*, 57.

4. Shattuck, *Letter*, 19, 32.

5. Dye and Smith, "Mother Love and Infant Death," 330, 343; Hoffert, "'Very Peculiar Sorrow,'" 601–16.

6. Brosco, "Early History," 479.

7. Meckel, *Save the Babies*; Condran and Murphy, "Defining and Managing Infant Mortality," 473–513.

8. Meckel, *Save the Babies*, 12–16; Brosco, "Early History," 478–79.

9. Reese, "Report on Infant Mortality," 94–95, 98–99, 102.

10. *Report of the City Registrar* (1854), 25; *Report of the City Registrar* (1857), 27; *Report of the City Registrar* (1864), 40, 43–44.

11. Condran and Murphy, "Defining and Managing Infant Mortality," 481–82.

12. [*Fourth*] *Annual Report of the State Board of Health of Massachusetts*, 201.

13. Reese, "Report on Infant Mortality," 96.

14. Meckel, *Save the Babies*, 27; Snow, *Report on Registration*, 7.

15. Meckel, *Save the Babies*, 34–35; Condran and Murphy, "Defining and Managing Infant Mortality," 478–82.

16. *Report of the City Registrar* (1864), 44; [*Fourth*] *Annual Report of the State Board of Health of Massachusetts*, 194.

17. Reese, "Report on Infant Mortality," 100; *Report of the City Registrar* (1864), 43–44.

18. Meckel, *Save the Babies*, 35–37.

19. Meckel, 63–91; Apple, "'To Be Used,'" 402–17; Julie Miller, "To Stop the Slaughter," 158–84; Levenstein, "'Best for Babies,'" 75–94; Waserman, "Henry L. Coit," 359–90.

20. Meckel, *Save the Babies*, 63–91; Newman, *Infant Mortality*, 257.

21. Meckel, *Save the Babies*, 135–36; "Visiting Nurses to Aid Poor Mothers," *New York Times*, 9 April 1909, 7.

22. AASPIM, *Transactions of the Fourth Annual Meeting*, quoted in CHBU, [*Second*] *Annual Report*, 10.

23. Lindenmeyer, *"Right to Childhood,"* 61–64; Meckel, *Save the Babies*, 178–85, 194–96.

24. Julia Lathrop, "The Federal Children's Bureau," in AASPIM, *Transactions of the Third Annual Meeting*, 47–48.

25. Van Blarcom, "Ophthalmia Neonatorum," 726, 731–33; F. Park Lewis to My Dear Doctor, 15 February 1908, box 13, folder Ophthalmia Neonatorum, MN-SBH-CMR.

26. Gordon Berry to H. M. Bracken, July 1916, box 2, folder "National Committee for the Prevention of Blindness, Ophthalmia Neonatorum," MN-SBH-CMR.

27. Campbell, "Prevention of Infantile Blindness," 285–86.

28. Walter Willcox to Cressy Wilbur, 4 December 1909, box 23, folder "General Correspondence, Wilbur, C. L. 1908–11"; and F. D. Beagle to Willcox, 13 March 1911, box 15, folder "Walter Willox, General Correspondence, Beagle, F. D.," both in WWP.

29. "What Women's Clubs and Nursing Organizations Can Do to Prevent Blindness," National Committee for the Prevention of Blindness Publications, no. 5, box 2, folder "National Committee for the Prevention of Blindness, Ophthalmia Neonatorum," MN-SBH-CMR.

30. "Summary of State Laws and Ruling Relating to the Prevention of Blindness from Babies' Sore Eyes," National Committee for the Prevention of Blindness Publications, box 2, folder "National Committee for the Prevention of Blindness, Ophthalmia Neonatorum," MN-SBH-CMR; *News Letter*, December 1918, 7.

31. Harris, "Laws, Provisions, and Methods," 143; "In Memory of Dr. Elisha Harris," 509–10.

32. Trask, *Vital Statistics*, 26.

33. Bracken to Cressy Wilbur, 8 April 1907, box 26, no folder, MN-SBH-CMR.

34. Dr. G. S. Luckett to Grace Abbott, 28 July 1927, box 266, file 4-2-1-2, CHBU-CF; Vaughan and Buck, "Diptheria Prevention in Detroit," 759; Randall, "Public Health Nurse," 747–48.

35. CHBU, [*Twelfth*] *Annual Report*, 5–6; CHBU, [*Nineteenth*] *Annual Report*, 3–4.

36. "Authorities Looking Out for Babies," *Milwaukee Journal*, 3 June 1898, 5.

37. Norton, "Economic Advisability," 341.

38. "Mother's Baby Books," 677; Hunter, *Infant Mortality*, 117; F. E. Harrington to Glen Steele, 4 May 1921, box 185, files 4-2-1 to 4-2-0, CHBU-CF.

39. West, *Infant Care*, 9; Ladd-Taylor, *Mother-Work*, 84.

40. Shupe to CHBU, 19 March 1923, file 4-2-1-2 (1 of 2); and Mrs. S. A. Cossairt to CHBU, 7 June 1924, file 4-2-1-2 (2 of 2), both in box 185, CHBU-CF.

41. Minutes, 10 April 1914, Indiana State Board of Health, Minutes of the Executive Board, Indiana State Archives; Indiana State Board of Health, *Indiana Mothers' Baby Book*.

42. Meigs, "Other Factors," 850.

43. CHBU, *Promotion of the Welfare* (1924), 25; CHBU, *Promotion of the Welfare* (1925), 37; CHBU, *Promotion of the Welfare* (1926), 29, 41, 47, 66; CHBU, *Promotion of the Welfare* (1928), 43, 53, 55, 60, 66, 78, 81, 84, 88, 91, 110, 125, 130, 133, 140–41, 143, 147; Vaughan, "Public Health Administration," 396.

44. CHBU, *Baby-Saving Campaigns*, 14.

45. Infant Welfare Society, "Annual Report 1918," box 6, folder 1, Infant Welfare Society Papers, Chicago History Museum.

46. Newsletter for Directors of State Child Hygiene Division, April 1920, box 2, folder 4, ISB-DICH-PFC.

47. CHBU, *Promotion of the Welfare* (1924), 6.

48. Estelle B. Hunter, *Office Administration*, 121–25, 147, 156–58, 187.

49. On coordination with visiting nurses in states and cities, see MacNutt, "Board of Health Nurse," 350, 353; Department of Public Safety, *Annual Report* (1915), 339–40; Blakeslee, "Birth Registration," 7; L. W. Hutchcroft to Robert Woodbury, 4 April 1924, box 185, file 4-2-1-2 (2 of 2); Blanche Haines to William Davis, 18 June, 20 August 1926, box 266, file 4-2-1-2-1; and Davis to Haines, 18 May 1929, box 374, file 4-2-1-2-1, all in CHBU-CF; CHBU, *Promotion of the Welfare* (1924), 13; and CHBU, *Promotion of the Welfare* (1926), 37.

50. Report of the Fargo Child Health Demonstration for the Month of September [1923], box 7, folder "Demonstrations, Fargo, N.D.," ACHA.

51. U.S. Congress, Senate, Committee on Commerce, *Federal Cooperation with States*, 288.

52. "Nursing News and Announcements," 604; "Visiting Nurses to Aid Poor Mothers," *New York Times*, 9 April 1909, 7.

53. CHBU, *Promotion of the Welfare* (1925), 35; Maryland State Board of Health, *Annual Report*, 17–18, 168.

54. CHBU, *Baby-Saving Campaigns*, 35; AASPIM, *Transactions of the Fourth Annual Meeting*, 368.

55. Newsletter for Directors of State Child Hygiene Division, April 1920, box 2, folder 4, ISB-DICH-PFC; Martin, "Public Health Nursing," 89.

56. A. T. Davis, "Aids in Securing," 27–28.

57. Meckel, *Save the Babies*, 136.

58. AASPIM, *Transactions of the Second Annual Meeting*, 20; AASPIM, *Transactions of the Third Annual Meeting*, 47; AASPIM, *Transactions of the Fourth Annual Meeting*, 49.

59. Lillian Smith, "A Breast-Feeding Survey in 11 Counties in Michigan," in CHBU, *Proceedings of the Fourth Annual Conference*, 89–94. Walter Willcox suggested that New York City should use its birth registration data and visiting nurses to conduct similar research. "Suggestions for a Division of Research in the Bureau of Records of the New York City Department of Health," [ca. 1910], box 38, folder "NYC Dept of Health, 1910–11," WWP.

60. Wolf, "'Don't Kill Your Baby,'" 219–53.

61. Hastings Hart, *Registration of Illegitimate Births*, 15–17.

62. Lundberg, *Children of Illegitimate Birth*, 8–9.

63. [Emma O. Lundberg], "Legislation for Children Born out of Wedlock," *Survey*, 13 March 1920; and "On Legislation for the Protection of Children Born out of Wedlock," press release, 6 March 1920, both in box 45, scrapbook 41, EGAP.

64. Prucha, *Great Father*, 288–91; USOIA, *Annual Report* (1912), 19–26.

65. USOIA, *Indian Babies*, 27.

66. USOIA, 27–28; CHBU, [*Fifth*] *Annual Report*, 22.

67. USOIA, *Indian Babies*, 5.

68. Meriam, *Problem of Indian Administration*, 266, 269. I have been unable to find either of these circular letters in the Bureau of Indian Affairs files, though I find letters that make reference to them.

69. Wilbur to Willcox, 16 January 1909, box 23, folder "General Correspondence, Wilbur, C. L., 1908–11," WWP.

70. Meritt to McKinley, 20 July 1920, Choctaw box 11, folder 00-1921 Choctaw 034, BIA-CCF.

71. Meritt to Mann, 28 February 1922, folder 009189-006-0370, Indian Health and Medical Affairs, Part 2: Diseases, nos. 702–7, 710, 730–31, files 1907–39, entry 121, BIA-CCF.

72. Meriam, *Problem of Indian Administration*, 266, 176.

73. As with Circular No. 1506, Circular No. 2410 is missing from the Bureau of Indian Affairs box and folder that should house it in the subseries "Orders, Circulars, and Circular Letters, Circulars 1904–34" at the National Archives and Records Administration in Washington, D.C. Evidence of its content is gleaned from letters sent to agencies that remind superintendents to follow its directives. See, e.g., C. F. Hauke to L. S. Bonnin, 16 August 1928, Cheyenne and Arapaho box 3, folder [1928] Cheyenne and Arapaho 033; Hauke to Albert McMillan, 1 July 1928, Five Tribes box 101, folder 00-1929 Five Tribes 034; and Meritt to Patrick Hamley, 16 March 1928, Havasupi box 1, folder 00-1928 Havasupi 034, all in BIA-CCF.

74. *Annual Report of the Commissioner of Indian Affairs to the Secretary of the Interior* (1917), 18.

75. USOIA, *Annual Report* (1897), 119.

76. *Report of the Commissioner of Indian Affairs to the Secretary of the Interior* (1917), 20.

77. George Ansley to Commissioner of Indian Affairs, 15 August 1924, New York box 4, folder 00-1924 New York 034, BIA-CCF.

78. Lucien Spencer to Commissioner of Indian Affairs, 10 April 1928, Seminole box 2, folder 00-1928 Seminole 034, BIA-CCF.

79. Meriam, *Problem of Indian Administration*, 238.

80. Cahill, *Federal Mothers and Fathers*; Theobald, *Reproduction on the Reservation*, 44–62.

81. Mary McKay to Commissioner of Indian Affairs, 15 January 1935, folder 002129-004-0830, Indian Health and Medical Affairs, Part 1: Reports on Medical and Nursing Activities, BIA-CCF.

82. L. W. Shotwell to Commissioner of Indian Affairs, 15 February 1934, folder 002129-004-0806, Indian Health and Medical Affairs, Part 1: Reports on Medical and Nursing Activities, BIA-CCF.

83. [Mary McKay] to Commissioner of Indian Affairs, 1 April 1935, folder 002129-027-0843, Indian Health and Medical Affairs, Part 1: Reports on Medical and Nursing Activities, BIA-CCF.

84. Theobald, "'Simplest Rules of Motherhood,'" 81; Shapiro and Schacter, "Birth Registration Completeness," 517.

85. Henry Wheeler to F. A. Gross, 14 July 1931, Fort Hall box 5, folder "Fort Hall Agency, 1930–June 30, 1935." For other claims that hospital births result in birth registration while nonhospital births might not, see F. S. Stacher to Commissioner of Indian Affairs, 11 July 1932, Eastern Navajo box 9, folder "Eastern Navajo, 1930–June 30, 1935"; and Charles Berry to Commissioner of Indian Affairs, 9 April 1934, Cheyenne and Arapaho box 2, folder "Cheyenne and Arapaho Agency, 1930–June 30, 1935." All in Records of the Statistics Division, RG 75, NARA-DC.

86. Shapiro and Schacter, "Birth Registration Completeness," 518.

CHAPTER 5

1. Erickson, "Child Labor Legislation," esp. 56–57.

2. Wilbur, *Federal Registration Service*, 18, 39.

3. Treas, "Age in Standards," 87.

4. Demographers report a "birth certificate effect" when it comes to age reporting. Birth registration leads those who are registered to more consistently report their ages and birth dates across a number of social institutions. Those who are not registered retain a looser and inconsistent sense of their birth date and age. In other words, registration fixes age as objective. See Rosenwaike and Hill, "Accuracy of Age Reporting," 310–24.

5. For another discussion of the importance of age-based Progressive Era legislation to the transformation of birth certificates into identity documents, see Landrum, "State's Big Family Bible," 47–52.

6. Minor, "Proof-of-Age Records," 127.

7. Brewer, *By Birth or Consent*, 149; James D. Schmidt, "'Restless Movements,'" 315–50; James D. Schmidt, *Industrial Violence*, 118–63.

8. Little, "'Keep Me with You.'"

9. Bensel, "American Ballot Box," 1–27; USCB, *Discussion of Age Statistics*, 7–15; Mason and Cope, "Sources of Age," 563–73; Craig Robertson, *Passport in America*, 96; Mollie

Ray Carroll to Grace Abbott, 11 February 1918, box 110, folder 25-4-1, CHBU-CF; Mark M. Smith, *Mastered by the Clock*; O'Malley, *Keeping Watch*.

10. Treas, "Age in Standards and Standards for Age," 67.

11. White, *Protecting the Innocents*, chap. 4.

12. Sundue, "'Beyond the Time,'" 47–65.

13. Field, *Struggle for Equal Adulthood*.

14. Field, "'If You Have the Right,'" 76.

15. Neal L. Anderson, "Child Labor Legislation," 79, 81; New York State Factory Inspectors, [*First*] *Annual Report*, esp. 8; Greenleaf, *Treatise*, esp. 289; *Dobson v. Cothran*, 34 S.C. 518 (1891); *The People v. Clifton E. Mayne*, 118 Cal. 516 (1897). See also Ehler, "Legal Importance," 105–7.

16. Landrum, "From Family Bibles," 124.

17. Field, "'If You Have the Right,'" 77.

18. Treas, "Age in Standards"; Field, "'Sixteen Years.'"

19. Treas, "Age in Standards"; Field, "'Sixteen Years.'" Navigating the evidentiary requirements of pension applications could be quite challenging for African Americans, and age was far from the only eligibility criterion that applicants had to establish. As with the establishment of age, for other categories, the process of qualification was racially uneven. See Brimmer, "Her Claim for Pension," 207–36; and Brimmer, "Black Women's Politics," 827–58.

20. Katz, *In the Shadow*, 107–13; Trattner, *From Poor Law*, 108–26; Mintz, *Huck's Raft*, 90–92, 156–61; Chudacoff, *How Old Are You?*, 29–48; Stephen Robertson, *Crimes against Children*.

21. Ryan, *Cradle of the Middle Class*; Zelizer, *Pricing the Priceless Child*; James D. Schmidt, *Industrial Violence*, 43–47; Stearns, *Childhood in World History*, 54–63.

22. Hindman, *Child Labor*, 31–36, 45–48; James D. Schmidt, *Industrial Violence*, 3–31; Trattner, *Crusade for the Children*, 32–33.

23. Derickson, "Making Human Junk," 1280–90; Sallee, *Whiteness of Child Labor Reform*.

24. Loughran, "Historical Development," 6–8; Trattner, *Crusade for the Children*, 145–60; Hindman, *Child Labor*, 187–212, 248–90.

25. James D. Schmidt, *Industrial Violence*, 165–74. For working-class parents' and children's ideas about children's economic contributions, see Lassonde, *Learning to Forget*; Hall et al., *Like a Family*, 60–65; Nasaw, *Children of the City*; Sallee, *Whiteness of Child Labor Reform*, 38–41; Stansell, *City of Women*, 52–54; and Lovejoy, *In the Shadow*, esp. 6.

26. New York State Department of Labor, [*First*] *Annual Report*, 136; New York State Factory Inspectors, [*First*] *Annual Report*, 15; Connecticut State Board of Education, *Annual Report*, 42; [*Second*] *Annual Report of the Factory Inspectors of Illinois*, 16. See also Child Labor Reports, 1887–88; Child Labor Reports, Windham County, 1886–87; and Child Labor Reports, September 1894–1895, all in Records of the Education Department, Connecticut State Archives; and Sarah McGarvey to Mary Bickford, 19 February 1918, box 114, folder 25-4-1; Florence Clark to Grace Abbott, 19 January 1918, box 125, folder 25-6-3; and Lydia Beasley to Miss Moore, 1 July 1918, box 105, folder 25-3-1-1-3, all in CHBU-CF-CL.

27. Reinhard, *Report and Testimony*, 1016–17, 1012–13.

28. Reinhard, 1257.

29. Child Labor Reports, Fairfield County, 1886–87, Records of the Education Department, Connecticut State Archives.

30. New York State Department of Labor, [*Third*] *Annual Report*, 54, 81, 88; Callcott, *Child Labor Legislation*, 21–27.

31. "Child Labor Decreasing," *New York Times*, 14 February 1903.

32. National Consumers' League, *Child Labor Legislation*, 35–37; National Child Labor Committee, *Uniform Child Labor Laws*, 17–23, 194; National Child Labor Committee, "Uniform Child Labor Law," 78–107; Terry, *Uniform State Laws*, 371–72; Ward, "Weakness," 179; CHBU, *Employment-Certificate System*, 4; Goldmark, *Child Labor Legislation*, 18; Sumner and Merritt, *Child Labor Legislation*, 100–183; CHBU, *Administration of the First Federal*, 17, 21.

33. Grace Abbott, untitled notes, ca. 1917; and Alexander McKelway to Florence Kelley, 30 June 1917, both in box 34, folder 4, EGAP; National Child Labor Committee to CHBU, memorandum re: Suggestions for Proofs of Age to Be Required for Issuance of Federal Certificates, n.d. [ca. 1917], box 103, folder 25-1-1, CHBU-CF-CL; CHBU, *Administration of the First Federal*; minutes, 48th Meeting of the Board of Trustees, 9 November 1916, box 7, Papers of the National Child Labor Committee, Library of Congress, Manuscripts Division, Washington, D.C.

34. CHBU, *Administration of the First Federal*, 23; Loughran, "Historical Development," 92.

35. Lindenmeyer, *"Right to Childhood,"* 196; Hindman, *Child Labor*, 81–84; Frances Perkins to George Buckley, memorandum, 18 July 1934; and Clara M. Beyer to Secretary of Labor, memorandum, 26 July 1934, both in box 35, folder 5, EGAP; "Statement of the National Child Labor Committee on the Fair Labor Standard Bill, Submitted to the Senate Committee on Education and Labor and House of Representatives Committee on Labor, by Courtenay Dinwiddie, General Secretary, National Child Labor Committee," box 65, folder 1, EGAP; U.S. Congress, Senate, Committee on Education and Labor, House of Representatives, Committee on Labor, *Fair Labor Standards Act*, 381–410; Gertrude Folks Zimand, "A Study Outline on Pending Federal Child Labor Legislation," 15 September 1937, box 64, folder 5, EGAP; Lumpkin, "Child Labor Provisions," 391–405; Elizabeth La Hines, "Women Leaders Join in Combat on Child Labor," *New York Times*, 29 October 1939.

36. Ward, "Weakness," 191.

37. Moran to Grace Abbott, 9 May 1918, box 125, folder 25-6-1, CHBU-CF-CL; Sumner and Hanks, *Administration of Child Labor Laws*, 38; USDL, *Cotton Textile Industry*, 159, 161; USDL, *Silk Industry*, 79–80; Ward, "Weakness," 192. On the Santurri case, see Edith Hall to Abbott, 23 May 1918, box 105, folder 25-3-1-1-1; and Mathilde Selig to Abbott, 3 May 1918, box 125, folder 25-6-1, both in CHBU-CF-CL.

38. Grace Abbott, untitled notes, 1917, box 34, folder 4, EGAP; CHBU, *Administration of the First Federal*, 24, 29–30, 165; CHBU, "Experiences in Child Labor-Labor Law Administration," transcript, radio broadcast aired 30 January 1923 through NAA, radio release no. 15, box 40, Radio Talks, scrapbook "Department of Commerce and Labor," EGAP. For agents' complaints about Bible records that were either difficult to verify or patently altered, see Ethel Bedient to Grace Abbott, 5 April 1918, box 110, folder 25-4-1; Ethel Hanks to Abbott, 19 August 1917, box 112, folder 25-4-1; Elizabeth Hughes to Abbott, 9 October, 4 November 1917, box 112, folder 25-4-1; and Nila Allen to Abbott, 1 October

1917, box 115, folder 25-4-1, all in CHBU-CF-CL. On problems with original Bible records located far from southern mill villages, see Hughes to Abbott, September, 9 November 1917, box 113, folder 25-4-1, CHBU-CF-CL. On trips by bureau agents and mill employees in search of Bible records, see Amazon Cotton Mills to CHBU, 3 September 1917, box 110, folder 25-4-1; and Hughes to Abbott, 17 December 1917, box 113, folder 25-4-1, both in CHBU-CF-CL.

39. Connecticut State Board of Education, *Annual Report*; W. L. Bodine, "Child Labor and School Attendance," *Chicago Daily Tribune*, 31 May 1903; Connecticut State Board of Education, *Report of the Board*, 47.

40. Lindenmeyer, *"Right to Childhood,"* 17–18; Kelley, *Some Ethical Gains*, 94–100.

41. Kelley, *Some Ethical Gains*, 94–95, 98, 100; Lathrop, "Federal Children's Bureau," 59; CHBU, *Birth Registration*, 10; Parker and Carpenter, "Julia Lathrop," 60–77; CHBU, *Administration of the First Federal*, 21; CHBU, *Employment-Certificate System*, 4. On the maternalist feminism of the Children's Bureau, see Muncy, *Creating a Female Dominion*; Skocpol, *Protecting Soldiers and Mothers*; Gordon, *Pitied but Not Entitled*; and Ladd-Taylor, *Mother-Work*.

42. Bird, *Employment Certificate System, Maryland*, 35–39; USCB, *Birth Statistics*, 4.

43. Bradley and Williamson, *Rural Children*, 101–2; Hunter, *Infant Mortality*, 20–21; Allen, *Infant Mortality*, 18–19; Dempsey, *Infant Mortality*, 65; Sherbon and Moore, *Maternity and Infant Care*, 27, 33–35, 54; "Birth Registration," undated manuscript [ca. 1920], box 142, file 12-8-3-1, CHBU-CF; Dart, *Maternity and Child Care*, 41; Hughes, *Infant Mortality*, 63–64; and William Davis to Frederic Beitler, 7 June 1924; John Hughes to Davis, 10 May 1924; and L. E. Ross to Robert Woodbury, 16 June 1924, all in box 185, folder 4-2-1-2, CHBU-CF.

44. Minutes, Field Work Committee, 15 June 1917, box 7, Papers of the National Child Labor Committee, Library of Congress, Manuscripts Division, Washington, D.C.

45. A. T. McCormack to Lathrop, 7 February 1917; and Lathrop to McCormack, 9 February 1917, both in box 105, folder 25-3-1-1-1, CHBU-CF-CL.

46. Lathrop to Bracken, 8 November 1916, box 2, folder "U.S. Department of Labor, Children's Bureau," MN-SBH-CMR.

47. Parker et al., "Departments of Work," 39.

48. CHBU, "Administrative Practice under the Barkley Bill as Compared with That Under the Federal Child Labor Act of 1916," prepared as part of Material for Senate Hearing on Child Labor Bills, 12 May 1936, box 35, folder 10, EGAP.

49. Sumner and Hanks, *Employment-Certificate System*, 33–58, 90–91; Hanks, *Employment-Certificate System, Wisconsin*, 55–57. See also USDL, *Cotton Textile Industry*, 159; USDL, *Silk Industry*, 79; Bird, *Employment Certificate System, Maryland*, 35–29; and Ward, "Weakness," 194–98.

50. C. L. Allgood to Grace Abbott, 28 January 1918, box 117, folder 25-4-1, CHBU-CF-CL; Matthews, *Illegally Employed Minor*, 68.

51. Grace Ward to Grace Abbott, 2 May 1918, box 125, folder 25-6-1; and Rideout to M. E. Gardner, 15 March 1918, box 117, folder 25-4-1-1, both in CHBU-CF-CL.

52. Bergeron to CHBU, 24 November 1921, box 185, folder 4-2-1-2, CHBU-CF.

53. Bergeron to CHBU; Garel to CHBU, 29 October 1923, box 185, folder 4-2-1-2, CHBU-CF.

54. *Report of the Massachusetts Child Labor Committee*, 9.

55. CHBU, *[Fourth] Annual Report*, 17.

56. Kelley, *Some Ethical Gains*, 10; Abbott and Breckinridge, *Truancy and Non-attendance*, 289–90. See also Ensign, *Compulsory School Attendance*.

57. Vaughan, "Public Health Administration," 398.

58. Guilfoy to Walter Willcox, 20 March 1911, box 38, folder "New York City Department of Health, 1910–11," WWP.

59. "Storage O.K., Say Teachers Wives," *Chicago Daily Tribune*, 7 October 1906; "Getting into School," 8; "Crowds for Schools," *New-York Tribune*, 5 September 1907; Loehr, "Philanthropy," 24; Green, "Why Should Births and Deaths," 44; State of Nevada, *Biennial Report*, 38; "Schools and Health," *Atlanta Constitution*, 12 July 1915; State Department of Education, *Act to Require School Attendance*; Wynne, "Practical Uses," 20–29; "Child Welfare Legislation," 149; Hemenway, "Birth and Death Certificates," 1–5; "Birth Registration Cards," 1764; Wilbur, *Federal Registration Service*, 47.

60. See also Landrum, "State's Big Family Bible," 119–21.

61. Capozzola, *Uncle Sam Wants You*, 44.

62. "How Old Are You?," *Michigan Bulletin of Vital Statistics*, 86; W. A. Evans, "How to Keep Well: Birth Registration," *Chicago Daily Tribune*, 17 September 1917.

63. Frederick Gilkyson to Provost Marshal General, 24 September 1918; and Crowder to Adjutant General of New Jersey, 27 September 1918, both in box 200 New Jersey 63–71, RG 163, NARA-MD.

64. William Guilfoy, "Registration of Births from the Viewpoint of War's Demands," in AASPIM, *Transactions of the Eighth Annual Meeting*, 134.

65. G. J. Hubbard to Provost Marshal General, 25 March 1918; and Crowder to Adjutant General of Alabama, 30 March 1918, both in box 77 Alabama 1–17; and Keith Neville to Provost Marshal General, 10 December 1917 and attachments, box 190 Nebraska 42–66, all in RG 163, NARA-MD.

66. J. C. Middlebrooks to J. Van Holt Nash, 14 June 1917; and Johnson to Adjutant General of Georgia, n.d., both in box 109 Georgia 13–17, RG 163, NARA-MD.

67. Lenhart, "Completeness of Birth Registration," 685–90.

CHAPTER 6

1. *Sunseri v. Cassagne*, 191 La. 209; 185 So. 1; 1938 La. LEXIS 1362 (1938); and *Sunseri v. Cassagne*, 195 La. 19; 196 So. 7; 1940 La. LEXIS 1051 (1940).

2. Gross, *What Blood Won't Tell*. Gross argues that reputation and association were always more important than documentation in adjudicating racial identity.

3. Gross (chap. 4) describes this process but not the role of birth certificates within the process. See also Bynum, "'White Negroes,'" 247–76.

4. "Proceedings of a Conference on Vital Statistics," 16.

5. Connecticut Secretary of State, *Report*, 7; "Transactions of Societies," 72.

6. *Annual Report of the Secretary of State of the State of Michigan* (1874), 19; *Annual Report of the Secretary of State of the State of Michigan* (1873), 22.

7. Plecker, "Standard Certificate of Birth," 1046–47.

8. *Virginia Health Bulletin*, January 1923, 10.

9. Anne Halkovich to Frank Morrison, memorandum, 8 February 1946, re: Trip Report to Tennessee, Ohio, and Alabama, box 87, folder Vital Statistics Forms, Census-ROADSS-TPM.

10. Instructions for Transcripts of Birth Certificates for 1920, box 2, MN-SBH-CMR.

11. USCB, *Physician's Handbook*.

12. Ripley, "Colored Population," 44.

13. "Vital Statistics," *Medical and Surgical Reporter*, 194.

14. Meritt to Buntin, 16 May 1928, Kiowa box 6, folder 00-1927-29 Kiowa 034; and C. F. Hauke to L. S. Bonnin, Cheyenne and Arapaho box 3, folder [1928] Cheyenne and Arapaho 033, both in BIA-CCF.

15. C. J. Rhoads to Forrest Stone, 20 October 1931, box 1, folder "Blackfeet, 1930–June 30, 1935"; and Rhoads to James Hyde, 18 October 1932, box 4, folder "Crow Agency, 1930–June 30, 1935," both in Records of the Statistics Division, RG 75, NARA-DC.

16. Frederic Snyder to Commissioner of Indian Affairs, 30 March 1928, Carson box 6, folder 00-1928 Carson 033, BIA-CCF.

17. For an exhaustive account of segregation laws across the states, see Stephenson, *Race Distinctions*.

18. Stremlau, *Sustaining the Cherokee Family*, 142.

19. Prucha, *Great Father*, 298–309; Stremlau, *Sustaining Cherokee Families*, 142–44, 185–86; Spruhan, "Legal History," 1–50.

20. Gross, *What Blood Won't Tell*, 140–68. See also Chang, *Color of the Land*.

21. Prucha, *Great Father*, 321–24; Kiel, "Bleeding Out," 89; Felix S. Cohen, *Handbook*, 5.

22. Garroutte, "Racial Formation of American Indians," 231.

23. Gross, *What Blood Won't Tell*, 24–25, 54, 57–58, 78, 103–4. See also Bela August Walker, "Fractured Bonds," 1–50.

24. Pascoe, *What Comes Naturally*; Bardaglio, *Reconstructing the Household*.

25. "News of Women's Patriotic Societies: Registration System for State Should Be Uniform," *Atlanta Constitution*, 31 March 1912.

26. "Social Progress," 191.

27. Lombardo, "Miscegenation, Eugenics, and Racism," 421–52, Plecker quote on 430; "The Acts of 1930 Which Affect the Administration of the Work of the Virginia Bureau of Vital Statistics," *Virginia Health Bulletin*, August 1930, 27; Thomason, "Racism and Racial Classification," 159.

28. "Ban on Race Amalgamation to Be Urged in Legislature by Dekalb Representative," *Atlanta Constitution*, 21 June 1925.

29. Plecker has featured in many histories. All of them connect his work passing and enforcing the RIA to the larger politics of white supremacy in the first half of the twentieth century. However, none connect his policing of vital registration documents to the larger history of birth certificates (and allied documents) as identification documents created and used by the state to administer its policies. See, e.g., Pascoe, *What Comes Naturally*; J. Douglas Smith, "Campaign for Racial Purity," 65–106; Holloway, *Sexuality, Politics, and Social Control*; J. Douglas Smith, *Managing White Supremacy*; and McRae, *Mothers of Massive Resistance*.

30. Plecker, "Virginia's Attempt," 111–15.

31. Plecker to Powell, 30 July 1924, box 41, JPP; minutes, 26 February 1925, folder "Minutes, 1924–43," vol. 4, Virginia State Board of Health, Library of Virginia.

32. "Virginia to Enforce New Segregation Act," *Pittsburgh Courier*, 5 July 1924.

33. Plecker to V. W. Davis, 13 May 1924; and to Clerks of Virginia, 10 June 1924, both in box 1, RCCR-CC.

34. Plecker to Register, 9 August 1924; and to H. L. Bough, 1 August 1924; Powell to Cox, 9 August 1924; and Plecker to C. W. Garrison, 5 January 1925, all in box 41, JPP.

35. *Virginia Health Bulletin*, March 1924, box 1, RCCR-CC.

36. *Virginia Health Bulletin*, March 1924; and Bureau of Vital Statistics, State Board of Health, *Eugenics in Relation to the New Family and the Law on Racial Integrity*, both in box 1, RCCR-CC; Plecker to Local Registrars, January 1943, box 9, Rennolds Papers, Library of Virginia.

37. Plecker to Samuel H. Nixon, 17 June 1946, box 42, JPP.

38. *Virginia Health Bulletin*, March 1924, box 1, RCCR-CC; minutes, Meeting of State Board of Health, 6 October 1936, folder "Minutes, 1924–43," vol. 4, Virginia State Board of Health, Library of Virginia; Eva Kelley to A. T. Shields, 15 October 1936; and Plecker to Shields, 2 April 1926, both in box 1, RCCR-CC; Plecker to H. D. Kissenger, 17 May 1939; and to Blanche Cunningham, 11 June 1940, both in box 41, JPP; Plecker to Walter Brigham, 28 August 1941, box 1, RCCR-CC; Plecker to M. A. Taff, 8 February 1945, box 42, JPP.

39. *Annual Report of the State Department of Health* (1930), 120; James Stockard to Halbert Dunn, memorandum, 17 March 1944, box 86, folder "TPM: Vital Statistics 1944," Census-ROADSS-TPM; Plecker to Collier, 6 April 1943; and Plecker to I. C. Riggin, 27 May 1946, both in box 42, JPP.

40. Plecker to W. E. Sandidge, 4 October 1924, box 41, JPP; Plecker to A. W. Robertson, 29 August 1924, box 1, RCCR-CC; "Virginia Race Purity Law Tested in Court," *Washington Post*, 8 September 1924; "Virginians Try Marriage Purity Law," *Chicago Defender*, 27 September 1924.

41. *Sorrells v. Shields*, in the Circuit Court of Rockbridge County, Certificate of Exceptions no. 1, folder 2, Rockbridge County Court Records, Circuit Court, Library of Virginia.

42. Plecker to J. J. Ambler, 27 May 1938, box 41, JPP.

43. Pascoe, *What Comes Naturally*, 138.

44. *Annual Report of the State Department of Health* (1930), 119; Plecker to M. B. Booker, 15 February 1924, box 41, JPP.

45. Saunders to Shields, 2 July 1924, box 1, RCCR-CC

46. Plecker to Glasgow, 14 August 1924. For similar letters to doctors, see Plecker to Davidson, 10 February 1925; and to W. A. Jeffress, 10 February 1925. All in box 1, RCCR-CC.

47. Plecker to Hartless, 15 August 1924. For similar letters to midwives, see Plecker to Mary Sorrells, 15 August 1924; and to Martha Wood, 23 November 1925. All in box 1, RCCR-CC.

48. Plecker to Vaden, 15 August 1924. For other cases in which the BVS refused to issue birth certificates, see Plecker to Lewis Tyree, 6 October 1930. Both in box 1, RCCR-CC.

49. Plecker to Beverly, 22 October 1929. Plecker wrote similar letters to other families.

See Plecker to William Adcock, 7 January 1930; to Mrs. Frank Clark, 1 May 1930; to Hamilton, 10 October 1930; to Hartless, 17 October 1930; to Neely Beverly, 25 February 1931; and to Mrs. W. B. Clark, 30 August 1924. All in box 1, RCCR-CC.

50. "Warning.—To be attached to the backs of birth or death certificates of those believed to be incorrectly recorded as to color or race," n.d., folder 1, Coates Papers, Library of Virginia. Plecker describes this practice in *Annual Report of the State Department of Health* (1930), 119. This is also described by U.S. Census Bureau agents in James Stockard to Halbert Dunn, memorandum, 17 March 1944, box 86, folder "TPM: Vital Statistics 1944," Census-ROADSS-TPM.

51. *Annual Report of the State Department of Health* (1930), 119.

52. Tucker to Plecker, 1 October 1942; and Plecker to Tucker, 8 October 1942, both in box 41, JPP.

53. Plecker to John Powell, 13 October 1942, box 42, JPP; James Stockard to Halbert Dunn, memorandum, 17 March 1944, box 86, folder "TPM: Vital Statistics 1944," Census-ROADDS-TPM.

54. James Stockard to Halbert Dunn, memorandum, 17 March 1944, box 86, folder "TPM: Vital Statistics 1944," Census-ROADDS-TPM; Plecker to Mrs. M. L. Williams, 17 April 1944; and to M. A. Taff, 8 February 1945, both in box 42, JPP; *Act to Amend and Reenact Sections 1575, 1578 and 1580 of the Code of Virginia*.

55. Plecker to Ware, 2 October 1935, box 41, JPP.

56. Plecker to H. V. Fitzgerald, 11 July 1940, box 41, JPP.

57. Plecker to M. A. Taff, 8 February 1945, box 42, JPP. The "no doubt" rule was created in the case of *Sunseri* (1940).

58. Dominguez, *White by Definition*, 36–45.

59. *State ex rel. Estelle Rodi, Wife of Theophile Soulet v. City of New Orleans et al.*, 94 So. 2d 108; 1957 La. App. LEXIS 1033.

60. *Soulet*, 94 So. 2d 108; 1957 La. App. LEXIS 1033.

61. For a critique of Louisiana's "no doubt" rule and an argument that accords too much power to vital statistics documents and denies due process, see Pugh, "Burden of Proof," 310–14.

62. Harris Hart to Division Superintendent, 30 September 1919, box 2, folder "Correspondence, 1916–July 1920," Rennolds Papers, Library of Virginia.

63. Plecker to W. H. Clark, 29 July 1924, box 41, JPP.

64. Plecker to Harry Davis, 4 October 1924, box 41, JPP.

65. Plecker to R. M. Irby, 6 October 1930, box 1, RCCR-CC; Plecker to Tyree, 6 October 1930, box 1, RCCR-CC.

66. *Report of the State Board of Health and the State Health Commissioner*, 304; Plecker to F. B. Gwynn, 10 September 1940, box 41, JPP; and to J. P. Beatty, 10 April 1945, box 42, JPP. See also *Virginia Health Bulletin*, March 1924, box 1, RCCR-CC; Plecker to A. T. Shields, 1 May 1925, box 1, RCCR-CC; Transcript of an Interview between William Archer Thaddeus Jones and Hon. Albert O. Boschen Held in the Office of the Bureau of Vital Statistics, 31 January 1925, box 41, JPP; and Plecker to County School Board of August County, 4 February 1943, box 42, JPP.

67. Plecker to H. V. Fitzgerald, 11 July 1940, box 41, JPP.

68. Plecker to Dear Sir, 12 February 1924, box 41, JPP.

69. Plecker to Robinson, 11 December 1926, box 4, Rennolds Papers, Library of Virginia.

70. Plecker to Elizabeth Tyler, 16 April 1936, box 41, JPP.

71. Plecker to A. T. Shields, 23 October 1929, box 1, RCCR-CC.

72. Plecker to Hamilton, 10 October 1930, box 1, RCCR-CC; and to Lizzie Ware, 2 October 1935, box 41, JPP.

73. Jennings to Albert Boschen, 27 January 1925, box 41, JPP.

74. Plecker to R. I. Overbey, 11 July 1940, box 41, JPP.

75. *Virginia Health Bulletin*, March 1924, 78; *Report of the State Board of Health and the State Health Commissioner*, 33.

76. Plecker to Neely Beverly, 25 February 1931, box 1; and to Jacob Henever, 1 May 1935, box 1, both in RCCR-CC.

77. Plecker to Jacob Henever, 1 May 1935, box 1, RCCR-CC.

78. Onwuachi-Willig, "Beautiful Lie," 2393–458.

79. Plecker to Sperka, 15 October 1930, box 1, RCCR-CC.

80. Plecker to Rogers, 12 March 1943, box 42, JPP.

81. Plecker generally aided and encouraged the prosecution or annulment of all illegal interracial marriages. See Plecker to J. P. Beatty, 10 April 1945, box 42, JPP.

82. Plecker to Horace Sutherland, 6 September 1940, box 41, JPP.

83. Plecker to Superintendent, 1 August 1940; and to W. G. Muncy, 3 August 1940. There are a few other cases in the extant correspondence; see Plecker to Stockes, 31 July 1940. All in box 41, JPP.

84. In 1965, federal Medicare funding was tied to hospital integration. Thomas, "Hill-Burton Act," 823–70.

85. Plecker to Charlotte Edmunds, 3 September 1942; and to Beale, 11 September 1942, both in box 41, JPP; Plecker to A. L. Herring, 27 October 1944, box 42, JPP.

86. Plecker to C. K. Holsinger, 11 June 1940, box 41, JPP.

87. Plecker to Charles Stokes, 31 July 1940, box 41; to Virginia Thomson, 17 February 1943, box 42; and to Sadie Bane, 24 April 1944, box 42, all in JPP.

88. Plecker to Nancy Hundley, 27 July 1943, box 42, JPP; J. Douglas Smith, *Managing White Supremacy*, 82.

89. "Mattaponi Indian Chief Says Tribe Not Negroid," *Richmond Times-Dispatch*, 14 July 1925.

90. For one such effort, see Coates Papers, Library of Virginia.

91. The reversal of Plecker's campaign and the reestablishment of "Indian" as a racial category in contemporary Virginia also involved the disavowal of African ancestry. See Coleman, *Blood That Stays Pure*; and Coleman, "From the 'Pocahontas Exception.'"

CHAPTER 7

1. Bartness to Minnesota Department of Health, Division of Vital Statistics, 15 January 1957; and Jane Winholz to Bartness, 1 February 1957, both in box 1, folder "Confidentiality of Adoption Records, 1943–65," MN-VSD-SF.

2. Bartness to Minnesota Department of Health, Division of Vital Statistics, 15 January 1957, box 1, folder "Confidentiality of Adoption Records, 1943–65," MN-VSD-SF.

3. CHBU, [*Fourth*] *Annual Report*, 17.

4. *Report of the City Registrar* (1887), page number unknown.

5. Duclos to H. M. Bracken, 1 May 1915; and Bracken to Phillip Hensler, 27 May 1915; and to Duclos, 7 June 1915, all in box 26, unlabeled folders, MN-SBH-CMR.

6. Lundberg and Lenroot, *Illegitimacy*, 20; Anderson quoted in Hastings Hart, *Registration of Illegitimate Births*, 5.

7. CHBU, *Birth Registration*; Duke, *Infant Mortality*, 49.

8. Bracken to Hastings Hart, 26 July 1915, box 26, MN-SBH-CMR; Hastings Hart, *Registration of Illegitimate Births*, 14–15; Lundberg and Lenroot, *Illegitimacy*, 35; Howard Moore, *Care of Illegitimate Children*; Bowen, "Birth Registration," 53–54.

9. Carp, *Family Matters*; Herman, *Kinship by Design*; Kunzel, *Fallen Women, Problem Girls*.

10. Tielebein to Gentlemen, Dept. Bureau of Labor, 10 September 1922; and to Ethel Waters, 15 October 1922, both in box 185, folder 4-2-1-2, CHBU-CF.

11. Quoted in Hastings Hart, *Registration of Illegitimate Births*, 5.

12. Rosen, *Reproductive Health, Reproductive Rights*, 45–61; CHBU, *Norwegian Laws*.

13. Lundberg and Lenroot, *Illegitimacy*, 19; CHBU, *Standards of Legal Protection*, 150.

14. CHBU, *Standards of Legal Protection*, 18.

15. CHBU, 47; H. M. Bracken to W. W. Hodson, 14 February 1917, box 9, folder 72, MN-SBH-CMR.

16. Hanna, "Guarding Illegitimate Status," 6.

17. Howard and Hemenway, "Birth Records," 643.

18. Thompson to Pierson, 3 February 1936, box 2, folder "Florida Health Department and Vital Statistics Division, Correspondence with, 1936–65," MN-VSD-SF.

19. Report of the Committee on Registration of Births out of Wedlock, presented to the Vital Statistics Section, American Public Health Association, Milwaukee, October 1935, box 490, file 4-2-1-2-4, CHBU-CF; "Registration of Births of Illegitimate and Adopted Children," 86; Howard and Hemenway, "Birth Records," 641–47; CHBU, *Paternity Laws*, 2.

20. Carp, *Family Matters*, 53–55; Colby, *Problems and Procedures in Adoption*, 120; Howard and Hemenway, "Birth Records," 647. The increase in adoption—and the presumption that adoptees were illegitimate—also led to changes in how Great Britain recorded such facts on its birth certificates. A 1926 law sealed the original birth certificates of adoptees but marked their new birth certificates with the stamp "adopted," thus essentially revealing illegitimacy. Deborah Cohen, *Family Secrets*, 140–41.

21. Report of the Committee on Registration of Births out of Wedlock, presented to the Vital Statistics Section, American Public Health Association, Milwaukee, October 1935, box 490, file 4-2-1-2-4, CHBU-CF; Howard and Hemenway, "Birth Records," 643.

22. Response from Margaret MacGunigal, [1936], box 490, file 4-2-1-2-4, CHBU-CF; "Lifting Stigma of Illegitimacy Goal of Health Officials' Drive," *New York Herald Tribune*, 10 October 1935; response from Lavinia Keys, [1936], box 490, file 4-2-1-2-4, CHBU-CF. On filius nullius, see Freund, *Illegitimacy Laws*, 9.

23. Minority Report of the Committee on Registration of Births out of Wedlock, 12 December 1935, box 490, file 4-2-1-2-4, CHBU-CF.

24. Response from Luetta Magruder, [1936]; and Carstens to Agnes Hanna, 3 March

1936, both in box 490, file 4-2-1-2-4, CHBU-CF; Pierson to W. A. Davis, 13 December 1937, box 1, folder "American Association of Registration Executives: Correspondence with President Davis, 1935–1938," MN-VSD-SF.

25. Smith to Hanna, 11 March 1936, box 490, file 4-2-1-2-4, CHBU-CF.

26. It is difficult to track the precise number of states that dropped legitimacy from the birth certificate, or to determine when they did so, because the decision was often administrative rather than statutory. In 1943, the Census Bureau claimed that nine states did not follow its standard for the "legitimacy question." It does not list these states. See "A Check List of Aspects of the Vital Records System Which Require Standardization and Improvement," material prepared for the meeting of the Census Advisory Committee, 19 January 1943, box 77, Census-CAC. A 1948 newspaper article also puts the number of states that do not record legitimacy at nine and lists them as California, Georgia, Mississippi, New Jersey, Nevada, Ohio, Oregon, Tennessee, and Washington. See "9 States' Birth Papers Leave Illegitimacy Out," *New York Herald Tribune*, 29 February 1948.

27. Minutes of the Subcommittee on Revision of Standard Certificates, 5 April 1938, box 74, Census-CAC; Dunn to Director, memorandum, 23 October 1943, box 85, Census-ROADSS-TPM; Minutes of the Meeting of the Council on Vital Records and Vital Statistics, 28–30 November 1944; and Minutes of the Meeting of the Council on Vital Records and Vital Statistics, 23–25 October 1945, both in box 118, folder "Vital Statistics, Council on Vital Records and Vital Statistics," Census-ROADSS-GR.

28. Minutes of the Meeting of the Council on Vital Records and Vital Statistics, Held at the Bureau of the Census, Washington, D.C., 30 April–2 May 1946, box 118, Census-ROADSS-GR; Huffman, "First Protection," 35; Rose McKee, "Social Workers Urge State Solons to Approve Use of 'Birth Cards,'" *Atlanta Constitution*, 28 November 1946; "Birth Record System Hides Illegitimacy," *Los Angeles Times*, 6 February 1950, 21; Rule et al., "Documentary Identification," 225.

29. "Study of the Experience of States Issuing Birth Cards," typescript memorandum, ca. 1951, box 3, folder "Working Group on Promoting and Testing Completeness of Vital Registration, 1949–51," MN-VSD-SF.

30. By contrast, in Great Britain the solution was, in 1947, to create a short-form birth certificate. This had already been in existence in most U.S. states for several decades. Deborah Cohen, *Family Secrets*, 144.

31. *Report of the City Registrar* (1852), 6; A. K. Bates to Secretary, State Board of Health, 1 July 1903; and Alfred Carlson to Minnesota State Board of Health, 2 June 1903, both in box 20, unlabeled folders, MN-SBH-CMR.

32. *Annual Report of the Commissioner of Health to the Governor of Virginia*, 105; "Demand for Birth Registration," 206–7; *Annual Report of the State Board of Health of Alabama*, 15; "Child Welfare Legislation," 149; Monger, "Cooperation," 19–23; "How Old Are You?," *Texas Health Magazine*, 5–7.

33. Sam Rogers to H. M. Bracken, 18 April 1917; and Bracken to William Davis, 20 June 1917; and to Harrison, 5 November 1917, all in box 9, folder 72 Vital Statistics 1917, MN-SBH-CMR.

34. Francis McDonald to Latimer, 23 June 1936, box 237, folder 703, SSB-MF; A. J. Altmeyer to Eatton Sumners, 12 May 1939, box 246, folder 751.5, SSB-MF; Leonard Calhoun to Robert Cassels, 4 March 1938, box 102, folder 750, Records of the Social Security Board,

Central File, Regional File, RG 47, NARA-MD; Altmeyer to R. N. Elliot, 13 July 1937, box 246, folder 751.5, SSB-MF.

35. Ernest Draper to John Winant, 26 June 1936, box 246; A. J. Altmeyer to Eatton Sumners, 12 May 1939; copy of U.S. Congress, House, H.R. 5232, 76th Cong., 1st sess., introduced 22 March 1939; and Frank Bane to William Mayer, 8 April 1938, all in box 246, folder 751.5, SSB-MF. The bill that was enacted was chap. 49, 74th Cong., 2d sess., 11 February 1936, introduced as HR 10464.

36. Pierson to T. F. Murphy, 7 May 1935, box 1, folder "Birth and Death Registration Test, 1933 and 1934"; and Report of Field Agent Mankato, 16 July 1937, box 1, folder "Field Trips, 1931–38," both in MN-VSD-SF.

37. Field Agent Report, Glencoe and Little Falls, 25 January and 16 February 1935; Field Agent Report, Investigations of Works Progress Administration Projects, 15 July 1938; and Field Agent Report, Investigation on 7–8 September 1938, all in box 1, folder "Field Trips, 1931–38," MN-VSD-SF; Field Agent Report, Investigations on 5 June 1940, Grand Rapids, box 1, folder "Field Trip Reports, 1939–48," MN-VSD-SF; Instructions for the Organization and Operation of the Vital Statistics Project, Indiana Works Progress Administration; and Final Report for the Vital Statistics Survey Project, Mississippi, both in box 111, Works Progress Administration Library and Archives, RG 69, NARA-MD; Minutes of the State Board of Health, 6 October 1936, Virginia State Board of Health, Library of Virginia.

38. "Many Seek Data on Age Benefits," *Sun*, 4 January 1940; Minutes of the Census Advisory Committee Meeting, 9–10 January 1942, box 76 "March 29 1940–January 10 1942," Census-CAC.

39. Whitfield to State Registrars of Vital Statistics, 31 July 1938, box 1, folder "American Association of Registration Executives: Correspondence of Director Pierson, 1937–46," MN-VSD-SF.

40. P. B. Jenkins to Gerda Pierson, 28 February 1938, box 1, folder "American Association of Registration Executives: Correspondence of Director Pierson, 1937–46," MN-VSD-SF; John Collinson to Director, memorandum, 7 June 1938, folder "TPM: Vital Statistics 1938"; and Halbert Dunn to Director, memorandum, 3 May 1939, folder "TPM: Vital Statistics 1939," both in box 83, Census-ROADSS-TPM.

41. Ernie Pyle, "Birth Certificate Epidemic in U.S.: You Need One of These to Get Defense Job," *Daily Boston Globe*, 19 May 1941.

42. Acting Secretary of the Navy and Acting Secretary of War to All Present and Prospective Army and Navy Contractors and Subcontractors, memorandum, [ca. 29 July 1941], box 121, folder "Vital Statistics: Form Letter Re Proof of Age, etc. 702.01–03," Census-ROADSS-GR.

43. Minnesota Department of Health, question 6 of Minnesota Questionnaire, 10 September 1941, box 2, folder "National Defense Employment-Related Increase in Requests, Correspondence, August 1941"; Minnesota Department of Health, explanatory statement supporting the 1943–45 deficiency, box 2, folder Legislation 1925–45; Gerda Pierson to Travis Burroughs, 7 August 1941; and Burroughs to Frederick Jackson et al., 7 August 1941, both in box 2, folder "National Defense Employment-Related Increase in Requests, Correspondence, August 1941," all in MN-VSD-SF.

44. Howard Kline to Halbert Dunn, memorandum, 20 May 1942; Charles Bennett

to Dunn, memorandum, 24 December 1942; and Howard Klein to Dunn, memorandum, [ca. April 1942], all in box 85, folder "TPM: Vital Statistics 1942," Census-ROADSS-TPM; Minutes of the Census Advisory Committee Meeting, 9–10 January 1942, box 76, Census-CAC; U.S. Congress, Senate, Committee on Military Affairs, *Hearing*, 19.

45. U.S. Congress, Senate, Committee on Military Affairs, *Hearing*, 5, 12; U.S. Congress, House of Representatives, Committee on the Census, *Hearings*, 17.

46. USCB, *Manual of Uniform Procedure for the Delayed Registration of Births*, 16 July 1941; and Secretary of War, Navy, and Commerce to State Bureaus of Vital Statistics, memorandum, 16 July 1941, both in box 121, Census-ROADSS-GR.

47. "A Bill to Establish a National Vital Statistics Registration Service," typescript, received 15 September 1941, box 3, folder "World War II–Related Vital Statistics Work, 1941–43," MN-VSD-SF; U.S. Congress, Senate, Committee on Military Affairs, *Hearing*; U.S. Congress, House of Representatives, Committee on the Census, *Hearings*.

48. Minutes of the Census Advisory Committee Meeting, 9–10 January 1942, box 76, Census-CAC; and Proceedings of Meeting of Health and Medical Committee, Office of Defense, Health and Welfare Service, 10 December 1941; A. W. Hedrich [chief, Maryland State Bureau of Vital Statistics], Memorandum of Conference Regarding Vital Statistics Survey, 12 December 1941; and Minutes of the Special Advisory Committee to the Division of Vital Statistics, 3 November 1941, all in box 3, folder "World War II–Related Vital Statistics Work, 1941–1943," MN-VSD-SF.

49. A. W. Hedrich to Riley, 17 April 1942, box 3, folder "World War II–Related Vital Statistics Work, 1941–43," MN-VSD-SF; "Effect of the War," 550–52.

50. Minutes of Census Advisory Committee Meeting, 10–11 July 1942; Minutes of Census Advisory Committee Meeting, 30–31 October 1942; and Commission on Vital Records Report, 12 October 1942, all in box 77, Census-CAC.

51. Charles Bennett to Halbert Dunn, memorandum, 24 December 1942, box 85, folder "TPM: Vital Statistics 1943," Census-ROADSS-TPM.

52. Woodward to William Grayson, 16 January 1943, box 3, folder "World War II–Related Vital Statistics Work, 1941–43," MN-VSD-SF.

53. Halbert Dunn to Gustav Carlson, memorandum, 11 June 1942, box 85, folder "TPM: Vital Statistics 1942," Census-ROADSS-TPM; Craig Robertson, *Passport in America*, 104–6.

54. Halbert Dunn to Gustav Carlson, memorandum, 11 June 1942, box 85, folder "TPM: Vital Statistics 1942," Census-ROADSS-TPM. See also Gerda Pierson to Richard Whitfield, 18 August 1938, box 1, folder "American Association of Registration Executives: Correspondence of Director Pierson, 1937–46," MN-VSD-SF.

55. Halbert Dunn to Director, memorandum, 3 May 1939, box 83, folder "TPM: Vital Statistics, 1939," Census-ROADSS-TPM.

56. Main Differences between the Existing State Vital Statistics Laws and the Model Draft, n.d. [ca. 1938], box 119, folder "Model Vital Statistics Act 700.78"; and Minutes of the Meeting of the Council on Vital Records and Vital Statistics, Held at the Bureau of the Census, Washington, D.C., 30 April–2 May 1946, box 118, both in Census-ROADSS-GR; Powell, "Birth Certificate Story," 27.

57. Powell, "Birth Certificate Story," 27.

58. Main Differences between the Existing State Vital Statistics Laws and the Model

Draft, n.d. [ca. 1938]; Vergil Reed to Secretary, Attention of the Solicitor, 15 October 1938. See also Introductory Remarks Concerning the Constitutional Statutory and Administrative Aspects of State Vital Statistics Laws. All in box 119, folder "Model Vital Statistics Act 700.78," Census-ROADSS-GR.

59. Memorandum for the Special Advisory Committee for Vital Statistics, n.d., box 119, folder "Model Vital Statistics Act 700.78," Census-ROADSS-GR.

60. Minutes of the Meeting of the Council on Vital Records and Vital Statistics, Held at the Bureau of the Census, Washington, D.C., 30 April–2 May 1946, box 118, Census-ROADSS-GR.

61. William Woodward to William Grayson, 16 January 1943; and to I. C. Riggin, 12 January 1943, both in box 3, folder "World War II–Related Vital Statistics Work, 1941–43," MN-VSD-SF.

CHAPTER 8

1. Plecker to R. B. Ware, 24 March 1943, box 42, JPP.

2. Plecker to George Warren, 17 February 1942, box 41, JPP; and to Herbert Smith, 22 April 1943, box 42, JPP; *Act to Amend and Reenact Sections 1575, 1578, and 1580 of the Code of Virginia.*

3. Plecker to Mrs. E. D. Branham, 16 September 1940, 20 March 1942; to William Bradby, 2 February 1942; to Rose Taylor, 27 March 1942; and to Mrs. Fred Caudill, 28 August 1942, all in box 41, JPP; Plecker to Nannette Dickerson, 9 February 1943; to Beatrice Pettway, 4 March 1943; to Clara Trent Pultz, 17 March 1943; to Harry W. Tyree, 31 March 1943; to Nellie Crum, 9 April 1943; to Lillie Carroll, 22 July 1943; to Jessie Lee Collins, 28 July 1943; to Ovis Shaw, 28 July 1943; to Mary Lula Mullins, 23 March 1944; to Edith Butcher, 9 May 1944; to James P. Greene, 1 June 1944; to Mrs. James A. Lethcoe, 29 August 1944; and to Dorothy Dix Dodson, 15 May 1946, all in box 42, JPP.

4. Plecker to Collins, 12 August 1944, box 42, JPP.

5. Plecker to Cleveland, 29 April 1944, box 42, JPP.

6. Plecker to Pugh, 19 July 1944, box 42, JPP.

7. Kesselman, *Social Politics*, 5, 7, 9–12; Garfinkel, *When Negroes March*, 19–20.

8. Kesselman, *Social Politics*, 12–15; Garfinkel, *When Negroes March*, 53–60; Ruchames, *Race, Jobs and Politics*, 17–22, 165; "Twelve States Launch FEPC Bill Drives," *Pittsburgh Courier*, 28 December 1946; Phenner, "State Fair Employment," 189–201, 191.

9. Norris to Thurgood Marshall, 7 January 1941, folder 001459-032-0440, Part 18, PNAACP.

10. Clarence Mitchell to Truman Gibson, 4 December 1944, folder 101101-019-0354, Records of the Office of the Assistant Secretary of War, RG 107, NARA-MD.

11. Fermaglich, "'What's Uncle Sam's Last Name?,'" 738.

12. Terrell to Collector of Internal Revenue, 9 December 1936, region 4, box 49, folder 750, Records of the Social Security Board, Central File, Regional File, RG 47, NARA-MD.

13. Alfred Edgar Smith, "Report of Activities, May 1 to May 31st Inclusive, Federal Works Progress Administration," folder 001398-020-0480, General Files, RG 69, NARA-MD.

14. Williams to Hastie, 27 February 1941, 22 November 1940, folder 101101-023-0192, Records of the Office of the Assistant Secretary of War, RG 107, NARA-MD.

15. "Birth Certificates No Longer Required for Defense Jobs," press release, ca. 15 July 1942, folder 001583-024-0419, Claude A. Barnett Papers, Chicago History Museum.

16. "Birth Certificate Is First Defense Job Qualification," *Call and Post*, 20 December 1941.

17. Shapiro and Schacter, "Birth Registration Completeness," 517, 521.

18. E. B. Meritt to Martin Jacoway, 13 October 1917, Choctaw box 11, folder 94198-17 Choctaw 034; C. F. Hauke to Lewis Calvin, 25 February 1918, Five Tribes box 101, folder 14024-1918 Five Tribes 034; and Victor Sloan to Cato Sells, 21 February 1918, Shawnee box 5, folder 15476-1918 Shawnee 034, all in BIA-CCF.

19. Alice Wardchow to John Collier, 17 November 1939, Shawnee box 5, folder 75690-1939 Shawnee 033, BIA-CCF.

20. Heaston to Department of the Interior, 15 July 1949; and Daiker to Heaston, 25 July 1949, both in Chickasaw box 1, folder 00-1949 Chickasaw 034, BIA-CCF.

21. John Beck to Superintendent, Indian Service, 12 January 1941; and J. M. Stewart to John Beck, 3 February 1942, both in folder 3279-1942 Five Tribes 033; and Darcy McNickle to A. M. Landman, 5 July 1944, folder 30382-1944 Five Tribes 034, all in Five Tribes box 21, BIA-CCF.

22. "Indian Registration," 3.

23. "Notes and Comments on the Contributions," i; "Indians, Too," 3; U.S. Congress, Senate, Committee on Indian Affairs, *Survey of Conditions.*

24. Minutes of the Meeting of the Metropolitan Council on Fair Employment Practice, 15 October 1942, folder 001434-017-0448, General Office File, Fair Employment Practices Committee, Part 13, PNAACP.

25. "The Much-Abused Birth Certificate," *Call and Post*, 16 May 1942; "Tricks Used to Keep from Hiring Negro Workers," *Atlanta Daily World*, 10 May 1942.

26. Bailey to NAACP, 6 March 1942, folder 001432-018-0001, General Office File, National Defense, Part 13, PNAACP.

27. "Hudson Naval Arsenal Refuses Qualified Negro Woman Trainee," press release, folder 001497-005-0001, Part 26, PNAACP.

28. Clarence Mitchell to Truman Gibson, 19 September 1944, folder 101101-018-0001, Records of the Office of the Assistant Secretary of War, RG 107, NARA-MD.

29. George Schuyler, "Views and Reviews," *Pittsburgh Courier*, stamped 25 April 1942, folder 001432-018-0001, General Office File, National Defense, Part 13, PNAACP.

30. Fermaglich, "'What's Uncle Sam's Last Name?'"

31. "Twelve States Launch FEPC Bill Drives," *Pittsburgh Courier*, 28 December 1946; *Inside Facts: The New York State Law against Discrimination*, pamphlet of the State Commission against Discrimination, rev. 1 December 1946, folder 001432-018-0635, General Office File, New York State Commission against Discrimination, Part 13, PNAACP; *Questioning Applicants for Employment: A Guide for Application Forms and Interviews under the Kansas Act against Discrimination*, pamphlet of the Commission on Civil Rights, ca. 1963, folder 252252-014-1233, Subgroup E, Addendum, Congress of Racial Equality Papers, MLK Center; Phenner, "State Fair Employment," 193–94.

32. U.S. Congress, Commission on Civil Rights, *Hearings*, 458.

33. Tuck, *Beyond Atlanta*, 23.

34. Young Men's Civic Club to My Dear Sirs [NAACP], 18 March 1939, folder 001517-001-0895, Part 04, PNAACP.

35. Althea Simmons to Roy Wilkins, memorandum, 10 September 1965, re: Report on SUMMER PROJECTS in Alabama, Mississippi, and South Carolina, folder 001519-003-0077, Supplement, Part 04, PNAACP.

36. Jackie German, "Rights Worker Live in Fear," in "Louisiana Summer, 1964, The Students Report to their Hometowns," folder 252251-026-0441, Series 5, Congress of Racial Equality Papers, Wisconsin Historical Society.

37. Associated Negro Press, "Desegregation Roundup," 14 September 1955, folder 001584-058-0001, Claude A. Barnett Papers, Chicago History Museum.

38. WATS Reports 142, 4 August 1965; and WATS Reports 154, 25 August 1965, both in folder 252253-016-0405, Subgroup A, Student Nonviolent Coordinating Committee Papers, MLK Center.

39. Clara Ashford et al. to Frances Keppel, 13 August 1965, folder 252253-071-0052, Appendix B, Student Nonviolent Coordinating Committee Papers, MLK Center.

40. "125,000 are Eligible to Register, Vote," *Louisiana Weekly*, 31 August 1963, 1–2, folder 252253-022-1032, Subgroup A, Student Nonviolent Coordinating Committee Papers, MLK Center.

41. Minutes of the 1962 CORE National Convention, Miami, Florida, 28 June–1 July 1962, folder 01355-010-0762, Part 2, Congress of Racial Equality Papers, Wisconsin Historical Society.

42. Ruby Hurley, "Annual Report, National Association for the Advancement of Colored People, Southeast Regional Office," folder 009058-017-0123, Part 29, PNAACP.

43. *May Day Is Birth-Registration Day*, 2, 9. See also Minutes of the Meeting of the Council on Vital Records and Vital Statistics, 28–30 November 1944, box 118, folder "VS: Council on Vital Records and Vital Statistics, 7001," Census-ROADSS.

44. Elisabeth H. Clayton, "Suggested Agencies and Groups to Interest in Birth Registration Campaign on May Day," 10 March 1945, box 118, folder "VS: Information Material," Census-ROADSS.

45. Halpin to Halbert Dunn, 8 May 1945, box 86, folder "TPM: 1945," Census-ROADSS.

46. Lenroot to Negro Leaders, 7 March 1945, box 118, folder "VS: Information Material," Census-ROADSS.

47. Elisabeth Clayton, *A Birth Certificate for Baby* (1946), in box 118, folder "VS: Information Material"; and Clayton to Halbert Dunn, memorandum, 25 February 1946, re: Trip to Louisiana, box 87, folder "TPM: Vital Statistics 1946," both in Census-ROADSS.

48. JAK, "Birth Registration," 134.

49. "Children on May First," *Atlanta Daily World*, 1 May 1945. See also "Urge Race Parents to Join in Drive," *Atlanta Daily World*, 5 June 1945.

50. Halbert Dunn, "The Development of the Division of Vital Statistics in the Bureau of the Census, Address before American Statistical Association, December 29, 1935"; and John Collinson to Director, memorandum, 11 May 1937, both in box 82, folder "TPM: Vital Statistics, 1937 or Earlier," Census-ROADSS-TPM.

51. "Registration among the Indians," 4; J. R. McGibony, Director of Health, to All Superintendents and Physicians, 9 April 1942, box 12, Orders, Circulars, and Circular Letters, RG 75, NARA-DC.

52. Gustav Carlson to Halbert Dunn, memorandum, 11 June 1942; Frances Sullivan to Dunn, memorandum, 13 October 1942; and Gordon Jackson to Dunn, memorandum, 31 December 1942, all in box 85, folder "TPM: Vital Statistics 1942," Census-ROADSS-TPM.

53. "Indian Registration in New Mexico," 2.

54. Paul Fickinger, for the Commissioner, to Superintendents for Distribution to Personnel, memorandum, 20 April 1945, box 14, Orders, Circulars, and Circular Letters, RG 75, NARA-DC; Elisabeth Clayton to Halbert Dunn, memorandum, 29 March, 25 May 1945, box 86, folder "TPM: Vital Statistics 1945," Census-ROADSS-TPM; Clayton to Frank Morrison, memorandum, 15 January 1946; and Dunn to Director, memorandum, 11 March 1946, both in box 87, "TPM: Vital Statistics 1946," Census-ROADSS-TPM.

55. Hadley, "Why Old Man Coyote's," 2–3.

56. "Áwéé Binaltsoos Beedáhazingo Adenchsin," 2.

57. U.S. Department of the Interior and Federal Security Agency, *A Birth Certificate Tells the Facts*, General 3, 1940–48, MS 218:2, Association of American Indian Affairs Archives, Mudd Library.

58. Hadley, "Health Conditions," 832–33.

59. Hadley, "Registration of Vital Events," 109.

60. Walter White, "Brandeis University Is Successful Venture in Prejudice-Free Learning," *Chicago Defender*, 15 November 1952, 11.

61. Brown, "First Serious Implementation," 182–90.

62. U.S. Department of Health, Education, and Welfare, Office of Education, "Texts of Notices, Letters and Choice Form Prescribed by the Commissioner of Education for Use with School Desegregation Plans," March 1966, folder 252252-005-0732, Subgroup A, Addendum, Congress of Racial Equality Papers, MLK Center.

63. "Answers Race Query with One Word—Human," *Chicago Defender*, 29 July 1950. Johnson is not identified as Black in the *Defender* article, but he is in the 1940 census. Johnson census record, 1940, Harrisburg, Dauphin, Pennsylvania, roll m-t0627–03481, p. 1B, enumeration district 22–37, Ancestry.com; "Funeral Services Held for Dr. L. Z. Johnson, Sr.," *Evening News*, 22 January 1949.

64. Prewitt, *What Is Your Race?*, 76. In the late twentieth and the twenty-first century, racial categorization on the U.S. Census remains a matter of contest.

65. "Refusal of Race Identification," 150; Minutes of the Meeting of the National Medical Committee of the NAACP, 20 June 1952, folder 001447-014-0389, Part 16, PNAACP, https://congressional.proquest.com/histvault?q=001447-014-0389.

66. "Harrisburg Doctor Refuses Race," 252; "Exit the Race Statistic," 326; "Refusal of Race Identification," 150.

67. Minutes of the Meeting of the National Medical Committee of the NAACP, 20 June 1952, folder 001447-014-0389, Part 16, PNAACP, https://congressional.proquest.com/histvault?q=001447-014-0389.

68. Legal Redress, Second Annual Freedom Fund Program, 31 October 1959, folder 001491-013-0310, Part 25, PNAACP, https://congressional.proquest.com/histvault?q=001491-013-0310.

69. Jean Roberts to Granger, 26 January 1956, box 1, folder "American Association of Registration Executives Correspondence, General, 1938–56," MN-VSD-SF.

70. Greenberg to Carter, 26 August 1960, folder 001475-008-0564, Part 22, PNAACP, https://congressional.proquest.com/histvault?q=001475-008-0564.

71. Greenberg to City of New York, Department of Health, 21 September 1960; and Erhardt to Greenberg, 26 September 1960, both in folder 001475-008-0564, Part 22, PNAACP.

72. Brower to Hazel Aune, 10 February 1956; Aune to Robert Barr, Attention: Brower, 15 February 1956; and appendix 1, Example of Utilization of Vital Statistics Classified by Race, draft, 2 June 1956, all in box 1, folder "American Association of Registration Executives Correspondence, General, 1938–56," MN-VSD-SF.

73. Polier to Dear Colleague, 30 December 1960, folder 001486–028–0184, Part 24, PNAACP.

74. Erhardt, "Race or Color," 666–67.

75. Erhardt, 667–68.

76. Erhardt, 668–69.

77. "For the Files," Sun, 1 January 1961.

78. "New York Will Drop Race in Birth Records," Chicago Daily Tribune, 27 December 1960.

79. "All Americans," New York Amsterdam News, 31 December 1960.

80. Borstelmann, Just Like Us, 46–47, 70–71.

81. Prewitt, What Is Your Race?, 84–85.

82. Morrie Ryskind, "Minority Report on Minorities: Liberals Should Tote the Score," Los Angeles Times, 2 January 1961.

83. Edwards, "Social Implications," 673–74.

84. Minutes of the Meeting of the Executive Committee, National Association for the Advancement of Colored People, 14 February 1966, folder 009052-001-0001, Part 01, PNAACP.

85. "Marriage Curb in South Is Seen for New Yorkers," New York Times, 28 December 1960; "New Orleans' New Fight," Pittsburgh Courier, 7 January 1961.

86. "Race Data Challenged," New York Times, 18 January 1962; "Bar Race Statements on Ill. Birth Certificates," Philadelphia Tribune, 28 November 1961; "Illinois Health Unite to Nix Birth Certificate Race Tag," Afro-American, 2 December 1962; Fisher to Alan Reitman, 4 January 1961, box 1025, folder 15, item 493, American Civil Liberties Union Papers, Mudd Library.

87. Aune, "Implications," 663–65.

88. "Public Health Conference on Records and Statistics," 992.

89. National Center for Health Statistics, Proceedings, 171.

90. Grover, 1968 Revision, 3–5, 28.

91. National Center for Health Statistics, Physicians' Handbook; National Center for Health Statistics, Hospital Handbook.

92. Woolsey, "1968 in Review," 3.

93. Act Eliminating the Recitation of Color; Act Permitting City and Town Clerks.

94. Act to Amend Sections 10000; Act to Amend Section 10613.

95. Certified Copies of Vital Records.

96. Act to Amend and Reenact Chapter 2.

97. Ford, "Administering Identity," 1257–61.

98. Centers for Disease Control, "Classification of American Indian Race," 220–23; Epstein, Moreno, and Bacchetti, "Underreporting of Deaths," 1363–66.

99. Minutes of the Minnesota Chippewa Indians Executive Committee Meeting, 15–18 May 1941, folder 002122-015-0336, BIA-CCF-MCM; Doerfler, "Tribal Citizenship," 786.

100. Minutes of the Cheyenne-Arapaho Tribes of Oklahoma Tribal Business Committee Meeting, 7 March 1962, folder 002124-012-0050, BIA-CCF-MCM; Minutes of the Cheyenne-Arapaho Tribes of Oklahoma Tribal Business Committee Meeting, 5 February 1965, folder 002124-012-0401, BIA-CCF-MCM.

101. Minutes of the Cheyenne River Sioux Indians Tribal Council Meeting, 2–4 December 1947, folder 002122-023-0792, BIA-CCF-MCM; Red Lake Chippewa Indians Tribal Council Meeting, 9 November 1960, folder 002125-012-0322, BIA-CCF-MCM.

102. Minutes of the Cheyenne River Sioux Indians Tribal Council Meeting, 3–6 December 1946, folder 002122-023-0345, BIA-CCF-MCM; Minutes of the Klamath Indians General Council Meeting, 10 February 1955, folder 002122-020-0098, BIA-CCF-MCM.

103. Minutes of the Navajo Tribal Council Advisory Committee Meeting, 24 January–2 February 1950, folder 002121-005-0430, BIA-CCF-MCM.

104. John Collier, memorandum re: Registration as an "Indian," 22 September 1936, box 1, folder Memoranda and Circulars, Other Enrollment Records, RG 75, NARA-DC.

105. Chairman of the Committee on Enrollment under Section 19, Indian Reorganization Act, to Commissioner of Indian Affairs, memorandum, 6 July 1936, box 3, folder Landless Indians, Other Enrollment Records, RG 75, NARA-DC.

106. Spruhan, "CDIB," 169–96.

107. "Certificate of Degree."

CONCLUSION

1. "'Bathroom Bill' Settlement Reached in North Carolina," *New York Times*, 23 July 2019.

2. Mottet, "Modernizing State Vital Statistics," 376–77.

3. "State-by-State Overview"; Associated Press, "Kansas to Allow."

4. "Identity Documents."

5. Tomchin, "Bodies and Bureaucracy," 813, 858.

6. Spade, "Documenting Gender," 806.

7. "How Trans-Friendly."

8. "Arkansas Bill Regarding Biological Sex Listing."

BIBLIOGRAPHY

PRIMARY SOURCES

ARCHIVES

Chicago History Museum, Chicago, Illinois
    Claude A. Barnett Papers, Associated Negro Press, 1918–67, Part 1: Associated Negro Press News Releases, 1928–64 (ProQuest History Vault)
    Infant Welfare Society Papers
Connecticut State Archives, Hartford, Connecticut
    Records of the Education Department
Hanna Holborn Gray Special Collections Research Center, University of Chicago Library
    Edith and Grace Abbott Papers
Herbert Hoover Presidential Library and Museum, West Branch, Iowa
    American Child Health Association Papers
Indiana State Archives, Indianapolis, Indiana
    Papers of John N. Hurty
    Indiana State Board of Health, Division of Infant and Child Hygiene, Policy Files and Correspondence
    Indiana State Board of Health, Minutes of the Executive Board
Library of Congress, Manuscripts Division, Washington, D.C.
    Papers of the NAACP (ProQuest History Vault)
        Part 01: Supplement, 1966–70, Group IV, Series A, Administrative File, Board of Directors
        Part 04: Voting Rights Campaign, 1916–60, Group I, Series C, Administrative File: Subject File—Discrimination
            Supplement: Voting Rights, General Office Files, 1956–65, Group III, Series A, General Office File, Subject File—Register and Vote
        Part 13: NAACP and Labor, Series B: Cooperation with Organized Labor, 1940–55, Group II, Series A, Subject Files on Labor Conditions and Employment Discrimination, 1940–55
            General Office File, Fair Employment Practices Committee
            General Office File, National Defense
            General Office File, New York State Commission against Discrimination
        Part 16: Board of Directors, Correspondence and Committee Materials, Series B: 1940–55, Group II, Series A, General Office File, Board of Directors
        Part 18: Special Subjects, 1940–55, Series C: General Office Files: Justice Department–White Supremacy, Group II, Series A, General Office File

Part 22: Legal Department Administrative Files, 1956–65, Group V, Series B, Administrative File, General Office File: Carter, Robert L., Outgoing Correspondence

Part 24: Special Subjects, 1956–65, Series B: Foreign Affairs–Leagues and Organizations, Group III, Series A, Administrative File, General Office File

Part 25: Branch Department Files, Series B: Regional Files and Special Reports, 1956–65, Group III, Series C, Branch Department Files, Special Reports

Part 26: Selected Branch Files, 1940–55, Series C: The Midwest, Group II, Series C: Branch Department Files, Geographical File

Part 29: Branch Department, Series A: Field Staff Files, 1965–72, Group VI, Series C: Branch Department Files, Field Staff: Regional Directors

Papers of the National Child Labor Committee

Walter F. Willcox Papers

Library of Virginia, Richmond, Virginia

Auditor of Public Accounts, Office Records: General Records—Correspondence, Orders and Oaths of Office, Letters Received, State Government Records Collection

John Brown Arithmetic Book, 1788–89, Accession 28978

James P. Coates Papers, 1833–1947

William G. Rennolds Papers

Rockbridge County Court Records, Circuit Court, Judgements: *Sorrels v. Shields* (Clerk), 1925

Rockbridge County Court Records, Clerk's Records, Clerk's Correspondence

Virginia State Board of Health, Minutes and Meetings Files, vol. 1, State Records Collection

Martin Luther King Jr. Center for Nonviolent Social Change, Inc., Atlanta, Georgia

Congress of Racial Equality Papers (ProQuest History Vault)

Addendum, 1944–68

Subgroup A: National Directors' Files, 1960–68, Series II: Floyd McKissick, 1960–68, Correspondence Files, 1960–68

Subgroup E: Community Relations Department, 1949–68, Series IV: Subject Files, 1960–67

Student Nonviolent Coordinating Committee Papers, 1959–72 (ProQuest History Vault)

Appendix B: Michael Kenney Papers, 1963–69

Subgroup A: Atlanta Office, Series VII: Communications Department Internal Communication, 1962–66

Massachusetts Historical Society, Boston, Massachusetts

Christ Church Records, 1724–1851

James Freeman Diary [1788–99]

Lemuel Shattuck Papers

Minnesota Historical Society, St. Paul, Minnesota

Minnesota State Archives

Minnesota State Health Department, Correspondence and Miscellaneous Records

Minnesota State Health Department, Vital Statistics Division, Subject Files

Mudd Library, Princeton University, Princeton, New Jersey
    American Civil Liberties Union Papers, 1912–90, Years of Expansion, 1950–90,
        Series 3: Subject Files: Due Process of Law, 1938–88 (Gale Primary Sources:
        Making of Modern Law)
    Association of American Indian Affairs Archives, General and Tribal Files, 1851–
        1983: Tribal Files (Gale Primary Sources: Indigenous Peoples: North America)
National Archives and Records Administration, College Park, Maryland
    RG 47, Records of the Social Security Administration
        Records of the Social Security Board, Central File, Master File, 1935–47
        Records of the Social Security Board, Central File, Regional File, 1935–47
    RG 69, Records of the Works Progress Administration
        General Files, File 102, 1936–37 (ProQuest History Vault)
        Works Progress Administration Library and Archives, State Project Reports and
            Research Publications
    RG 90, Records of the Public Health Service
        Records of the National Board of Health
            Copies of Letters Sent, April 1879–January 1882
            Minutes of the Board
    RG 102, Records of the U.S. Children's Bureau
        Central Files
        Central Files Relating to Child Labor, 1914–40
    RG 107, Records of the Secretary of War
        Records of the Office of the Assistant Secretary of War, Entry 188: Civilian Aide to
            the Secretary—Subject File [General Correspondence (Judge Hastie), 1940–48]
            (ProQuest History Vault)
    RG 163, Records of the Selective Service System, WWI
        Records of the Office of the Provost Marshal General, States Files 1917–19
National Archives and Records Administration, Washington, D.C.
    RG 29, Administrative Records of the Census Bureau
        Census Advisory Committee, Minutes of Meetings, Correspondence, and Reports
        Records of the Office of Assistant Director for Statistical Standards
            Records Relative to Vital Statistics
            Records Concerning Trips, Papers Read, and Meetings Attended, 1934–49
    RG 75, Records of the Bureau of Indian Affairs
        Central Classified File
            Indian Health and Medical Affairs, Part 1: Reports on Medical and Nursing
                Activities (ProQuest History Vault)
            Indian Health and Medical Affairs, Part 2: Diseases (ProQuest History
                Vault)
            Major Council Meetings of American Indian Tribes (ProQuest History
                Vault)
        Orders, Circulars, and Circular Letters and Replies to Them, 1932–50
        Other Enrollment Records, Applications, and Other Records
        Records of the Statistics Division, Correspondence Concerning Reports,
            1930–35

National Library of Medicine, Bethesda, Maryland
    Louis I. Dublin Papers
South Carolina Historical Society, Charleston, South Carolina
    St. Michael's Church Records
University of Virginia Library, Special Collections, Charlottesville, Virginia
    Papers of John Powell
Wisconsin Historical Society, Library–Archives Division, Madison, Wisconsin
    Congress of Racial Equality Papers, 1941–67 (ProQuest History Vault)
        Part 2: Southern Regional Office, 1959–66, Series 2, Louisiana Office
        Series 5, Departments and Related Organizations, 1946–1970, Community
            Relations Department, National Projects

BOOKS AND ARTICLES

Abbott, Edith, and Sophonisba Breckinridge. *Truancy and Non-attendance in Chicago Schools.* Chicago: University of Chicago Press, 1917.
Ahmrad, Jad, prod. "The Girl Who Doesn't Exist." *Radiolab,* 29 August 2016. Podcast, 34:44. http://www.wnycstudios.org/story/invisible-girl.
Allen, Nila F. *Infant Mortality: Results of a Field Study in Saginaw, Mich., Based on Births in One Year.* Washington, D.C.: Government Printing Office, 1919.
American Association for the Study and Prevention of Infant Mortality. *Transactions of the First Annual Meeting.* Baltimore: American Association for the Study and Prevention of Infant Mortality, 1910.
———. *Transactions of the Second Annual Meeting.* Baltimore: American Association for the Study and Prevention of Infant Mortality, 1912.
———. *Transactions of the Third Annual Meeting.* Baltimore: American Association for the Study and Prevention of Infant Mortality, 1913.
———. *Transactions of the Fourth Annual Meeting.* Baltimore: American Association for the Study and Prevention of Infant Mortality, 1914.
———. *Transactions of the Eighth Annual Meeting.* Baltimore: American Association for the Study and Prevention of Infant Mortality, 1918.
American Child Health Association. *The Expectant Mother in the House of Health.* New York: American Child Health Association, 1924.
"American Intelligence and Editorial." *New York Journal of Medicine and Collateral Sciences* 10 (January 1848): 111–20.
"American Medical Association." *Medical Examiner* 11 (1855): 348–71.
"American Medical Association." *New Jersey Medical Reporter and Transactions of the New Jersey Medical Society,* 1853, 291–310.
"The American Public Health Association." *Medical Examiner* 14 (15 May 1873): 116–20.
American Statistical Association. *Constitution and By-laws of the American Statistical Association: With a List of Officers, Fellows, and Members and an Address.* Boston: T. R. Marvin, 1840.
Anderson, Neal L. "Child Labor Legislation in the South." *Annals of the American Academy of Political and Social Science* 25, no. 3 (1905): 77–93.
"Annual Meeting of the Medical Society of the State of New York." *Medical and Surgical Reporter* 16 (1867): 132–34.

"Annual Report of the City Inspector, of the City of New York, for the Year 1844." *New York Journal of Medicine and Collateral Sciences* 5 (September 1845): 222–27.

"Arkansas Bill Regarding Biological Sex Listing on Birth Certificates (HB 1894)." Rewire News Legislative Tracker. 6 September 2019. https://rewire.news/legislative -tracker/law/arkansas-bill-regarding-biological-sex-listing-birth-certificates-hb -1894.

Arnold, Richard D. *Letters of Richard D. Arnold, M.D.* Edited by Richard H. Shryock. Durham, N.C.: Seeman, 1929.

Associated Press. "Kansas to Allow Trans Residents to Change Birth Certificates." NBC News. 25 June 2019. https://www.nbcnews.com/feature/nbc-out/kansas-allow -trans-residents-change-birth-certificates-n1021411.

Aune, Hazel. "Implications of the Race-Color Item for National Vital Statistics." *American Journal of Public Health and the Nation's Health* 52, no. 4 (April 1962): 663–65.

"Áwéé Binaltsoos Beedáhazingo Adenchsin." *Registrar*, 15 October 1947, 2.

B. "Vital Statistics of Fayette County, KY." *Western Journal of Medicine and Surgery* 8 (November 1851): 453–55.

Balfe, J. P. "Birth Registration in Connecticut." *American Journal of Public Health* 8, no. 10 (October 1918): 776–79.

Billings, John S. "Original Lectures." *Medical News* 55 (1889): 561–72.

———. "The Registration of Vital Statistics." *American Journal of the Medical Sciences* 85 (January 1883): 33–49.

Bird, Frances Henry. *Employment Certificate System, Maryland*. Pt. 3 of *Administration of Child Labor Laws*, by U.S. Children's Bureau. Washington, D.C.: Government Printing Office, 1919.

"Birth Registration Cards and Vaccination Required of Virginia School Children." *Public Health Reports* (1925): 1764.

Blair, Mrs. Elmer, Mrs. George O. Welch, and Mrs. Francis D. Everett. "Public Health." *General Federation of Women's Clubs Magazine*, January 1916, 24–26.

Blakeslee, G. Arthur. "Birth Registration." *City Health* 3 (October 1920): 6–7.

Bowen, Louise de Koven. "Birth Registration and Establishment of Paternity." Speech printed in U.S. Children's Bureau, *Standards of Legal Protection*, 53–54.

Bradley, Frances Sage. *The Care of the Baby*. New York: Russell Sage Foundation, 1917.

———. "Report of the Child Health Committee." *General Federation of Women's Clubs Magazine*, April 1916, 24.

Bradley, Frances Sage, and Margaretta A. Williamson. *Rural Children in Selected Counties of North Carolina*. Washington, D.C.: Government Printing Office, 1918.

Brown, Violet Palmer, and Jessie E. Spafford. "Report on Birth Registration during 1917." *Bulletin of the Illinois Federation of Women's Clubs* 10, no. 2 (1918): 29–30.

Callcott, Mary Stevenson. *Child Labor Legislation in New York: The Historical Development and the Administrative Practices of Child Labor Laws in the State of New York, 1905–1930*. New York: Macmillan, 1931.

Campbell, Charles. "Prevention of Infantile Blindness." *Annals of the American Academy of Political and Social Science* 37, no. 2 (March 1911): 273–87.

"The Care of Your Baby." *Public Health Reports* 37, no. 5 (1922): 200–239.

"Certificate of Degree of Indian or Alaska Native Blood Instructions." Bureau of

Indian Affairs (website). Accessed 16 September 2020. https://www.bia.gov/sites/bia
.gov/files/assets/foia/raca/pdf/idc1–029262.pdf.

Chapin, Charles. *A Report on State Public Health Work Based on a Survey of State
Boards of Health*. Chicago: American Medical Association, 1916.

"Child Welfare Legislation." *Bulletin of the Kansas State Board of Health* 14 (1918):
148–60.

The Cleveland Year Book. Cleveland, Ohio: Cleveland Year Book, 1921.

Cohen, Felix S. *Handbook of Federal Indian Law*. Washington, D.C.: Government
Printing Office, 1945.

Colby, Mary Ruth. *Problems and Procedures in Adoption*. Washington, D.C.: Government Printing Office, 1941.

"Conference of Boards of Public Health, Held at New York, May 21 and 22, 1874." *Journal of Social Science* 7 (September 1874): 210–28.

Cooper, Thomas, ed. *The Statutes at Large of South Carolina*. Vol. 2, *Containing the
Acts from 1682–1716, Inclusive, Arranged Chronologically*. Columbia, S.C.: A. S. John-
ston, 1837.

Cox, Christopher. "A Report upon the Necessity for a National Sanitary Bureau." In
*Selections from Public Health Reports and Papers Presented at the Meetings of the
American Public Health Association, 1873–1883*, 522–32. New York: Hurd and Hough-
ton, 1875; Arno, 1977.

Dart, Helen M. *Maternity and Child Care in Selected Rural Areas of Mississippi*. Washington, D.C.: Government Printing Office, 1921.

Davis, A. T. "Aids in Securing Better Registration." *American Journal of Public Health*
16, no. 1 (January 1926): 25–29.

Davis, William H. "A Check for the Registration of Births." *American Journal of Public
Health* 7, no. 9 (September 1917): 762–64.

———. "1926 Progress Report in the Campaign to Bring Every State into the Registration Area before 1930." Pt. 4 of "The Past and Future Development of Vital Statistics
in the United States." *Journal of the American Statistical Association* 21, no. 155
(September 1926): 274–79. https://doi.org/10.2307/2277054.

———. "Report of Committee on Registration Affairs." *American Journal of Public
Health* 14, no. 12 (December 1924): 1015. https://doi.org/10.2105/AJPH.14.12.1015.

"The Demand for Birth Registration." *Florida Health Notes* 9 (1914): 206–7.

Dempsey, M. V. *Infant Mortality: Results of a Field Study in Brockton, Massachusetts,
Based on Births in One Year*. Washington, D.C.: Government Printing Office, 1919.

Dickinson, May. *Children Well and Happy: A Manual for the Girls' Health League*.
Boston: LeRoy Phillips, 1918.

Douglass, Frederick. *Narrative of the Life of Frederick Douglass, an American Slave:
Written by Himself*. Boston: Anti-Slavery Office, 1845.

Dublin, Louis I. "The Present Status of Birth Registration in American Cities and Its
Relation to the Infant Mortality Rate." *Publications of the American Statistical Association* 15 (March 1917): 533–47.

Dublin, Louis I., William H. Davis, Wilmer R. Batt, Frederick L. Hoffman, Blanche M.
Haines, and B. J. Lloyd. "The Growth of the Birth and Death Registration Areas:

Report of the Committee." *American Journal of Public Health and the Nation's Health* 18, no. 5 (May 1928): 606–8. https://doi.org/10.2105/ajph.18.5.606.

Duke, Emma. *Infant Mortality: Results of a Field Study in Johnstown, PA., Based on Births in One Calendar Year.* Washington, D.C.: Government Printing Office, 1915.

Editor [John Forry]. "Nature and History of Vital Statistics—Being a Chapter from an Unpublished Volume." *New York Journal of Medicine and Collateral Sciences* 3 (November 1844): 320–34.

Edwards, G. Franklin. "Social Implications of Race-Color Designations." *American Journal of Public Health and the Nation's Health* 52, no. 4 (April 1962): 671–75.

"The Effect of the War on Vital Statistics." In "A Review of Vital Statistics, 1941." *Vital Statistics—Special Reports* 17, no. 29 (August 1943): 550–55.

Ehler, Elmer W. "The Legal Importance of Birth Registration." In American Association for the Study and Prevention of Infant Mortality, *Transactions of the Third Annual Meeting*, 102–8.

EJ. "Report of the Births, Marriages, and Deaths of Massachusetts, for the Year 1850." *American Journal of the Medical Sciences* 24 (July 1852): 147–64.

Ensign, Forest Chester. *Compulsory School Attendance and Child Labor: A Study of the Historical Development of Regulations Compelling Attendance and Limiting the Labor of Children in a Selected Group of States.* Iowa City, Iowa: Athens, 1921.

Erhardt, Carl L. "Race or Color on Vital Records: Why Confidential?" *American Journal of Public Health and the Nation's Health* 52, no. 4 (April 1962): 666–70.

Erickson, Halford. "Child Labor Legislation and Methods of Enforcement in Northern Central States." *Annals of the American Academy of Political and Social Science* 25 (May 1905): 53–65.

"Exit the Race Statistic." *Journal of the National Medical Association* 42 (1950): 326.

Feezer, Lester W. "Collection of Birth Reports in Thinly Settled Communities." *American Journal of Public Health* 8, no. 12 (1918): 906–9.

Fox, Carroll. "Public Health Administration in North Dakota." *Public Health Reports* 30, no. 51 (1915): 3658–88. https://doi.org/10.2307/4573073.

Franklin, Benjamin. "Benjamin Franklin on the Causes and Consequences of Population Growth." *Population and Development Review* 11, no. 1 (1985): 107–12. https://doi.org/10.2307/1973381.

Freund, Ernst. *Illegitimacy Laws of the United States and Certain Foreign Countries.* Washington, D.C.: Government Printing Office, 1919.

Fuller, Clara K. *History of Morrison and Todd Counties, Minnesota: Their People, Industries and Institutions.* Indianapolis, Ind.: B. F. Bowen, 1915.

Garfinkel, Herbert. *When Negroes March: The March on Washington Movement in the Organizational Politics of the FEPC.* Glencoe, Ill.: Free Press, 1959.

General Federation of Women's Clubs. *Twelfth Biennial Convention.* Chicago: General Federation of Women's Clubs, 1914.

"Getting into School." *Youth's Companion*, 3 January 1907, 8.

Goldmark, Josephine C. and Madeline Wallin Sikes, eds. "Child Labor Legislation: Schedules of Existing Statutes [. . .]." Supplement, *Annals of the American Academy of Political and Social Science* 18 (January 1907): S18.

Goodwin, Etta R. "Methods of Popularizing Birth Registration." In American Association for the Study and Prevention of Infant Mortality, *Transactions of the Eighth Annual Meeting*, 149–51.

Green, Frederick R. "Why Should Births and Deaths be Registered in Illinois." *Transactions of the Illinois State Academy of Science* 6 (1913): 34–44.

Greenleaf, Simon. *A Treatise on the Law of Evidence*. Vol. 2. Boston: Little, Brown, 1842.

Griscom, John H. *The Sanitary Condition of the Laboring Population of New York, with Suggestions for Its Improvement*. New York: Harper and Brothers, 1845.

Grover, Robert D. *The 1968 Revision of the Standard Certificates, Vital and Health Statistics: Documents and Committee Reports*. Series 4. No. 8. Washington, D.C.: Government Printing Office, 1968.

Grubbs, S. B. "Public Health Administration in Illinois." *Public Health Reports* 30, no. 21 (1915): 1479–545.

Guilfoy, William H. "The Enforcement of Registration of Births and Deaths in Metropolitan Areas—History, Methods, Results and Checks." *Michigan Bulletin of Vital Statistics* 20 (July 1917): 96–100.

Hadley, J. Nixon. "Health Conditions among Navajo Indians." *Public Health Reports* 70 (1955): 831–36.

———. "Registration of Vital Events among Indians." *Vital Statistics—Special Reports* 33, no. 6 (June 1950): 109–26.

———. "Why Old Man Coyote's Children Didn't Go to School." *Registrar*, 15 November 1946, 2–3.

Hanks, Ethel Edna. *Employment-Certificate System, Wisconsin*. Pt. 4 of *Administration of Child Labor Laws*, by U.S. Children's Bureau. Washington, D.C.: Government Printing Office, 1921.

Hanna, Agnes K. "Guarding Illegitimate Status." *Child Welfare League of America Bulletin* 13, no. 4 (May 1934): 3–7.

Harris, Elisha. "General Sanitary Laws, State and Local Organization for Sanitary Administration." In *Selections from Public Health Reports and Papers Presented at the Meetings of the American Public Health Association, 1873–1883*, 472–82. New York: Hurd and Houghton, 1875; Arno, 1977.

———. "Laws, Provisions, and Methods for Securing the Benefits of General Vaccination throughout the Country." *Public Health Papers and Reports* 3 (1876): 140–53.

———. "Report of the Committee on Vital Statistics." *Public Health Papers and Reports* 7 (1881): 429–35.

"Harrisburg Doctor Refuses Race Identification on Birth Certificate." *Journal of the National Medical Association* 42 (1950): 252.

Hart, Hastings. *The Registration of Illegitimate Births: A Preventative of Infant Mortality*. New York: Russell Sage Foundation, 1916.

Hart, Sophie Chantal. "The North Atlantic Section." *Journal of the Association of Collegiate Alumnae* 10 (May 1917): 612–14.

"Health Maryland: Practice of Midwifery; Notification of Cases of Ophthalmia Neonatorum; Acts of 1912, Chapter 94, Approved April 4, 1912." *Public Health Reports* 27, no. 51 (1912): 2139–40.

Hemenway, Henry Bixby. "Birth and Death Certificates as Legal Evidence." *American Journal of Public Health* 11, no. 1 (January 1921): 1–5.

Holt, W. Stull. *The Bureau of the Census: Its History, Activities and Organization.* Washington, D.C.: Brookings Institute, 1929.

"How a Life Insurance Company Helps in Birth Registration." *American Journal of Public Health* 7, no. 6 (June 1917): 576.

Howard, Sheldon L. "Division of Vital Statistics." *Illinois Health News* 5 (January 1919): 40–50.

Howard, Sheldon L., and Henry Bixby Hemenway. "Birth Records of Illegitimates and of Adopted Children." *American Journal of Public Health and the Nation's Health* 21, no. 6 (June 1931): 641–47.

"How Old Are You?" *Michigan Bulletin of Vital Statistics* 20 (June 1917): 86.

"How Old Are You?" *Texas Health Magazine,* June 1920, 5–7.

"How Trans-Friendly Is the Driver's License Gender Change Policy in Your State?" National Center for Transgender Equality. Accessed 6 September 2019. https://transequality.org/sites/default/files/docs/id/Drivers%20License%20Grades%20Sep%202019.docx.pdf.

Huffman, Helen C. "A First Protection for the Child Born Out of Wedlock." *Child* 11 (1946): 34–37.

Hughes, Elizabeth. *Infant Mortality: Results of a Field Study in Gary, Ind., Based on Births in One Year.* Washington, D.C.: Government Printing Office, 1923.

Hunter, Estelle B. *Infant Mortality: Results of a Field Study in Waterbury, Conn., Based on Births in One Year.* Washington, D.C.: Government Printing Office, 1918.

———. *Office Administration for Organizations Supervising the Health of Mothers, Infants, and Children of Preschool Age.* Washington, D.C.: Government Printing Office, 1922.

"Identity Documents." Lambda Legal. Accessed 6 September 2019. https://www.lambdalegal.org/know-your-rights/article/trans-identity-documents.

Indiana State Board of Health. *The Indiana Mothers' Baby Book: A Brief Treatise for Mothers* [. . .]. 2nd ed. Indianapolis: Indiana State Board of Health, 1919.

"Indian Registration." *Registrar,* 15 November 1945, 2–3.

"Indian Registration in New Mexico." *Registrar,* 15 April 1943, 2.

"Indians, Too—." *Registrar,* 15 August 1942, 3.

"In Memory of Dr. Elisha Harris." *Public Health Papers and Reports* 10 (1884): 509–10.

"Investigation Made by Miss Gertrude Barnes, a Visiting Nurse, for a Committee on Prevention, of Society for Promoting the Interest of the Blind, Cleveland, Ohio." *American Journal of Nursing* 11, no. 5 (1911): 387–90.

JAK. "Birth Registration." *Journal of the National Medical Association* 37 (1945): 134.

JHG. "Fourth Annual Report to the Legislature [. . .]." *New York Journal of Medicine and Collateral Sciences* 6 (1846): 263–70.

Kelley, Florence. *Some Ethical Gains through Legislation.* New York: Macmillan, 1905.

Lathrop, Julia. "The Federal Children's Bureau." *Child Labor Bulletin* 2 (May 1913): 56–62.

Lenhart, Robert F. "Completeness of Birth Registration in the United States in 1940." *American Journal of Public Health and the Nation's Health* 33, no. 6 (June 1943): 685–90.

Loehr, Mrs. Leon Lee. "Philanthropy." *Illinois Club Bulletin* 4 (1913): 24.

Loughran, Miriam E. "The Historical Development of Child-Labor Legislation in the United States." PhD diss., Catholic University of America, 1921.

Love, Nat. *The Life and Adventures of Nat Love Better Known in the Cattle Country as Deadwood Dick by Himself.* Los Angeles: printed by the author, 1907. https://search.alexanderstreet.com/view/work/bibliographic_entity%7Cdocument%7C4391340.

Lovejoy, Owen. *In the Shadow of the Coal Breaker.* New York: National Child Labor Committee, 1907.

Lumpkin, Katharine Du Pre. "The Child Labor Provisions of the Fair Labor Standards Act." *Law and Contemporary Problems* 6 (Summer 1939): 391–405.

Lundberg, Emma O. *Children of Illegitimate Birth and Measures for their Protection.* Washington, D.C.: Government Printing Office, 1926.

Lundberg, Emma O., and Katherine F. Lenroot. *Illegitimacy As a Child-Welfare Problem.* Pt. 1. Washington, D.C.: Government Printing Office, 1920.

MacNutt, J. Scott. "The Board of Health Nurse: What She Can Do for the Public Welfare in a Small City." *American Journal of Public Health* 3, no. 4 (April 1913): 344–53.

Martin, A. J. "Public Health Nursing in Syracuse." *Milbank Memorial Fund Quarterly Bulletin* 5 (October 1927): 85–90.

Matthews, Ellen N. *The Illegally Employed Minor and the Workmen's Compensation Law.* Washington, D.C.: Government Printing Office, 1932.

May Day Is Birth-Registration Day: A Handbook for Communities. Washington, D.C.: Government Printing Office, 1945.

Meanes, Lenna L., and M. L. Turner. "Committee on Women's and Children's Welfare." *Journal of the American Medical Association* 68 (June 1917): 1755–56.

"Medical General Convention." *New York Journal of Medicine and Collateral Sciences* 6 (May 1846): 1–7.

"Meeting of the American Medical Association, Second Day—Morning Session." *Ohio Medical and Surgical Journal* 5 (1853): 427–47.

"Meeting of the American Public Health Association." *Medical and Surgical Reporter* 33, no. 4 (December 1875): 445–49.

Meigs, Grace L. "Other Factors in Infant Mortality Than the Milk Supply and Their Control." *American Journal of Public Health* 6, no. 8 (August 1916): 847–53.

Meriam, Lewis. "Auditing the Birth Account: A Necessary Process in our Social Bookkeeping." In *Proceedings of the National Conference of Charities and Correction, at the Fortieth Annual Session, July 5–12, 1913,* 173–80. Fort Wayne, Ind.: Fort Wayne Printing, 1913.

———. *The Problem of Indian Administration.* Baltimore: Johns Hopkins University Press, 1928.

"Midwife Inspection in State of New York." *American Journal of Public Health* 6, no. 3 (March 1916): 291–92.

"Midwifery—Practice of—Schools For." *Public Health Reports* 30 (1915): 2686–91.

Minnesota Federation of Women's Clubs. *Annual Report 1915–1916.* Minneapolis: Minnesota Federation of Women's Clubs, 1916.

Minor, Jeanie V. "Proof-of-Age Records." *Annals of the American Academy of Political and Social Science* 35 (March 1910): 127–29.

"Minutes of the Eleventh Annual Meeting of the American Medical Association, Held in the City of Washington, May 4, 1858." *Medical and Surgical Reporter* 11 (1858): 361–85.

Monger, Jonathon Emerson. "Cooperation of State and Federal Governments in Registration of Births and Deaths." *Michigan Bulletin of Vital Statistics* 22 (February 1919): 19–23.

———. "Why Births and Deaths Should Be Registered." *Michigan Bulletin of Vital Statistics* 20 (1917): 139–43.

Moore, Elizabeth. *Maternity and Infant Care in a Rural County in Kansas.* Washington, D.C.: Government Printing Office, 1917.

Moore, Eva Perry. "Committee on Resolutions." *Journal of the Association of Collegiate Alumnae* 6 (March 1913): 50–51.

Moore, Howard. *The Care of Illegitimate Children in Chicago.* Chicago: Juvenile Protective Association of Chicago, 1912.

"Mother's Baby Books: Instruction for Mothers in the Care of Infants." *Public Health Reports* 29 (1914): 677.

"The Moving Picture and Public Health." *American Journal of Public Health* 2, no. 11 (November 1913): 903–4.

National Center for Health Statistics. *Hospital Handbook on Birth and Fetal Death Registration.* Washington, D.C.: Government Printing Office, 1967.

———. *Physicians' Handbook on Medical Certification: Death, Fetal Death, Birth.* Washington, D.C.: Government Printing Office, 1967.

———. *Proceedings of the Public Health Conference on Records and Statistics, 11th National Meeting, June 1966.* Public Health Service Publication No. 1594. Washington, D.C.: Government Printing Office, 1967.

National Child Labor Committee. "The Uniform Child Labor Law." *Child Labor Bulletin* 1 (August 1912): 78–107.

———. *Uniform Child Labor Laws, Proceedings of the Seventh Annual Conference.* Philadelphia: American Academy of Political and Social Science, 1911.

National Consumers' League. *Child Labor Legislation.* New York: National Consumers' League, 1904.

Newman, George. *Infant Mortality: A Social Problem.* New York: E. P. Dutton, 1907.

"News and Miscellany." *Medical and Surgical Reporter* 6 (1861): 344.

Norton, J. Pease. "The Economic Advisability of a National Department of Health." *Albany Law Journal* (November 1906): 338–44.

"Notes and Comments on the Contributions." *Indians at Work* 9 (May–June 1942): i.

Nurse Instruction for Civil Service Examinations. New York: Civil Service Chronicle, 1916.

"Nursing News and Announcements." *American Journal of Nursing* 9 (May 1909): 604.

Our Baby's Book: The Story of Baby's First Years. Minneapolis, Minn.: Carleton J. West, 1929.

Parker, Mabel Hammond. "Departments of Work." *Illinois Federation Bulletin* 7 (May 1916): 32–58.

Petrie, W. F. "Practical Workings of Michigan's Birth Registration Law." *Publications of the American Statistical Association* 10, no. 80 (1907): 506–9.

Petty, William. *Essays on Mankind and Political Arithmetic*. London: Robert Clavel and
   Henry Mortlock, 1698; Project Gutenberg, 2014. http://www.gutenberg.org/files/5619
   /5619-h/5619-h.htm.
Phenner, Michael E. "State Fair Employment Practice Acts and Multi-state Employers."
   Notre Dame Lawyer 36 (March 1961): 189–201.
Plecker, Walter. "A Standard Certificate of Birth." *American Journal of Public Health* 5,
   no. 10 (October 1915): 1044–47.
———. "Virginia's Attempt to Adjust the Color Problem." *American Journal of Public
   Health* 15, no. 2 (February 1925): 111–15.
Powell, Ernestine Breisch. "The Birth Certificate Story." *Women's Law Journal* 13 (1944):
   13–29.
Price, Marshall Langton. "Vital Statistics." *American Journal of Public Hygiene* 18
   (1908): 364–65.
"Proceedings of a Conference on Vital Statistics." *National Board of Health Bulletin*,
   no. S5 (January 1880): S1–23.
*Proceedings of the Eighteenth Annual Meeting of the Lake Mohonk Conference of the
   Friends of the Indian*. Reported and compiled by Isabel C. Barrows. New York: n.p.,
   1901.
*Proceedings of the Fifth Annual Meeting of the Lake Mohonk Conference of Friends of
   the Indian*. Philadelphia: Sherman, 1887.
"The Proposed State Board of Health." *Medical and Surgical Reporter* 30 (April 1874):
   339–40.
"Public Health Conference on Records and Statistics." *Public Health Reports* 79 (1964):
   991–96.
Randall, Marian G. "The Public Health Nurse in a Rural Health Department: An
   Introductory Report on the Study in Progress in Cattaraugus County." *American
   Journal of Public Health and the Nation's Health* 21, no. 7 (July 1931): 737–50.
Rawlings, Isaac D. "Symposium on the Next Step for State Health Departments."
   American Journal of Public Health 12, no. 12 (December 1922): 1009–12.
Reese, Meredith. "A Report on Infant Mortality in Large Cities [. . .]." *Transactions of
   the American Medical Association* 10 (1857): 94–102.
"Refusal of Race Identification on Birth Certificate." *Journal of the National Medical
   Association* 44 (1952): 150.
"Registration." *Western Journal of Medicine and Surgery* 6 (December 1850): 547–48.
"Registration among the Indians." *Registrar*, 15 January 1940, 4.
"Registration of Births of Illegitimates and Adopted Children." In "American Public
   Health Association Year Book, 1933–1934." Supplement, *American Journal of Public
   Health and the Nation's Health* 24, no. S2 (February 1934): S84–87.
"The Registration Report of Michigan." *Medical and Surgical Reporter* 27 (December
   1872): 519–20.
Reinhard, Philip W. *Report and Testimony Taken before the Special Committee of the
   Assembly Appointed to Investigate the Condition of Female Labor in the City of New
   York*. Vol. 2. Albany, N.Y.: Wynkoop, Hallenback, Crawford, 1896.
Ripley, William Z. "Colored Population of African Descent." In *The Federal Census:*

Critical Essays, edited by the American Economic Association, 38–48. New York: Macmillan, 1899.

Routzahn, Evart G. "Education and Publicity." *American Journal of Public Health* 11, no. 11 (November 1925): 1032–36.

Ruchames, Louis. *Race, Jobs and Politics: The Story of the FEPC.* New York: Columbia University Press, 1953.

Rude, A. E. *The Midwife Problem.* Washington, D.C.: Government Printing Office, 1923.

Schmidt, Violet Jayne. "Report of the Vice-President for the Northeast Central Section." *Journal of the Association of Collegiate Alumnae* 10 (September 1916): 49–56.

"Second Annual Report of the Legislature [. . .]." *American Journal of the Medical Sciences* 8 (July 1844): 190–91.

Secretary of the Commonwealth. *Instructions Concerning the Registration of Births, Marriages, and Deaths, in Massachusetts.* Boston: William White, 1860.

"Securing Birth Reports without Prosecution." *Public Health News* 1 (1916): 233–35.

Shapiro, Sam, and Joseph Schacter. "Birth Registration Completeness United States, 1950." *Public Health Reports* 67 (1952): 513–24.

Shattuck, Lemuel. *A Complete System of Family Registration.* Boston: Ticknor, 1841.

———. "Ecclesiastical Register; Or a Complete System of Ecclesiastical and Parochial Registration." *American Quarterly Register* 12 (1840): 285–92.

———. *Letter to the Secretary of State on the Registration of Births, Marriages and Deaths in Massachusetts.* Boston: n.p., 1845.

———. *Report of a General Plan for the Promotion of Public and Personal Health, Devised, Prepared and Recommended by the Commissioners Appointed under a Resolve of the Legislature of Massachusetts, Relating to a Sanitary Survey of the State.* Boston: Dutton and Wentworth, 1850.

Sherbon, Florence B., and Elizabeth Moore. *Maternity and Infant Care in Two Rural Counties in Wisconsin.* Washington, D.C.: Government Printing Office, 1919.

Sidwell, Francis Haldeman. "Report of the Vice-President of the South Atlantic Section." *Journal of the Association of Collegiate Alumnae* 9 (1916): 55–56.

Smith, Richard Mayo. "An Outline of Statistics." *Publications of the American Economic Association* 3 (1888): 14–78.

———. "A Permanent Census Bureau." *Political Science Quarterly* 11, no. 4 (1896): 589–600.

Snow, Edwin M. *Report on Registration, Presented to the Quarantine and Sanitary Convention.* n.p., 1860.

"Social Progress." *Crisis,* 1 February 1917, 191–93.

"State-by-State Overview: Rules for Changing Gender Markers on Birth Certificates." Transgender Law Center. Updated April 2017. http://transgenderlawcenter.org/wp -content/uploads/2016/12/Birth-Cert-overview-state-by-state.pdf.

State Department of Education [of South Carolina]. *An Act to Require School Attendance.* Columbia, S.C.: R. L. Bryan, 1915.

"State Laws and Regulations Pertaining to Public Health: Ohio." *Public Health Reports* 29 (1914): 1272.

"State Laws and Regulations Pertaining to Public Health: Wisconsin." *Public Health Reports* 31 (1916): 979.

Steele, G. *Maternity and Infant Care in a Mountain County in Georgia.* Washington, D.C.: Government Printing Office, 1923.

Stephenson, Gilbert Thomas. *Race Distinctions in American Law.* New York: D. Appleton, 1910.

"Summary of the Transactions of the College of Physicians of Philadelphia." *American Journal of the Medical Sciences* 70 (April 1858): 377–426.

Sumner, Helen L., and Ethel E. Hanks. *Employment-Certificate System in New York.* Pt. 2 of *Administration of Child Labor Laws,* by U.S. Children's Bureau. Washington, D.C.: Government Printing Office, 1917.

Sumner, Helen L., and Ella A. Merritt. *Child Labor Legislation in the United States.* Washington, D.C.: Government Printing Office, 1915.

Talbot, Holmer. *Post-war Activities, New Jersey State Council of Defense, a Report.* New Jersey: n.p., 1920.

Terry, Charles Thaddeus. *Uniform State Laws in the United States, Fully Annotated.* New York: Baker, Voorhis, 1920.

"Tommy's Birth Certificate." *Healthologist* 2 (October 1912): 18–19.

"Transactions of Societies: Art. VIII—Summary of the Transactions of the College of Physicians of Philadelphia." *American Journal of the Medical Sciences* 83 (July 1861): 69–100.

Trask, John W. *Vital Statistics: A Discussion of What They Are and Their Uses in Public Health Administration.* Washington, D.C.: Government Printing Office, 1914.

Tucker, George. *Progress of the United States in Population and Wealth in Fifty Years.* New York: Press of Hunt's Merchants' Magazine, 1843.

U.S. Bureau of Naturalization. *Suggestions for Americanization Work among Foreign-Born Women.* Washington, D.C.: Government Printing Office, 1921.

U.S. Census Bureau. *Birth Statistics for the Registration Area of the United States, 1916, Second Annual Report.* Washington, D.C.: Government Printing Office, 1918.

———. *A Discussion of Age Statistics.* Washington, D.C.: Government Printing Office, 1904.

———. *Legal Importance of Registration of Births and Deaths: Report of Special Committee on Vital Statistics to the Conference on Commissioners on Uniform State Laws.* Washington, D.C.: Government Printing Office, 1908.

———. *Physician's Handbook on Birth and Death Registration, Containing International List of Causes of Death.* 9th rev. ed. Washington, D.C.: Government Printing Office, 1943.

———. *Registration of Births and Deaths: Drafts of Laws and Forms of Certificates, Information for Local Officers.* Washington, D.C.: Government Printing Office, 1903.

U.S. Census Office. *Compendium of the Tenth Census.* Vol. 2. Washington, D.C.: Government Printing Office, 1883.

———. *Legislative Requirement for Registration of Vital Statistics.* Washington, D.C.: Government Printing Office, 1903.

U.S. Children's Bureau. *Administration of the First Federal Child-Labor Law.* Washington, D.C.: Government Printing Office, 1921.

———. *Baby-Saving Campaigns: A Preliminary Report on What American Cities Are Doing to Prevent Infant Mortality.* Washington, D.C.: Government Printing Office, 1914.

———. *Baby-Week Campaigns: Suggestions for Communities of Various Sizes.* Washington, D.C.: Government Printing Office, 1915; rev. ed., 1917.

———. *Birth Registration: An Aid in Protecting the Lives and Rights of Children.* Washington, D.C.: Government Printing Office, 1914.

———. *Birth-Registration Test.* 2nd ed. Washington, D.C.: Government Printing Office, 1916.

———. *Child-Welfare Programs: Study Outlines for the Use of Clubs and Classes.* Washington, D.C.: Government Printing Office, 1920.

———. *The Employment-Certificate System: A Safeguard for the Working Child.* Washington, D.C.: Government Printing Office, 1921.

———. *Infant Mortality, Montclair, N.J.: A Study of Infant Mortality in a Suburban Community.* Washington, D.C.: Government Printing Office, 1915.

———. *Norwegian Laws Concerning Illegitimate Children.* With introduction and translated by Leifur Magnusson. Washington, D.C.: Government Printing Office, 1918.

———. *An Outline of a Birth Registration Test.* Washington, D.C.: Government Printing Office, 1919.

———. *Paternity Laws: Analysis and Tabular Summary of State Laws Relating to Paternity and Support of Children Born out of Wedlock, in Effect January 1, 1938.* Washington, D.C.: Government Printing Office, 1938.

———. *Proceedings of the Fourth Annual Conference of State Directors in Charge of the Local Administration of the Maternity and Infancy Act.* Washington, D.C.: Government Printing Office, 1927.

———. *Proceedings of the Third Annual Conference of State Directors in Charge of the Local Administration of the Maternity and Infancy Act.* Washington, D.C.: Government Printing Office, 1926.

———. *Standards of Legal Protection for Children Born out of Wedlock: A Report of Regional Conferences Held under the Auspices of the U.S. Children's Bureau and the Inter-city Conference on Illegitimacy.* Washington, D.C.: Government Printing Office, 1921.

U.S. Congress. "Printing of Mortality Statistics." 33rd Cong., 1854. *Congressional Globe* 24 (1854): 45–46.

U.S. Congress. Commission on Civil Rights. *Hearings Before the United States Commission on Civil Rights, Detroit, Michigan.* 86th Cong., 14 and 15 December 1960. Statement of Chrysler Corp.

U.S. Congress. House of Representatives. Committee on the Census. *Hearings Before the Committee on the Census, Authorizing the Director of the Census to Issue Birth Certificates.* 77th Cong., 2d sess., 4, 9, and 10 June 1942.

U.S. Congress. Senate. *An Act to Provide for the Registration of Married Indians, and for* the Licensing, the Legal Performance, and the Recording of Marriages among Reservation Indians, or between Reservation Indians and Others; and to Make Definite and to Record the Family Relations of Indians Who Have Not Yet Received Allotments of Land in Severalty. S. 4713. 56th Cong., 1st sess. Introduced in the Senate 15 May 1900.

U.S. Congress. Senate. Committee on Commerce. Federal Cooperation with States in Promotion of General Health of Rural Population of the United States and Welfare and Hygiene of Mothers and Children: Hearings on S. 572 Before the Committee on Commerce. 72nd Cong., 1st sess., 4 and 5 February 1932.

U.S. Congress. Senate. Committee on Education and Labor. House of Representatives. Committee on Labor. Fair Labor Standards Act of 1937, Pt. 2: Hearings on S. 2475 and H.R. 7200 Before the Senate Committee on Education and Labor and House Committee on Labor. 75th Cong., 1937.

U.S. Congress. Senate. Committee on Indian Affairs. Survey of Conditions of the Indians in the United States: Hearings Before a Subcommittee of the Committee on Indian Affairs, United States Senate. Pt. 41, "Osage Indian Matters, 22777." 78th Cong., 1st sess. 1943.

U.S. Congress. Senate. Committee on Military Affairs. Hearing on S. 2299 Before a Subcommittee of the Committee on Military Affairs. 77th Cong., 2 April 1942.

U.S. Department of Labor. Cotton Textile Industry. Vol. 1 of Report on Condition of Woman and Child Wage-Earners in the United States. Washington, D.C.: Government Printing Office, 1910.

———. The Silk Industry. Vol. 4 of Report on Condition of Woman and Child Wage-Earners in the United States. Washington, D.C.: Government Printing Office, 1911.

U.S. Office of Indian Affairs. Indian Babies: How to Keep Them Well. Washington, D.C.: Government Printing Office, 1916.

Van Blarcom, Carolyn Conant. "Ophthalmia Neonatorum as a Cause of Blindness." American Journal of Nursing 10 (July 1910): 724–33.

Vaughan, Henry F. "Public Health Administration." American Journal of Public Health 17, no. 4 (April 1927): 396–99.

Vaughan, Henry F., and Carl E. Buck. "Diptheria Prevention in Detroit." American Journal of Public Health and the Nation's Health 21, no. 7 (July 1931): 751–61.

"Vital Statistics." Medical and Surgical Reporter 20, no. 10 (1869): 194.

"Vital Statistics of Kentucky." Western Journal of Medicine and Surgery 1, no. 4 (April 1854): 293–96.

"Vital Statistics of Massachusetts." Medical and Surgical Reporter 3, no. 11 (November 1866): 403–4.

Walker, Francis A., comp. Statistical Atlas of the United States, Based on the Results of the Ninth Census, 1870. New York: J. Bien, 1874.

Ward, Grace F. "Weakness of the Massachusetts Child Labor Laws." In Labor Laws and Their Enforcement, with Special Reference to Massachusetts, edited by Susan M. Kingsbury, 159–219. New York: Longmans, Green, 1911.

Warner, Oliver. Instructions Concerning the Registration of Births, Marriages, and Deaths, in Massachusetts. Boston: William White, 1860.

Watson, Henry. Narrative of Henry Watson, a Fugitive Slave: Written by Himself. Boston: Bela Marsh, 1848. https://docsouth.unc.edu/neh/watson/watson.html.

Webster, Mrs. Garrett. "A Boy's Life in Photographs." *Ladies Home Journal*, November 1898, 6.

West, Mrs. Max [Mary Mills]. *Infant Care*. Washington, D.C.: Government Printing Office, 1914.

White House Conference on Child Health and Protection. *Obstetric Education: Report of the Subcommittee on Obstetric Teaching and Education*. New York: Century, 1932.

Wilbur, Cressy L. "The Chief Statistician on Vital Statistics." *Outlook*, 11 January 1913, 94–96.

———. *The Federal Registration Service of the United States: Its Development, Problems, and Defects*. Washington, D.C.: Government Printing Office, 1916.

———. "Notes on Recent Progress in Vital Statistics in the United States." *Publications of the American Statistical Association* 8, no. 61 (1903): 269–79.

Willcox, Wilbur F. "A Difficulty with American Census Taking." *Quarterly Journal of Economics* 14, no. 4 (1900): 459–74.

Wilson, Mrs. Andrew. "Child Welfare Work in Wheeling, West Virginia." *Public Health Nurse* 11 (February 1919): 138–42.

"Women's Clubs to Check Birth Registration." *Florida Health Notes* 9 (April 1914): 70–71.

Woolsey, Theodore D. "1968 in Review." *Registrar and Statistician* 34, no. 1 (January 1969): 1–4.

Wright, Carroll D. "Studies in Statistics." *Journal of the American Economic Association* 6, nos. 1/2 (1891): 64–71.

Wynne, Shirley W. "Practical Uses of Vital Statistics." *Michigan Bulletin of Vital Statistics* 21 (1918): 20–29.

Zimmerman, Mrs. George. "Civics and Baby Week in Ohio." *General Federation of Women's Clubs Magazine*, May 1916, 18.

PERIODICALS

Aberdeen (S.D.) Daily News
Afro-American (Baltimore)
Atlanta Constitution
Atlanta Daily World
Boston Daily Advertiser
Boston Globe
Bulletin, Chicago School of Sanitary Instruction
Butte (Mont.) Weekly Miner
Call and Post (Cleveland, Ohio)
Chicago Daily Tribune
Chicago Defender
Columbian Register (New Haven, Conn.)
Congregationalist (Boston)
Daily Boston Globe
Daily Cleveland Herald
Daily Evening Bulletin (San Francisco, Calif.)
Evening News (Harrisburg, Pa.)
Los Angeles Times
Lowell (Mass.) Daily Citizen and News
Milwaukee Daily Sentinel
Milwaukee Journal
Milwaukee Sentinel
News Letter [of the National Committee for the Prevention of Blindness]
New York Amsterdam News
New York Herald Tribune
New York Observer and Chronicle
New York Times
New-York Tribune
North American and United States Gazette (Philadelphia)

Philadelphia Tribune
Pittsburgh Courier
Richmond (Va.) Times-Dispatch
St. Louis Globe-Democrat

Sun (Baltimore)
Virginia Health Bulletin
Washington Post

ANNUAL REPORTS

Years after the title indicate the year of the report—often provided in a given annual report's title—rather than the year of publication, if they differ.

Annual Report of the Commissioner of Health to the Governor of Virginia for the Year Ending September 30, 1912.
Annual Report of the Factory Inspectors of Illinois.
Annual Report of the Secretary of State of the State of Michigan, Relating to the Registry and Return of Births, Marriages, and Deaths. 1870–74.
Annual Report of the State Board of Health of Alabama. 1917.
Annual Report of the State Board of Health of Massachusetts.
Annual Report of the State Department of Health and the State Health Commissioner to the Governor of Virginia. 1926, 1930.
Board of Indian Commissioners. Thirty-First Annual Report of the Board of Indian Commissioners.
———. Thirty-Second Annual Report of the Board of Indian Commissioners.
Connecticut Secretary of State. Report of the Secretary of State, Relating to the Registration of Births, Marriages and Deaths. 1850.
Connecticut State Board of Education. Annual Report of the Board of Education of the State of Connecticut, Submitted to the Governor, January 9, 1888.
———. Report of the Board of Education of the State of Connecticut to the Governor. 1899.
Connecticut State Librarian. Report of the State Librarian, Relating to the Registration of Births, Marriages and Deaths. 1854, 1862.
Department of Public Safety. Annual Report, Sub-department of Health, to the Mayor and City Council of Baltimore.
Indiana State Board of Health. Annual Report of the State Board of Health of Indiana.
Kansas State Board of Health. Biennial Report.
Maryland State Board of Health. Annual Report of the State Board of Health of Maryland for the Year Ending December 31, 1925.
New York State Department of Labor. Annual Report of the Commissioner of Labor and the Annual Report on Factory Inspection.
New York State Factory Inspectors. Annual Report of the Factory Inspectors of the State of New York.
Report of the City Registrar of the Births, Marriages, and Deaths, in the City of Boston. 1852–87.
Report of the Massachusetts Child Labor Committee. 1915.
Report of the State Board of Health and the State Health Commissioner to the Governor of Virginia. 1926.
State of Nevada. Biennial Report of the State Board of Health, for Period Ending December 21, 1912.

U.S. Census Bureau. *Report of the Director of the Census to the Secretary of the Interior, 1903.*
U.S. Children's Bureau. *Annual Report of the Chief of the Children's Bureau to the Secretary of Labor.*
———. *The Promotion of the Welfare and Hygiene of Maternity and Infancy: The Administration of the Act of Congress of November 21, 1921.* 1923–29.
U.S. Office of Indian Affairs. *Annual Report of the Commissioner of Indian Affairs.* 1874–1912.

COURT CASES

Dobson v. Cothran, 34 S.C. 518 (1891).
Ohio v. Boone, No. 12846, 1911 Ohio LEXIS 97.
The People v. Clifton E. Mayne, 118 Cal. 516 (1897).
State ex rel. Estelle Rodi, Wife of Theophile Soulet v. City of New Orleans et al., 94 So. 2d 108; 1957 La. App. LEXIS 1033 (1957).
Sunseri v. Cassagne, 191 La. 209; 185 So. 1; 1938 La. LEXIS 1362 (1938).
Sunseri v. Cassagne, 195 La. 19; 196 So. 7; 1940 La. LEXIS 1051 (1940).

LAWS

An Act Concerning the Registration of Births, Marriages, and Deaths. Chap. 25. Acts and Joint Resolutions of the General Assembly of the Commonwealth of Virginia. (1853): 40–43.
An Act Eliminating the Recitation of Color, Weight and Use of Prophylactic on Records of Birth and Providing for Certain Statistical Information. Chap. 0358. Session Laws Massachusetts. (1968): 213–14.
An Act for Registering Births, Christenings, and Burials. Chap. 4, 1713. The Acts of Assembly Now in Force in the Colony of Virginia. Vol. 1 (1752): 88.
An Act Permitting City and Town Clerks or the State Secretary to Omit the Color of Child in Issuing Copies of Certificates of Birth. Chap. 0478. Session Laws Massachusetts. (1969): 332.
An Act to Amend and Reenact Chapter 2 of Title 40 of the Louisiana Revised Statute of 1950. Chap. 776. Louisiana Revised Statutes. Vol. 2 (1979): 776.
An Act to Amend and Reenact Sections 1575, 1578 and 1580 of the Code of Virginia, 1919. H. B. No. 55. Journal of the Senate of the Commonwealth of Virginia. (1942): 175.
An Act to Amend Section 10613 of, and to Add Article 3.5 (Commencing with Section 10425) to Chapter 8 of Division 9 of, the Health and Safety Code, Relating to Vital Statistics. Chap. 610. Statutes of California and Digests of Measures. (1989): 2:2053–54.
An Act to Amend Sections 10000, 10008, 10125, 10575, 10575.1, and 10675 of, and to Add Sections 10001.1., 10125 5, 10126, 10127, 10128, 10129, 10130, 10130.5, and 10131 to, the Health and Safety Code, Relating to Vital Statistics, and Making an Appropriation Therefor. Chap. 1386 §2. Statutes of California and Digests of Measures. (1978): 3:4592–94.
Certified Copies of Vital Records; Other Copies. Vol. 2. Chap. 711, §32.1–272 (f). Code of Virginia. (1979).

SECONDARY SOURCES

Anderson, Margo J. *The American Census: A Social History.* New Haven, Conn.: Yale University Press, 1988.

Apple, Rima. "'To Be Used Only under the Direction of a Physician': Commercial Infant Feeding and Medical Practice, 1870–1940." *Bulletin of the History of Medicine* 54, no. 3 (Fall 1980): 402–17.

Balogh, Brian. *A Government out of Sight: The Mystery of National Authority in Nineteenth-Century America.* New York: Cambridge University Press, 2009.

Bardaglio, Peter W. *Reconstructing the Household: Families, Sex, and the Law in the Nineteenth-Century South.* Chapel Hill: University of North Carolina Press, 1998.

Barnhill, Georgia Brady. "'Keep Sacred the Memory of Your Ancestors': Family Registers and Memorial Prints." In Simons and Benes, *Art of Family,* 60–74.

Bashford, Alison. *Global Population: History, Geopolitics, and Life on Earth.* New York: Columbia University Press, 2014.

Bashford, Alison, and Joyce E. Chaplin. *The New Worlds of Thomas Robert Malthus: Rereading the "Principle of Population."* Princeton, N.J.: Princeton University Press, 2016.

Benes, Peter. "Family Representations and Remembrances: Decorated New England Family Registers, 1770 to 1850." In Simons and Benes, *Art of Family,* 13–59.

Bensel, Richard. "The American Ballot Box: Law, Identity, and the Polling Place in the Mid-nineteenth Century." *Studies in American Political Development* 17, no. 1 (April 2003): 1–27.

Borstelmann, Thomas. *Just Like Us: The American Struggle to Understand Foreigners.* New York: Columbia University Press, 2020.

Bouk, Dan. *How Our Days Became Numbered: Risk and the Rise of the Statistical Individual.* Chicago: University of Chicago Press, 2015.

Breckenridge, Keith, and Simon Szreter, eds. *Registration and Recognition: Documenting the Person in World History.* Oxford: Oxford University Press, 2012.

———. "Recognition and Registration: The Infrastructure of Personhood in World History." In Breckenridge and Szreter, *Registration and Recognition,* 1–36.

Brennan Center for Justice. *Citizens without Proof: A Survey of Americans' Possession of Documentary Proof of Citizenship and Photo Identification.* New York: Brennan Center for Justice at New York University School of Law, 2006.

Brewer, Holly. *By Birth or Consent: Children, Law and the Anglo-American Revolution in Authority.* Chapel Hill: University of North Carolina Press, 2005.

Brimmer, Brandi. "Black Women's Politics, Narratives of Sexual Immorality, and Pension Bureaucracy in Mary Lee's North Carolina Neighborhood." *Journal of Southern History* 80, no. 4 (November 2014): 827–58.

———. "'Her Claim for Pension Is Lawful and Just': Representing Black Union Widows in Late-Nineteenth Century North Carolina." *Journal of the Civil War Era* 1, no. 2 (June 2011): 207–36.

Brosco, Jeffrey P. "The Early History of the Infant Mortality Rate in America: 'A Reflection upon the Past and a Prophecy of the Future.'" *Pediatrics* 103, no. 2 (1999): 478–85.

Brown, Frank. "The First Serious Implementation of Brown: The 1964 Civil Rights Act and Beyond." *Journal of Negro Education* 73, no. 3 (2004): 182–90. https://doi.org/10.2307/4129604.

Brumberg, H. L., D. Dozor, and S. G. Golombek. "History of the Birth Certificate: From Inception to the Future of Electronic Data." *Journal of Perinatology* 32 (2012): 407–11. https://doi.org/10.1038/jp.2012.3.

Burns, Kathryn. *Into the Archive: Writing and Power in Colonial Peru.* Durham, N.C.: Duke University Press, 2010.

———. "Notaries, Truth, and Consequences." *American Historical Review* 110, no. 2 (April 2005): 350–79. https://doi.org/10.1086/531318.

Bynum, Virginia. "'White Negroes' in Segregated Mississippi: Miscegenation, Racial Identity, and the Law." *Journal of Southern History* 64, no. 2 (May 1998): 247–76. https://doi.org/10.2307/2587946.

Cahill, Cathleen. *Federal Fathers and Mothers: A Social History of the United States Indian Service, 1869–1933.* Chapel Hill: University of North Carolina Press, 2011.

Caplan, Jane, and John Torpey, eds. *Documenting Individual Identity: The Development of State Practices in the Modern World.* Princeton, N.J.: Princeton University Press, 2001.

———. Introduction to Caplan and Torpey, *Documenting Individual Identity,* 1–12.

Capozzola, Christopher. *Uncle Sam Wants You: World War I and the Making of the Modern American Citizen.* New York: Oxford University Press, 2008.

Carp, E. Wayne. *Family Matters: Secrecy and Disclosure in the History of Adoption.* Cambridge, Mass.: Harvard University Press, 1998.

Cassedy, James H. *Demography in Early America: Beginnings of the Statistical Mind, 1600–1800.* Cambridge, Mass.: Harvard University Press, 1969.

———. "The Roots of American Sanitary Reform, 1843–1847: Seven Letters from John H. Griscom to Lemuel Shattuck." *Journal of the History of Medicine and Allied Sciences* 30 (1975): 136–47.

Centers for Disease Control. "Classification of American Indian Race on Birth and Infant Death Certificates—California and Montana." *Morbidity and Mortality Weekly* 42 (April 1993): 220–23.

Chang, David. *The Color of the Land: Race, Nation, and the Politics of Landownership in Oklahoma, 1832–1929.* Chapel Hill: University of North Carolina Press, 2010.

Chaplin, Joyce E. *Benjamin Franklin's Political Arithmetic: A Materialist View of Humanity.* Washington, D.C.: Smithsonian Institution, 2009.

Chudacoff, Howard. *How Old Are You? Age Consciousness in American Culture.* Princeton, N.J.: Princeton University Press, 1989.

Clemens, Elisabeth S. "Lineages of the Rube Goldberg State: Building and Blurring Public Programs, 1900–1940." In *Rethinking Political Institutions: The Art of the State,* edited by Ian Shapiro, Stephen Skrowneck, and Daniel Galvin, 187–215. New York: New York University Press, 2006.

Cohen, Deborah. *Family Secrets: Living with Shame from the Victorians to the Present Day.* London: Viking, 2013.

Cohen, Patricia Cline. *A Calculating People: The Spread of Numeracy in Early America.* New York: Routledge, 1999.

Cohn, Bernard S. *Colonialism and Its Forms of Knowledge: The British in India*. Princeton, N.J.: Princeton University Press, 1996.

Coleman, Arica L. *The Blood That Stays Pure: African Americans, Native Americans, and the Predicament of Race and Identity in Virginia*. Bloomington: Indiana University Press, 2013.

———. "From the 'Pocahontas Exception' to a 'Historical Wrong': The Hidden Cost of Formal Recognition for American Indian Tribes." *Time*, 9 February 2018. https://time.com/5141434/virginia-indian-recognition-pocahontas-exception.

Condran, Gretchen A., and Jennifer Murphy. "Defining and Managing Infant Mortality: A Case Study of Philadelphia, 1870–1920." *Social Science History* 32, no. 4 (2008): 473–513.

Critical Genealogies Collaboratory. "Standard Forms of Power: Biopower and Sovereign Power in the Technology of the U.S. Birth Certificate, 1903–1935." *Constellations* 25, no. 4 (July 2018): 641–56.

Curtis, Bruce. *The Politics of Population: State Formation, Statistics, and the Census of Canada, 1840–1875*. Toronto, Ontario: University of Toronto Press, 2001.

Dandeker, Christopher. *Surveillance, Power and Modernity: Bureaucracy and Discipline from 1700 to the Present Day*. Cambridge, UK: Polity, 1990.

Davis, Robert C. "The Beginnings of American Social Research." In *Nineteenth-Century American Science: A Reappraisal*, edited by G. C. Daniels, 152–78. Evanston, Ill.: Northwestern University Press, 1972.

Derickson, Alan. "Making Human Junk: Child Labor as a Health Issue." *American Journal of Public Health* 82, no. 9 (1992): 1280–90. https://doi.org/10.2105/ajph.82.9.1280.

Doerfler, Jill. "Tribal Citizenship." In *Encyclopedia of United States Indian Policy and Law*, edited by Paul Finkelman and Tim Alan Garrison, 784–87. Vol. 2. Washington, D.C.: CQ Press, 2009.

Dominguez, Virginia R. *White by Definition: Social Classification in Creole Louisiana*. New Brunswick, N.J.: Rutgers University Press, 1986.

Duffy, John. *The Healers: The Rise of the Medical Establishment*. New York: McGraw Hill, 1976.

———. *The Sanitarians: A History of American Public Health*. Urbana: University of Illinois Press, 1992.

Dye, Nancy Schrom, and Daniel Blake Smith. "Mother Love and Infant Death, 1750–1920." *Journal of American History* 73, no. 2 (September 1986): 329–53. https://doi.org/10.2307/1908225.

Edge, P. Granville. "Vital Registration in Europe: The Development of Official Statistics and Some Differences in Practice." *Journal of the Royal Statistical Society* 91, no. 3 (1928): 346–93. https://doi.org/10.2307/2341602.

Epstein, Myrna, Raul Moreno, and Peter Bacchetti. "The Underreporting of Deaths of American Indian Children in California, 1979 through 1993." *American Journal of Public Health* 87, no. 8 (August 1997): 1363–66.

Eyler, John M. *Victorian Social Medicine: The Ideas and Methods of William Farr*. Baltimore: Johns Hopkins University Press, 1979.

Faust, Drew Gilpin. *This Republic of Suffering: Death and the American Civil War*. New York: Alfred A. Knopf, 2008.

Fermaglich, Kirsten. "'What's Uncle Sam's Last Name?' Jews and Name Changing in New York City during the World War II Era." *Journal of American History* 102, no. 3 (December 2015): 719–45. https://doi.org/10.1093/jahist/jav509.

Field, Corinne T. "'If You Have the Right to Vote at 21 Years, Then I Have': Age and Equal Citizenship in the Nineteenth-Century United States." In Field and Syrett, *Age in America*, 69–85.

———. "'Sixteen Years, and No Longer': Chronological Age, Childhood Dependency, and Racial Inequality in the Administration of U.S. Civil War Pensions." Paper presented at Writing History Through Children, Northwestern University, Evanston, Illinois, 5–6 October 2018.

———. *The Struggle for Equal Adulthood: Gender, Race, Age, and the Fight for Citizenship in Antebellum America*. Chapel Hill: University of North Carolina Press, 2014.

Field, Corinne, and Nicholas Syrett, eds. *Age in America: The Colonial Era to the Present*. New York: New York University Press, 2015.

Finnegan, William. "The Deportation Machine." *New Yorker*, 29 April 2013, 24–29.

Ford, Christopher A. "Administering Identity: The Administration of 'Race' in Race-Conscious Law." *California Law Review* 82, no. 5 (1994): 1231–85. https://doi.org/10.2307/3480910.

Foucault, Michel. *The History of Sexuality*. Vol. 1, *An Introduction*. Translated by Robert Hurley. New York: Vintage Books, 1990.

Garroutte, Eva Marie. "The Racial Formation of American Indians: Negotiating Legitimate Identities within Tribal and Federal Law." *American Indian Quarterly* 25, no. 2 (2001): 224–39.

Gitelman, Lisa. *Paper Knowledge: Toward a Media History of Documents*. Durham, N.C.: Duke University Press, 2014.

Glass, David. *Numbering the People: The Eighteenth-Century Population Controversy and the Development of Census and Vital Statistics in Britain*. New York: Gordon and Cremonesi, 1978.

Goldin, Janet. *Babies Made Us Modern: How Infants Brought America into the Twentieth Century*. New York: Cambridge University Press, 2018.

Gordon, Linda. *Pitied but Not Entitled: Single Mothers and the History of Welfare, 1890–1935*. Cambridge, Mass.: Harvard University Press, 1994.

Groebner, Valentin. *Who Are You? Identification, Deception, and Surveillance in Early Modern Europe*. Translated by Mark Kyburz and John Peck. New York: Zone Books, 2007.

Gross, Ariela J. *What Blood Won't Tell: A History of Race on Trial in America*. Cambridge, Mass.: Harvard University Press, 2008.

Gutman, Robert. *Birth and Death Registration in Massachusetts, 1639–1900*. New York: Milbank Memorial Fund, 1959.

Hacking, Ian. "Biopower and the Avalanche of Printed Numbers." *Humanities in Society* 5 (1982): 279–95.

———. *The Taming of Chance*. New York: Cambridge University Press, 1990.

Hall, Jacquelyn Dowd, James L. Leloudis, Robert R. Korstad, Mary Murphy, and Lu Ann Jones. *Like a Family: The Making of a Southern Cotton Mill World*. Chapel Hill: University of North Carolina Press, 1987.

Hannah, Matthew G. *Governmentality and the Mastery of Territory in Nineteenth-Century America*. New York: Cambridge University Press, 2000.

Harmon, Alexandra. "Tribal Enrollment Councils: Lessons on Law and Indian Identity." *Western Historical Quarterly* 32, no. 2 (2001): 175–200. https://doi.org/10.2307/3650772.

Headrick, Daniel R. *When Information Came of Age: Technologies of Knowledge in the Age of Reason and Revolution, 1700–1850*. New York: Cambridge University Press, 2000.

Herman, Ellen. *Kinship by Design: A History of Adoption in the Modern United States*. Chicago: University of Chicago Press, 2008.

Hetzel, Alice M. *History and Organization of the Vital Statistics System*. Hyattsville, Md.: National Center for Health Statistics, 1997.

Higgs, Edward. *Identifying the English: A History of Personal Identification 1500 to the Present*. New York: Continuum International, 2011.

———. *The Information State in England: The Central Collection of Information on Citizens since 1500*. New York: Palgrave Macmillan, 2004.

Hindman, Hugh. *Child Labor: An American History*. Armonk, N.Y.: M. E. Sharpe, 2002.

Hodgson, Dennis. "Ideological Currents and the Interpretation of Demographic Trends: The Case of Francis Amasa Walker." *Journal of the History of the Behavioral Sciences* 28, no. 1 (January 1992): 28–44.

Hoff, Derek S. *The State and the Stork: The Population Debate and Policy Making in U.S. History*. Chicago: University of Chicago Press, 2012.

Hoff, Haley. "Get Real: Implications and Impositions of the Real ID Act of 2005 on Vulnerable Individuals and States." *Catholic University Law Review* 68, no. 2 (Spring 2019): 379–400.

Hoffert, Sylvia D. "'A Very Peculiar Sorrow': Attitudes toward Infant Death in the Urban Northeast, 1800–1860." *American Quarterly* 39, no. 4 (Winter 1987): 601–16.

Holloway, Pippa. *Sexuality, Politics, and Social Control in Virginia, 1920–1945*. Chapel Hill: University of North Carolina Press, 2006.

Hoxie, Frederick E. *A Final Promise: The Campaign to Assimilate the Indians, 1880–1920*. Lincoln: University of Nebraska Press, 1984.

Hoy, Benjamin. "Uncertain Counts: The Struggle to Enumerate First Nations in Canada and the United States, 1870–1911." *Ethnohistory* 62, no. 4 (2015): 729–50.

Hunter, Wendy. *Undocumented Nationals: Between Statelessness and Citizenship*. New York: Cambridge University Press, 2019.

Hunter, Wendy, and Robert Brill. "'Documents Please': Advances in Social Protection and Birth Certification in the Developing World." *World Politics* 68, no. 2 (2016): 191–228. https://doi.org/10.1017/S0043887115000465.

Igo, Sarah E. *The Known Citizen: A History of Privacy in Modern America*. Cambridge, Mass.: Harvard University Press, 2018.

Jacobs, Margaret. *White Mother to a Dark Race: Settler Colonialism, Maternalism, and the Removal of Indigenous Children in the American West and Australia, 1880–1940.* Lincoln: University of Nebraska Press, 2009.

Jobe, Margaret. "Native Americans and the U.S. Census: A Brief Historical Survey." *Journal of Government Information* 30, no. 1 (2004): 66–80. https://doi.org/10.1016/j.jgi.2001.10.001.

John, Richard. "Recasting the Information Infrastructure for the Industrial Age." In *Nation Transformed by Information: How Information Has Shaped the United States from Colonial Times to the Present,* edited by Alfred D. Chandler and James W. Cortada, 55–106. New York: Oxford University Press, 2000.

———. *Spreading the News: The American Postal System from Franklin to Morse.* Cambridge, Mass.: Harvard University Press, 1995.

Katz, Michael. *In the Shadow of the Poorhouse: A Social History of Welfare in America.* Rev. ed. New York: Basic Books, 1996.

Kesselman, Louis. *The Social Politics of the FEPC: A Study in Reform Pressure Movements.* Chapel Hill: University of North Carolina Press, 1948.

Kiel, Doug. "Bleeding Out: Histories and Legacies of 'Indian Blood.'" In *The Great Vanishing Act: Blood Quantum and the Future of Native Nations,* edited by Kathleen Ratteree and Norbert Hill, 80–97. Golden, Colo.: Fulcrum, 2017.

King, Wilma. *Stolen Childhood: Slave Youth in Nineteenth-Century America.* Bloomington: Indiana University Press, 1997.

Klepp, Susan E. *Revolutionary Conceptions: Women, Fertility, and Family Limitation in America, 1760–1820.* Chapel Hill: University of North Carolina Press, 2017.

Koopman, Colin. *How We Became Our Data: A Genealogy of the Informational Person.* Chicago: University of Chicago Press, 2019.

Kuczynski, Robert. "The Registration Laws in the Colonies of Massachusetts Bay and New Plymouth." *Publications of the American Statistical Association* 7, no. 51 (1900): 1–9.

———. *West Indian and American Territories.* Vol. 3 of *Demographic Survey of the British Colonial Empire.* London: Oxford University Press, 1953.

Kunzel, Regina. *Fallen Women, Problem Girls: Unmarried Mothers and the Professionalization of Benevolence, 1890–1945.* New Haven, Conn.: Yale University Press, 1993.

Ladd-Taylor, Molly. *Mother-Work: Women, Child Welfare, and the State, 1890–1930.* Urbana: University of Illinois Press, 1995.

Landrum, Shane. "From Family Bibles to Birth Certificates: Young People, Proof of Age, and American Political Cultures, 1820–1915." In Field and Syrett, *Age in America,* 124–47.

———. "The State's Big Family Bible: Birth Certificates, Personal Identity, and Citizenship in the United States, 1840–1950." PhD diss., Brandeis University, 2014.

Lassonde, Stephen. *Learning to Forget: Schooling and Family Life in New Haven's Working Class, 1870–1940.* New Haven, Conn.: Yale University Press, 2005.

Lauer, Josh. *Creditworthy: A History of Consumer Surveillance and Financial Identity in America.* New York: Columbia University Press, 2017.

Leavitt, Judith Walzer. *Brought to Bed: Childbearing in America, 1750 to 1950.* New York: Oxford University Press, 1986.

LeBrón, Alana M. W., William D. Lopez, Keta Cowan, Nicole L. Novak, Olivia Temrowski, Maria Ibarra-Frayre, and Jorge Delva. "Restrictive ID Policies: Implications for Health Equity." *Journal of Immigrant and Minority Health* 20, no. 2 (April 2018): 255–60.

Lee, Erika. *At America's Gates: Chinese Immigration during the Exclusion Era, 1882–1943.* Chapel Hill: University of North Carolina Press, 2003.

Levenstein, Harvey. "'Best for Babies' or 'Preventable Infanticide'? The Controversy over Artificial Feeding of Infants in America, 1880–1920." *Journal of American History* 70, no. 1 (1983): 75–94.

Lindenmeyer, Kriste. *"A Right to Childhood": The U.S. Children's Bureau and Child Welfare, 1912–46.* Urbana: University of Illinois Press, 1997.

Litoff, Judy. *American Midwives: 1860 to the Present.* Westport, Conn.: Greenwood, 1978.

Little, Ann M. "'Keep Me with You, So That I Might Not Be Damned': Age and Captivity in Colonial Borderlands Warfare." In Field and Syrett, *Age in America*, 23–46.

Lombardo, Paul A. "Miscegenation, Eugenics, and Racism: Historical Footnotes to Loving v. Virginia." *U.C. Davis Law Review* 21, no. 2 (1988): 421–52.

Looijesteijn, Henk, and Marco H. D. Van Leeuwen. "Establishing and Registering Identity in the Dutch Republic." In Breckenridge and Szreter, *Registration and Recognition*, 211–51.

Mackenzie, Beatrice. "To Know a Citizen: Birthright Citizenship Documentary Regimes in U.S. History." In *Citizenship in Question: Evidentiary Birthright and Statelessness*, edited by Benjamin N. Lawrance and Jacqueline Stevens, 117–31. Durham, N.C.: Duke University Press, 2017.

Mason, Karen Oppenheim, and Lisa G. Cope. "Sources of Age and Date-of-Birth Misreporting in the 1900 U.S. Census." *Demography* 24, no. 4 (November 1987): 563–73.

McCormick, Ted. "Governing Model Populations: Queries, Quantification, and William Petty's 'Scale of Salubrity.'" *History of Science* 51, no. 2 (June 2013): 179–97.

———. "Statistics in the Hands of an Angry God? John Graunt's *Observations* in Cotton Mather's New England." *William and Mary Quarterly* 72, no. 4 (2015): 563–86.

McRae, Elizabeth Gillespie. *Mothers of Massive Resistance: White Women and the Politics of White Supremacy.* New York: Oxford University Press, 2018.

Meckel, Richard A. *Save the Babies: American Public Health Reform and the Prevention of Infant Mortality, 1850–1929.* Baltimore: Johns Hopkins University Press, 1990.

Michael, Jerrod M. "The National Board of Health, 1879–1883." *Public Health Reports* 126, no. 1 (2011): 123–29.

Miller, Julie. "To Stop the Slaughter of the Babies: Nathan Straus and the Drive for Pasteurized Milk, 1893–1920." *New York History* 74, no. 2 (1993): 158–84.

Mintz, Stephen. *Huck's Raft: A History of American Childhood.* Cambridge, Mass.: Harvard University Press, 2004.

———. "Reflections on Age as a Category of Historical Analysis." *Journal of the History of Childhood and Youth* 1, no. 1 (2008): 91–94.

Mottet, Lisa. "Modernizing State Vital Statistics Statutes and Policies to Ensure Accurate Gender Markers on Birth Certificates: A Good Government Approach to

Recognizing the Lives of Transgender People." *Michigan Journal of Gender and Law* 19, no. 2 (2013): 373–470.

Muncy, Robyn. *Creating a Female Dominion in American Reform, 1900–1935.* New York: Oxford University Press, 1991.

Nasaw, David. *Children of the City: At Work and at Play.* New York: Oxford University Press, 1986.

Ngai, Mae M. *Impossible Subjects: Illegal Aliens and the Making of Modern America.* Princeton, N.J.: Princeton University Press, 2005.

Novak, William J. "The Myth of the 'Weak' American State." *American Historical Review* 113, no. 3 (2008): 752–72.

———. *The People's Welfare: Law and Regulation in Nineteenth-Century America.* Chapel Hill: University of North Carolina Press, 1996.

O'Malley, Michael. *Keeping Watch: A History of American Time.* New York: Viking, 1990.

Onwuachi-Willig, Angela. "Beautiful Lie: Exploring Rhinelander v. Rhinelander as a Formative Lesson on Race, Identity, Marriage, and Family." *California Law Review* 95, no. 6 (2007): 2393–458.

Parker, Jacqueline K., and Edward M. Carpenter. "Julia Lathrop and the Children's Bureau: The Emergence of an Institution." *Social Service Review* 55, no. 1 (March 1981): 60–77.

Pascoe, Peggy. *What Comes Naturally: Miscegenation Law and the Making of Race in America.* New York: Oxford University Press, 2009.

Patriarca, Silvana. *Numbers and Nationhood: Writing Statistics in Nineteenth-Century Italy.* Cambridge: Cambridge University Press, 1996.

Pearson, Susan J. "'Age Ought to Be a Fact': The Campaign against Child Labor and the Rise of the Birth Certificate." *Journal of American History* 101, no. 4 (March 2015): 1144–65.

———. "A New Birth of Regulation: The State of the State after the Civil War." *Journal of the Civil War Era* 5, no. 3 (September 2015): 422–39.

———. *The Rights of the Defenseless: Protecting Animals and Children in Gilded Age America.* Chicago: University of Chicago Press, 2011.

Poovey, Mary. *A History of the Modern Fact: Problems of Knowledge in the Sciences of Wealth and Society.* Chicago: University of Chicago Press, 1998.

Porter, Theodore M. *The Rise of Statistical Thinking, 1820–1900.* Princeton, N.J.: Princeton University Press, 1986.

Prevost, Jean-Guy. "Controversy and Demarcation in Early-Twentieth-Century Demography: The Rise and Decline of Walker's Theory of Immigration and the Birth Rate." *Social Science History* 22, no. 2 (1998): 131–58.

Prewitt, Kenneth. *What Is Your Race? The Census and Our Flawed Efforts to Classify Americans.* Princeton, N.J.: Princeton University Press, 2013.

Prucha, Francis. *The Great Father: The United States Government and the American Indians.* Abridged ed. Lincoln: University of Nebraska Press, 1986.

Pugh, George W. "Burden of Proof: 'No Doubt at All.'" *Louisiana Law Review* 29 (1969): 310–14.

Rapoport, Abby. "Want to Vote? Bring Your Birth Certificate and the Original Magna Carta." *American Prospect*, January/February 2013, 63.

Robertson, Craig. *The Passport in America: The History of a Document.* New York: Oxford University Press, 2010.

Robertson, Stephen. *Crimes against Children: Sexual Violence and Legal Culture in New York City, 1880–1960.* Chapel Hill: University of North Carolina Press, 2005.

Rockwell, Stephen J. *Indian Affairs and the Administrative State in the Nineteenth Century.* New York: Cambridge University Press, 2010.

Rosen, Robyn L. *Reproductive Health, Reproductive Rights: Reformers and the Politics of Maternal Welfare, 1917–1940.* Columbus: Ohio State University Press, 2003.

Rosenthal, Caitlin. *Accounting for Slavery: Masters and Management.* Cambridge, Mass.: Harvard University Press, 2018.

Rosenwaike, Ira, and Mark E. Hill. "The Accuracy of Age Reporting among Elderly African Americans: Evidence of a Birth Registration Effect." *Research on Aging* 18, no. 3 (September 1996): 310–24.

Ross, Dorothy. *The Origins of American Social Science.* New York: Cambridge University Press, 1991.

Rowse, Tim. "Population Knowledge and the Practice of Guardianship." *American Nineteenth Century History* 15, no. 1 (2014): 15–42.

Rule, James B., Douglas McAdam, Linda Stearns, and David Uglow. "Documentary Identification and Mass Surveillance in the United States." *Social Problems* 31, no. 2 (December 1983): 222–34.

Rusnock, Andrea A. *Vital Accounts: Quantifying Health and Population in Eighteenth-Century England and France.* New York: Cambridge University Press, 2002.

Ryan, Mary. *Cradle of the Middle Class: The Family in Oneida County, New York, 1790–1865.* New York: Cambridge University Press, 1981.

Sallee, Shelly. *The Whiteness of Child Labor Reform in the New South.* Athens: University of Georgia Press, 2004.

Schmidt, James D. "The Ends of Innocence: Age as a Mode of Inquiry in Sociolegal Studies." *Law and Social Inquiry* 32, no. 4 (December 2007): 1027–57.

———. *Industrial Violence and the Legal Origins of Child Labor.* New York: Cambridge University Press, 2010.

———. "'Restless Movements Characteristic of Childhood': The Legal Construction of Child Labor in Nineteenth-Century Massachusetts." *Law and History Review* 23 (Summer 2005): 315–50.

Scholten, Catherine M. "'On the Importance of the Obstetrick Art': Changing Customs of Childbirth in America, 1760 to 1825." *William and Mary Quarterly* 34, no. 3 (July 1977): 426–45.

Schor, Paul. *Counting Americans: How the U.S. Census Classified the Nation.* New York: Oxford University Press, 2017.

Schweber, Libby. *Disciplining Statistics: Demography and Vital Statistics in France and England, 1830–1885.* Durham, N.C.: Duke University Press, 2006.

Scott, James. *Seeing Like a State: How Certain Schemes to Improve the Human Condition Have Failed.* New Haven, Conn.: Yale University Press, 1998.

Shoemaker, Nancy. "The Census as Civilizer: American Indian Household Structure in the 1900 and 1910 U.S. Censuses." *Historical Methods* 25, no. 1 (January 1992): 4–11.

Simons, D. Brenton. "New England Family Record Broadsides and Portraiture, and the Letterpress Artist of Connecticut." In Simons and Benes, *Art of Family*, 91–113.

Simons, D. Brenton, and Peter Benes, eds. *The Art of Family: Genealogical Artifacts in New England*. Boston: New England Historic Genealogical Society, 2002.

Skocpol, Theda. *Protecting Soldiers and Mothers: The Political Origins of Social Policy in the United States*. Cambridge, Mass.: Harvard University Press, 1995.

Smith, J. Douglas. "The Campaign for Racial Purity and the Erosion of Paternalism in Virginia, 1922–1930: 'Nominally White, Biologically Mixed, and Legally Negro.'" *Journal of Southern History* 68, no. 1 (2002): 65–106.

———. *Managing White Supremacy: Race, Politics, and Citizenship in Jim Crow Virginia*. Chapel Hill: University of North Carolina Press, 2002.

Smith, Mark M. *Mastered by the Clock: Time, Slavery, and Freedom in the American South*. Chapel Hill: University of North Carolina Press, 1997.

Spade, Dean. "Documenting Gender." *Hastings Law Journal* 59, no. 1 (March 2008): 731–842.

Spruhan, Paul. "CDIB: The Role of the Certificate of Degree of Indian Blood in Defining Native American Legal Identity." *American Indian Law Journal* 6, no. 2 (2018): 169–96.

———. "A Legal History of Blood Quantum in Federal Indian Law to 1935." *South Dakota Law Review* 51, no. 1 (2006): 1–50.

Stansell, Christine. *City of Women: Sex and Class in New York, 1789–1860*. Urbana: University of Illinois Press, 1987.

Stearns, Peter N. *Childhood in World History*. New York: Routledge, 2006.

Stremlau, Rose. "'To Domesticate and Civilize Wild Indians': Allotment and the Campaign to Reform Indian Families, 1875–1887." *Journal of Family History* 30 (2005): 265–86.

———. *Sustaining the Cherokee Family: Kinship and the Allotment of an Indigenous Nation*. Chapel Hill: University of North Carolina Press, 2011.

Sundue, Sharon Braslaw. "'Beyond the Time of White Children': African American Emancipation, Age, and Ascribed Neoteny in Early National Pennsylvania." In Field and Syrett, *Age in America*, 47–65.

Szreter, Simon. "Registration of Identities in Early Modern English Parishes and among the English Overseas." In Breckenridge and Szreter, *Registration and Recognition: Documenting the Person in World History*, 67–92.

———. "The Right of Registration: Development, Identity Registration, and Social Security—a Historical Perspective." *World Development* 35, no. 1 (2007): 67–86.

Theobald, Brianna. *Reproduction on the Reservation: Pregnancy, Childbirth, and Colonialism in the Long Twentieth Century*. Chapel Hill: University of North Carolina Press, 2019.

———. "'The Simplest Rules of Motherhood': Settler Colonialism and the Regulation of American Indian Reproduction, 1910–1976." PhD diss., Arizona State University, 2015.

Thomas, Karen Kruse. "The Hill-Burton Act and Civil Rights: Expanding Hospital Care for Black Southerners, 1939–1960." *Journal of Southern History* 72, no. 4 (2006): 823–70.

Thomason, Brian William. "Racism and Racial Classification: A Case Study of the

Virginia Racial Integrity Legislation." PhD diss., University of California, Riverside, 1978.

Tomchin, Olga. "Bodies and Bureaucracy: Legal Sex Classification and Marriage-Based Immigration for Trans* People." *California Law Review* 101, no. 3 (2013): 813–62.

Trattner, Walter. *Crusade for the Children: A History of the National Child Labor Committee and Child Labor Reform in America*. Chicago: Quadrangle Books, 1971.

———. *From Poor Law to Welfare State: A Social History of Welfare in America*. New York: Free Press, 1999.

Treas, Judith. "Age in Standards and Standards for Age: Institutionalizing Chronological Age as Biographical Necessity." In *Standards and Their Stories: How Quantifying, Classifying, and Formalizing Practices Shape Everyday Life*, edited by Martha Lampland and Susan Leigh Star, 65–87. Ithaca, N.Y.: Cornell University Press, 2009.

Tuck, Stephen G. N. *Beyond Atlanta: The Struggle for Racial Equality in Georgia, 1940–1980*. Athens: University of Georgia Press, 2001.

United Nations Children's Fund. *Every Child's Birth Right: Inequities and Trends in Birth Registration*. New York: UNICEF, 2013.

Walker, Bela August. "Fractured Bonds: Policing Whiteness and Womanhood through Race-Based Marriage Annulments." *DePaul Law Review* 58 (2008): 1–50.

Waserman, Manfred J. "Henry L. Coit and the Certified Milk Movement in the Development of Modern Pediatrics." *Bulletin of the History of Medicine* 46 (1972): 359–90.

Watner, Carl. "The Compulsory Birth and Death Certificate in the United States." In *National Identification Systems: Essays in Opposition*, edited by Carl Watner and Wendy McElroy, 70–86. Jefferson, N.C.: McFarland, 2004.

Weil, Francois. *Family Trees: A History of Genealogy in America*. Cambridge, Mass.: Harvard University Press, 2013.

Wertz, Richard, and Dorothy Wertz. *Lying-In: A History of Childbirth in America*. New York: Free Press, 1977.

Westover, Tara. *Educated: A Memoir*. New York: Random House, 2018.

White, Holly N. S. *Protecting the Innocents: Legal and Cultural Debates about Age and Ability in the Early United States*. Charlottesville: University of Virginia Press, forthcoming.

Wilson, Amy Blank. "It Takes ID to Get ID: The New Identity Politics in Services." *Social Service Review* 83, no. 1 (March 2009): 111–32. https://doi.org/10.1086/599025.

Wolf, Jacqueline H. "'Don't Kill Your Baby': Feeding Infants in Chicago, 1903–1924." *Journal of the History of Medicine and Allied Sciences* 53, no. 3 (1998): 219–53.

Wulf, Karin. "Bible, King, and Common Law: Genealogical Practices and Family History Practices in British America." *Early American Studies* 10, no. 3 (2012): 467–502.

Zakim, Michael. *Accounting for Capitalism: The World the Clerk Made*. Chicago: University of Chicago Press, 2018.

———. "Paperwork." *Raritan* 33, no. 4 (2014): 34–56.

Zelizer, Viviana. *Pricing the Priceless Child: The Changing Social Value of Children*. Princeton, N.J.: Princeton University Press, 1994.

INDEX

Jamestown, 31–32
Jarvis, Edward, 134
Jennings, Clarence, 215
Jennings, John, 168
Jews, 259–60, 275
John, Dorothy, 203
Johns, Dorothy, 216
Johnson, Leonard Z., 271
Jones, Alice, 216–17
Jones, Anita, 111–12
Jones, W. A. T., 215
Jones, William, 90

Keating-Owen Act (1916), 172–73, 178–79
Keith (Mr.), 75
Kelley, Eva, 202
Kelley, Florence, 168, 173; *Some Ethical Gains through Legislation* (1905), 97–98, 177
Keys, Lavinia, 235
King, William, 55
King family, 211–12, 214

labor unions, on child labor, 166
Lake Mohonk Conference, 83–90
Lands (Mr.), 72
Lathrop, Julia, 98, 121, 137, 147; *Child Labor Bulletin*, 177. *See also* Children's Bureau
Lawson, William (Mrs.), 196–97
legitimacy: and adoption, 233–34; illegitimacy and targeted interventions, 230, 236; illegitimate births as underreported, 225–30; and infant mortality, 147, 228; and marriage after birth, 233; and miscegenation, 218; and registration tests, 101; removal from all birth certificates, 230, 234–39, 247–48; and state interference, 147–48
Lenhart, Robert, 187
Lenroot, Katharine, 230–31, 265
Lenz (Mr.), 71
Leupp, Francis, 90
Levy, Magnus, 169
life insurance policies, 176

literacy, 142, 162, 165
Love, Nate, 28
Lovejoy, Owen, 168
Lundberg, Emma, 230–31
Lyttle, Mark, 4

MacGunigal, Margaret, 235
Magruder, Luetta, 236
Mallery, Garrick, 84
Mann, F. T., 152
manumission and freedom suits, 301n13
March on Washington Movement, 255–56
Marcley, Jessie, 101–2
marriage, 25, 29–30. *See also* miscegenation laws
Marshall, Herbert, 272–73
Mather, Cotton, 35
May Day campaigns, 264–65, 267
McKinley, F. J., 151–52
McLean, John, 169
McNickle, Darcy, 267
McRaven, Donald, 256
Mercer, A. Maceo, 271–72, 277–78
Meriam, Lewis, 99, 104, 152–53. *See also* Children's Bureau
Meritt, E. B., 151–52, 192
Metropolitan Life Insurance Company, 114, 141; *The Baby*, 141
midwives: and African Americans' use of, 62, 110–11, 145, 265; education on birth registration, 110–12; and language barriers and illiteracy as barrier to registering births, 60–66; licensure and registry of, 61, 63–66, 110; and Native Americans' use of, 153–56; outlawing of midwifery, 65; and rural areas, 61–62
milk stations, 135
miscegenation laws, 189, 193, 197–98, 203–5, 215–18, 278
model law: administration of, 60, 75, 77, 97; implementation of, 56–57; lack of, 104, 114–17; updated versions of, 247–49, 290–91
Moon, William H., 218